The Best of
Mennonite
Fellowship
MEALS

The Best of
Mennonite
Fellowship
MEALS

More than 900 favorite recipes
to share with friends
at home or at church

Phyllis Pellman Good *and*
Louise Stoltzfus

Intercourse, PA 17534
800/762-7171
www.goodbks.com

Design by Dawn J. Ranck
Cover design and illustrations by Cheryl Benner

THE BEST OF MENNONITE FELLOWSHIP MEALS
Copyright © 1991, 2003 by Good Books, Intercourse, Pennsylvania, 17534
International Standard Book Number: 1-56148-048-7 (paperback edition)
International Standard Book Number: 1-56148-409-1 (comb-bound paperback edition)
Library of Congress Catalog Card Number: 91-74051

Library of Congress Cataloging-in-Publication Data
Good, Phyllis Pellman
   The best of Mennonite fellowship meals : favorite recipes to share with
friends at home or church / Phyllis Pellman Good, Louise Stoltzfus.
      p.cm.
   Includes index.
      1. Cookery, Mennonite. I. Stoltzfus, Louise
II. Title.
TX715.G61726 1991
641.5--dc20   91-74051
                                                              CIP

Table of Contents

Food for Fellowship

We have observed the growth of a wonderful practice in many Mennonite congregations during the last several years—the church fellowship meal! Where we once invited "company" home for Sunday dinner, today we are more likely to share a carry–in lunch in the church fellowship hall after morning worship.

It's a custom worth fostering, we believe, especially when we see so little of each other apart from Sunday morning. Furthermore, it seems more appropriate to relax in the spirit of community rather than to be entertained by one starring (and probably tense and exhausted!) cook.

Familiar Favorites

Collected here are favorite recipes from Mennonite fellowship meals, offered by the cooks who prepare them. "People ask me to bring this," some explained with gentle pride. "I love watching people go for this dish" or "I take this because I never have any leftovers" admitted others!

A Multi–Cultural Event

Food fuels friendships and begins to undo prejudices. In that spirit, this book contains favorite dishes from the many food traditions which are now part of the Mennonite family of faith. In some places throughout North America, Mennonite fellowship meals are multi-cultural events, reflecting the make–up of their congregations. Experiment with the Lao, Chinese, Belizean, Mexican, native–American and African-American dishes that are part of this collection.

For Eating at Home

Not only are all these recipes fellowship meal favorites, they also feed family and friends equally well at home. One note if you prepare these dishes for eating at home—the number of servings included with each recipe assumes the traditional bounty of a fellowship meal. Consequently, we have assumed more servings per recipe than is likely to be adequate for home use.

About Titling Recipes

While most Mennonite cooks take pride in the food they fix, they are also a modest lot. We took one liberty as editors that may challenge the humility of a few who submitted recipes to us: in some cases we included the name of the submitter in the title of the recipe, in an effort to distinguish it from similar surrounding recipes. (We figured that was in keeping with our tradition of crediting the maker of a favorite dish by the name we give it—"Aunt Anna May's Snickerdoodles," for example.) We do apologize if we have embarrassed anyone with this decision.

If You're in Charge

In the interest of easing your planning for a fellowship meal we have included a chapter about overcoming common hurdles—what to do when your oven space is limited; what if there are too few electrical outlets; how to overcome tight quarters for eating.

If You Don't Know What to Make

To give you inspiration when you've been asked to bring finger food, when you're looking for something children will enjoy or when you want to make an unusual dish, we offer special indexes at the back of the book to those categories, plus several others.

May you find this food delectable and nourishing, not only for your bodies, but for your friendships and families also. There is incomparable warmth in eating together. This is food for fellowship. Thank you, countless cooks, for offering your best dishes so bountifully!

–Phyllis Pellman Good
–Louise Stoltzfus

Breads, Rolls and Muffins

Homemade Bread

Carol Sommers
Millersburg, OH
Martins Creek Mennonite Church

Makes 2 loaves

2 cups lukewarm water
1 pkg. yeast
⅔ cup shortening
⅔ cup white sugar
1 tsp. salt
1 egg
6 cups bread flour

1. Dissolve yeast in warm water. Add shortening, sugar, salt, egg and 3 cups flour. Mix until smooth.
2. Add remaining flour, mixing with a spoon. Let rise until double in size.
3. Shape into loaves, dinner rolls or sweet rolls. Put dough into greased pans and let rise again until double in size.
4. Bake at 350° about 40-50 minutes or until light brown. Be careful not to overbake.

Pumpernickel Bread

Helene Funk,
Laird, SK
Tiefengrund Rosenort Mennonite Church

Makes 3-4 loaves

3 Tbsp. yeast
2 tsp. sugar
1 cup warm water
3¼ cups water
½ cup dark molasses
1 Tbsp. margarine
1 tsp. salt
3½ cups whole wheat flour
4½ cups white flour
3½ cups rye flour
1 Tbsp. cocoa (optional)
1 cup bran
¾ cup yellow cornmeal
½ cup millet (optional)
2 cups mashed potatoes
2 tsp. caraway seeds
½ cup flax

1. Dissolve yeast with sugar in 1 cup warm water. Let stand 10 minutes until bubbly. Stir well.
2. Combine 3¼ cups water, molasses and margarine in saucepan. Heat over low heat until margarine is dissolved. Add salt and yeast mixture.
3. Combine all flours and cocoa. Add bran, cornmeal, millet and mashed potatoes. Add to liquid yeast mixture and beat until thoroughly mixed. Stir in caraway seeds and flax and mix well.
4. Let dough rest 15 minutes. Knead until smooth. Let rise until double in bulk, about 1 hour.
5. Punch down. Let rise again for 30 minutes. Divide into 3-4 pieces and shape into loaves or balls and place in greased tins. Cover and let rise in warm place, about 45 minutes.
6. Bake at 325° for 45-50 minutes or until done.

Poppy Seed Bread

Julie Hurst
Leola, PA

Makes 1 loaf pan

1 cup sugar
2 eggs
1 cup evaporated milk
1 cup cooking oil
2 cups flour
2 tsp. baking powder
¼ tsp. salt
1 tsp. vanilla
¼ cup poppy seeds

1. Combine sugar, eggs, milk and oil.
2. Sift together flour, baking powder and salt. Add to egg mixture with vanilla. Fold in poppy seeds.
3. Put in greased loaf pan.
4. Bake at 375° for 1 hr.

Cheddar Cheese Corn Bread

Pat Augsburger Blum
Berkeley, CA

Makes 8 servings

1 cup cornmeal
1 cup flour
1 Tbsp. baking powder
1 tsp. salt
1 Tbsp. sugar
2 eggs
1 cup milk
¼ cup melted butter
¼ cup grated cheddar cheese

1. Mix all dry ingredients.
2. Beat together eggs and milk until smooth. Stir into dry ingredients until moistened.
3. Stir butter and cheese into batter and pour into an 8-inch greased skillet.
4. Bake at 400° for 25-30 minutes.

Corn Bread

Joyce M. Marable
Lancaster, PA
South Christian Street Mennonite Church

Makes 8-10 servings

2 cups all-purpose flour
1 cup cornmeal
¼ cup sugar
2 tsp. baking powder
½ tsp. salt
1 cup milk
¼ cup cooking oil
1 egg

1. Combine all dry ingredients. Stir in milk, oil and egg, mixing until dry ingredients are moistened. (Mixture may be lumpy.)
2. Spoon into greased 9-inch baking pan.
3. Bake at 400° for 25-30 minutes or until light golden brown.

Belizean Creole Bread

Debbie Rowley and
Leanora Harwood
Lancaster, PA
South Christian Street Mennonite Church

Makes 6 servings

3 cups flour
1 tsp. salt
3 Tbsp. sugar
3 Tbsp. shortening
1½ cups coconut milk
2 Tbsp. sugar
1 Tbsp. yeast

1. Combine flour, salt and 3 Tbsp. sugar. Cut shortening into dry ingredients and mix well.
2. Combine coconut milk, 2 Tbsp. sugar and yeast. Let sit until yeast sets.
3. Gradually add yeast mixture to dry mixture. Mix well and knead for 10 minutes. Place in greased bowl and let rise for 15 minutes.
4. Punch down and knead for 10 minutes. Cut dough into desired shape, flatten pieces a little and place on greased baking sheet. Let rise again.
5. Bake at 350° until nice and brown.

Short'nin' Bread

Alice Whitman
Lancaster, PA
South Christian Street Mennonite
Church

¼ **lb. butter, softened**
¼ **cup light brown sugar**
1½ **cups flour**

1. Cream butter and sugar together. Add flour and mix thoroughly.
2. Roll dough out quickly to ½-inch thickness on floured board. Cut into shapes with a biscuit cutter.
3. Lay dough shapes on lightly greased and floured baking sheet.
4. Bake at 350° for 15-20 minutes, watching carefully.

Bannock

Edith von Gunten
and Bernice Potoski
Riverton, MB
Native Ministries

Makes 8-10 servings

6 **cups flour**
2 **Tbsp. baking powder**
1 **tsp. salt**
6 **heaping Tbsp. lard**
Warm milk or warm water
Raisins (optional)

1. Combine flour, baking powder and salt. Add lard and mix by hand.
2. When mixture is crumbly, add enough warm milk or water to knead mixture into a ball. Raisins may be

added for special occasions.
3. Press dough onto a greased cookie sheet. Prick all over with fork.
4. Bake at 400-425° for 20 minutes.
5. Dough may also be cut into squares and deep fried in cooking oil.

Natives traditionally prepare bannock by rolling it thinly onto a green stick and baking it over an open fire.

Sweet French Bread

Sadie Yoder
Quarryville, PA
Bart Mennonite Church

Makes 5 loaves

3 **cups warm water**
2 **pkgs. yeast**
3 **eggs**
1 **Tbsp. salt**
1 **Tbsp. cooking oil**
1¼ **cups sugar**
10 **cups flour**

1. Combine all ingredients except flour and mix well.
2. Gradually add flour and knead. Dough may be sticky.
3. Let dough rise until double in bulk. Punch down.
4. Divide dough into 5 pieces. With a rolling pin roll each piece into an oblong shape. Roll up into an oblong loaf. (Or you may use this dough recipe for sticky buns.)
5. Place all 5 loaves on a cookie sheet beside each other. Allow to rise.
6. Bake at 350° for 25-30 minutes.

Monkey Bread

Kathy Falk
Champaign, IL
Bethel Mennonite Church

Makes 10-15 servings

3 **cans buttermilk biscuits**
½ **cup white sugar**
2 **Tbsp. cinnamon**
1 **cup brown sugar**
8 **Tbsp. margarine**
1 **cup chopped nuts**

1. Put 1 can biscuits together with ⅓ of the total white sugar and cinnamon in a bag and shake until biscuits are covered. Repeat precedure with remaining cans of biscuits.
2. Melt brown sugar and margarine together and bring to a boil. Boil for 1 minute.
3. In lightly greased angel food or bundt cake pan layer ingredients in following order: 1 can biscuits, ⅓ cup nuts, ⅓ of brown sugar mixture. Continue same order with each can biscuits.
4. Bake at 350° for 35 minutes. Let set 10 minutes before removing from pan.

Cinnamon Bread or Rolls

Becky Bixler
Iowa City, IA
First Mennonite Church

Makes 2 loaves or 2 pans rolls

1 pkg. yeast
¼ cup warm water
1 cup milk, scalded
¼ cup sugar
¼ cup margarine
1 tsp. salt
3-4 cups flour
1 egg
½ cup sugar
2 tsp. cinnamon
Softened butter *or* margarine

1. Soften yeast in warm water.

2. Combine milk, ¼ cup sugar, margarine and salt. Cool to lukewarm. Add about half of flour and mix well. Add softened yeast and egg. Beat well.

3. Stir in remaining flour to make a moderately soft dough. Turn out onto a lightly floured surface. Knead until smooth and elastic, about 8-10 minutes.

4. Place in lightly greased bowl, turning once to coat surface. Cover and let rise in warm place until double, about 1½-2 hours.

5. Punch down, shape into a ball, cover and let rest 10 minutes.

6. Divide dough in half. Roll into a 9" x 12" rectangle. Mix ½ cup sugar and cinnamon. Spread dough with softened butter or margarine

and sprinkle with cinnamon mixture.

7. Roll up and either cut each roll into 9 cinnamon rolls or bake in two loaf pans. Cover and let rise until double, about 1 hour.

8. Bake at 350° for 25-30 minutes.

Banana Bread

Ginny Buckwalter
Scarborough, ON
Warden Woods Mennonite Church

Makes 12 servings

½ cup margarine
1 cup brown sugar or less
2 eggs
2 large bananas, mashed
1 tsp. baking soda
¼ tsp. salt
1 cup white flour
1 cup whole wheat flour
½ cup yogurt or buttermilk
1 tsp. vanilla *or* lemon extract
½ cup chopped pecans

1. Cream together margarine, sugar and eggs. Stir in mashed bananas.

2. Mix all dry ingredients and add to banana mixture, alternating with yogurt or buttermilk. Add vanilla or lemon extract. Fold in chopped nuts. Put in greased loaf pan.

3. Bake at 350° for 50 minutes or until it tests done.

Beth's Banana Bread

Elizabeth Weaver Bonnar
Thorndale, ON
Valleyview Mennonite Church

Makes 8-10 servings

⅓ cup Canola oil
2 eggs, beaten (or use an egg substitute)
6 medium bananas, mashed
1¾-2¼ cups whole wheat flour
¼ tsp. salt
1¼ tsp. baking soda
¼ cup hot water
1 cup chopped walnuts

1. Beat oil and eggs and mix well. Stir in bananas.

2. Sift together all dry ingredients and add to batter, alternating with hot water. Mix until smooth. Fold in the walnuts.

3. Bake in greased loaf pan at 325° for about 50 minutes.

4. Cool on wire rack for ½ hour before slicing.

5. Serve with honey or maple syrup.

I created this recipe from one called Whole Wheat Banana Nut Bread because I wanted a recipe without sugar for persons with diabetes and hypoglycemia. When I take it to fellowship meals, I always put a sign next to it which says, "No sugar."

Banana Nut Bread

Edith Stoltzfus
Mantua, OH
Aurora Mennonite Church

Makes 8-10 servings

⅓ cup shortening
½ cup sugar
2 eggs
1¾ cups flour
2 tsp. baking powder
½ tsp. salt
¼ tsp. baking soda
1 cup mashed, ripe bananas
½ cup chopped walnuts

1. Cream shortening and sugar together. Add eggs and beat well. Add dry ingredients alternately with bananas, beating well after each addition. Stir in walnuts.
2. Pour into well-greased loaf pan.
3. Bake at 350° for 45-50 minutes or until it tests done. Remove from pan while still warm.

Fresh Apple Bread

Viola Weidner
Allentown, PA
First Mennonite Church

Makes 12 or more servings

2 cups flour
1 tsp. baking powder
1 tsp. baking soda
½ tsp. salt
1 tsp. cinnamon
½ cup shortening
1 cup sugar
2 eggs
2 cups chopped apples
½ cup chopped black walnuts
1 tsp. vanilla

1. Sift all dry ingredients together.
2. Cream shortening and sugar and add eggs. Beat well. Add apples, walnuts and vanilla. Mix well. Stir in dry ingredients.
3. Pour batter into a well-greased loaf pan.
4. Bake at 350° for 1 hour or until center is set. Turn pan on side to cool.

Pumpkin Bread

Mattie Miller
Sugarcreek, OH
Walnut Creek Mennonite

Shirley Hershey
Bloomingdale, NJ
Garden Chapel Mennonite Church

Makes 2 medium loaves

2 cups pumpkin
3 cups sugar
1 tsp. nutmeg
1 tsp. cloves
1 tsp. cinnamon
1½ tsp. salt
2 tsp. baking soda
4 eggs
⅔ cup hot water
1 cup cooking oil
3½ cups flour
1 cup chopped nuts

1. Combine pumpkin, sugar, spices, salt and baking soda. Add eggs and mix well.
2. Add water, oil and flour and mix well. Fold in nuts.
3. Grease and flour loaf pans and fill each one ⅔ full.
4. Bake at 350° for 1 hour.

Zucchini Bread

Audrey J. Brubaker
York, PA
Church of the Nazarene

Makes 24 servings

3 eggs
1 cup cooking oil
1 cup white sugar
1 cup brown sugar
2 cups grated zucchini with skin
2 cups flour
½ tsp. salt
¼ tsp. baking powder
2 tsp. baking soda
1 tsp. cinnamon
1 tsp. vanilla
1 cup chopped nuts (optional)

1. Combine all ingredients and mix thoroughly.
2. Pour into 2 greased loaf pans.
3. Bake at 325° for 45 minutes to 1 hour.

Zucchini Oatmeal Bread

Lorene Good
Armington, IL
Hopedale Mennonite Church

Makes 2 small loaves

3 eggs
1 cup cooking oil
1 cup sugar
2 cups grated zucchini
1 cup quick oats
1 tsp. vanilla
2 cups flour
1 tsp. salt
1 tsp. baking soda
¼ tsp. baking powder
3 tsp. cinnamon
½ cup raisins (optional)
½ cup chopped nuts

1. Beat eggs until light and foamy. Add oil, sugar, zucchini, oats and vanilla. Mix slightly, but well.
2. Sift together flour, salt, baking soda, baking powder and cinnamon. Add to batter and mix until blended. Fold in raisins and nuts.
3. Spoon batter into greased and floured loaf pans.
4. Bake at 325° for 1 hour.

Honey Oatmeal Wheat Bread

Evelyn Cross
Prescott, AZ
Prescott Mennonite Church

Makes 3 loaves

3 cups boiling water
1½ cups oatmeal
¾ cup warm water
3 pkgs. yeast
½ cup honey or brown sugar
⅓ cup Canola oil
2 tsp. salt
3-4 cups whole wheat flour
4-5 cups unbleached flour

1. Pour boiling water over oatmeal in large mixing bowl. Cool to lukewarm.
2. Dissolve yeast in warm water. Let stand until foamy.
3. Add yeast to oatmeal mixture. Add honey or brown sugar and oil. Blend well. Add salt. Add whole wheat flour, stirring well after each addition. Gradually add unbleached flour, forming a soft dough.
4. Turn out onto floured board and knead 5-10 minutes. Place dough in greased bowl, cover with damp towel and let rise until double in size.
5. Punch down and form dough into 3 loaves. Let rise about 20 minutes.
6. Bake at 350° for 30 minutes. Put out on rack or board for cooling.

Variations:
This dough will also make approximately 2 ½ dozen sandwich buns or 3 ½-4 dozen dinner rolls. Change baking time for buns or rolls to 15-20 minutes.

Oatmeal Bread

Louise A. Bartel
North Newton, KS
Bethel College Mennonite Church

Makes 15-20 servings

1 pkg. dry yeast
½ cup warm water
1 cup quick oats
½ cup whole wheat flour
½ cup brown sugar *or* molasses
1 Tbsp. salt
2 Tbsp. margarine
2 cups boiling water
5-6 cups flour

1. Dissolve yeast in warm water. Set aside.
2. Combine oats, whole wheat flour, sugar or molasses, salt and margarine. Pour boiling water over mixture and mix well. Cool to lukewarm and add yeast.
3. Gradually add flour, stirring with spoon, then kneading by hand. Let rise until double in bulk and punch down. Shape into two loaves and allow to rise again.
4. Bake at 350° for 40 minutes.

Lemon Bread

Kathy Hertzler
Lancaster, PA
Charlotte Street Mennonite Church

Makes 3 miniature loaf pans

Batter:
1 cup butter *or* margarine
2 cups sugar
4 eggs
½ tsp. salt (optional)
½ tsp. baking soda
3 cups all-purpose flour
1 cup buttermilk
1 cup finely chopped pecans
Rind of 1 lemon, grated

Glaze:
Juice from 2 lemons *or*
  ¼ cup lemon juice
1 cup powdered sugar

1. To prepare batter cream together butter or margarine and sugar in large bowl on high speed. Blend in eggs, one at a time, beating after each addition.

2. In another bowl combine salt, baking soda and flour. Add to creamed mixture, alternating with buttermilk. Add pecans and lemon rind, stirring by hand.

3. Grease and flour loaf pans. Line bottom of pan with parchment or waxed paper. Spoon batter into pans.

4. Bake at 300° for 1 hour and 20 minutes or until bread tests done with a wooden toothpick.

5. Let bread cool in pans for 10 minutes. Remove from pans to cooling racks.

6. To prepare glaze combine all ingredients. Punch holes in bread with a toothpick while bread is still warm. Pour glaze slowly over bread. Cool completely before slicing, wrapping or freezing.

I usually cut this bread at church, arrange it in a basket with a cloth and serve it with homemade jam.

Homemade Rolls

Ruth S. Weaver
Reinholds, PA
South Seventh Street Mennonite Church

Makes 20 servings

5¾-6¾ cups bread flour
⅓ cup instant non-fat dry milk solids
¼ cup sugar
1 Tbsp. salt
2 pkgs. dry yeast
⅓ cup margarine, softened
2 cups warm tap water

1. In large bowl mix 2 cups flour, milk, sugar, salt and yeast. Add margarine.

2. Gradually add tap water (120 to 130°) to dry ingredients and beat 2 minutes at medium speed with a mixer. Add 1 more cup flour and beat 2 minutes on high speed. Stir in enough flour to make a stiff dough.

3. Turn out onto a lightly floured board and knead about 8-10 minutes. Place in greased bowl, turning to grease top of dough.

4. Cover and let rise in warm place until doubled in bulk (about 45 minutes). Punch down and allow to rise again for 20 minutes.

5. Divide dough in half and cut each half into 10 equal pieces. Form into rolls and place on greased baking sheet about 2 inches apart. Cover and let rise again about 1 hour.

6. Bake at 375° for 15-20 minutes. Remove from baking sheet and brush with melted margarine.

Not many other people bring homemade bread or rolls, and I always bake them several days before the fellowship meal so I have no last minute rush.

Mom's Dinner Rolls

Veva Zimmerman Mumaw
Hatfield, PA

Makes 2 dozen rolls

1 pkg. dry yeast
¼ cup warm water
¾ cup milk, scalded
¼ cup shortening
¼ cup sugar
1 tsp. salt
1 egg, beaten
3 cups flour

1. Soften yeast in warm water. Allow to set for a little while.

2. Combine scalded milk, shortening, sugar and salt. Cool mixture to lukewarm. Add to yeast mixture.

3. Add beaten egg and flour and knead. Let rise.

4. Punch down and shape into rolls. Let rise again.

5. Bake at 400° for 12-15 minutes.

Whole Wheat Rolls

Faye Pankratz
Inola, OK
Eden Mennonite Church

Makes 2 dozen rolls

2 pkgs. dry yeast
1/2 cup warm water
1 tsp. sugar
1 3/4 cups milk, scalded
1/4 cup sugar
1 Tbsp. salt
3 Tbsp. shortening
2 cups whole wheat flour
3 egg whites
3 cups white flour or more

1. Combine yeast and warm water in small bowl. Sprinkle 1 tsp. sugar over yeast and water. Set aside.
2. Pour scalded milk over 1/4 cup sugar, salt and shortening in large bowl. Cool until lukewarm. Add yeast mixture and stir well.
3. Add whole wheat flour and egg whites. Beat well and gradually add white flour until you have soft dough.
4. Turn onto floured surface and knead until dough is elastic. Place in greased bowl, turning dough to grease top. Cover with clean cloth and let rise until doubled in bulk.
5. Punch down and shape into rolls. Place on greased cookie sheets and let rise until double.
6. Bake at 350° for 20 minutes or until lightly browned.

Whole Wheat Cottage Cheese Rolls

Rebecca Byler
Mt. Eaton, OH
Longenecker Mennonite Church

Makes 24 servings

3 3/4 cups whole wheat flour
2 pkgs. dry yeast
1/2 tsp. baking soda
1 1/2 cup cream-style cottage cheese
1/2 cup water
1/4 cup honey
2 Tbsp. margarine
1 tsp. salt
2 eggs

1. Stir together 1 1/2 cups flour, yeast and baking soda.
2. Heat together cottage cheese, water, honey, margarine and salt until moderately warm. Add mixture to dry ingredients along with the eggs. Beat at slow speed for 1 minute. Beat at high speed for 3 minutes.
3. By hand stir in enough remaining flour to make moderately stiff dough. Knead on floured surface, using up to 1/4 cup more flour, until smooth. Place in greased bowl and let rise until double.
4. Punch down and shape into 24 rolls. Place in greased muffin tins or on baking sheets in whatever shape desired. Let rise until nearly double.
5. Bake at 350° for 12-15 minutes.

Potato Rolls

Virginia Moyer
New Oxford, PA

Makes 4 dozen medium rolls

1 1/2 cups lukewarm potato water
2/3 cup sugar
1 1/2 tsp. salt
1 cake compressed yeast
2 eggs
2/3 cup shortening, softened
1 cup lukewarm mashed potatoes
7-7 1/2 cups sifted flour

1. Combine potato water, sugar and salt. Crumble yeast into mixture, stirring until dissolved.
2. Add eggs, shortening and mashed potatoes and mix well.
3. Gradually add flour, stirring first with a spoon, then by hand. Knead until smooth.
4. Refrigerate dough. About 2 hours before baking, form into desired shape and let rise 1 1/2 to 2 hours.
5. Bake at 400° for 12-15 minutes.

Butterhorn Rolls

Melanie Frayle
Ridgeway, ON
Riverside Chapel

Dorothea M. Eigsti
Morton, IL

Makes approximately 4 dozen

1 Tbsp. yeast
1 cup warm water
1 cup milk
6 Tbsp. sugar
1½ tsp. salt
6 Tbsp. shortening
1 egg
6 cups flour
Melted butter

1. Soften yeast in warm water. Set aside.
2. Scald milk and add sugar, salt and shortening. When cooled to lukewarm, add 1 cup flour and beat well. Add egg and yeast and mix thoroughly. Add enough flour to make a soft dough.
3. Knead dough until smooth. Cover and let rise until double in bulk. Knead down. Divide dough into 3 portions, cover and let rise about 15 minutes.
4. Roll each ball of dough into a circular shape about ¼ inch thick. Cut into pie-shaped pieces. Brush each piece with melted butter and roll up, beginning at the wide end. Curve into crescents on greased baking sheet. Let rise until double in bulk.
5. Bake at 375° for 10-12 minutes.

Onion Bacon Oatmeal Buns

Kathy Hertzler
Lancaster, PA
Charlotte Street Mennonite Church

Makes 30 servings

¾ lb. bacon
2 cups diced onion
2 cups boiling water
½ cup oatmeal
½ cup cornmeal
3 Tbsp. cooking oil
2 Tbsp. dry yeast
⅓ cup warm water
¼ cup dark molasses
⅔ cup brown sugar
1 egg
2 tsp. salt (not optional)
5 cups all-purpose flour,
    more as needed
1 cup whole wheat flour

1. Cut bacon into ¼-inch pieces and fry. Drain all but 3 Tbsp. bacon drippings and saute onions until slightly brown. Set bacon and onions aside.
2. Pour boiling water over oatmeal and cornmeal, stirring to prevent lumps. Add cooking oil.
3. Dissolve yeast in warm water (110 to 115°). Add yeast, molasses, brown sugar, egg and salt to oatmeal mixture.
4. Mix flours together and beat ½ of flour into batter to make a soft dough. Add onion and bacon pieces. Add remaining flour. Knead until smooth, adding extra flour to prevent a sticky dough.
5. Cover bowl and let dough rise until double in bulk. Punch down and let rise again for approximately 1 hour.
6. Punch down again. Pull off lemon-sized pieces of dough and form into round bun shapes. Place on greased baking sheets about 1 ½ to 2 inches apart. Let rise until double in size.
7. Bake at 375° for 18-20 minutes. Check oven to make sure bottoms are not too brown. Cool before storing.

Powder Buns

Debbie Rowley and
Leanora Harwood
Lancaster, PA
South Christian Street Mennonite Church

Makes 2 dozen buns

4 cups flour
3 tsp. baking powder
¼ tsp. salt
¾ cup margarine
1½ cups sugar
1 coconut, grated
1 tsp. cinnamon
1 tsp. nutmeg
½ cup milk
1 tsp. vanilla

1. Mix all ingredients well with a knife or by hand. Do not knead.
2. Shape dough into 2 dozen balls. Place on greased cookie sheet and flatten.
3. Bake at 350° for 20 minutes.

Oil Rolls

Vera Kuhns
Harrisonburg, VA
Parkview Mennonite Church

Makes 2 dozen rolls

2 pkgs. dry yeast
2 cups warm water
4 Tbsp. sugar
3 tsp. salt
½ cup cooking oil
6-7 cups all-purpose flour
1 egg, slightly beaten

1. In large mixing bowl soften yeast in warm water. Add sugar, salt and oil. Stir to dissolve sugar.
2. Gradually add about 5 cups flour, enough to make soft dough.
3. Turn out onto floured surface. Cover and let rest 8-10 minutes.
4. Knead in remaining flour, making a smooth and elastic dough. Place in bowl and let rise in warm place until double in size, about 1½ hours.
5. Turn out onto lightly floured surface. Form dough into large ball and let rest 10 minutes.

6. Divide dough into 2 balls. Divide each ball into 12 equal pieces. Roll each small piece of dough into a pencil-like strand 9 inches long and ½ inch in diameter. Form into loose knot.
7. Place each bowknot 2 to 3 inches apart on greased baking sheet. Brush with egg. Let rise.
8. Bake at 375° for about 20 minutes.

Cornmeal Rolls

Frances Schrag
Newton, KS
First Mennonite Church

Makes 75-100 small rolls

2 cups milk
⅔ cup cornmeal
½ cup sugar
8 Tbsp. butter *or* margarine
1½ tsp. salt
2 pkgs. active dry yeast
½ cup warm water
2 eggs
7 cups flour

1. Cook milk and cornmeal until thick, stirring constantly. Add sugar, margarine and salt. Let cool to lukewarm.
2. In small bowl combine yeast and water. Add yeast mixture and eggs to cornmeal mixture. Gradually add flour to make soft dough.
3. Turn out onto lightly floured surface and knead about 5 minutes, adding small amount of flour to prevent sticking. Cover and let

rise until double in size.
4. Punch down and form into rolls. Let rise until double.
5. Bake at 350° for 15-20 minutes.

Bran Rolls

Johanna Badertscher
Apple Creek, OH

Makes 32 rolls

1 cup wheat bran
1 cup boiling water
½ cup honey *or* brown sugar
1½ tsp. salt
1 cup cooking oil
2 pkgs. yeast
1 cup warm water
2 eggs
6½ cups flour

1. Combine bran, boiling water, honey or brown sugar, salt and cooking oil. Cool to lukewarm.
2. Dissolve yeast in warm water and add to bran mixture.
3. Beat in eggs and 3½ cups flour. Knead in remaining 3 cups flour to make a smooth, soft dough.
4. Place in greased bowl and let rise until double in size or seal tightly and place in refrigerator until ready to use.
5. Shape into rolls. Place rolls in greased pans and let rise until double in size.
6. Bake at 375° for 20 minutes.

Variation:
This dough makes wonderful hamburger rolls. After shaping, place on greased cookie sheets at least 1 inch apart.

Oatmeal Rolls

Miriam Christophel
Battle Creek, MI
Pine Grove Mennonite Church

Makes 24 rolls

2⅓ cups water
1 cup dry oatmeal
3 Tbsp. butter *or* margarine
2 pkgs. dry yeast
⅔ cup brown sugar, packed
1 Tbsp. white sugar
1½ tsp. salt
5-5¾ cups all-purpose flour

1. In a saucepan bring 2 cups water to a boil. Add oatmeal and butter or margarine. Simmer 1 minute. Remove to a large mixing bowl and let cool to about 120°.

2. Heat ⅓ cup water to warm. Add yeast and dissolve.

3. To the oatmeal mixture add brown sugar, white sugar, salt, yeast and half the flour. Mix well.

4. Add remaining flour, enough to make a soft dough. Turn out onto a floured board and knead 6-8 minutes or until smooth and elastic. Add additional flour if necessary.

5. Place dough in greased bowl, turning once to grease top. Cover and let rise until double in size, about 1 hour.

6. Punch dough down, divide in half and shape each half into 12 balls. Place 1 inch apart on two greased 9" x 13" baking pans. Cover and let rise until double in size, about 45-60 minutes.

7. Bake at 350° for 20-30 minutes.

Orange Bowknots

Helen E. Reusser
Kitchener, ON
Mannheim W.M.S.C

Makes 30 plus rolls

Dough:
1 pkg. dry yeast
¼ cup warm water
1 cup milk, scalded
½ cup shortening
⅓ cup sugar
1 tsp. salt
5-5½ cups sifted flour
2 eggs, beaten
2 Tbsp. grated orange rind
¼ cup orange juice

Orange Frosting:
1 tsp. grated orange rind
2 Tbsp. orange juice
1 cup powdered sugar, sifted

1. To prepare dough soften yeast in warm water.

2. Combine hot milk, shortening, sugar and salt. Cool to lukewarm. Add 2 cups flour and beat well. Add eggs and beat well. Stir in softened yeast. Add orange rind, orange juice and enough remaining flour to make a soft dough. Cover

and let rest for 10 minutes.

3. Knead dough 8-10 minutes until smooth and elastic. Place in greased bowl, turning once to grease surface. Cover and let rise until double, about 2 hours. Punch down. Cover and let rest 10 minutes.

4. Roll dough into a 10" x 18" rectangle, ½" thick. Cut strips 10" long and ¾" wide. Roll each strip back and forth under fingers and tie into a loose knot. Arrange on greased baking sheet. Cover and let rise until almost double, about 45 minutes.

5. Bake at 400° for 8-10 minutes until gently browned.

6. To prepare frosting combine all ingredients.

7. Brush frosting on each bowknot with a pastry brush. Serve.

Cream Cheese Rolls

Vera Kuhns
Harrisonburg, VA
Parkview Mennonite Church

Makes 2 dozen rolls

Dough:
2 pkgs. dry yeast
2 cups warm water
4 Tbsp. sugar
3 tsp. salt
½ cup cooking oil
6-7 cups all-purpose flour
1 egg, slightly beaten

Cream Cheese Filling:
8-oz. pkg. cream cheese
1 small egg
¼ cup sugar
1 tsp. vanilla

1. In large mixing bowl soften dry yeast in warm water. Add sugar, salt and oil. Stir to dissolve sugar.
2. Gradually add about 5 cups flour, enough to make a soft dough. Turn out onto floured surface. Cover and let rest 8-10 minutes.
3. Knead in remaining flour until dough is smooth and elastic. Place in bowl and let rise in warm place until double in size, about 1½ hours.
4. Meanwhile, prepare cream cheese filling by combining all ingredients. Mix well. Set aside.
5. Turn dough out onto lightly floured surface and divide it in half. Divide each half into 12 equal pieces. Form each piece into a roll. Place 2-3 inches apart on greased baking sheet. Brush with slightly beaten egg. Let rise.

6. Immediately before putting into oven, place 1 tsp. filling in center of each roll.
7. Bake at 375° for about 20 minutes.

Rollkuchen

Jessie Penner
Bakersfield, CA

Makes 20-25 servings

2 eggs, beaten
½ cup cream
½ Tbsp. sugar
1 tsp. salt
2 tsp. baking soda
1 cup milk
2-3 cups flour

1. Beat eggs until light and lemon colored. Add cream, sugar, salt and baking soda. Gradually add milk, alternating with flour until you have a soft dough.
2. Roll out onto floured board. Cut dough into 2"-3" squares.
3. Fry Rollkuchen in deep fat.
4. Serve with jelly or watermelon.

Easy Zwieback

Lucille Taylor
Hutchinson, KS
First Mennonite Church

Makes 20 servings

2 cups milk
1 Tbsp. dry yeast
12 Tbsp. margarine
2 Tbsp. sugar
1 Tbsp. salt, scant
5 cups flour

1. Dissolve yeast in ¼ cup lukewarm milk. Set aside.
2. Combine 1¾ cups milk, margarine, sugar and salt and heat until fairly warm.
3. Add three cups flour and beat well. Add yeast mixture to the sponge.
4. Add another cup flour and beat again.
5. Knead in remaining cup flour or enough flour to make a fairly soft dough. Let rise.
6. Shape into 20 buns on 2 cookie sheets by pinching off pieces of dough. Make another 20 balls slightly smaller than the first ones and set the smaller balls on top of the larger ones.
7. Let rise in warm place until almost double in bulk.
8. Bake at 400° for 15 minutes or until brown. Place on rack to cool.

Zwieback

Susan Ortman Goering
Boulder, CO
Boulder Mennonite Church

Makes 6-7 dozen servings

4 cups skim milk
2 pkgs. yeast
$\frac{1}{2}$ cup sugar
1 Tbsp. salt
1 cup cooking oil
10 cups flour

1. Scald milk and cool to lukewarm. Add yeast and sugar to milk and dissolve. Add salt, oil and enough flour to make a cake-like batter. Beat thoroughly.
2. Continue adding flour until you have kneaded a smooth, medium-soft dough. Let rise until double in bulk.
3. Shape dough into Zwieback (a small bun topped with a slightly smaller one). Place on greased baking sheet. Let rise again.
4. Bake at 400° for 15 minutes or until golden brown.

This recipe was developed to reduce saturated fat. Compared to typical Zwieback recipes, they are lighter and quicker.

Bagels

Bob Litt
London, OH

Makes 32 servings

2 Tbsp. active dry yeast
1 tsp. sugar
$1\frac{1}{2}$ cups warm water
$\frac{1}{4}$ cup sugar
4-4$\frac{1}{2}$ cups flour
2 eggs
Cornmeal
Egg whites
Chopped onion or poppy seeds

1. Dissolve yeast and 1 tsp. sugar in warm water. Let stand until foamy.
2. Add $\frac{1}{4}$ cup sugar, 2 cups flour and eggs. Beat until well mixed, approximately 200 strokes.
3. Slowly add remaining flour to make soft dough. Turn out onto lightly floured surface. Knead dough until smooth and elastic, approximately 8-10 minutes.
4. Place dough in greased bowl, turning to coat top of dough. Cover and let stand in warm, dry place until doubled in size, approximately $1\frac{1}{2}$ hours.
5. Punch down and divide in half until you have 32 pieces. Shape into ball and punch finger through each piece to make a bagel shape. Let rise until double in size.
6. Boil each bagel for 3 minutes, turning after first minute.
7. Grease baking pan and coat with cornmeal. Bake at 375° for 25-30 minutes.
8. Top each bagel with egg white and either onion or poppy seeds.

Rhubarb Muffins

Mary Vaughn Warye
West Liberty, OH
Oak Grove Mennonite Church

Makes 18 servings

$1\frac{1}{4}$ cups brown sugar
$\frac{1}{2}$ cup cooking oil
1 egg, beaten
2 tsp. vanilla
1 cup buttermilk
$1\frac{1}{2}$ cups diced rhubarb
$\frac{1}{2}$ cup chopped walnuts
$\frac{1}{4}$ tsp. black walnut flavoring
$2\frac{1}{2}$ cups flour
1 tsp. baking soda
1 tsp. baking powder
$\frac{1}{2}$ tsp. salt
1 tsp. butter, melted
$\frac{1}{3}$ cup white sugar
1 tsp. cinnamon

1. In large bowl combine brown sugar, oil, egg, vanilla and buttermilk. Mix well. Stir in rhubarb, walnuts and flavoring.
2. In smaller bowl combine flour, baking soda, baking powder and salt. Add dry ingredients to rhubarb mixture. Stir only until moistened.
3. Spoon batter into prepared muffin tins. Combine melted butter, white sugar and cinnamon. Spoon over top of each muffin, lightly pressing it down.
4. Bake at 375° for 20-25 minutes.

Pumpkin Muffins

Sharon Hartman
Winston-Salem, NC
Oak Hill Mennonite Church

Makes 2 dozen muffins

4 eggs, lightly beaten
2 cups white sugar or less
1½ cups cooking oil
1¾ cups pumpkin
3 cups all-purpose flour
1 Tbsp. cinnamon
2 tsp. baking powder
2 tsp. baking soda
1 tsp. salt
2 cups raisins
Brown sugar

1. Blend eggs, sugar, oil and pumpkin and beat thoroughly. Add all dry ingredients and mix until smooth. Stir in raisins.
2. Fill greased muffin cups ⅔ full and sprinkle tops with brown sugar.
3. Bake at 375° for 15-20 minutes.

The Best Blueberry Muffins

Laura Grimm
Dalton, OH

Makes 12 servings

½ cup butter
1 cup white sugar
2 large eggs
1 tsp. vanilla
2 tsp. baking powder
¼ tsp. salt
2½ cups blueberries

1½ cups all-purpose flour
¼ cup soy flour
¼ cup whole wheat flour
2 Tbsp. wheat germ
½ cup milk
1 Tbsp. white sugar
¼ tsp. ground nutmeg

1. In medium bowl beat butter until creamy. Add 1 cup sugar and beat until fluffy. Add eggs, vanilla, baking powder and salt and blend.
2. Mash ½ cup blueberries with a fork. Mix into batter.
3. In small bowl mix all flours and wheat germ. With a spatula fold half of flour into batter. Add half of milk. Fold in remaining flour and milk and mix just enough to wet dry ingredients.
4. Fold remaining blueberries into batter.
5. Scoop batter into 12 greased muffin cups. Mix 1 Tbsp. sugar and nutmeg and sprinkle small amount on each muffin.
6. Bake at 375° for 25-30 minutes. Let muffins cool at least 30 minutes before removing from muffin tins.

Lemon Blueberry Muffins

Ellen Helmuth
Debec, NB
New Brunswick Monthly Meeting, Society of Friends

Makes 18-20 servings

4 eggs
1 cup cooking oil
1½ cups sugar
1 tsp. vanilla
Rind and juice of 1 lemon
½ cup cornmeal
2½ cups flour
2 tsp. baking powder
1 tsp. baking soda
1 cup milk
1½ cups blueberries

1. Beat eggs. Add oil, sugar, vanilla, lemon rind and juice. Stir in cornmeal.
2. Sift flour, baking powder and baking soda together.
3. To the batter add milk, dry ingredients and blueberries. Stir gently until well mixed. Fill greased muffin cups.
4. Bake at 375° for 20 minutes.

Banana Chocolate Chip Muffins

Karen and Leonard Nolt
Boise, ID
Hyde Park Mennonite Church

Makes 18 servings

3-4 large bananas, mashed
¾ cup sugar
1 egg, beaten
1½ cups flour
1 tsp. baking soda
1 tsp. baking powder
½ tsp. salt
⅓ cup margarine, melted
½ cup chocolate chips

1. Blend bananas, sugar and egg together. Add flour, baking soda, baking powder and salt. Blend well. Stir in margarine and chocolate chips.
2. Fill paper-lined muffin tins ⅓ full.
3. Bake at 375° for 15-20 minutes.

Banana Date Muffins

Nancy Roth
Colorado Springs, CO
Remnant of Israel Congregation

Makes 16-18 servings

1½ cups whole wheat flour
½ cup bran
½ cup sugar
½ cup chopped dates
1 cup shredded apples

1 Tbsp. baking powder
3 large bananas, mashed
2 egg whites
½ cup skim milk

1. Mix all ingredients except egg whites and skim milk in a large bowl.
2. Lightly beat egg whites. Gradually add skim milk while beating eggs. Add to other ingredients and blend well.
3. Fill greased muffin tins ⅔ full.
4. Bake at 350° for 20-25 minutes or until wooden pick comes out clean.

All-Bran Date Muffins

Mrs. Lewis L. Beachy
Sarasota, FL
Bahia Vista Mennonite Church

Makes 12-16 servings

1 cup chopped dates
1 cup chopped nuts
1 tsp. baking soda
1 Tbsp. shortening
1 cup boiling water
¾ cup brown sugar
1 egg, well beaten
1 cup flour
1 cup All-Bran
1 tsp. baking powder

1. Combine dates, nuts, baking soda and shortening. Pour boiling water over mixture and let cool.
2. Add sugar, egg, flour, All-Bran and baking powder. Fold together until blended. Do not use mixer.

3. Spoon batter into well-greased muffin tins.
4. Bake at 350° for 20-25 minutes.

Sunshine Muffins

Ellen Helmuth
Debec, NB
New Brunswick Monthly Meeting, Society of Friends

Makes 15-18 muffins

1 cup whole wheat flour
1 cup unbleached flour
2 tsp. baking powder
1 cup sugar
1 tsp. cinnamon
2 cups grated carrots
⅓ cup raisins
⅓ cup sunflower seeds
⅓ cup coconut
⅓ cup chocolate chips
3 eggs
1 cup cooking oil
1 tsp. vanilla
1 banana, mashed or
** 2 apples, grated**

1. Combine all dry ingredients. Stir in carrots, raisins, sunflower seeds, coconut and chocolate chips.
2. In separate bowl beat eggs. Add oil and vanilla. Add to dry ingredients along with bananas or apples. Spoon batter into greased muffin cups, filling ¾ full.
3. Bake at 400° for 20-25 minutes.

Apple Oat Bran Muffins

Ruth Brunk
Sarasota, FL
Bahia Vista Mennonite Church

Makes 18-24 muffins

2 eggs, lightly beaten
¼ cup butter, softened
½ cup honey
½ cup plain yogurt
¾ cup milk
1 cup rolled oats
1 cup oat bran
2 medium apples
1½ cups whole wheat
  flour
1½ tsp. baking powder
¾ tsp. baking soda
1 tsp. cinnamon

1. Combine eggs, butter, honey, yogurt, milk, rolled oats and oat bran.
2. Peel, core and chop apples and fold into batter.
3. Sift all dry ingredients and add to batter, stirring until moistened. Spoon into greased muffin tins.
4. Bake at 425° for 20-25 minutes. Remove from pan and cool on rack.

Refrigerator Oatmeal Muffins

Edith Petri
Wood Dale, IL
Lombard Mennonite Church

Makes 6 dozen muffins

6 cups old-fashioned
  oatmeal
2 cups boiling water
1 cup shortening, melted
1½ cups sugar
4 eggs, beaten
1 quart buttermilk
5 cups flour
5 tsp. baking soda
2 tsp. salt
Chopped raisins or dates

1. Pour boiling water over 2 cups oatmeal and let stand.
2. Mix together remaining oatmeal, shortening, sugar, eggs and buttermilk.
3. Sift together flour, baking soda and salt and stir into batter along with oatmeal soaked in boiling water. Fold in chopped raisins or dates.
4. Store in refrigerator and bake as needed.
5. Bake at 400° for 20 minutes.

Soups

White Chili with Cashews

Marjorie Rush
West Lafayette, IN

Makes 8 servings

3 Tbsp. butter
1 medium onion, chopped
1 green pepper, chopped
2 ribs celery, chopped
2 cups cooked, drained
    white beans
15-oz. can whole kernel corn
16-oz. can tomatoes
2-3 tsp. chili powder
1 tsp. cumin
2 cloves garlic, minced
1 tsp. dried basil
1 tsp. dried oregano
1 bay leaf
½ tsp. pepper
1 cup raisins
1 cup raw cashews
½ cup grated cheddar cheese

1. In a large saucepan melt butter. Sauté onion, green pepper and celery until crisp and tender, about 10 minutes. Add beans, corn, tomatoes, chili powder, cumin, garlic, basil, oregano, bay leaf and pepper. Bring to a boil. Reduce heat and simmer for 30 minutes.

2. Stir in raisins and cashews. Continue to simmer until raisins are plump and cashews are tender, about 20 minutes.

3. Remove bay leaf. Ladle soup into serving dish and top with grated cheese.

Chick Pea Chili

Thelma Wolgemuth
Immokalee, FL
People's Chapel

Makes 6-8 servings

1 small onion, minced
2 cloves garlic, minced
15-oz. can chick peas,
    drained
2 8-oz. cans tomato sauce
1 Tbsp. chili powder
1 tsp. ground cumin
½ tsp. dried oregano
Cayenne pepper to taste
⅔ cup low-fat yogurt
2 cups cooked brown rice

1. Sauté onion and garlic over medium heat in a large saucepan. Stir in chick peas, tomato sauce, chili powder, cumin, oregano and cayenne. Simmer, uncovered, about 30 minutes, stirring occasionally. (If mixture becomes too thick, add water.)

2. Pour into serving dish and top with yogurt.

3. Serve with hot, cooked rice on the side.

Chili

Pat Augsburger-Blum
Berkeley, CA

Makes 10-12 servings

1 onion, chopped
4 cloves garlic, minced
1 Tbsp. cooking oil
4 lbs. ground beef
4 8-oz. cans tomato sauce
4 cups water or more
8 Tbsp. mild chili powder
3 Tbsp. cocoa
2 Tbsp. sugar
4 tsp. salt
4 tsp. oregano
2 tsp. cumin
3 16-oz. cans red kidney beans

1. In a large saucepan sauté onion and garlic in oil. Add meat and brown. Drain excess fat.
2. Stir in all other ingredients. Simmer for 1 hour.

Chili Con Carne

Shirley Hershey
Bloomingdale, NJ
Garden Chapel

Makes 8 servings

2 lbs. ground beef
1 medium onion, chopped
1 cup chopped celery
1 clove garlic, minced
2 Tbsp. cooking oil
2 cups tomatoes
1 cup tomato purée
2 tsp. ground cumin
2 tsp. chili powder

1 tsp. salt
2 16-oz. cans kidney beans

1. In a heavy skillet sauté ground beef, onion, celery and garlic.
2. Stir in tomatoes, tomato purée, cumin, chili powder and salt.
3. Cover and simmer for 45 minutes to 1 hour.
4. Fold in kidney beans and adjust seasoning. Continue to simmer for 30 minutes longer. Serve.

Variation:
Add 1 cup frozen corn and ½ cup seeded, chopped jalapeño peppers.

Elaine Klaassen
Minneapolis, MN,
Faith Mennonite Church

Mild Chili Con Carne

Anna Petersheim
Paradise, PA
Kinzer Mennonite Church

Makes 4-5 main servings

1 lb. ground beef
1 tsp. minced onion
1 Tbsp. flour
½ tsp. salt
1½ tsp. chili powder
1 cup hot water
2 cups tomatoes
2 cups kidney beans

1. Brown ground beef and onion. Drain excess fat.
2. Add flour to ground beef and brown. Add salt, chili powder, water and tomatoes.
3. Cover and simmer

slowly for 1 hour. Add more water if necessary.
4. Add kidney beans and bring to a boil.
5. Or this may be slow-cooked in crockpot on low for 4-6 hours.

Variations:
Instead of thickening chili with flour, add ½ cup macaroni during last ½ hour of simmering time.

Iona S. Weaver
Lansdale, PA,
Norristown New Life Church

Add ½ cup diced peppers to meat and onions while browning them.

Lucille Weaver,
Perkasie, PA

New Year's Soup

Rhoda M. Peachey
Reedsville, PA
Allensville Mennonite Church

Makes 4 quarts

1 lb. dried beans
2 Tbsp. salt
1½-2 lbs. ground turkey
2 quarts water
1 large onion, chopped
28-oz. can whole tomatoes
1 clove garlic, minced
Juice of 1 lemon
1 tsp. chili powder (optional)

1. Wash beans. Place in large kettle and cover with salt water to 2 inches above bean line. Soak beans overnight and drain in morning.
2. Brown ground turkey and add to beans. Add all re-

maining ingredients and simmer for 3 hours.

3. To make in crockpot cook on high for 3 hours.

4. Serve hot and enjoy.

Bean Soup

Lois Fenton
Philadelphia, MO
Pea Ridge Mennonite Church

Makes 12-16 servings

2 lbs. lean ground beef *or* ground turkey
1 large onion, chopped
2 28-oz. cans tomatoes, chopped
5 16-oz. cans variety of beans
15-oz. can tomato sauce
Chili powder to taste
Salt to taste

1. Brown ground meat with onion. Drain excess fat if necessary.

2. In a large soup kettle or Dutch oven combine tomatoes, beans and tomato sauce. Add meat mixture and stir.

3. Add seasonings and simmer for 30 minutes, adding water to make desired consistency.

4. Serve with crackers, French bread, carrot sticks and fresh apples.

St. Paul Bean Pot Soup

Jane Miller
Minneapolis, MN
St. Paul Mennonite Fellowship

Makes 8-10 servings

2½ cups dried beans
2½ quarts water
2 Tbsp. chicken bouillon
1 cup chopped onion
15-oz. can tomato sauce
1½ Tbsp. chili powder
2 tsp. garlic powder
Pepper

1. Soak beans in water overnight.

2. Transfer to crockpot and cook on high 4-5 hours.

3. Two hours into cooking time add all remaining ingredients to the crockpot.

4. Serve with rice.

Basic Bean Soup

Marjorie Weaver Nafziger
Harman, WV

Makes 8-10 servings

2 cups dried beans
1¾-2 quarts water
1 ham bone
1 onion, chopped
2-3 stalks celery, chopped
2-3 carrots, chopped
3-4 cups canned tomatoes
Salt and pepper to taste

1. On Saturday night bring the beans and water to a boil. Transfer to crockpot

turned on high.

2. Add all remaining ingredients and turn crockpot on low overnight.

3. Take along to church on Sunday morning and plug into outlet in Sunday school room if none are available in kitchen.

Sausage Bean Chowder

Nancy Bradford
Gap, PA
Bart Mennonite Church

Makes 3 quarts

2 lbs. bulk pork sausage
4 cups water
2 16-oz. cans kidney beans
2 16-oz. cans whole tomatoes
2 medium onions, chopped
2 medium potatoes, cubed
½ cup chopped green pepper
1 large bay leaf
½ tsp. salt
½ tsp. dried whole thyme
¼ tsp. garlic powder
¼ tsp. pepper

1. Brown sausage in a Dutch oven, stirring to crumble. Drain off excess fat.

2. Stir in all remaining ingredients and bring to a boil.

3. Cover, reduce heat and simmer for 1 hour.

4. Remove bay leaf before serving.

Green Bean Soup

Dorothy Jane Thomas
Marion, SD
Evangelical Mennonite Brethren
Ladies Mission Fellowship

Makes about ½ gallon

1 smoked ham bone
2 medium potatoes, chopped
1 large carrot, diced
3-4 sprigs summer savory
1 quart green beans
1-2 Tbsp. sour cream

1. Cook ham bone in water to cover until tender. During last ½ hour of cooking time add potatoes, carrot and summer savory.
2. Remove ham bone and take off all meat. Return meat to soup kettle. Add green beans and heat through.
3. Immediately before serving, stir in sour cream.

Yellow Pea Soup

Elaine Klaassen
Minneapolis, MN
Faith Mennonite Church

Makes 5-6 servings

16-oz. pkg. dried yellow
peas
7 cups water
16-oz. can sauerkraut
3 Tbsp. butter
½ cup sour cream
Salt to taste

1. Cook the dried peas in 7 cups water until mushy. Add

undrained sauerkraut and simmer at least ½ hour to let flavors blend.
2. Stir in butter and sour cream. Salt to taste. Simmer for 15 minutes. Serve immediately.

Russian Lentil Fruit Stew

Naomi E. Fast
Newton, KS
Goessel Mennonite Church

Makes 8-10 servings

1 lb. lean beef cubes
6 cups cold water
1 cup dry lentils
2 Tbsp. cooking oil
2 medium potatoes, cubed
½ cup dried apricots
½ cup dried prunes
Salt and pepper to taste
½ cup coarsely chopped
walnuts

1. Cover beef cubes with cold water and simmer for 1-1½ hours. Add dry lentils and cook over medium-low heat for 20 minutes.
2. In a skillet brown potatoes in oil until all surfaces are lightly browned. Add potatoes, apricots and prunes to lentils and beef. Continue cooking over low heat for 25-30 minutes.
3. Adjust liquid to make a stew consistency. Salt and pepper to taste.
4. Add walnuts and cook several minutes longer. Serve with yogurt.

Lentil Vegetable Soup

Mary C. Jungerman
Boulder, CO
Boulder Mennonite Church

Makes 8-10 servings

2 cups lentils
8 cups water
2 slices bacon, diced
½ cup chopped onion
½ cup chopped celery
¼ cup chopped carrots
3 Tbsp. snipped parsley
1 clove garlic, minced
2½ tsp. salt
¼ tsp. pepper
½ tsp. dried oregano
2 cups chopped tomatoes
2 Tbsp. wine vinegar

1. Rinse lentils. Drain and place in large soup kettle. Add water and all remaining ingredients except tomatoes and vinegar.
2. Cover and simmer 1 ½ hours.
3. Add tomatoes and vinegar. Cover and simmer for 30 minutes longer.
4. Adjust seasoning and serve.

Lentil Stew

Susan Ortman Goering
Boulder, CO
Boulder Mennonite Church

Makes 8-10 servings

1 lb. dried lentils
1 Tbsp. salt
¼ tsp. thyme

¼ tsp. marjoram
4-5 large carrots, sliced
1 large onion, chopped
2 16-oz. cans tomatoes
3 cups grated Swiss cheese

1. Wash lentils.
2. Put all ingredients except cheese into crockpot. Add enough water to fill crockpot.
3. Cook on high for 2 hours, stirring occasionally.
4. Immediately before serving, stir in grated cheese.

Wild Rice Soup

Elaine Unruh
Minneapolis, MN
Mennonite Brethren Church of New
Hope

Makes 8-10 servings

1½ cups uncooked wild
    rice
3½ cups water
2 tsp. salt
4 Tbsp. butter
2 Tbsp. minced onion
¾ cup flour
4 cans chicken broth
1 tsp. salt
⅔ cup minced ham
⅔ cup finely grated carrot
¼ cup slivered almonds
2 cups half-and-half

1. In a saucepan combine rice, water and 2 tsp. salt. Simmer for 45 minutes.
2. In a large soup kettle melt butter. Sauté onion until tender. With a wire whisk stir in flour.
3. Gradually add chicken

broth and cook until mixture thickens, stirring constantly.
4. Stir in rice and 1 tsp. salt. Add ham, carrot and almonds. Simmer for 5 minutes.
5. Immediately before serving, blend in half-and-half.

Potato Chowder

Makes 8-10 servings

4 cups peeled, diced
    potatoes
½ cup finely chopped onion
1 cup grated carrot
1 tsp. salt
¼ tsp. pepper
1 Tbsp. dried parsley flakes
4 chicken bouillon cubes
6 cups scalded milk
4 Tbsp. butter
¼ cup flour

1. In large Dutch oven or kettle combine potatoes, onion, carrot, salt, pepper, parsley and bouillon cubes. Add enough water to just cover vegetables.
2. Cook until vegetables are tender, about 15-20 minutes. Do not drain.
3. Scald milk by heating until tiny bubbles form around edges of pan. Remove 1 ½ cups milk from saucepan. Stir butter and flour into this milk with a wire whisk.
4. Add remaining milk to vegetables.
5. Gradually stir thickened milk into kettle until well blended.

6. Simmer 15 minutes on low heat.

Potato Broccoli Soup

Evelyn Cross
Prescott, AZ
Prescott Mennonite Church

Makes 8-10 servings

4 chicken bouillon cubes
1 quart water
2½ cups peeled, cubed
    potatoes
1 cup diced celery
1 cup diced carrots
1 small onion, diced
3-4 cups chopped broccoli
2 cans cream of chicken soup
1 cup cubed cheese
    (half Velveeta)
½ cup water

1. Dissolve bouillon cubes in water.
2. Add potatoes, celery, carrots and onion. Cook until vegetables are almost tender. Add broccoli and cook a few minutes longer.
3. Add cream of chicken soup, cheese and water. Stir slowly and gently until cheese melts and is hot. Do not bring to a boil.
4. Keep warm in a crockpot until ready to serve.

Mary Zehr's Broccoli Soup

Mary Zehr
Mt. Pleasant, PA
Mennonite Church of Scottdale

Makes 6-8 servings

4 slices bacon
1/3 cup chopped onion
6 cups shredded potatoes
4 cups water
2 tsp. salt
1/2 tsp. pepper
3 Tbsp. butter
3 Tbsp. flour
12-oz. can evaporated milk
1 1/2 cups milk
4 slices American cheese
4 cubes chicken bouillon
10-oz. pkg. chopped broccoli

1. Fry, drain and crumble bacon. Set aside.
2. Sauté onion in bacon fat.
3. Rinse shredded potatoes thoroughly.
4. In a kettle combine onion, potatoes, water, salt and pepper. Cook for 40 minutes.
5. In a separate saucepan melt butter. Add flour, stirring until bubbly. Gradually add evaporated milk, regular milk, cheese and bouillon cubes. Cook over medium heat until thick and creamy, stirring constantly.
6. Immediately before serving, add broccoli and cheese mixture to kettle with potatoes. Heat through.
7. Sprinkle bacon over top and serve.

Ham Broccoli Soup

Ethel O. Yoder
Goshen, IN
College Mennonite Church

Makes 6-8 cups

2 cups chopped, fresh broccoli
1/2 cup finely chopped celery
3 Tbsp. minced onion
1/4 cup margarine
1/4 cup flour
2 cups milk
1 1/2 cups chicken broth
1/4 tsp. celery salt
1/4 tsp. pepper
3/4 cup finely chopped ham
3/4 cup shredded cheese

1. Cook broccoli in small amount of water for about 5 minutes. Drain and set aside.
2. In large skillet sauté celery and onion in margarine until tender. Stir flour into mixture.
3. Gradually add milk and chicken broth, stirring after each addition. Cook until thick and smooth, stirring constantly.
4. Add seasonings, broccoli and ham. Simmer for 10 minutes, stirring frequently. Add cheese and stir until melted. Serve.

Mary Martin's Broccoli Soup

Mary E. Martin
Goshen, IN
Benton Mennonite Church

Makes 6 servings

16-oz. can chicken broth
12 ozs. fresh broccoli, cut up
4 Tbsp. margarine
1/2 medium onion, chopped
1/2 tsp. salt
1/4 tsp. pepper
1/4 tsp. onion salt
1/4 tsp. garlic salt
1 cup milk
1/4 cup cream
1/2 cup buttermilk
4 Tbsp. flour
2 Tbsp. sour cream (optional)
3 Tbsp. margarine

1. Bring broth to boil in large kettle. Add broccoli and simmer until tender.
2. Sauté onion in 2 Tbsp. margarine. Stir onion and seasonings into broccoli and simmer.
3. In a small saucepan heat milk, cream and buttermilk.
4. Melt 2 Tbsp. margarine in a skillet. Add flour and stir in warm milk. Cook mixture until thick, stirring constantly.
5. Add thickened milk to broccoli. Remove from heat and stir in sour cream and 3 Tbsp. margarine. Serve.

Hamburger Soup

Susie Janzen
Wichita, KS
Lorraine Avenue Mennonite Church

Makes 30-40 servings

5 lbs. ground beef
18 cups water
4 16-oz. cans tomatoes,
    cut up
16 carrots, sliced
18 potatoes, cubed
3 medium onions, chopped
3 cups chopped celery
6 tsp. salt
1 tsp. pepper
2 heads cabbage, cut up

1. Brown ground beef in a kettle. Drain excess fat.
2. Add water and all remaining ingredients. Bring to a boil.
3. Reduce heat, cover and simmer 45-60 minutes or until vegetables are tender.

Spinach Soup

Sadie Yoder
Quarryville, PA
Bart Mennonite Church

Makes 12-14 servings

1 tsp. butter
1½ cups chopped onion
1 quart puréed spinach
½ tsp. garlic powder
1 tsp. salt
½ tsp. celery salt
Dash pepper
1 cup evaporated milk
1 pint milk

1. In a saucepan melt butter. Sauté onion until wilted. Add spinach, garlic powder, salt, celery salt, pepper and evaporated milk. Heat through.
2. Add 1 pint milk and simmer until heated through.
3. Serve with crackers or croutons.

In the summer when garden spinach grows fast, I cut, wash and steam it lightly. Then I purée it in my blender and freeze it in 1-quart containers. My husband likes this soup and so do I.

Zucchini Soup

Marlys Wiens
Minneapolis, MN
Faith Mennonite Church

Makes 12 servings

½ lb. bacon
1 green pepper, cut in strips
1 medium onion, chopped
3 cups chopped celery
2 4-oz. cans mushrooms
1 quart tomatoes
15-oz. can tomato sauce
5-6 small zucchini, sliced
1 cup water
½ tsp. salt
¼ tsp. black pepper
1½ tsp. basil
1 tsp. sugar

1. Fry, drain and crumble bacon.
2. In bacon grease sauté green pepper, onion and celery. Drain.
3. In a soup kettle combine all ingredients. Cook slowly until zucchini is tender.

Cabbage Soup

Reta Martin
Waterloo, ON
St. Jacobs Mennonite Church

Makes 8-10 servings

1 lb. ground beef
1 Tbsp. cooking oil
1 cup chopped onion
½ cup chopped celery
½ cup chopped green
    pepper
2 cups diced potatoes
1 cup diced carrots
14-oz. can pork and beans
28-oz. can tomatoes *or* 4
    cups tomato juice
4 cups hot water
2 tsp. salt or less
¼ tsp. pepper
½ tsp. paprika
Dash rosemary and cumin
2 cups shredded cabbage

1. Brown ground beef in oil along with onion, celery and green pepper. Drain excess fat.
2. Combine all ingredients except cabbage in large soup kettle. Simmer for 1 hour.
3. Add cabbage and simmer 1 hour longer.

Minestrone Soup

Lydia Konrad
Edmonton, AB
Lendrum Mennonite Brethren
Church

Makes 10-12 servings

1½ lbs. lean ground beef
1 cup diced onions
1 cup diced zucchini
1 cup cubed potatoes
1 cup sliced carrots
½ cup diced celery
1 cup shredded cabbage
15-oz. can tomatoes, chopped
1½ quarts water
1 bay leaf
½ tsp. thyme
5 tsp. salt
Pepper to taste
1 tsp. Worcestershire sauce
¼ cup rice
½ cup grated Parmesan
    cheese

1. Brown ground beef in large soup kettle. Add vegetables, water and spices and bring to a boil.
2. Sprinkle rice into mixture. Cover and simmer for at least 1 hour.
3. Sprinkle with Parmesan cheese and serve with brown bread.

Italian Vegetable Soup

Verna Birky
Albany, OR
Albany Mennonite Church

Makes 12 servings

1 lb. ground beef
1 cup diced onion
1 cup diced celery
1 cup diced carrots
2 cloves garlic, minced
16-oz. can tomatoes
15-oz. can tomato sauce
15-oz. can kidney
    beans, undrained
2 cups water
5 tsp. beef bouillon granules
1 Tbsp. dried parsley flakes
½ tsp. oregano
½ tsp. sweet basil
¼ tsp. black pepper
2 cups shredded cabbage
1 cup green beans, cut up
½ cup elbow macaroni
Parmesan cheese

1. Brown ground beef in large, heavy kettle or skillet. Drain.
2. Add all ingredients except cabbage, green beans, macaroni and cheese. Bring to a boil over low heat. Cover and simmer for 20 minutes.
3. Add cabbage, green beans and macaroni. Simmer until vegetables are tender. Add water if needed.
4. Sprinkle with Parmesan cheese and serve.

Hungry Man's Soup

Bernice Potoski
Riverton, MB
Native Ministries

Makes 10 servings

2 lbs. ground beef
1 medium onion, diced
4 medium carrots, diced
2 cups diced turnips
4 cups diced cabbage
5 cups diced potatoes
10 cups water
2 tsp. salt
½ tsp. pepper
19-oz. can tomatoes
2 cans tomato soup
1 cup water
¾ cup flour

1. Brown ground beef lightly. Drain excess fat.
2. In a large kettle combine ground beef, onion, carrots, turnips, cabbage, potatoes, 10 cups water, salt and pepper. Cook on medium-low heat until vegetables are tender. Add tomatoes and tomato soup. Bring to a boil and simmer on low boil for 30-45 minutes.
3. Combine 1 cup water and flour to make a paste. Thicken soup slightly with paste.
4. Cook for 15 minutes longer. Serve.

Menudo

Mabel E. De Leon
La Junta, CO
Emmanuel Mennonite Church

Makes 10 servings

2½ lbs. beef tripe, cubed
4 pigs' feet
1 tsp. oregano
1 ½ tsp. salt
3 Tbsp. chili powder
2 ½ quarts water
2 #303 cans white hominy
1 small onion, chopped

1. Combine beef tripe, pigs' feet, oregano, salt, chili powder and water in a soup kettle. Bring to a boil and simmer for 4 hours or cook in a pressure cooker for 35-45 minutes.
2. Add hominy and onion and cook until tender.
3. May be served as a soup or with tortillas.

Beef Barley Soup

Vera M. Kuhns
Harrisonburg, VA
Parkview Mennonite Church

Makes 8-10 servings

3 beef shanks, seared
12 cups water
1 cup barley
1 large potato, diced
1 large carrot, diced
1 large onion, diced
1 tsp. salt
¼ tsp. pepper
¼ tsp. garlic
7 beef bouillon cubes

1. In a large pot brown meat. Add all other ingredients. Stir to mix well.
2. Cover and bake at 250°-275° for 2-3 hours.
3. Serve with homemade bread and a salad. Soup has more flavor when reheated.

Borscht

Helga Neudorf
North Vancouver, BC

Makes 10-12 servings

4-lb. beef brisket
3 quarts cold water
¼ cup chopped dill
½ cup chopped parsley
Salt and pepper to taste
4-5 large onions, chopped
2 large carrots, shredded
½ cup shredded beets
2 cups diced potatoes
2 cups tomatoes
1 head cabbage, shredded

1. Bring meat to a boil in water. Cook until tender. Cut meat into bite-sized pieces.
2. Skim all excess fat from broth and return meat to broth. Add dill and parsley. Simmer for about 15 minutes. Salt and pepper to taste.
3. Add onions, carrots, beets and potatoes. Simmer until vegetables are tender.
4. Add tomatoes and cabbage and cook until cabbage wilts and is tender.
5. Serve. Borscht is even better after it has been reheated.

Springtime Soup

Clara L. Hershberger
Goshen, IN
Goshen Mennonite Church

Makes 10-12 servings

1 lb. ground beef
1 cup chopped onion
4 cups water
1 cup diced carrots
1 cup diced celery
1 cup diced potatoes
2 tsp. salt or less
1 tsp. Worcestershire sauce
¼ tsp. pepper
1 bay leaf
⅛ tsp. basil
6 tomatoes, chopped
Fresh parsley

1. In large saucepan cook and stir ground beef until browned. Drain excess fat.
2. In large, heavy soup pot cook and stir onions with meat until onions are clear and tender, about 5 minutes.
3. Stir in all remaining ingredients except parsley. Bring to a boil.
4. Reduce heat, cover and simmer until vegetables are just tender.
5. Immediately before serving, add fresh parsley.

Chicken Borscht

Paul Isaak
Rocky Ford, CO
Rocky Ford Mennonite Church

Makes 70-75 servings

23 lbs. chicken
14 quarts water
12 tsp. salt
24 cups diced potatoes
24 cups diced carrots
7 medium onions, diced
7 cups cooked tomatoes
5 heads cabbage, shredded
12-15 peppercorns
3-4 bay leaves
12-15 whole allspice
Chicken bouillon to taste

1. Cook chicken in salted water. Remove skin and debone chicken. Set aside.
2. Skim fat off broth. Add potatoes, carrots and onions. Cook in broth until vegetables are almost tender. Add chicken, tomatoes and cabbage.
3. Place peppercorns, bay leaves and allspice in a cloth bag and suspend bag in soup.
4. Simmer until cabbage is tender. Remove spice bag and add chicken bouillon for additional flavor.

Chicken Soup

Carol Enns
Minneapolis, MN
Faith Mennonite Church

Makes 10 servings

3-5 lb. chicken
Water to cover
10-12 peppercorns
1 ginger root
Anise seed (optional)
2 bay leaves
1 lb. egg noodles
Salt to taste
Fresh parsley

1. Cover chicken with cold water in a kettle. Bring to a boil. Skim excess fat off top. Cover and simmer for 2-3 hours.
2. During last ½ hour of simmering time put spices in a spice ball and add to broth.
3. Remove chicken and spice ball from broth. Add noodles to broth and cook until tender. (Add water if necessary.)
4. Meanwhile, cut chicken from bones. Add diced chicken to broth. Heat through. Immediately before serving, add fresh parsley.

Chicken Escarole Soup

Helen Bowman
Columbiana, OH
Midway Mennonite Church

Makes 10-12 cups

2-3 lb. chicken
2 ribs celery with leaves
1 medium onion, quartered
Parsley
7 cups water
4 chicken bouillon cubes
¾ cup thinly chopped carrots
½ cup chopped onion
⅓ cup uncooked rice
¼ tsp. pepper
½ lb. escarole

1. Cook chicken, celery ribs, unpeeled onion and parsley with water and bouillon until chicken is soft. Remove chicken and strain broth. Discard vegetables.
2. Return strained broth to soup kettle. Cut chicken from bone.
3. Bring broth to a boil. Add carrots, onion, rice and pepper. Cook until vegetables are soft.
4. Add diced chicken. Bring to simmer and add escarole which has been cut crosswise into thin slices. Heat through and serve.

Laotian Noodle Soup

Boulieng Luangviseth
Regina, SK
Laotian Fellowship

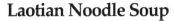

Makes 2-4 servings

2 chicken legs
4-oz. pkg. rice noodles
Warm water to cover
4-5 cups cold water
1 tsp. salt
1 tsp. fish sauce
½ cup dry shrimp
2 green onions, chopped

1. With a sharp knife cut meat from chicken legs. Cube meat and set aside.
2. Soak rice noodles in warm water for 10-15 minutes. Drain thoroughly.
3. Bring 4-5 cups water to a boil. Add chicken, salt, fish sauce and shrimp. Let boil for 10-15 minutes or until meat is tender. Add noodles and boil a few more minutes. Sprinkle with green onions and remove from heat. Serve.

Salmon Chowder

Marjorie Anderson
Lima, OH

Makes 8-10 servings

1 cup diced potato
1 small onion, minced
2 cups hot water
¼ cup butter
¼ cup flour
3 cups milk
7-oz. can pink salmon
1 cup canned tomatoes
2 tsp. salt
¼ tsp. pepper

1. Cook potato and onion in hot water. Do not allow potato to become mushy.
2. Melt butter in a saucepan. Stir in flour. Gradually add milk, stirring constantly until thickened.
3. Pick through salmon to remove all bones.
4. Cut tomatoes into bite-sized pieces.
5. Combine all ingredients in soup kettle. Stir and heat.

Seafood Gumbo

Dorothy L. Ealy
Los Angeles, CA
Calvary Christian Fellowship

Makes 12 servings

3 onions, chopped
½ stalk celery, chopped
2 cloves garlic, minced
2 15-oz. cans tomatoes
6-oz. can tomato paste
2 lbs. raw shrimp
1 gallon water
Salt to taste

1. Combine onions, celery, garlic, tomatoes and tomato paste in heavy Dutch oven.
2. Bake at 250° for 3 hours, removing cover for last ½ hour. Stir once or twice while baking.
3. Peel and devein shrimp.
4. Move gumbo into large soup kettle. Add 1 gallon water and heat through. Add shrimp and cook for 15-20 minutes. Season with salt.
5. Serve with hot rice.

Salads

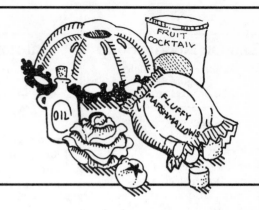

Vegetable Salads

Salad Slaw and Dressing

Rosemary K. Hartzler
High Point, NC
Greensboro Mennonite Church

Makes 10-12 servings

1 medium head cabbage, shredded
1 green pepper, chopped
2-3 stalks celery, chopped
1 onion, chopped
3-4 carrots, grated
Salt to taste
1 cup sugar
1½ tsp. garlic salt
1½ tsp. minced onion
½ cup ketchup
½ cup vinegar
1½ tsp. paprika
1 cup cooking oil

1. Combine all prepared vegetables in large bowl and sprinkle with salt to taste. Let stand 1 hour.
2. In large saucepan combine sugar, garlic salt, onion, ketchup, vinegar, paprika and cooking oil. Bring to a boil and boil for 1 minute. Remove from heat and cool.
3. Squeeze excess juice out of cabbage mixture. Combine with dressing and refrigerate.

Lanae Waltner's Coleslaw

Lanae Waltner
Freeman, SD

Makes approximately 32 servings

10 lbs. cabbage
3 cups sour cream
1 cup sugar
½ cup white vinegar
1½ tsp. salt
1 tsp. pepper

1. Grate cabbage.

2. Combine all other ingredients.
3. Immediately before serving, pour dressing over cabbage and mix thoroughly.

Sensational Slaw

Viola Stauffer
Milford, NE
Bellwood Mennonite Church

Makes 8-10 servings

3 cups shredded cabbage
¾ cup chopped green onions
1 cup pineapple tidbits, drained
1 cup shredded cheese
½ cup sliced olives
¼ cup whipping cream
½ cup mayonnaise
1 tsp. lemon juice
Salt and pepper to taste

1. Combine cabbage, onions, pineapple, cheese and olives.
2. Whip cream. Fold in mayonnaise, lemon juice, salt and pepper.

and pepper.

   3. Pour dressing over salad and refrigerate at least 2 hours before serving.

Betty Pellman's Coleslaw

Betty Pellman
Millersville, PA
Rossmere Mennonite Church

Makes 6-8 servings

½ **head firm cabbage, grated**
1 **medium carrot, grated**
½ **small onion, grated**
½ **cup mayonnaise**
1-2 **Tbsp. sugar**
1-2 **Tbsp. vinegar**

   1. Mix cabbage, carrot and onion together.

   2. In small bowl whip mayonnaise until creamy. Add sugar and vinegar to taste. Pour over grated vegetables and mix well.

Confetti Coleslaw

Mattie Miller
Sugarcreek, OH
Walnut Creek Mennonite Church

Makes 8 servings

3-oz. **pkg. lime gelatin**
1 **cup boiling water**
½ **cup cold water**
1 **Tbsp. vinegar**
½ **cup mayonnaise**
1 **cup shredded cabbage**

½ **cup shredded carrots**
½ **cup finely diced celery**
⅓-½ **cup raisins**

   1. Dissolve gelatin in boiling water. Stir in cold water and vinegar.

   2. Gradually add gelatin to mayonnaise, stirring until well blended. Chill until slightly thickened.

   3. Fold in cabbage, carrots, celery and raisins. Pour into dish or 1-quart mold. Chill until firm.

Bavarian Inn Cabbage Salad

Colleen Heatwole
Burton, MI
New Life Christian Fellowship

Makes 12 servings

1 **lb. shredded cabbage**
2 **Tbsp. sugar**
¾ **tsp. salt**
4 **tsp. Ivory-Jel *or* instant clear-gel**
4 **Tbsp. mayonnaise**
2 **Tbsp. vinegar**
½ **cup half-and-half**
1 **red *or* green pepper, sliced**
½ **cup shredded carrot**

   1. Mix sugar, salt and Ivory-Jel. Stir mayonnaise into dry ingredients. Add vinegar and half-and-half. Pour dressing over shredded cabbage.

   2. Garnish with red or green pepper and shredded carrot. Refrigerate until ready to serve.

This is an authentic Michigan dish and is served in Frankenmuth, MI at Bavarian and Zenders restaurants. They sell Ivory-jel at their restaurants. Clear-gel works almost as well.

Red Cabbage with Apples

Naomi E. Fast
Newton, KS
Goessel Mennonite Church

Makes 10-12 servings

4 **cups shredded red cabbage**
2 **tart apples, finely chopped**
1 **cup finely chopped onion**
1½ **tsp. salt**
2 **tsp. sugar**
¼ **tsp. black pepper, freshly ground**
¼-⅓ **cup red wine vinegar**

   1. In a large bowl combine all ingredients, toss lightly and cover tightly with plastic wrap. Refrigerate at least 2 hours.

   2. Serve as either a salad or a meat relish. (Finely chopped ingredients are the secret to success.)

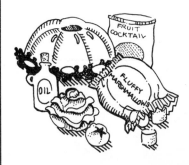

Cabbage Ramen

Winifred Ewy, Newton, KS; Bonnie
and Vern Ratzlaff, Tuba City, AZ;
Mabel S. Neff, Quarryville, PA

Makes 8-10 servings

Salad:
1/2 head cabbage, shredded
2 Tbsp. sesame seeds
2 Tbsp. sunflower seeds
1/2 cup slivered almonds
4 green onions, chopped
1 pkg. French Onion Ramen
   noodles, uncooked

Dressing:
1/2 cup cooking oil
3 Tbsp. sugar
3 Tbsp. vinegar
1/2 tsp. soy sauce
1/2 tsp. pepper
Dash salt

1. Combine all salad ingredients except flavoring package which comes with noodles.
2. Combine all dressing ingredients and pour over salad. Fold in Ramen noodle flavoring. Refrigerate several hours or overnight.

Variation:
Substitute 1 medium head Chinese cabbage for 1/2 head regular cabbage.

**Marilyn Yoder
Archbold, OH,**
West Clinton Mennonite Church

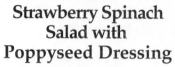

Indian Spinach Salad

Florence Lehman
Kidron, OH
Salem Mennonite Church

Makes 6-8 servings

Salad:
6 cups chopped spinach
1 1/2 cups chopped apples
1/2 cup raisins
1/2 cup peanuts
2 Tbsp. minced green onion

Dressing:
1/4 cup cooking oil
1/4 cup white wine vinegar
2 Tbsp. chopped chutney
2 tsp. sugar
1/2 tsp. salt
1 1/2 tsp. curry powder
1 tsp. dry mustard

1. Combine all salad ingredients in a large bowl.
2. Combine all dressing ingredients and mix well. Chill.
3. Immediately before serving, shake dressing thoroughly and pour over spinach. Toss and serve.

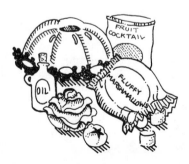

Strawberry Spinach Salad with Poppyseed Dressing

Jeanette Zacharias
Morden, MB
Barn Swallow Quilters

Makes 6-8 servings

Salad:
10-12 ozs. fresh spinach
2 cups halved strawberries
2 small oranges, peeled & sliced
1/3 cup sliced, toasted almonds

Dressing:
1/2 cup mayonnaise
1/2 cup sour cream
1 Tbsp. poppy seed
1 Tbsp. honey
1 Tbsp. orange juice
1 tsp. grated orange rind
1/4 tsp. ground ginger

1. Thoroughly mix all dressing ingredients. Chill several hours to blend flavors.
2. Wash and drain spinach and tear it into bite-sized pieces. Arrange in large bowl. Top with strawberries, orange slices and almonds.
3. Drizzle dressing over salad and serve.

Variation:
Substitute the following dressing recipe: 1/2 cup sugar, 2 Tbsp. sesame seeds, 1 Tbsp. poppy seeds, 1 1/2 tsp. minced green onion, 1/4 tsp. Worcestershire sauce, 1/4 tsp. paprika, 1/2 cup cooking oil and 1/4 cup cider vinegar. Thoroughly mix all ingredients. Chill and drizzle over salad.

**Ila Yoder, Hesston, KS; Yvonne E.
Martin, Mechanicsburg, PA;
Eleanor Kathler, Steinbach, MB**

Spinach Salad

Ruth Zercher
Grantham, PA
Grantham Brethren in Christ Church

Makes 10-15 servings

1 lb. fresh spinach
1 head bibb lettuce
¼ cup salted cashew nuts
1 cup cooking oil
1 tsp. celery seed
⅓ cup sugar
1 tsp. salt
1 tsp. dry mustard
1 tsp. grated onion
¼ cup vinegar

1. Wash spinach and lettuce and tear into bite-sized pieces. Combine spinach, lettuce and nuts in serving bowl, reserving a few nuts for garnish.
2. Combine all other ingredients in blender and mix well.
3. Immediately before serving, pour dressing over greens and nuts. Sprinkle reserved nuts over top.

Korean Spinach Salad

Marcella Stalter
Flanagan, IL
Waldo Mennonite Church;

Edith Stoltzfus
Mantua, OH
Aurora Mennonite Church

Makes 8-10 servings

Salad:
1 pkg. fresh spinach
½ lb. bacon
1 small can water chestnuts
1 small can bean sprouts
3 hard-boiled eggs, diced

Dressing:
1 cup cooking oil
¼ cup vinegar
1 onion, chopped
1 Tbsp. Worcestershire sauce
2 tsp. salt
⅓ cup ketchup
¾ cup sugar

1. Wash and drain spinach. Break into bite-sized pieces.
2. Fry, drain and crumble bacon. Toss bacon and spinach with water chestnuts, bean sprouts and eggs.
3. Combine all dressing ingredients and mix well. Pour dressing over salad and serve.

Variation:
Add ½ lb. sliced mushrooms to salad ingredients.
Doris Ebersole
Archbold, OH
Zion Mennonite Church

Spinach Salad with Garlic Dressing

Dorothy Shank
Goshen, IN
College Mennonite Church

Makes 6-8 servings

Salad:
1 lb. fresh spinach
6 slices bacon
¼ lb. mushrooms, sliced
4 hard-cooked eggs,
  quartered lengthwise
1-2 pimentos, chopped
  coarsely

Dressing:
⅓ cup cooking oil
¼ cup vinegar
1 clove garlic, crushed
1 Tbsp. steak sauce
½ tsp. salt
Dash of pepper

1. In large salad bowl tear spinach into bite-sized pieces.
2. Fry, drain and crumble bacon. Toss spinach and bacon with mushrooms, eggs and pimentos.
3. Combine all dressing ingredients in a covered jar and shake to mix. Pour over salad and toss lightly.

Ferne Burkhardt's Spinach Salad

Ferne Burkhardt
Petersburg, ON
Mannheim Mennonite Church

Makes 10-12 servings

Salad:
1 lb. raw spinach
¼ cup crumbled bacon

Dressing;
1 cup sour cream
2 Tbsp. white vinegar
1 tsp. prepared mustard
1 tsp. grated onion
Salt and pepper to taste
Sugar to taste

1. Tear spinach leaves into bite-sized pieces.
2. Combine all dressing ingredients and mix well. Toss with spinach.
3. Top with bacon.

Variations:

Add one or several of the following ingredients: tangerine segments, handful of raisins, ½ cup sliced mushrooms, handful of bean sprouts or handful of sunflower seeds.

Irene Riegsecker's Spinach Salad

Irene Riegsecker
Sarasota, FL
Bahia Vista Mennonite Church

Makes 10-12 servings

Salad:
1 lb. spinach
3 hard-boiled eggs, chopped
½ lb. bacon

Dressing:
1¾ cups sugar
⅔ cup vinegar
1½ cups cooking oil
1 tsp. dry mustard
1 tsp. salt
1 tsp. minced onion

1. Combine spinach and eggs in serving bowl.
2. Fry, drain and crumble bacon. Toss with spinach and egg.
3. Combine all dressing ingredients and beat until very thick. Pour ½ of dressing over salad. Refrigerate remaining dressing to use another time.

Variation:
Add ½ lb. fresh mushrooms to the salad ingredients.
Melba Eshleman
Manheim, PA
Chestnut Hill Mennonite Church

In Search of the Perfect Broccoli or Cauliflower Salad

Broccoli, bacon and raisin salads with a mayonnaise and sugar dressing have become a familiar sight at fellowship meals. Each of us has our own preferences about which combinations work best—from less sugar to more vinegar and from broccoli with raisins to cauliflower with eggs. Here are some of those variations, each of which can bear your own particular adaptation.

Low-Calorie Cauliflower Salad

Joy Sutter
Iowa City, IA

Makes 8 servings

Salad:
3 stalks celery, chopped
1 small onion, chopped
20-oz. pkg. frozen peas
1 head cauliflower, chopped

Dressing:
1 cup plain yogurt
1 cup low-calorie
    mayonnaise
1 pkg. low-calorie Hidden
    Valley Ranch dressing mix

1. Chop and toss all vegetables together in a bowl.
2. Combine yogurt, mayonnaise and dressing mix.

Pour over vegetables.
3. Refrigerate at least 2 hours before serving.

Cauliflower Salad

Mary Ann Gaeddert
Georgetown, KY
Faith Baptist Church

Makes 6-8 servings

Salad:
3 cups chopped cauliflower
**½ cup chopped green
  pepper**
4 ozs. sliced black olives
2 ozs. chopped pimento
**¼ cup chopped green
  onions**

Dressing:
2 Tbsp. lemon juice
2 Tbsp. vinegar
¼ cup cooking oil
½ tsp. salt

1. Combine all vegetables.
2. Combine all dressing ingredients and pour over vegetables.
3. Chill and serve.

Cauliflower Lettuce Salad

Ruth Liechty
Goshen, IN
Berkey Avenue Mennonite Fellowship

Makes 16-20 servings

Salad:
½ head lettuce
½-1 head cauliflower
4 hard-boiled eggs, diced
¼ lb. grated cheddar cheese
¼ lb. bacon

Dressing:
1 ½ cups mayonnaise
⅓ cup Parmesan cheese
¼ cup sugar

1. Combine lettuce, cauliflower, eggs and cheddar cheese.
2. Mix together mayonnaise, Parmesan cheese and sugar. Toss dressing with salad.
3. Fry, drain and crumble bacon. Sprinkle over salad and serve.

Hazel Miller's Cauliflower Salad

Hazel Miller
Hudson, IL
Carlock Mennonite Church

Makes 12-15 servings

Salad:
1 large head lettuce
½ large head cauliflower
1 lb. bacon
**1 ½ cups grated Colby *or*
  Monterey Jack cheese**

Dressing:
½ cup imitation sour cream
**½ cup low-calorie
  mayonnaise**
¼ cup lemon juice
2 Tbsp. sugar substitute
1 tsp. prepared mustard
2 tsp. onion salt

1. Sometime during the day before the fellowship meal, chop lettuce and cauliflower into large serving bowl. Cover with plastic wrap and store in refrigerator.
2. Fry, drain and crumble bacon. Put into small plastic container and seal. Store in refrigerator.
3. Grate cheese, put into small container and store in refrigerator.
4. Combine all dressing ingredients and mix well. Pour into jar and store in refrigerator.
5. Take each container along to church. Immediately before meal is served, combine all ingredients in large serving bowl.

Cauliflower Broccoli Salad

E.B. Heatwole
Rocky Ford, CO
Rocky Ford Mennonite Church

Makes 25 servings

Salad:
½ lb. bacon
1 ½ bunches broccoli
2 heads cauliflower
1 medium red onion, diced

Dressing:
1½ cups mayonnaise
½ cup sugar
⅓ cup vinegar

1. Fry, drain and crumble bacon.
2. Wash and separate broccoli and cauliflower into bite-sized pieces. Combine with onion and bacon.
3. Combine mayonnaise, sugar and vinegar and pour over salad. Allow to marinate at least 2 hours.

Variations:
Add 1 cup raisins to salad ingredients.
Lorene Good
Armington, IL,
Hopedale Mennonite Church

Add 4 chopped, hard-boiled eggs to salad ingredients.
Nancy Bradford
Gap, PA
Bart Mennonite Church

Add 2 pkgs. shelled sunflower seeds to salad ingredients.
Irene Epp
Kindersley, SK
Superb Mennonite Church

Add ½ cup Parmesan cheese and 2 cups grated mozzarella cheese to salad ingredients.
Shirley Hochstetler
Kidron, OH
Sonnenberg Mennonite Church

Add ½ cup peanuts or sliced almonds to salad ingredients.
Nancy S. Lapp
Goshen, IN
Assembly Mennonite Church

Substitute 1 cup sour cream for 1 cup mayonnaise. Add a dash of salt and a dash of Worcestershire sauce to the dressing ingredients.
Melanie Frayle
Ridgeway, ON
Riverside Chapel

24-Hour Salad

Laura Bauman
Elmira, ON
Rockway Mennonite Church

Lois Brubacher
Waterloo, ON

Makes 8-10 servings

Salad:
1 head romaine lettuce
1½ cups cauliflower
6-8 slices bacon
1 red onion, sliced

Dressing:
½ cup Parmesan cheese
2 Tbsp. sugar
1 cup mayonnaise

1. Wash and dry romaine. Break into bite-sized pieces. Layer into a deep, glass dish.
2. Cut cauliflower into fine slices and layer over lettuce.

3. Fry, drain and crumble bacon and layer over cauliflower.
4. Layer onion over bacon.
5. Combine all dressing ingredients and spread over top of salad evenly. Cover tightly and refrigerate for 24 hours.
6. Toss well immediately before serving.

Christine Guth's Broccoli Salad

Christine Guth
Goshen, IN
East Goshen Mennonite Church

Makes 8 servings

1 large bunch broccoli
¼ cup sunflower seeds
½ cup raisins
1 cup plain yogurt
2 Tbsp. vinegar
2 tsp. honey

1. Cut broccoli into bite-sized pieces. Peel stems and chop, adding to salad. Add sunflower seeds and raisins.
2. Mix yogurt, vinegar and honey together.
3. Pour yogurt dressing over salad and toss to mix well. Refrigerate several hours or overnight before serving.

Virginia Bender's Broccoli Salad

Virginia Bender
Dover, DE
Presbyterian Church of Dover

Makes 6-8 servings

1 large bunch broccoli
½ lb. Swiss cheese
3 large tomatoes
1 medium onion
16-oz. can kidney beans
1 bottle Zesty Italian
  dressing

1. Cut broccoli into bite-sized pieces. Cut cheese into cubes. Cut tomatoes into wedges. Slice onion into rings.
2. Toss all ingredients together. Allow to marinate for several hours before serving.

Broccoli, Cauliflower and Carrot Salad

Clara L. Yoder
Wadsworth, OH
Salem Mennonite Church

Makes 8 servings

2 10-oz. pkgs. broccoli
10-oz. pkg. cauliflower
3 large carrots, chopped
1 cup diced celery
1 cup diced onion
1 green pepper, sliced
1 tsp. mustard
1 cup sugar
1 Tbsp. cornstarch
¾ cup vinegar
1 tsp. salt

1. Cook first three vegetables separately to a crisp stage. Drain each one and cool.
2. Combine all vegetables in large serving bowl.
3. In a saucepan combine mustard, sugar, cornstarch, vinegar and salt. Cook until clear. Pour over vegetables.
4. Cover and chill overnight or at least 12 hours before serving.

Broccoli, Cauliflower and Pea Salad

Virginia Graber
Freeman, SD
Salem Zion Mennonite Church

Makes 10-12 servings

2 cups chopped broccoli
2 cups chopped cauliflower
2 cups frozen peas, thawed
1 large onion, chopped
2 cups chopped celery
¾ cup sour cream
¾ cup mayonnaise
2 Tbsp. sugar
2 Tbsp. vinegar
¼ tsp. salt

1. Combine all ingredients.
2. Refrigerate overnight and serve.

Variation:
Add 1 can sliced water chestnuts to ingredients.
Jeanne Heyerly
Reedley, CA
Reedley First Mennonite Church

Green and White Vegetable Salad

Joan B. Lange
New Oxford, PA
The Brethren Home
Retirement Village

Makes 8 servings

Salad:
1 bunch fresh broccoli
1 medium head cauliflower
1½ cups finely chopped
  celery
6 green onions, chopped

Dressing:
¾ cup mayonnaise
¼ cup whipping cream
2 Tbsp. sugar
¼ tsp. pepper

1. Wash broccoli and cauliflower. Break or chop into small pieces.
2. Combine all vegetables in large bowl.
3. Combine all dressing ingredients, mixing well. Pour over vegetables and toss lightly to coat.
4. Cover and chill thoroughly before serving.

Jean Blake's Broccoli Salad

Jean Blake
Poolesville, MD
Dawsonville Mennonite Church

Makes 8-12 servings

Salad:
1-2 lbs. fresh broccoli
1 lb. bacon
1 medium onion, chopped
1 cup raisins

Dressing:
2 cups mayonnaise
1 cup sugar
4 Tbsp. vinegar

1. Chop broccoli into bitesized pieces.
2. Fry, drain and crumble bacon.
3. Layer ingredients into 9" x 13" container in following order: broccoli, onion, raisins, bacon.
4. Combine mayonnaise, sugar and vinegar. Pour over layers. Cover and refrigerate 2-3 hours or overnight.

Variation:
Substitute ½ cup chopped cabbage for chopped onion.

Alma C. Ranck
Paradise, PA
Paradise Mennonite Church

Broccoli Salad

Thelma P. Plum
Waynesboro, PA
Waynesboro Church of the Brethren

Martha A. Miller
Harrisonburg, VA

Makes 8-12 servings

Salad:
1 medium head broccoli
1 red onion
½ lb. bacon
1 cup grated cheddar cheese

Dressing:
½ cup mayonnaise
¼ cup sugar
1 Tbsp. vinegar

1. Chop broccoli and onion into a bowl.
2. Fry, drain and crumble bacon.
3. Combine mayonnaise, sugar and vinegar to make a dressing. Pour dressing over broccoli and onion.
4. Sprinkle crumbled bacon and shredded cheese over top.
5. Refrigerate several hours or overnight before serving.

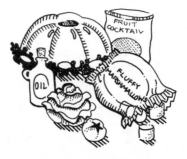

Lorraine Amstutz's Broccoli Salad

Lorraine Stutzman Amstutz
Bluffton, OH

Makes 10-12 servings

Salad:
4-6 slices bacon
3 cups chopped, fresh broccoli
4 hard-boiled eggs
½ cup chopped onion
¼ cup raisins
1 cup chopped celery
½ cup diced cheese
Sunflower seeds

Dressing:
1 cup mayonnaise
¼ cup sugar
2 Tbsp. vinegar

1. Fry, drain and crumble bacon. Combine bacon, broccoli, eggs, onion, raisins, celery, cheese and sunflower seeds.
2. In small bowl combine mayonnaise, sugar and vinegar. Pour dressing over salad and mix well.
3. Chill and serve.

Helen Peachey's Broccoli Salad

Helen M. Peachey
Harrisonburg, VA
Lindale Mennonite Church

Makes 10-12 servings

Salad:
2 bunches fresh broccoli
1 medium red onion, sliced
¼ cup raisins
8 slices bacon
¼ cup sunflower seeds

Dressing:
1 cup mayonnaise
¼ cup sugar
2 Tbsp. vinegar

1. Chop broccoli and onion into bowl. Add raisins.
2. Fry, drain and crumble bacon and add to salad.
3. Combine mayonnaise, sugar and vinegar and mix well.
4. Fold dressing and sunflower seeds into vegetables.
5. Refrigerate 1-2 hours before serving.

Donna Horst's Potato Salad

Donna Horst
Leola, PA
Groffdale Mennonite Church

Makes 15-20 servings

Salad:
12 cups potatoes
12 hard-boiled eggs
1 cup finely chopped celery
1 finely chopped onion

Dressing:
3 cups mayonnaise
6 tsp. mustard
1¼ cups sugar
½ cup milk
4 tsp. salt or less
¼ cup vinegar

1. Cook, cool and shred potatoes to make 12 cups.
2. Shred the eggs and combine all salad ingredients.
3. Combine all dressing ingredients and pour over potatoes.

Barbara Hershey's Potato Salad

Barbara Hershey
Lancaster, PA
Rossmere Mennonite Church

Makes 6 servings

Salad:
6 cups potatoes
4 hard-boiled eggs
¼ cup shredded onion
¼ cup chopped parsley
1½ tsp. salt
½ tsp. pepper

Dressing:
½ cup sugar
1 Tbsp. cornstarch
1 tsp. dry mustard
½ tsp. salt
¾ cup water
¼ cup vinegar
2 eggs
1 cup mayonnaise

1. Cook and cube potatoes to make 6 cups. Chop hard-boiled eggs.
2. Combine all salad ingredients.
3. In a saucepan combine sugar, cornstarch, mustard, salt, water, vinegar and eggs. Bring to a boil. Fold in mayonnaise and cool completely.
4. Pour dressing over salad and serve.

Eleanor Kathler's Potato Salad

Eleanor Kathler
Steinbach, MB

Makes 6 servings

2 lbs. potatoes
1 cup low-fat yogurt
3 Tbsp. light mayonnaise
¼ cup minced green onion
1 tsp. curry powder
1 tsp. Dijon mustard
½ tsp. salt
⅓ cup chopped fresh dill
¼ tsp. pepper
Watercress (optional)

1. Cook potatoes until tender. Peel only if skins are tough. Cut into thin slices.
2. In a serving bowl mix together yogurt, mayonnaise, onion, curry, mustard and salt. Add potatoes, dill and pepper.
3. Stir gently and garnish with watercress if desired.

Linda Welty's Potato Salad

Linda Welty
La Junta, CO
Emmanuel Mennonite Church

Makes 10-12 servings

10 medium potatoes
5 medium sweet pickles, diced
½ cup pickle juice
1 medium onion, chopped
¾ tsp. salt
½ tsp. pepper
¼ cup sugar
1 Tbsp. mustard
1 cup mayonnaise
6 hard-boiled eggs, diced

1. Cook, cool and shred potatoes.
2. Combine pickles, juice and onion. Add salt, pepper, sugar, mustard, mayonnaise and 4 eggs. Gently fold potatoes into mixture.
3. Garnish with 2 sliced hard-boiled eggs and serve.

Three-Bean Salad

June Marie Weaver,
Harrisonburg, VA,
Harrisonburg Mennonite Church;

Priscilla Falb, Dalton, OH
Martins Mennonite Church

Makes 12 servings

16-oz. can green beans
16-oz. can yellow beans
16-oz. can kidney beans
1 medium onion, sliced
¾ cup sugar

⅔ cup vinegar
⅓ cup cooking oil
1 tsp. salt
¼ tsp. pepper
¼ tsp. oregano

1. Drain each can of beans and combine with onion in serving bowl.
2. In a saucepan combine sugar, vinegar, oil, salt, pepper and oregano. Heat until sugar dissolves. Pour over bean mixture.
3. Refrigerate at least 12 hours before serving.

Four-Bean Salad

Lola L. Miller
Quakertown, PA,
West Swamp Mennonite Church;

Helen Rose Pauls
Sardis, BC,
Sardis Community Church

Makes 12 servings

Salad:
16-oz. can green beans
16-oz. can yellow beans
16-oz. can kidney beans
16-oz. can lima beans
1 medium onion, sliced
1 medium green pepper, sliced

Dressing:
½ cup sugar
½ cup wine vinegar
½ cup cooking oil
½ tsp. basil leaves
1 tsp. salt
½ tsp. dry mustard
½ tsp. dry tarragon leaves
2 Tbsp. fresh parsley

1. Drain all beans and combine with onion and green pepper in large serving dish.
2. Combine all dressing ingredients. Pour over bean mixture. Refrigerate at least 12 hours before serving.

Variation:
Substitue 16-oz. can chickpeas for the lima beans. Also toss occasionally during refrigeration so all the beans will be marinated.

Viola Weidner
Allentown, PA
First Mennonite Church

Five-Bean Salad

Edna M. Detwiler
Honey Brook, PA

Makes 20-25 servings

⅓ cup chopped onion
⅓ cup chopped celery
⅓ cup chopped green pepper
16-oz. can kidney beans, drained
16-oz. can lima beans, drained
16-oz. can yellow beans, drained
16-oz. can green beans, drained
16-oz. can chickpeas, drained
2 cups sugar
1½ cups vinegar
½ cup water

1. Mix onion, celery, pepper and beans together.
2. In a saucepan bring

sugar, vinegar and water to a boil. Pour dressing over bean mixture.

3. Refrigerate and marinate for at least 24 hours. Serve.

Kidney Bean Salad

Gail U. Pentz
Sarasota, FL
Bahia Vista Mennonite Church

Makes 6 servings

2 cups kidney beans
¼ cup diced celery
3 medium pickles, chopped
1 small onion, minced
2 hard-boiled eggs, chopped
½ tsp. salt
1/8 tsp. pepper
¼ cup mayonnaise

1. Cook, drain and cool kidney beans. Combine beans, celery, pickles and onion. Add eggs, salt and pepper.

2. Gently fold in mayonnaise and refrigerate until ready to serve.

Variation:
Add ½ tsp. curry powder to the ingredients.
Iona S. Weaver, Lansdale, PA,
Norristown New Life Church

Green Bean Salad

Twila Nafziger
Wadsworth, OH
Bethel Mennonite Church

Makes 6-8 servings

16-oz. can French-cut green beans, drained
16-oz. can baby peas, drained
1 cup finely chopped celery
1 medium onion, minced
3-oz. can pimentos, finely chopped
1 cup sugar
1 cup vinegar
½ cup cooking oil
1 Tbsp. water
1 tsp. pepper
1 tsp. salt

1. In a serving bowl combine green beans, peas, celery, onion and pimentos.

2. In a separate bowl combine sugar, vinegar, oil, water, salt and pepper. Pour dressing over salad. Mix gently and refrigerate for at least 24 hours before serving.

Calico Cheese Salad

Doreen Snyder
Waterloo, ON
Erb Street Mennonite Church

Makes 6-8 servings

16-oz. can red kidney beans
16-oz. can whole kernel corn
1 cup chopped celery
¼ lb. cheddar cheese, cubed

½ cup oil and vinegar dressing
Lettuce leaves (optional)

1. Drain and rinse kidney beans. Toss with corn, celery, cheese and dressing. Cover and chill at least 3 hours to blend flavors, stirring several times.

2. Drain, reserving dressing for future use. Serve in lettuce-lined bowl if desired.

Pea Salad

Jeanette Friesen
Loveland, CO
Boulder Mennonite Church

Makes 6 cups

2 10-oz. pkgs. frozen peas
½ lb. cheddar cheese, cubed
¾ cup chopped celery
¼ cup finely chopped onion
⅓ cup low-fat sour cream
⅓ cup mayonnaise
2 Tbsp. milk
1 tsp. prepared mustard
½ tsp. salt
¼ tsp. pepper
¼ tsp. Tabasco sauce

1. Combine peas, cheese, celery and onion in a serving bowl.

2. In a small bowl combine sour cream, mayonnaise, milk, mustard, salt, pepper and Tabasco sauce, mixing until smooth.

3. Immediately before serving, pour dressing over salad and toss to coat.

Calico Bean Salad

Eileen Lehman,
Kidron, OH
Sonnenberg Mennonite Church

Makes 10 servings

Salad:
2 cups fresh green beans
2 cups fresh yellow beans
1 cup chopped carrots
1½ cans kidney beans,
    drained
16-oz. can chickpeas,
    drained
½ cup chopped celery
½ cup chopped onion
½ cup chopped green
    pepper

Dressing:
¾ cup vinegar
¾ cup sugar
1 tsp. salt
½ tsp. dry mustard
½ tsp. black pepper
⅓ cup cooking oil

1. Cook and drain green beans, yellow beans and carrots. Cool and add kidney beans, chickpeas, celery, onion and green pepper.
2. In a saucepan combine all dressing ingredients. Bring to a boil. Cool.
3. Stir dressing into salad. Refrigerate overnight before serving.

Tazoo Salad

Becky Bixler
Iowa City, IA
First Mennonite Church

Makes 8 servings

16-oz. can medium pitted
    ripe olives
2 small zucchini, thinly
    sliced
2 8-oz. jars marinated
    artichoke hearts
2 medium tomatoes, cut up
2 green onions, thinly sliced
Salt and pepper to taste

1. Drain jar of olives. Mix with zucchini, undrained artichoke hearts, tomatoes, onions, salt and pepper in a large bowl.
2. Marinate for at least 4 hours. Drain before serving.

Antipasto Salad

Grace Krabill
Goshen, IN
College Mennonite Church

Makes 6 servings

Salad:
8-oz. can cut green beans,
    drained
8-oz. can garbanzo beans,
    drained
½ cup sliced ripe olives
½ cup sliced pepperoni
2-oz. can sliced pimento,
    drained
Bibb lettuce

Dressing:
⅓ cup olive oil
2 Tbsp. lemon juice
1 tsp. dried oregano, crushed
¼ tsp. salt
⅛ tsp. garlic powder
⅛ tsp. pepper

1. In medium bowl combine green beans, garbanzo beans, olives, pepperoni and pimento.
2. Combine all dressing ingredients in a jar. Cover and shake well. Pour dressing over vegetable mixture and toss gently to coat.
3. Cover and refrigerate several hours or overnight, stirring occasionally.
4. Immediately before serving, drain salad. Serve on lettuce-lined plate.

Vegetable Marinade Salad

Esther Porter
Minneapolis, MN
Faith Mennonite Church

Makes 8 servings

Salad:
16-oz. can French-style
    green beans
16-oz. can peas
2 medium carrots, sliced
2 cups diced celery
2 medium onions, sliced
½ cup stuffed olives,
    halved
1 cup alfalfa sprouts
    (optional)
1 cup cooked soybeans
    (optional)

Dressing:
¾ cup orange juice
¼ cup lemon juice
¼ cup vinegar
¼ cup sugar
¼ cup cooking oil
½ tsp. paprika
2 tsp. salt

1. Combine all vegetables in glass serving bowl.
2. Combine all dressing ingredients and stir until sugar is dissolved. Pour dressing over vegetables.
3. Cover and refrigerate for 24 hours or overnight. Serve with a slotted spoon.

Marinated Italian Vegetables

Judith E. Bartel
North Newton, KS
Bethel College Mennonite Church

Makes 12 servings

Salad:
1 head cauliflower, chopped
6 carrots, sliced
16-oz. can sliced green beans
6-oz. can pitted black olives
1 medium red onion, sliced
½ lb. fresh mushrooms, sliced
1 pint cherry tomatoes, halved
1 green pepper, sliced

Dressing:
1 cup cooking oil
1 cup red wine vinegar
1 Tbsp. sugar
1 tsp. dry mustard
Dash pepper

2 pkgs. Italian salad dressing mix

1. Combine all dressing ingredients and mix well. Pour into large serving bowl.
2. Drain green beans and olives and add all vegetables to bowl of marinade. Toss to cover all vegetables.
3. Marinate overnight, stirring occasionally. Drain before serving.

Tabouli

Ellen Helmuth
Debec, NB
New Brunswick Monthly Meeting
Society of Friends

Makes 6-8 servings

1 cup dry bulgur wheat
1½ cups boiling water
1 tsp. salt
¼ cup lemon juice
¼ cup olive oil
1 cup chopped fresh parsley
1 cup chopped fresh mint
2-3 tomatoes, chopped
2 cloves garlic, crushed
½ cup chopped scallions
   or onions, chopped
Pepper to taste

1. Pour boiling water over bulgur wheat and let stand approximately ½ hour until wheat is fluffy. Drain or squeeze liquid from wheat.
2. Add all remaining ingredients and mix well.
3. Chill overnight before serving.

Gazpacho

Maxine Hershberger
Dalton, OH
Salem Mennonite Church

Makes 6 servings

1 cup finely chopped tomato
½ cup chopped green pepper
½ cup chopped celery
½ cup chopped cucumber
¼ cup finely chopped onion
2 tsp. snipped parsley
1 tsp. snipped chives
1 small clove garlic, minced
2-3 Tbsp. tarragon wine vinegar
2 Tbsp. olive oil
1 tsp. salt
¼ tsp. black pepper
½ tsp. Worcestershire sauce
2 cups tomato juice
1 cup croutons

1. Combine all ingredients except croutons in a glass bowl. Toss to mix well.
2. Cover and chill at least 4 hours before serving.
3. Sprinkle croutons on top and serve.

This may be used as a salad or a soup.

Marinated Tomatoes

Erma Wenger
Lancaster, PA
Mellinger Mennonite Church

Makes 8 servings

1 clove garlic, minced
½ tsp. salt
1 tsp. sugar
¼ tsp. pepper
2 tsp. prepared mustard
¼ cup olive oil
2 Tbsp. tarragon vinegar
1 onion, thinly sliced
¼ cup chopped fresh parsley
4-6 firm tomatoes, sliced

1. Combine all ingredients except tomatoes.
2. Slice tomatoes into serving dish. Pour marinade over tomatoes. Chill several hours before serving. Flavors improve with longer refrigeration.

Herbed Tomatoes

Johanna Dyck
Coaldale, AB
Coaldale Mennonite Church

Makes 6 servings

4 medium tomatoes, thickly
  sliced
¼ cup sliced onion rings
½ cup cooking oil
¼ cup vinegar
¼ cup parsley
¼ tsp. pepper
½ tsp. salt
½ tsp. thyme *or* marjoram

1. Slice tomatoes and onions into serving dish.
2. Shake together all other ingredients and pour over vegetables. Marinate for several hours before serving.

Marinated Carrot Salad

Margaret Rich, North Newton, KS;
Alice Suderman, New Hope, MN;
Jeanne Heyerly, Reedley, CA

Makes 10-12 servings

2 lbs. carrots, sliced
1 green pepper, sliced in
  rings
1 medium onion, sliced in
  rings
1 can tomato soup
¼ cup cooking oil
⅓-½ cup vinegar
½ cup sugar
1 tsp. Worcestershire sauce
1 tsp. prepared mustard
½ tsp. salt

1. Cook carrots about 10 minutes or until just tender. Drain and arrange in serving dish with green pepper and onion.
2. In a saucepan combine all remaining ingredients and bring to a boil. Simmer about 15 minutes to blend flavors. Pour over vegetables.
3. Refrigerate and marinate at least 12 hours before serving.

Green Pepper and Tomato Salad

Linda Sponenburgh
DeLand, FL

Makes 12-16 servings

8 medium tomatoes
4 green peppers
1 medium onion
2 Tbsp. sugar or more
4 Tbsp. vinegar or less
1 tsp. salt
1 tsp. pepper

1. Peel and slice tomatoes. Seed and slice green peppers into thin rings. Chop onion.
2. Combine tomatoes, peppers and onion. Toss gently and set aside.
3. Combine all remaining ingredients. Pour over tomato mixture and toss gently. Cover and chill overnight.
4. If desired, drain before serving.

Tomato Aspic

Betty Hostetler
Belleville, PA
Allensville Mennonite Church

Makes 6-8 servings

2¼ cups tomato juice
1 tsp. sweet basil
1 tsp. sugar
½ tsp. salt
2 stalks celery, chopped
1 small onion, chopped
2 pkgs. unflavored gelatin

¼ cup cold water
Lettuce leaves
Fresh parsley *or* watercress

1. In a saucepan combine tomato juice, basil, sugar, salt, celery and onions. Simmer 20 minutes. Strain mixture.
2. Soften gelatin in cold water. Dissolve gelatin mixture in hot tomato mixture. Let set until mixture begins to thicken.
3. Stir and pour into well-greased mold. Chill until firm.
4. Unmold and serve on lettuce leaves garnished with parsley or watercress.

Carrot Raisin Salad

Christine Guth
Goshen, IN
East Goshen Mennonite Church

Makes 6-8 servings

1 lb. carrots, grated
½ cup raisins *or* currants
¾ cup plain yogurt
¼ cup mayonnaise
2 tsp. honey

1. Combine all ingredients and mix well.
2. Refrigerate several hours or overnight. Stir well before serving.

Cucumber Salad

Diena Schmidt
Henderson, NE
Bethesda Mennonite Church

Makes 6-8 servings

4 large cucumbers, peeled and sliced
1 medium onion, sliced
1 cup mayonnaise
4 Tbsp. vinegar
⅓ cup sugar
¼ tsp. salt

1. Slice cucumbers and onions into serving dish.
2. Combine mayonnaise, vinegar, sugar and salt. Pour over cucumbers and stir to mix.
3. Refrigerate at least 2-3 hours before serving.

Jello Carrot Salad

Carolyn Baer
Conrath, WI
Shiloh Mennonite Church

Makes 12 servings

15¼-oz. can crushed pineapple
6-oz. pkg. orange jello
2 cups boiling water
2 cups cold water and juice
1 cup finely diced celery
2 cups shredded carrots
Lettuce leaves

1. Drain pineapple and reserve juice.
2. Dissolve jello in boiling water.

3. Add enough cold water to reserved pineapple juice to make 2 cups. Add to jello mixture. Chill.
4. When jello is partially set, fold in pineapple, celery and carrots. Pour into mold and chill until firm.
5. Unmold and serve on lettuce leaves.

Cucumber Lime Salad

Judy Hall
Molalla, OR
Zion Mennonite Church

Makes 12-15 servings

2 medium cucumbers
6-oz. pkg. lime gelatin
1 cup boiling water
½ cup cold water
½ cup mayonnaise
¼ cup liquid from jar of jalapeño peppers

1. Peel and shred cucumbers.
2. Dissolve gelatin in hot water. Stir in cold water, mayonnaise, pepper liquid and cucumbers.
3. Refrigerate to set.
4. Before gelatin sets completely, stir again and return to refrigerator.

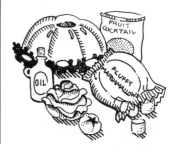

Cucumber Cottage Cheese Salad

Esther Eshleman
Mechanicsburg, PA

Makes 8 servings

3-oz. pkg. lemon gelatin
½ cup boiling water
1 cucumber, grated
1 small onion, grated
12 ozs. cottage cheese
2 Tbsp. vinegar
½ cup mayonnaise

1. Dissolve gelatin in boiling water. Stir in remaining ingredients. Stir well and pour into a mold.
2. Chill in refrigerator until set, approximately 4 hours.

Jellied Rhubarb Salad

Hettie Conrad
Colorado Springs, CO

Makes 6-8 servings

4 cups diced rhubarb
½ cup water
¾ cup sugar
6-oz. pkg. strawberry jello
½ cup cold water
1 Tbsp. grated orange rind
¼ cup chopped nuts
1 cup finely chopped celery
Lettuce leaves
Cottage cheese

1. Simmer rhubarb, water and sugar until rhubarb is tender, about 10 minutes. Remove from heat, sprinkle in

jello and stir until dissolved.
2. Add cold water, orange rind, nuts and celery. Pour into ring mold and chill until firm.
3. Turn out onto a platter of lettuce leaves. Fill center of ring with cottage cheese and serve.

Curried Rice Salad

Mary Leatherman
Doylestown, PA
Doylestown Mennonite Church

Makes 10-12 servings

6 cups cooked rice
½ cup chopped green pepper
⅓ cup chopped pimento
2 Tbsp. chopped onion
½ cup cooking oil
⅓-½ cup vinegar
2 Tbsp. sugar
2 Tbsp. lemon juice
1½ tsp. curry
1 tsp. salt

1. Toss rice, green pepper, pimento and onion together in a large serving dish.
2. In small bowl combine oil, vinegar, sugar, lemon juice, curry and salt.
3. Pour dressing over salad and toss gently.
4. Refrigerate at least 6-8 hours before serving.

Easy Wild Rice Salad

Sara Fretz-Goering
Silver Spring, MD
Hyattsville Mennonite Church

Makes 6-8 servings

1 box wild rice
1 cup cooked white rice
½ cup mayonnaise
2 Tbsp. olive oil
½ tsp. lemon juice
2 tsp. curry powder (optional)
1 cup assorted vegetables

1. Cook wild rice as directed on package. Cool.
2. In small bowl combine mayonnaise, olive oil, lemon juice and curry.
3. Prepare an assortment of raw vegetables. (Whatever you have on hand.)
4. In medium serving bowl toss wild rice, white rice, dressing and vegetables. Serve.

Rice Salad

Irene Epp
Kindersley, SK
Superb Mennonite Church

Makes 12 servings

Salad:
1 cup uncooked long-grain rice
1 bunch broccoli
½ lb. peas
½ lb. mushrooms, sliced
1 pint cherry tomatoes, halved

4 green onions, sliced
Red *or* green peppers
   (optional)

Dressing:
1 cup cooking oil
2 Tbsp. lemon juice
2 Tbsp. vinegar
1 tsp. dry mustard
½ tsp. salt
½ tsp. pepper
2 cloves garlic, minced
   (optional)

1. Cook and cool rice. Cut broccoli into bite-sized pieces.

2. Combine all salad ingredients in a large bowl and toss.

3. Combine all dressing ingredients in a jar. Cover and shake well.

4. Pour dressing over rice mixture and toss well. Refrigerate at least 12 hours before serving.

Lentil Confetti Salad

Thelma Wolgemuth
Immokalee, FL
People's Chapel

Makes 4-6 servings

½ cup lentils, washed and
   drained
1½ cups water
2 cups cooked brown rice
1 medium tomato, chopped
½ cup chopped green
   pepper
¼ cup chopped onion
2 Tbsp. chopped celery
½ cup low-calorie Italian
   salad dressing

1. In a saucepan bring lentils and water to a boil. Reduce heat and simmer for 20 minutes or until lentils are tender. Drain.

2. Combine all remaining ingredients. Add lentils. Toss well and chill.

Pasta a la Caprese

Rosalee Maust Otto
Champaign, IL

Makes 10-12 servings

12 plum *or* 4 large tomatoes,
   thinly sliced lengthwise
3-4 cloves garlic, mashed
1 green pepper, thinly sliced
20 leaves fresh basil, torn
½ cup olive oil
1 tsp. salt
5-6 twists from pepper mill
1 lb. rotini *or* ziti
8 ozs. grated mozzarella
   cheese
Parmesan cheese

1. Combine tomatoes, garlic, green pepper, basil, oil, salt and pepper in a large bowl at least 1 ½ hours before serving. Let stand at room temperature.

2. Cook and drain pasta. Stir into marinade. Cool for several minutes. Add mozzarella and stir.

3. Top with Parmesan cheese and serve.

This is a seasonal dish because it must have fresh basil and is certainly best with homegrown tomatoes. I grow basil especially for this salad.

Lois Mast's Pasta Salad

Lois Mast
Indianapolis, IN

Makes 10-12 servings

Salad:
1 lb. box rigatoni noodles
1 medium cucumber, peeled
   and diced
1 medium onion, diced
3-oz. jar pimentos
½ cup chopped celery
½ cup chopped green
   pepper
¼ cup chopped parsley

Dressing:
1 cup cider vinegar
1 cup cooking oil
1¼ cups sugar
1 tsp. salt
1½ tsp. pepper
1 tsp. garlic powder
2 tsp. prepared mustard

1. Cook noodles according to package directions. Drain and cool. Put in serving bowl and set aside.

2. In a saucepan combine vinegar, oil and sugar. Bring to a boil. Remove from heat and cool. Add salt, pepper, garlic powder and mustard and mix well.

3. Pour dressing over noodles and stir gently. Add all remaining salad ingredients and mix well.

Pasta and Broccoli Salad

Mary Herr and Elsie Lehman
Three Rivers, MI
The Hermitage Community Retreat Center

Makes 4-6 servings

Salad:
1 cup broccoli flowerets
8-oz. pkg. pasta shells
1 small red pepper, cut into strips
1 small onion, thinly sliced
2 ozs. Swiss cheese, cut into strips
1 Tbsp. chopped walnuts

Dressing:
1 Tbsp. Oriental sesame oil
$1\frac{1}{2}$ tsp. red wine vinegar
1 tsp. dried marjoram, crumbled
1 clove garlic, minced
$\frac{1}{4}$ tsp. black pepper

1. To prepare dressing combine oil, vinegar, marjoram, garlic and black pepper in serving bowl and whisk to mix. Set aside.

2. Cook broccoli for 3 minutes in large kettle of boiling water. Scoop out with small strainer. Shake to remove excess water and stir into dressing.

3. In the same kettle of boiling water, cook the pasta according to directions. Drain well and stir into broccoli and dressing mixture. Add all remaining salad ingredients.

4. Toss well, cover and refrigerate until needed.

Sandy Richardson's Pasta Salad

Sandy Zeiset Richardson
Leavenworth, WA

Makes 12 servings

1 pkg. pesto sauce mix
4 ozs. olive oil
1 clove garlic, minced
16-oz. pkg. spiral pasta
15-oz. can black olives
$1\frac{1}{2}$ cups halved cherry tomatoes
1 cup sliced bell peppers
$\frac{1}{2}$ cup sunflower seeds

1. Combine pesto sauce mix with olive oil and garlic.

2. Cook pasta according to package directions. Drain.

3. In a large serving bowl combine pasta, olives, tomatoes, peppers and sunflower seeds. Pour pesto sauce over salad and toss.

4. Refrigerate at least 4 hours before serving.

Feta Vegetable Pasta Salad

Mary Alice Miller
Elkhart, IN
Prairie Street Mennonite Church

Makes 12-15 servings

2 cups spiral pasta
8 ozs. feta cheese
1 cup sliced green pepper
$\frac{1}{4}$ cup sliced red onion
$\frac{1}{4}$ cup sliced cucumber
$\frac{1}{4}$ cup sliced zucchini
$\frac{1}{4}$ cup diced carrots
$\frac{1}{4}$ cup diced celery
2 cups broccoli flowerets
2 cups diced tomatoes
$\frac{1}{4}$ cup creamy Italian dressing

1. Cook pasta according to directions. Drain and chill.

2. Drain and crumble feta cheese.

3. In large serving dish combine all ingredients except tomatoes and dressing.

4. Immediately before serving, fold in tomatoes and dressing.

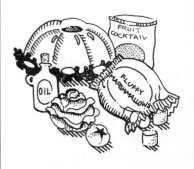

Macaroni Salad

Audrey J. Brubaker
York, PA
Church of the Nazarene

Makes 15-20 servings

1 lb. macaroni
1½ cups sugar
1 cup mayonnaise
¼ cup vinegar
¾ cup evaporated milk
3 Tbsp. mustard
¼ tsp. salt
4 hard-boiled eggs, sliced
1 cup chopped celery
2 tsp. celery seed

1. Cook macaroni according to directions. Drain and cool.
2. Combine sugar, mayonnaise, vinegar, milk, mustard and salt and mix well. Pour over cooled macaroni.
3. Add eggs, celery and celery seed.
4. Refrigerate until serving time.

Chef Salad

Lou Maniaci
Gladstone, MI
Soo Hill Christian Church

Makes 25-30 servings

1½-2 heads lettuce
6 stalks celery, sliced
10 green onions, chopped
5 carrots, thinly sliced
6 tomatoes, sliced
1 cup broccoli flowerets
1 cup chopped cauliflower

1 cucumber, sliced
5 hard-boiled eggs, sliced
1 red pepper, sliced
Garlic powder
1 large bottle low-calorie dressing

1. Prepare all vegetables at home and put into separate containers.
2. Immediately before fellowship meal is served, tear lettuce into large serving dish. Drain any accumulated liquid from vegetables and add to lettuce in bowl. Toss lightly. (Waiting to tear up lettuce allows for judging how much is needed. No one likes to take leftover salad home.)
3. Sprinkle garlic powder over salad and toss again. Serve with salad dressing on the side.

Japanese Salad

Wilma Roeschley
Hinsdale, IL
Lombard Mennonite Church

Makes 4-6 servings

Salad:
1½ heads lettuce
1 can chow mein noodles
3 green onions, sliced
1 small pkg. sliced almonds
¼ cup sesame seeds

Dressing:
4 Tbsp. sugar
1 tsp. salt
½ tsp. pepper
4 Tbsp. vinegar
½ cup cooking oil

1. Break lettuce into bite-sized pieces in a serving bowl. Add all other salad ingredients and toss lightly.
2. Combine all dressing ingredients and mix well.
3. Immediately before serving, pour dressing over salad and toss well.

Mama's Salad

Lois Taylor Erb
Morgantown, PA

Makes 16 servings

Salad:
2 heads iceberg lettuce
4 hard-boiled eggs, sliced
1 large sweet onion, sliced
8 cherry tomatoes, halved
Fresh parsley

Dressing:
1 cup mayonnaise
2 Tbsp. sugar
2 Tbsp. vinegar
⅓ cup milk

1. To prepare dressing combine all ingredients and blend well.
2. Tear lettuce into bite-sized pieces in large serving dish. Pour ¼ of dressing over lettuce.
3. Add ingredients in the following order: sliced eggs, ¼ of dressing, sliced onion, ¼ of dressing, cherry tomatoes, ¼ of dressing.
4. Garnish with fresh parsley and serve.

Mandarin Salad

Mary L. Gaeddert
North Newton, KS
Bethel College Mennonite Church;

Donna Horst
Leola, PA
Groffdale Mennonite Church

Makes 8 servings

Salad:
1/4 head iceberg lettuce
1/4 head romaine lettuce
2 green onions, thinly sliced
1/2 cup chopped celery
11-oz. can mandarin
 oranges, drained and
 chilled
1/4 cup sliced almonds
4 tsp. sugar

Dressing:
1/4 cup cooking oil
2 Tbsp. vinegar
1 Tbsp. snipped parsley
1/2 tsp. salt
2 Tbsp. sugar
Dash pepper

1. Prepare lettuce, romaine, onions and celery in a bowl and chill. Keep oranges in a separate jar and keep cool.
2. Cook almonds and sugar over low heat, stirring constantly until sugar is melted and almonds are coated. Cool and break apart. Set aside.
3. Shake all dressing ingredients together in a jar and keep cool.
4. Immediately before serving, layer mandarin oranges over lettuce mixture. Sprinkle dressing over top. Add almonds and toss all ingredients.

Lettuce and Dressing

Laura E. Benner
Sellersville, PA
Steel City Mennonite Church

Makes 10-12 servings

1 medium head lettuce
2 hard-boiled eggs, sliced
1/4 cup mayonnaise
1/2 tsp. salt
1 1/2 Tbsp. sugar
1 1/2 Tbsp. vinegar
1/2 tsp. prepared mustard
1 cup milk

1. Cut lettuce into serving bowl. Add eggs and toss.
2. In small bowl combine mayonnaise, salt, sugar, vinegar and mustard and beat until smooth. Add milk and mix well.
3. Immediately before serving, fold dressing into salad.

Old-Fashioned Egg Salad

Anna Weinhold
Ephrata, PA
Ephrata Mennonite Church

Makes 6-8 servings

Salad:
1 head lettuce
6 hard-boiled eggs, sliced
1 large onion, sliced
1/4 cup grated sharp cheese

Dressing:
1/4 cup cooking oil
2 Tbsp. vinegar
1 tsp. Worcestershire sauce
1 Tbsp. minced parsley
1 tsp. salt
1/4 tsp. pepper
Dash paprika

1. Break lettuce into bite-sized pieces into a salad bowl. Alternate layers of eggs, onion and cheese.
2. Combine all dressing ingredients in a jar. Shake well.
3. Immediately before serving, pour over salad and toss lightly.

Deviled Eggs

Linda Welty
La Junta, CO
Emmanuel Mennonite Church

Makes 12 servings

6 hard-boiled eggs
1/2 tsp. salt
1/2 tsp. dry mustard

¼ tsp. pepper
3 Tbsp. mayonnaise
Paprika

1. Cool, peel and cut eggs in half lengthwise. Remove yolks and mash with a fork.
2. Add all remaining ingredients to egg yolks and mix well. Fill each egg half with mixture. Sprinkle with paprika.

Variations:

Add ½ tsp. vinegar and 1 tsp. minced onion to egg yolk mixture. Top each egg half with ½ of an olive.

Linda Sponenburgh
DeLand, FL

Add ¾ tsp. Worcestershire sauce to egg yolk mixture. Sprinkle tops of eggs with paprika.

Leora Gerber
Dalton, OH

To hard-boil eggs bring to a full, rolling boil. Turn off heat and let eggs sit in water for 20 minutes. This saves energy.

Loretta Lapp
Kinzer, PA

Red Beet Eggs

Joyce G. Slaymaker
Strasburg, PA
Refton Brethren in Christ

Makes 2 dozen eggs

2 dozen hard-boiled eggs, peeled
3½ cups vinegar
4 cups sugar
2 tsp. salt

2 cups red beet juice
3 tsp. red food coloring (optional)

1. Dissolve sugar and salt in vinegar.
2. In a large saucepan bring red beet juice to a boil. Add vinegar mixture and food coloring and bring to a boil again. Remove from heat and set aside to cool for several minutes.
3. Pour liquid over eggs and let stand at least 24 hours.

Honey Dressing for Tossed Salad

Ruth Heatwole
Charlottesville, VA
Charlottesville Mennonite Church

Makes 1 pint dressing

¾ cup cooking oil
⅓ cup honey
⅓ cup vinegar
1 Tbsp. lemon juice
1 tsp. minced onion
⅔ cup sugar
1 tsp. dry mustard
1 tsp. paprika
¼ tsp. salt
1 tsp. celery seed

1. Place ingredients in blender in the order listed. Blend until sugar has completely dissolved.
2. Refrigerate for future use.
3. Shake well before serving.

Russian Dressing

Frances Schrag
Newton, KS
First Mennonite Church

½ cup mayonnaise
1 Tbsp. chili sauce *or* ketchup
1 tsp. finely chopped onion
½ tsp. horseradish
¼ tsp. Worcestershire sauce
1 Tbsp. finely chopped parsley

1. Combine all ingredients and mix well.
2. Serve with choice of tossed salad.

Maple Dressing

Esther Lehman
Lowville, NY
Croghan Mennonite Church

Makes 2 cups dressing

1 cup cooking oil
⅔ cup white vinegar
½ cup sugar
1½ Tbsp. prepared mustard
½ cup maple syrup

1. Combine all ingredients and mix well.
2. Serve with choice of tossed salad.

Maple Dressing Variation

Esther Lehman
Lowville, NY
Croghan Mennonite Church

Makes 1¼ cups dressing

¼ cup maple syrup
½ cup vinegar
½ cup cooking oil
3 Tbsp. ketchup
½ tsp. salt
⅛ tsp. pepper
¼ tsp. garlic powder
¼ tsp. onion salt

1. Shake all ingredients together in a jar.
2. Serve with choice of tossed salad.

Sweet French Dressing

Anna Marie Ramer
New Paris, IN

Makes approximately 1 pint dressing

½ cup sugar or less
¼ cup vinegar
⅓ cup ketchup
1 cup cooking oil
1 Tbsp. minced onion
1 tsp. salt
1 Tbsp. Worcestershire sauce

1. Mix all ingredients thoroughly and store in refrigerator.
2. Serve with choice of tossed salad.

Dressing for Lettuce or Cabbage Salad

Esther Lehman
Lowville, NY
Croghan Mennonite Church

Makes 1 pint dressing

1 tsp. salt
½ tsp. pepper
2 Tbsp. mayonnaise
1 small onion, chopped
1 cup sugar or less
1 tsp. celery seed
⅓ cup vinegar
3 tsp. prepared mustard *or*
    1 tsp. dry mustard
1 cup cooking oil

1. Combine all ingredients and blend well.

2. Serve with choice of lettuce or cabbage salad.

Broccoli Cauliflower Marinade

Mary Ethel Lahman Heatwole
Harrisonburg, VA
Harrisonburg Mennonite Church

Makes enough marinade for 1 head cauliflower or 1 bunch broccoli

1½ cups cooking oil
1 cup vinegar
1 Tbsp. sugar
1 Tbsp. dill weed
1 Tbsp. Accent
1 tsp. salt
1 tsp. pepper
1 tsp. garlic salt

1. Combine all ingredients and mix well.
2. Pour over prepared vegetables. Marinate in refrigerator for at least 6 hours before serving.

An Easy Lettuce Salad

Seven-layer lettuce salad, a great favorite at church fellowship meals, abounds in variations. Add, subtract and mix as you please.

In what is perhaps the best demonstration of this popular recipe's versatility, several submitters provided only a list of ingredients without giving any specific measurements. We salute their creativity and hope that your version of this recipe will please you as well.

Fresh Lettuce Salad

Jennie Stutzman
Corry, PA
Beaverdam Mennonite Church

Makes 8 servings

Salad:
1 large bowl fresh leaf
    lettuce
6 slices bacon
1 onion, sliced
4 hard-boiled eggs, diced

Dressing:
1 tsp. shortening, melted
2 Tbsp. flour
1 tsp. salt
1/2 cup sugar
1/3 cup white vinegar
2/3 cup water

1. Wash and tear lettuce into bite-sized pieces.
2. Fry, drain and crumble bacon. Toss lettuce and bacon with onion and eggs.
3. Combine all dressing ingredients in a saucepan. Cook until thickened, stirring constantly. Pour hot dressing over salad if desired; or chill dressing before pouring over salad.

Variation:
In the dressing ingredients substitute 1 tsp. bacon fat for shortening. Omit salt. Mix dressing as directed.
Anna Buckwalter
Ronks, PA

South-of-the-Border Salad

A. Catharine Boshart
Lebanon, PA
Hereford Mennonite Home Church

Makes 4-6 servings

Salad:
1/2 head lettuce, shredded
1 green pepper, cut in strips
6 ozs. pitted ripe olives
3 tomatoes, sliced
1 cup grated, low-fat
    cheddar cheese

Dressing:
1 lb. turkey bacon
1 onion, thinly sliced
1 Tbsp. cornstarch
1/2 tsp. chili powder
1/2 tsp. cumin
1 tsp. salt
1/2 cup vinegar

1. Combine all salad ingredients except cheese in large serving bowl.
2. Cut bacon into 1/2-inch pieces and cook until crisp. Drain, reserving 1/4 cup drippings in skillet.
3. Sauté onion in bacon drippings. Stir in cornstarch, chili powder, cumin and salt. Add vinegar and heat to boiling. Pour hot bacon dressing over salad ingredients. Add bacon pieces and toss well to coat.
4. Top with cheese and serve immediately.

Super Salad

Beulah Kauffman
Elkhart, IN

Makes 16 servings

1 head lettuce, shredded
1/2 cup diced celery
1/2 cup chopped green onion
1 can water chestnuts, sliced
2 10-oz. pkgs. frozen peas
2 cups mayonnaise
1 Tbsp. sugar
1/2 cup Parmesan cheese
1/2 lb. bacon
5 hard-boiled eggs, chopped
5-6 tomatoes, cut in wedges

1. Layer lettuce, celery, green onion, water chestnuts and peas into large container. Spread with mayonnaise. Sprinkle with sugar and Parmesan cheese. Refrigerate overnight.
2. Fry, drain and crumble bacon. Add bacon, eggs and tomatoes just before serving.

Seven-Layer Lettuce Salad

Audrey J. Brubaker, York, PA;
Janice Crist, Quinter, KS;
Anna S. Petersheim, Paradise, PA;
Viola Weidner, Allentown, PA

Makes 10-12 servings

8 slices bacon
2 cups mayonnaise
2 Tbsp. sugar
1 head lettuce
1 cup finely diced celery
4 hard-boiled eggs, sliced
10-oz. pkg. frozen peas
1 small onion, diced
4 ozs. cheddar cheese, grated

1. Fry, drain and crumble bacon.
2. Combine mayonnaise and sugar and mix well.
3. Wash lettuce and tear into bite-sized pieces.
4. Layer ingredients into serving dish in following order: lettuce, celery, eggs, peas, onion, bacon, mayonnaise dressing and cheese.
5. Let stand in refrigerator 10-12 hours before serving.

Variations:
Add 1 cup grated raw carrots and ½ cup diced green pepper to layers.
Carol Weber, Lancaster, PA; Kathryn Metzler, Lancaster, PA; Rachel Kauffman, Alto, MI; Grace A. Zimmerman, Reinholds, PA; Mary Klassen, Winnipeg, MB

Use 2 cups low-calorie mayonnaise and add only 2 tsp. sugar.
Lorraine Martin
Dryden, MI

I eliminate the sugar from this recipe, serve it in my grandmother's antique glass bowl and put a label in front of it which says, "No Sugar."
Elizabeth Weaver Bonnar, Thorndale, ON

Add 1 finely chopped head cauliflower and 1 finely chopped head broccoli to the layers.
Toledo, OH
Bancroft Mennonite Church,

Add shrimp, cooked chicken or ham as one of the layers.
Miriam Showalter
Salem, OR

Layered Salad

Sarah Klassen
Winnipeg, MB
River East Mennonite
Brethren Church

Makes 10 servings

Salad:
8 slices bacon
½ small head iceberg lettuce
½ small head romaine lettuce
6 hard-boiled eggs, sliced
12-oz. pkg. frozen peas
1 green pepper, chopped
7 green onions, chopped
½ cup chopped black olives

Dressing:
1 cup mayonnaise
1 cup sour cream
½ tsp. black pepper
1 tsp. dill
1 Tbsp. sugar
1 ½ cups grated cheese
4 slices bacon

1. Fry, drain and crumble all 12 slices bacon.
2. Wash lettuce and tear into bite-sized pieces.
3. Layer salad ingredients into 9" x 13" pan in following order: lettuce, eggs, peas, pepper, onions, olives and 8 slices bacon.
4. To prepare dressing combine mayonnaise, sour cream, pepper, dill and sugar. Spread over top layer of salad. Sprinkle with cheese and remaining 4 slices bacon.
5. Cover tightly and refrigerate overnight or for 24 hours if possible.

Festive Layered Salad

Evelyn Cross
Prescott, AZ
Prescott Mennonite Church

Makes 10-12 servings

1 cup macaroni
1 head romaine lettuce
4 carrots, grated
10-oz. pkg. frozen peas, thawed
1 small red onion, separated into rings
½ lb. cooked, cubed ham
½ cup shredded Swiss cheese
1½ cups mayonnaise
2 Tbsp. snipped fresh dill
2 hard-boiled eggs, cut into wedges

1. Cook macaroni according to package directions. Drain and cool.
2. Wash and thoroughly

drain lettuce. Tear into bite-sized pieces. Arrange in an even layer in the bottom of a large dish. Arrange carrots in an even layer over lettuce. Add layer of macaroni, peas, onion and ham. Sprinkle with cheese.

3. Combine mayonnaise and dill in a small bowl. Mound dressing in center of salad. Arrange egg wedges around the dressing. Cover and chill for several hours or overnight.

4. Immediately before serving, toss well to coat all ingredients with dressing.

Meat Salads

Chicken Curry Layer Salad

Lydia S. Martin
Harrisonburg, VA
Lindale Mennonite Church

Makes 12 servings

6 cups shredded lettuce
2 pkgs. frozen peas
3 cups chopped, cooked
 chicken
3 cups chopped tomatoes
2 cups sliced cucumbers
2 cups mayonnaise
1 Tbsp. sugar

1½ tsp. curry powder
3 cups croutons

1. Layer lettuce, peas, chicken, tomatoes and cucumbers into 5-quart salad bowl.

2. Combine mayonnaise, sugar and curry powder. Mix well. Spread over salad. Cover and refrigerate overnight.

3. Immediately before serving, sprinkle with croutons.

Super Chicken Salad

Becky Bixler
Iowa City, IA
First Mennonite Church

Makes 8 servings

1 Tbsp. olive oil
2 cooked chicken breasts,
 cut up
½ cup chopped pecans
1 cup sliced mushrooms
1 can artichokes, quartered
⅓ cup water chestnuts
¼ cup sliced black olives
½ cup chopped celery
1 medium zucchini, sliced
10-12 cherry tomatoes
1 cup Italian dressing

1. Sauté chicken, pecans and mushrooms in olive oil. Remove from heat.

2. Combine all ingredients in large salad bowl. Refrigerate several hours or overnight.

Chicken Salad

Norma Troyer
Mio, MI
Fairview Mennonite Church

Makes 20-25 servings

1 cup uncooked rice
1 pint salad dressing
½ cup vinegar
1 quart chopped, cooked
 chicken
2 cups diced celery
½ cup chopped sweet
 pepper
1 pint cooked peas
6 hard-boiled eggs, diced
½ tsp. salt
Dash pepper
2 cups sliced almonds

1. Cook rice according to directions. Cool.

2. Mix salad dressing and vinegar. Fold all ingredients except almonds into dressing. Chill for at least 3 hours.

3. Immediately before serving, garnish with almonds.

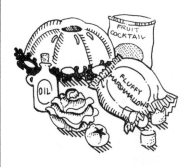

Chunky Salad

Betty Herr
Beallsville, MD
Dawsonville Mennonite Church

Makes 8-10 servings

1 apple, chopped
1 orange, peeled and
    chopped
1 cup halved grapes
$\frac{1}{2}$ cup walnuts
$\frac{1}{2}$ cup mayonnaise
1 cup cubed cheddar cheese
2 cups diced, cooked turkey
Salt and pepper to taste
Lettuce leaves

1. Toss all ingredients together except lettuce leaves.
2. Serve on platter of lettuce leaves.

Chicken and Rice Salad

Margaret Oyer
Gibson City, IL
East Bend Mennonite Church

Makes 12 servings

$\frac{1}{4}$ cup corn oil
$\frac{1}{4}$ cup vinegar
$\frac{1}{4}$ cup finely chopped
    onion
1 tsp. salt
$\frac{1}{8}$ tsp. pepper
3 cups cooked rice
3 cups cubed, cooked
    chicken
2 cups chopped celery
$\frac{1}{4}$ cup chopped green
    pepper (optional)

$1\frac{1}{2}$ cups mayonnaise
$\frac{1}{2}$ cup slivered almonds
1 Tbsp. butter

1. Combine corn oil, vinegar, onion, salt and pepper. Add to rice and toss lightly until seasonings are well mixed with rice. Refrigerate for 1 hour to marinate.
2. Add chicken, celery, green pepper and mayonnaise. Mix thoroughly and refrigerate.
3. About 1 hour before serving, sauté almonds in butter until lightly browned. Drain and cool. Add to chicken and rice mixture and refrigerate until ready to serve.

Chicken Salad Indonesia

Tena Neufeld
Delta, BC
Peace Mennonite Church

Makes 6-8 servings

2-3 Tbsp. cider vinegar
2 Tbsp. cooking oil
$\frac{3}{4}$ cup mayonnaise
$2\frac{1}{2}$ cups cooked, diced
    chicken
2 cups cooked rice
1 cup pineapple tidbits,
    drained
1 cup mandarin orange
    sections, drained
1 cup chopped celery
$\frac{1}{2}$ cup salted peanuts
$\frac{1}{2}$ cup raisins
Lettuce leaves
Pineapple bits *or*
    orange slices

1. In large bowl combine vinegar, oil and mayonnaise. Add remaining ingredients except lettuce leaves and pineapple bits or orange slices.
2. Toss until all ingredients are well coated. Cover and refrigerate until thoroughly chilled, about 4 hours or overnight.
3. Serve salad on bed of lettuce leaves, garnished with pineapple bits or orange slices.

Party Chicken Salad

Hulda G. Stucky
Wichita, KS
Lorraine Avenue Mennonite Church

Makes 8-10 servings

3 cups cooked, chopped
    chicken breasts
2 cups diced celery
8-oz. can pineapple chunks,
    drained
$\frac{1}{4}$ cup chopped sweet
    pickle
$\frac{1}{4}$ cup sliced ripe olives
1 cup white seedless grapes,
    halved
1 cup chopped walnuts
$\frac{2}{3}$ cup light mayonnaise
3 Tbsp. lemon juice
Lettuce leaves

1. Toss all ingredients except lettuce leaves. Chill.
2. Serve on lettuce leaves.

Turkey Salad

Eva Blosser
Dayton, OH
Huber Mennonite Church

Makes 8 servings

3 cups cubed, cooked turkey
1 cup diced celery
1 cup sliced green, seedless
grapes
1/2 tsp. salt
3/4 cup mayonnaise
1 hard-boiled egg, sliced
Lettuce leaves

1. Combine turkey, celery, grapes and salt. Moisten with mayonnaise.
2. Serve on lettuce leaves garnished with egg slices.

Chicken Macaroni Salad

Lorie Willms
St. Catharines, ON
Bethany Mennonite Church

Makes 6 servings

1 cup macaroni
3 hard-boiled eggs, diced
1 cup chopped, cooked
chicken
1 Tbsp. chopped onion
1/2 cup chopped celery
1/2 cup chopped mushrooms
1 Tbsp. chopped sweet
pepper
Mayonnaise to taste
Salt and pepper to taste

1. Cook macaroni according to directions. Drain and

rinse in cold water.
2. Combine all ingredients. Let stand in refrigerator for several hours to blend the flavors.

Variation:
Add 2 tsp. prepared mustard to the ingredients. Garnish with snipped fresh parsley.
Miriam E. LeFever
East Petersburg, PA

Japanese Chicken Salad

Lola L. Miller
Quakertown, PA
West Swamp Mennonite Church

Makes 10-12 servings

4 Tbsp. sugar
4 Tbsp. white vinegar
1/2 cup cooking oil
3 tsp. Accent or less
1/4 tsp. pepper
1 tsp. salt
3/4 cup slivered almonds
1 can chow mein noodles
1/8-1/4 cup poppy seeds
4 chicken breasts, cooked
and chopped
1 head lettuce, shredded
1/4 cup chopped onion

1. The evening before serving this recipe combine sugar, vinegar, oil, Accent, pepper and salt. Store in refrigerator.
2. Combine almonds, chow mein noodles and poppy seeds in separate container in refrigerator.
3. Prepare chicken breast and refrigerate.

4. Immediately before serving, toss all ingredients together.

Hmong Chicken Salad

Hmong Christian Church
Kitchener, ON

Makes 4 servings

5 1/4 ozs. bean thread
2 chicken breasts
2 eggs
3 carrots, grated
1 small bunch Chinese
parsley, snipped
1 small bunch fresh mint,
snipped
1/2 cup cooking oil
2 tsp. fish sauce
Juice of 1 lemon
1 tsp. brown sugar
Salt and pepper to taste

1. Bring bean thread to a boil with water. Boil for 4 minutes. Drain well.
2. Cook chicken breasts until soft. Cool. Cut chicken into small pieces.
3. Beat eggs and fry them. Cut into small pieces.
4. Combine bean thread, chicken, eggs, carrots, parsley and mint in a medium bowl.
5. Combine oil, fish sauce, lemon juice, sugar, salt and pepper and mix well. Pour over salad ingredients and mix well. Serve.

Pasta, Ham and Pineapple Salad

Elaine Klaassen
Minneapolis, MN
Faith Mennonite Church

Makes 4 or more servings

2 cups pasta
1 cup crushed pineapple
1 cup mayonnaise
1/4-1/2 lb. boiled, cubed ham

1. Cook and drain the pasta.
2. In a large bowl blend undrained pineapple and mayonnaise. Add ham. Stir in pasta.
3. Chill and serve.

Hot Rice, Ham and Cheese Salad

Anna Weber
Atmore, AL
Mennonite Christian Fellowship

Makes 6-8 servings

1 cup uncooked rice
2 cups water
1/4 cup finely chopped onion
2 Tbsp. soy sauce
1 medium clove garlic, minced
2 cups diced, cooked ham
1/2 cup chopped celery
1/2 cup mayonnaise
1 Tbsp. vinegar
1/8 tsp. cayenne pepper
1 cup shredded Swiss cheese

1. Combine rice, water, onion, soy sauce and garlic in a skillet. Cover and cook 20 minutes or until rice is tender and liquid is absorbed.
2. Add ham and celery and heat through.
3. Stir in all remaining ingredients. Serve.

Crab and Pasta Salad

Miriam M. Witmer
Manheim, PA
Erisman Mennonite Church

Makes 12-15 servings

Salad:
4 cups pasta
1 carrot, grated
2 cups broccoli buds
2 cups cauliflower buds
1/2 cup chopped onion
2 cups pressed crab meat

Dressing:
1 pkg. Italian dressing mix
1/4 cup vinegar
2 Tbsp. water
1/2 cup cooking oil

1. Cook pasta according to directions. Drain and cool. Combine all salad ingredients.
2. Combine all dressing ingredients.
3. Toss salad with dressing and serve.

Crab-Stuffed Eggs

Judith E. Bartel
North Newton, KS
Bethel College Mennonite Church

Makes 24 servings

12 hard-boiled eggs
1-lb. can crab meat
3 Tbsp. mayonnaise
1/4 cup sour cream
4 tsp. grated onion
1/2 tsp. salt
1/4 cup finely chopped celery
4 drops Tabasco sauce
1/2 tsp. Worcestershire sauce
1/8 tsp. white pepper
1 Tbsp. Dijon mustard
Pimento *or* fresh parsley

1. Peel and carefully cut each hard-boiled egg in half lengthwise. Remove egg yolk from egg whites. Reserve egg whites.
2. Mash egg yolks with fork.
3. Combine and thoroughly mix all other ingredients except pimento or fresh parsley. Add mashed egg yolks and mix well.
4. Fill each egg white with yolk mixture, heaping lightly in rounded mound shape. Garnish with pimento or fresh parsley.
5. Cover and refrigerate overnight.

Brown Rice Shrimp Salad

Rachel Senner
Freeman, SD
Salem Mennonite Church

Makes 6 or more servings

1 cup uncooked brown rice
1/3 cup cooking oil
2 Tbsp. lemon juice
1 Tbsp. grated orange peel
1 tsp. salt or less
1/4 tsp. pepper
2 oranges, peeled and
    chopped
3 green onions and tops,
    diced
2 small cans shrimp, drained

1. Prepare rice according to package directions, omitting butter.
2. In small bowl combine oil, juice, orange peel, salt and pepper, mixing well. Stir into hot rice. Cover and refrigerate at least 2-3 hours.
3. Immediately before serving, stir in oranges and green onions. Gently fold in shrimp.

Chinese Rice Salad

Lois Cressman
Plattsville, ON
Nith Valley Mennonite Church

Makes 6-8 servings

Salad:
2 cups cooked rice
1 cup tuna, ham *or* chicken
1 cup peas
1 cup chopped celery
1/2 cup chopped pepper
1/2 cup chopped onion

Dressing:
1/3 cup cooking oil
3 Tbsp. soy sauce
3 Tbsp. vinegar
1 1/2 tsp. curry
3/4 tsp. salt
1/2 tsp. celery seed
1/2 tsp. garlic salt

1. Toss all salad ingredients together.
2. Mix all dressing ingredients and pour over salad. Let stand at least 3-4 hours before serving.
3. Taste improves as salad marinates.

Mexican Salad

Jan Pembleton
Arlington, TX
Hope Mennonite Church

Makes 8-10 servings

Salad:
1 head lettuce
1 lb. ground beef or turkey
2 tomatoes, chopped
16-oz. can kidney beans,
    drained
1 1/2 cups grated cheddar
    cheese
1/4 cup diced onion
1 can olives, sliced
1 avocado, diced
1 pkg. taco chips, crushed

Sauce:
8 ozs. Thousand Island
    dressing
1 Tbsp. dry taco seasoning
1 Tbsp. hot sauce
1/3 cup sugar

1. Wash lettuce and tear into bite-sized pieces.
2. Brown, drain and cool ground meat.
3. Combine all salad ingredients except taco chips. Set aside.
4. Combine all sauce ingredients. Pour sauce over salad and toss thoroughly.
5. Immediately before serving, add taco chips.

Variations:
Substitute the following ingredients for sauce: 1 cup mayonnaise, 2 Tbsp. sweet relish and 1/4 cup ketchup. Serve sauce on the side.

Lydia Yoder,
London, OH,
Shiloh Mennonite Church

Substitute 15-oz. can chickpeas for kidney beans.

Christine Bauman,
Souderton, PA

Sprinkle with chili powder before tossing ingredients.

Adeline Schiedel,
Cambridge, ON,
Preston Mennonite Church

Serve this dish with dressing, picanté sauce and green chilies on the side.

Eunice Stoner,
Farmington, NM

Lorna Sirtoli's Taco Salad

Lorna A. Sirtoli
Cortland, NY
Nazarene Church of Cortland

Makes 15 servings

1 lb. ground beef
1 onion, chopped
1 bunch fresh spinach, chopped
5-6 large radishes, chopped
2 medium cucumbers, sliced
1 head lettuce, shredded
1 cup cubed cheddar cheese
1 cup shredded cheddar cheese
16-oz. can kidney beans, drained
1 onion, sliced
1 bag corn chips, crushed
12-oz. bottle Catalina dressing

1. Brown ground beef and onion. Drain and cool.
2. Combine all other ingredients except dressing in large serving dish. Add ground beef and toss thoroughly.
3. Immediately before serving, add dressing and mix well.

Variation:
Add 1 can chopped black olives to ingredients.

Bonnie and Vern Ratzlaff
Tuba City, AZ
Moencopi Mennonite Church

Genie Kehr's Taco Salad

Genie Kehr
Goshen, IN
Berkey Avenue Mennonite Fellowship

Makes 18-20 servings

1 large head lettuce, finely chopped
1 green pepper, chopped
3 tomatoes, diced
2 carrots, shredded
1 16-oz. can kidney beans, drained
2 lbs. ground beef, fried and drained
2 pkgs. dry taco seasoning
1 lb. cheese, grated
12-oz. bottle Russian dressing
1 bag taco chips, crushed

1. Prepare each ingredient and put into separate plastic containers for carrying to fellowship meal.
2. Immediately before serving, mix all ingredients in large bowl or serving dish.

Mosaic Salad

Twila Nafziger
Wadsworth, OH
Bethel Mennonite Church

Makes 12-16 servings

2 cups pasta
1 stick pepperoni, sliced
¼ lb. salami, sliced
¼ lb. herb salami, sliced
¼ lb. bologna, sliced

¼ lb. cheddar cheese, cubed
¼ lb. Provolone cheese, cubed
¼ lb. mozzarella cheese, cubed
¼ cup green olives, sliced
¼ cup black olives, sliced
¼ cup Greek olives, sliced
1 cup chopped broccoli
1 cup chopped cauliflower
1 cup diced carrots
½ cup diced onion
1 cup chopped red peppers
1 cup chopped green peppers
1 cup chopped zucchini
¾ cup Italian dressing

1. Cook pasta according to directions. Drain and cool.
2. Combine all ingredients in a large bowl and toss with dressing.
3. Serve with rolls or bread sticks.

Fruit Salads

Fruit Salad with Macaroni

LaNae Waltner
Freeman, SD

Makes 12 servings

Salad:
½ cup uncooked macaroni
1 cup pineapple tidbits, drained

1 cup diced peaches, drained
1 cup diced pears, drained
2-3 bananas, sliced
Maraschino cherries
    (optional)

Dressing:
½ Tbsp. flour
¼ cup sugar
2 egg yolks, beaten
½ cup pineapple juice
1 Tbsp. vinegar *or* lemon
    juice

1. Cook macaroni according to directions. Drain and rinse.

2. Drain each cup fruit, reserving ½ cup pineapple juice.

3. To prepare dressing combine flour and sugar in a saucepan. Stir in egg yolks, fruit juice and vinegar. Cook until thickened. Cool.

4. Combine all ingredients in a large serving dish.

Cheese Gelatin Salad

Laura Nisly
Grantham, PA
Slate Hill Mennonite Church

Makes 12-15 servings

6-oz. pkg. orange gelatin
2 cups hot water
20-oz. can crushed
    pineapple, drained
1 cup apricot nectar
2 cups miniature
    marshmallows
1 cup whipped topping
1 cup grated cheese
½ cup chopped nuts

1. Dissolve gelatin in hot water.

2. Drain pineapple, reserving juice. Add juice to apricot nectar to make 2 cups, adding more apricot nectar if needed.

3. Stir pineapple, pineapple juice and apricot nectar into gelatin. Pour into 9" x 13" pan. Cover with marshmallows. Chill until firm.

4. Spread whipped topping over gelatin. Sprinkle with cheese and nuts. Serve.

Edie's Fruit and Cheese Salad

Edith M. Weaver
College Park, MD
Hyattsville Mennonite Church

Makes 12-14 servings

2 6-oz. pkgs. lemon gelatin
20-oz. can crushed pineapple
4 bananas, sliced
1 cup miniature
    marshmallows
1 egg, beaten
½ cup sugar
1 Tbsp. flour, rounded
1 cup pineapple juice
¾ cup whipping cream
1 cup grated cheese

1. Prepare gelatin according to directions.

2. Drain pineapple, reserving juice.

3. Combine partially set gelatin, pineapple and bananas. Pour into 9" x 13" pan. Cover with marshmallows and chill until firm.

4. In a saucepan combine egg, sugar, flour and pineapple juice (add water to make 1 cup if necessary). Cook mixture until thickened, stirring frequently. Let cool. Fold in whipping cream.

5. Pour thickened mixture over firmly chilled gelatin. Top with grated cheese and serve.

Pineapple Cheese Salad

Barbara A. Yoder
Indianapolis, IN
First Mennonite Church

Makes 6-8 servings

2 Tbsp. flour
4 Tbsp. sugar
½ tsp. salt
1 egg, beaten
1 cup orange juice
1 cup grated cheese
1 cup pineapple chunks
1 cup chopped walnuts

1. Combine flour, sugar and salt. Add egg and juice. Cook until thickened. Cool.

2. Pour dressing into serving dish. Stir in cheese, pineapple and nuts. Chill and serve.

Apple Waldorf Salad

Violet Jantzi
Medina, NY
Harris Hill Mennonite Church

Makes 6-8 servings

2 cups diced apples,
   unpeeled
1 cup chopped celery
1/2 cup chopped nutmeats
1 cup sugar
2 Tbsp. flour
1 egg, beaten
2 Tbsp. water
1 cup water
1 Tbsp. butter *or* margarine
1 tsp. vinegar
Pinch of salt

1. Combine apples, celery
and nutmeats in a serving
bowl.
2. In a saucepan stir to-
gether sugar, flour, egg and 2
Tbsp. water. Add 1 cup
water and butter. Bring to a
boil and cook until thickened, stirring constantly.
Add vinegar and salt. Let
cool. Pour over apple mixture.
3. Refrigerate until ready
to serve.

Apple Salad

Esther Lehman
Lowville, NY
Croghan Mennonite Church

Makes 8-12 servings

4 yellow apples
4 red apples
2-3 stalks celery, chopped
1 cup seedless grapes,
   halved
2 Tbsp. crunchy peanut
   butter
1/2 cup sugar or less
1 cup mayonnaise *or* sour
   cream

1. Wash, core and dice apples into large serving bowl.
Add chopped celery and
halved grapes.
2. Blend together peanut
butter, sugar and mayon-
naise. Fold into fruit and
serve.

Cider Waldorf Mold

Dorothy Shank
Goshen, IN
College Mennonite Church

Makes 8-10 servings

4 cups apple cider
6-oz. pkg. orange gelatin
Dash salt (optional)
2 medium apples, diced
1/2 cup diced celery
1/2 cup chopped walnuts

1. Bring 2 cups cider to
boiling. Add gelatin and salt,
stirring to dissolve gelatin.

Add remaining cider.
2. Pour 1 cup gelatin mixture into 5-cup mold. Chill
until partially set. Cut 1/2 of
one apple into thin wedges.
Arrange apple slices over
gelatin. Chill until firm.
3. Chill remaining gelatin
until partially set.
4. Fold remaining apples,
celery and walnuts into remaining gelatin. Spoon over
first layer of almost firm gelatin.
5. Chill until firm.

Waldorf Crown Salad

Annabelle Kratz
Clarksville, MD
Hyattsville Mennonite Church

Makes 6-8 servings

6-oz. pkg. strawberry gelatin
2 cups boiling water
1 1/2 cups cold water
1 cup cubed apples
1/2 cup thinly sliced celery
1/4 cup chopped walnuts
1 cup sour cream
1/2 cup mayonnaise
1 1/2 cups miniature
   marshmallows
Lettuce leaves
Apple slices

1. Dissolve gelatin in boiling water. Stir in cold water.
Chill until partially set.
2. Fold in apples, celery
and walnuts. Pour into 5-cup
ring mold. Chill until firm.
3. Blend sour cream and
mayonnaise until smooth.
Fold in marshmallows.
4. Unmold gelatin onto

bed of lettuce leaves. Fill center with sour cream mixture. Garnish with apple slices.

California Salad

Rebecca Byler
Mt. Eaton, OH
Longenecker Mennonite Church

Makes 6 servings

20-oz. can pineapple
   chunks, drained
2 oranges, cut up
1 cup chopped nuts
Miniature marshmallows
   (optional)
1 Tbsp. flour
¼ cup sugar
½ Tbsp. margarine
1 cup pineapple juice
1 egg, beaten
2 bananas, sliced

1. Drain pineapple, reserving juice. In serving dish combine pineapple, oranges, nuts and marshmallows.
2. In a saucepan combine flour, sugar and margarine. Slowly stir in juice. Bring to a boil and cook until thickened. Gradually add beaten egg and boil for 1 minute longer. Cool.
3. Immediately before serving, pour dressing over fruit. Fold in dressing and sliced bananas.

Lee Snyder's Fruit Salad

Lee Snyder
Harrisonburg, VA
Community Mennonite Church

Makes 10-12 servings

2 eggs, beaten
2 Tbsp. vinegar
2 Tbsp. lemon juice
4 Tbsp. sugar
Dash salt
2 Tbsp. margarine
1 cup diced apples
20-oz. can pineapple
   chunks, drained
1 cup halved grapes
11-oz. can mandarin
   oranges, drained
1 cup chopped walnuts
1 cup whipped topping

1. Beat eggs. Add vinegar, lemon juice, sugar and salt. Cook until thick and smooth, stirring constantly. Remove from heat and stir in margarine. Cool mixture.
2. In a serving dish combine apples, pineapple, grapes, oranges and walnuts. Fold in chilled dressing and whipped topping.
3. Serve.

Helen Claassen's Fruit Salad

Helen Classsen
Elkhart, IN
First Norwood Mennonite Church

Makes 10-12 servings

Salad:
16-oz. can peaches, drained
   and sliced
20-oz. can pineapple
   chunks, drained
2 oranges, cut up
2 cups miniature
   marshmallows

Dressing:
2 eggs, slightly beaten
2 Tbsp. pineapple juice
1 Tbsp. vinegar
2 Tbsp. sugar
Dash salt
1 cup whipped topping

1. Combine all dressing ingredients except whipped topping in a saucepan. Cook, stirring constantly until thickened. Cool.
2. Fold whipped topping into cooled dressing. Add well-drained fruit, oranges and marshmallows. Mix well and refrigerate.

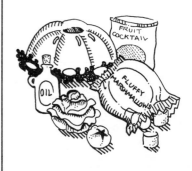

Banana Salad

Ruth Ellen Yoder
West Liberty, OH
South Union Mennonite Church

Makes 10-12 servings

1 egg
¾ cup sugar
4 Tbsp. lemon juice
8 bananas, sliced
½ cup pineapple
1 cup miniature marshmallows
¾ cup peanuts

1. Beat the egg. Add sugar and lemon juice. In a saucepan cook over low heat until thickened, stirring constantly. Cool.
2. Take dressing, fruits, marshmallows and peanuts along to fellowship meal in separate containers.
3. Immediately before serving, slice bananas into dressing. Add pineapple, marshmallows and ½ cup peanuts and stir gently.
4. Sprinkle peanuts over top and serve.

Grandma Moley's Fruit Salad

Elva Evers
North English, IA
Wellman Mennonite Church

Makes 6-8 servings

1 can pineapple chunks
1 orange
1 lemon

6-8 pkgs. sugar substitute
2 Tbsp. minute tapioca
6 small apples, cored and diced
2 bananas, sliced

1. Drain pineapple chunks, reserving juice.
2. Squeeze juice from orange and lemon. Combine all juices, sugar and tapioca. Let stand for about 5 minutes.
3. Heat mixture in microwave for 8-10 minutes, stirring every 2 minutes, until it thickens and tapioca is transparent. Cool.
4. Combine apples and pineapple. Fold in cooled dressing.
5. Immediately before serving, slice in bananas.

Honeymoon Salad

Elsie Neufeldt
Saskatoon, SK
Nutana Park Mennonite Church

Makes 4-6 servings

½ pkg. miniature marshmallows
1 cup minced maraschino cherries
⅓ cup maraschino cherry juice
10-oz. can mandarin oranges, drained
14-oz. can crushed pineapple, drained
½ pint sour cream
1 cup flaked coconut

1. Measure all ingredients into a serving bowl. Gently stir to blend. Cover and chill.
2. Serve.

Dawn Roggie's Fruit Salad

Dawn Roggie
Lowville, NY
Lowville Mennonite Church

Makes 12-15 servings

11-oz. can mandarin oranges
20-oz. can pineapple tidbits
16-oz. can fruit cocktail
1 pkg. instant vanilla pudding
½ cup minute tapioca
1 tsp. frozen orange juice
2 bananas, sliced

1. Drain oranges, pineapple and fruit cocktail, reserving juices.
2. Prepare vanilla pudding according to directions, using reserved fruit juices for required liquid. Add water if needed.
3. Prepare minute tapioca according to directions. Combine pudding and tapioca. Stir in orange juice. Cool pudding and fold in all fruit.
4. Refrigerate until ready to serve.

Fruit Salad Supreme

Miriam Showalter
Salem, OR
Salem Mennonite Church

Makes 15-20 servings

3 17-oz. cans fruit cocktail
2 11-oz. cans mandarin
   oranges
20-oz. can pineapple tidbits
½ cup pineapple juice
1 small pkg. instant vanilla
   pudding
1 cup sour cream
1 cup whipped topping

1. Drain fruit cocktail, oranges and pineapple, reserving ½ cup pineapple juice.
2. Beat dry vanilla pudding with pineapple juice for 1 minute. Add sour cream. Blend in whipped topping.
3. Fold all fruit into dressing and chill several hours before serving.

Fast Family Favorite Fruit Salad

Lorraine J. Kaufman
Moundridge, KS
West Zion Mennonite Church

Makes 10 servings

29-oz. can apricot halves
20-oz. can pineapple chunks
11-oz. can mandarin oranges
1 cup apricot juice
1 small pkg. instant vanilla
   pudding
2-3 bananas, sliced
Lettuce leaves

1. Drain all canned fruit, reserving 1 cup apricot juice.
2. Combine pudding mix with apricot juice. Fold drained fruit into pudding. Cover and chill several hours or overnight.
3. Immediately before serving, fold in bananas.
4. Serve in lettuce-lined glass dish.

Cranberry Crimson Mold

Jean E. Herr
Quarryville, PA

Makes 10 servings

6-oz. pkg. strawberry gelatin
1½ cups boiling water
½ cup mayonnaise
12-oz. container cranberry
   sauce
1 cup applesauce

1. Dissolve gelatin in boiling water. Gradually whisk mayonnaise into gelatin until smooth. Stir in cranberry and applesauce.
2. Pour into lightly greased 5-cup ring mold.
3. Chill until firm, about 4 hours.

Cranberry Apple Salad

Jane M. Zimmerman
Blue Ball, PA
Bethany Mennonite Church

Makes 12-15 servings

½ lb. cranberries
2-3 tart apples
1 cup sugar
6-oz. pkg. cherry gelatin
2 cups boiling water

1. Grind cranberries and apples together.
2. Dissolve sugar and gelatin in boiling water.
3. Blend finely ground cranberries and apples into gelatin mixture. Pour into mold or 8" x 12" pan.
4. Refrigerate until set. Cut into squares and serve.

Cranberry Gelatin Salad

Ruth E. Harder
Dallas, TX

Makes 8-10 servings

3-oz. pkg. raspberry gelatin
1 tsp. plain gelatin
1 cup boiling water
1 cup chopped apples
½ cup chopped celery
16-oz. can whole cranberries
⅔ cup condensed milk
1 Tbsp. lemon juice
½ cup chopped walnuts (optional)

1. Combine raspberry gelatin, plain gelatin and boiling water. Let cool until slightly thickened. Fold in apples, celery and cranberries.
2. Whip condensed milk with lemon juice until very stiff. Blend into gelatin mixture. Fold in chopped walnuts if desired.
3. Refrigerate until firm.

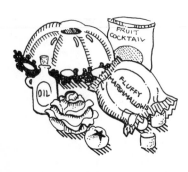

Thanksgiving Fruit Salad

Mary Vaughn Warye
West Liberty, OH
Oak Grove Mennonite Church

Makes 8-10 servings

1 cup pineapple tidbits
2 3-oz. pkgs. cherry gelatin
2 cups hot water
1 cup cold water
2 Tbsp. lemon juice
Dash salt
¾ cup sugar
1½ cups coarsely ground fresh cranberries
½ cup finely ground orange with peel
1 cup orange sections, halved
¾ cup diced celery
⅓ cup chopped walnuts

1. Drain pineapple, reserving ⅓ cup juice.
2. Dissolve gelatin in hot water. Stir in cold water, reserved pineapple juice, lemon juice and salt. Chill until partially set.
3. Meanwhile, stir sugar into ground cranberries and orange.
4. Stir ground fruit mixture, pineapple, orange sections, celery and walnuts into partially set gelatin.
5. Pour into mold and chill until set.

Variations:
Add 1 cup red grapes to the partially set gelatin.

Betty Rutt,
Elizabethtown, PA

Substitute strawberry gelatin for cherry. Omit celery and use only ¼ cup sugar.

Lora S. Oyer,
Chenoa, IL,
Meadows Mennonite Church

Red Gelatin Salad

Adeline Schiedel
Cambridge, ON
Preston Mennonite Church

Makes 10-12 servings

2 3-oz. pkgs. raspberry gelatin
2 cups boiling water
1 cup cold water or cranberry cocktail
½ cup sliced almonds
⅓ cup cranberry sauce
⅛ tsp. cloves
¼ tsp. cinnamon
1 cup chopped apple
½ cup chopped celery
½ cup sliced almonds

1. Dissolve gelatin in boiling water. Add cold water. Pour ¾ cup of mixture into the bottom of a 2-quart mold. Decorate with ½ cup sliced almonds. Chill until firm. Keep remaining gelatin mixture at room temperature.
2. Mix cranberry sauce into remaining gelatin mixture, stirring with a whisk to break up solid mass. Add cloves, cinnamon, apple, celery and ½ cup sliced almonds. Pour over first gelatin layer and chill until firm.

Layered Cranberry Salad

LaVerna Klippenstein
Winnipeg, MB
Home Street Mennonite Church

Makes 10-12 servings

16-oz. can crushed pineapple
Water
2 3-oz. pkgs. cherry gelatin
16-oz. can whole cranberry
   sauce
1 cup sour cream

1. Thoroughly drain and reserve juice from crushed pineapple.
2. To pineapple juice add enough water to measure 2 cups.
3. In a saucepan bring juice and water to a boil. Stir in gelatin until dissolved.
4. Remove from heat. Stir in pineapple and cranberry sauce. Pour ½ of mixture into a glass serving bowl and chill until set. Keep remaining gelatin mixture at room temperature.
5. Spread sour cream over firm gelatin and pour reserved gelatin mixture over sour cream. Refrigerate until firm.

Surprise Orange Salad

Betty Herr, Beallsville, MD; Mary Ethel Lahman Heatwole, Harrisonburg, VA; Esther Lehman, Lowville, NY

Makes 10-12 servings

2 cups cottage cheese
3-oz. pkg. orange gelatin
1 cup whipped topping
11-oz. can mandarin oranges
15-oz. can crushed pineapple

1. Combine cottage cheese, dry gelatin and whipped topping and mix well.
2. Drain fruit thoroughly. Add drained fruit to cottage cheese mixture and mix well. Refrigerate for several hours or overnight.

Cranberry Salad

Esther B. Loux
Souderton, PA
Blooming Glen Mennonite Church

Makes 10 servings

6-oz. pkg. cherry gelatin
1 cup boiling water
16-oz. can cranberry sauce
20-oz. can crushed
   pineapple, drained
1 cup finely chopped celery
1 cup finely chopped nuts

1. Dissolve gelatin in water. Chill until slightly set.
2. Press cranberry sauce through a sieve.

3. Fold all ingredients into partially set gelatin. Pour into large mold. Chill until firm.

Variations:
Top with miniature marshmallows before serving.
Pauline A. Bauman
Bluffton, OH
First Mennonite Church

Substitute raspberry flavored gelatin and omit the celery.
Ruth Heatwole,
Charlottesville, VA,
Charlottesville Mennonite Church

Orange Cranberry Gelatin Salad

Wilma Shank
Sturgis, MI
Goshen Mennonite Assembly

Makes 6-8 servings

3-oz. pkg. orange gelatin
1 cup boiling water
16-oz. can whole cranberry
   sauce
½ cup orange juice
1 whole orange, peeled
½ cup chopped celery
½ cup chopped walnuts

1. Dissolve gelatin in boiling water. Add cranberry sauce, stirring with a wire whisk to break up solid mass. Add orange juice.
2. Remove seeds from orange and cut into small pieces. Fold orange slices, celery and walnuts into gelatin. Turn into 1-quart mold or glass serving dish. Chill until firm.

Orange Sherbet Salad

Gladys Thiessen
Hillsboro, KS
Hillsboro Mennonite Church

Makes 12-15 servings

2 3-oz. pkgs. orange gelatin
3-oz. pkg. lemon gelatin
2 cups hot water
1 pint orange sherbet
20-oz. can crushed pineapple
11-oz. can mandarin oranges
½ cup cold water

1. Dissolve orange and lemon gelatin in hot water. Stir in sherbet.
2. Fold pineapple with juice, oranges with juice and water into gelatin mixture. Pour into 9" x 13" pan. Chill until firm.
3. Cut into squares before serving.

Simplicity Orange Salad

Naomi E. Fast
Newton, KS
Goessel Mennonite Church

Makes 6 servings

2 cups fresh orange juice
6-oz. pkg. orange gelatin
2 cups buttermilk
1 pint cottage cheese
Choice of fruit

1. Heat orange juice to near boiling point. Add orange gelatin, stirring until dissolved. Set aside to cool.

2. When liquid is room temperature, stir in buttermilk. Pour into greased 1½-quart ring mold. Chill until set.
3. Immediately before serving, unmold onto serving plate. Fill center with cottage cheese. Garnish with choice of fruit slices and serve.

Orange Gelatin Mold

Jeannine Janzen
Elbing, KS
Zion Mennonite Church

Makes 8-10 servings

8-oz. can crushed pineapple
11-oz. can mandarin oranges
6-oz. pkg. orange gelatin
12-oz. can frozen orange
 juice concentrate
¾-1 cup 7-Up

1. Drain juice from pineapple and oranges. In a saucepan bring juices to a boil. Dissolve gelatin in hot juice.
2. Add orange juice and 7-Up. Fold in pineapple and oranges. Pour into mold and refrigerate.
3. Chill until firm. Serve.

Seven-Up Salad

Rebecca Byler
Mt. Eaton, OH
Longenecker Mennonite Church

Makes 6 servings

1 cup hot water
3-oz. pkg. lemon gelatin
1 cup 7-Up
8-oz. pkg. cream cheese,
 softened
1 cup crushed pineapple,
 drained
¼ cup chopped nuts
1 tsp. sugar
1 tsp. vanilla

1. Pour hot water over gelatin and let dissolve. Cool. Stir in 7-Up.
2. Whip cream cheese, drained pineapple, nuts, sugar and vanilla together. Slowly fold into gelatin mixture.
3. Refrigerate until firm. Serve.

Pineapple, Apple, Carrot Salad

Ruth Weber
Ephrata, PA
Charlotte Street Mennonite Church

Makes 6 servings

3-oz. pkg. lime or orange
 gelatin
1 cup boiling water
15-oz. can crushed
 pineapple, drained
1 cup pineapple juice
1½ cups grated carrots

½ cup chopped walnuts
1 apple, chopped
Lettuce leaves

1. Dissolve gelatin in hot water. Stir in pineapple juice which has been drained from crushed pineapple. (If crushed pineapple yields less than 1 cup juice, add ice cubes to make 1 cup.) Chill until slightly thickened.

2. Fold all remaining ingredients into gelatin mixture. Pour into mold and chill until set.

3. Unmold onto lettuce leaves and serve with mayonnaise.

Pear Gelatin Salad

Erma J. Sider
Fort Erie, ON
Riverside Chapel Brethren in Christ

Makes 6-8 servings

3-oz. pkg. lime gelatin
1 cup boiling water
¾ cup fruit juice
1 cup sliced canned pears
1 cup pineapple pieces
½ cup cottage cheese
2 Tbsp. mayonnaise
1 kiwi

1. Dissolve gelatin in boiling water and fruit juice. Cool until slightly thickened.

2. Combine pears, pineapple, cottage cheese and mayonnaise. Fold mixture into gelatin. Chill until firm.

3. Immediately before serving, arrange wedges of kiwi in center of dish.

Lime Pineapple Salad

Edna M. Detwiler
Honey Brook, PA
West Chester Mennonite Church

Makes 12 servings

6-oz. pkg. lime gelatin
2 cups boiling water
8-oz. pkg. cream cheese
½ cup mayonnaise
3 Tbsp. lemon juice
1¼ cups ice water
20-oz. can crushed
  pineapple, drained
½ cup chopped nuts

1. Dissolve gelatin in boiling water, stirring until dissolved.

2. Cream the cream cheese until smooth. Gradually add mayonnaise.

3. Fold cream cheese mixture into gelatin, stirring until smooth. Add lemon juice and ice water. Add pineapple and nuts.

4. Pour into mold and chill until firm.

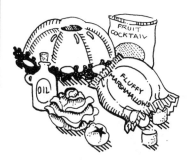

Pacific Lime Mold

Helene Funk
Laird, SK
Tiefengrund Rosenort

Makes 6-8 servings

3-oz. pkg. lime gelatin
1 cup boiling water
9-oz. can crushed pineapple
1 cup creamy cottage cheese
½ cup mayonnaise
¼ cup chopped walnuts
1 tsp. horseradish (optional)

1. Dissolve gelatin in boiling water, stirring for about 5 minutes.

2. Drain juice from pineapple and stir juice into gelatin mixture. Chill and beat until mixture appears creamy.

3. Fold in all remaining ingredients, reserving some walnuts for garnish.

4. Sprinkle walnuts over top and chill until firm.

Variations:
Add 1 cup evaporated milk before chilling mixture the first time. Omit horseradish and stir in ½ cup chopped celery in step 3.

Ruth Brunk
Sarasota, FL
Bahia Vista Mennonite Church

Add 4 marshmallows, quartered in step 3.

Pauline Wyatt
Tangent, OR
Albany Mennonite Church

Refresher Salad

Melba Eshelman
Manheim, PA
Chestnut Hill Mennonite Church

Makes 8-10 servings

20-oz. can crushed pineapple
2 3-oz. pkgs. unflavored
  gelatin
1½ cups boiling water
1 cup sugar
2 bananas, sliced
11-oz. can mandarin
  oranges, drained
Rind and juice of 1 lemon
6-7 maraschino cherries,
  chopped

1. Drain pineapple, reserving juice. Add enough water to juice to make 1 pint. Dissolve gelatin in juice.
2. Add boiling water, sugar, bananas, mandarin oranges, lemon rind and juice, maraschino cherries and pineapple, stirring until sugar dissolves.

Cottage Cheese Pineapple Salad

Helen White
Edmonton, AB
Holyrood Mennonite Church

Makes 6-8 servings

3-oz. pkg. lime gelatin
¼ tsp. salt
1 cup hot water
1 cup crushed pineapple
11-oz. can mandarin oranges
¾ cup pineapple juice

1 cup cottage cheese
½ cup flaked coconut

1. Dissolve gelatin and salt in hot water.
2. Drain crushed pineapple and mandarin oranges, reserving pineapple juice.
3. Add ¾ cup pineapple juice to gelatin mixture. Fold in pineapple, cheese, coconut and mandarin oranges, saving some mandarin orange sections for garnish.
4. Chill until firm.
5. Immediately before serving, garnish with orange sections.

Buttermilk Salad

Anna Weber
Atmore, AL
Mennonite Christian Fellowship

Makes 6 or more servings

15-oz. can crushed pineapple
6-oz. pkg. lime gelatin
2 cups buttermilk
1 cup whipped topping

1. Bring pineapple and juice to a boil. Add gelatin, stirring until dissolved. Add buttermilk and cool until slightly thickened.
2. Fold in whipped topping and chill until firm.
3. Chill until firm.

Pineapple Salad

Joyce Hofer
Morton, IL
Trinity Mennonite Church

Makes 15 servings

6-oz. pkg. lemon gelatin
2 cups hot water
1 cup cold water
20-oz. can crushed pineapple
4 small bananas, sliced
½ cup sugar
2 Tbsp. flour
¾-1 cup pineapple juice
1 egg, beaten
1 cup whipped topping

1. Dissolve gelatin in hot water. Add cold water and cool.
2. Drain pineapple, reserving juice. Stir pineapple and bananas into gelatin. Pour into 9" x 13" pan and refrigerate until set.
3. Combine sugar, flour and juice and microwave on high for 5 minutes, stirring two times.
4. Mix beaten egg into sugar mixture and microwave on medium for 3 minutes, stirring one time. Cool.
5. Fold whipped topping into cooled sugar mixture and layer over gelatin mixture.
6. Chill and serve.

Golden Salad

Joan Sala
Gilbertsville, PA
Boyertown Mennonite Church

Makes 12 servings

20-oz. can crushed pineapple
3 pkgs. unflavored gelatin
1 cup unsweetened orange
  juice
1 cup water
6 pkgs. sugar substitute
2 oranges, cut up
2 apples, chopped
1 banana, sliced
1 cup fresh strawberries,
  sliced

1. Drain crushed pineapple to obtain 1 cup juice. Add water to make 1 cup if needed.
2. Bring pineapple juice to a boil. Remove from heat and dissolve gelatin in juice. Add orange juice, water and sugar substitute. Cool.
3. Combine pineapple, oranges, apples, banana and strawberries. Pour gelatin mixture over fruit. Spoon into lightly greased 6-cup mold or large glass bowl.
4. Refrigerate until set.

Yum Yum Pineapple Salad

Dorothea M. Eigsti
Morton, IL

Makes 10-12 servings

2 Tbsp. unflavored gelatin
½ cup cold water
2 cups crushed pineapple
Juice of 1 lemon
1 cup sugar
1 cup whipping cream
1 cup grated cheese
1-2 Tbsp. finely chopped
  green pepper (optional)
2 Tbsp. finely chopped
  celery
½ cup mayonnaise
Lettuce leaves

1. Soak gelatin in cold water for at least 5 minutes.
2. Heat pineapple. Add lemon, sugar and gelatin, stirring until sugar and gelatin are dissolved. Cool mixture.
3. Whip cream until stiff.
4. When gelatin mixture is partially set, fold in cheese and stiffly beaten cream. Mix well. Spoon into mold and refrigerate until firm.
5. Combine green pepper, celery and mayonnaise to make a dressing.
6. Unmold gelatin salad onto lettuce leaves. Cut into serving pieces and serve with green pepper and celery dressing.

Strawberry Pineapple Salad

Ruth Ann Zeiset
Mohnton, PA
Hampden Mennonite Church

Makes 10 servings

3-oz. pkg. sugar-free
  strawberry gelatin
¾ cup boiling water
10-oz. pkg. frozen,
  unsweetened strawberries
8-oz. can crushed pineapple
1 medium banana, sliced
1 cup plain, low-fat yogurt

1. Dissolve gelatin in boiling water. Chill until mixture is consistency of egg white. Fold in strawberries, pineapple with juice and banana.
2. Pour ½ of mixture into lightly greased 9" x 13" pan. Chill until firm. Store remaining gelatin at room temperature.
3. Spread yogurt evenly over chilled and set gelatin. Pour remaining gelatin over yogurt.
4. Chill until firm. Cut into squares and serve.

Refreshing Fruit Salad

Thelma Wolgemuth
Immokalee, FL
People's Chapel

Makes 8 servings

3-oz. pkg. strawberry gelatin
1 cup boiling water
1 cup frozen strawberries
   with juice
8-oz. can crushed pineapple
1 banana, mashed
1 cup finely chopped nuts
1 cup sour cream

1. Dissolve gelatin in boiling water.
2. Combine strawberries with juice, pineapple with juice, banana and nuts. Pour gelatin over fruit and mix well.
3. Pour ½ of gelatin salad into glass dish and chill until firm. Keep remaining gelatin at room temperature.
4. Spread sour cream over firm gelatin layer. Pour remaining gelatin salad over sour cream. Chill until firm.

Three-Layer Gelatin Salad

Johanna Dyck
Coaldale, AB
Coaldale Mennonite Church

Makes 15 servings

3-oz. pkg. strawberry gelatin
2 cups water
1½ pkgs. unflavored gelatin
½ cup cold water
1 cup light cream
1 cup sugar
2 cups sour cream
1 tsp. vanilla
3-oz. pkg. raspberry gelatin
1 cup boiling water
1 small can blueberries

1. Dissolve strawberry gelatin in 2 cups water. Chill in a large, glass bowl until set.
2. Soak unflavored gelatin in cold water.
3. Heat light cream and sugar, stirring until sugar dissolves. Remove from heat and add unflavored gelatin, stirring until dissolved. Set aside to cool.
4. When cool, add sour cream and vanilla. Let stand several minutes. Pour over layer of strawberry gelatin. Return to refrigerator until second layer sets.
5. Dissolve raspberry gelatin in boiling water. Fold in blueberries. Chill until slightly thickened. Pour over second layer.
6. Chill until firm. Serve.

Apricot Gelatin Salad

Wilma Roeschley
Hinsdale, IL
Lombard Mennonite Church

Makes 6-8 servings

2 3-oz. pkgs. apricot gelatin
1½ cups boiling water
6-oz. can frozen orange juice
   concentrate
2 Tbsp. lemon juice
7-oz. can Sprite
16-oz. can baby apricots
8-oz. can crushed pineapple
⅓ cup chopped nuts

1. Dissolve gelatin in boiling water. Add all other ingredients and stir.
2. Refrigerate until firm. Serve.

Apricot Mold

Gladys D. Kulp
Middletown, VA
Stephens City Mennonite Church

Makes 12-16 servings

11 ozs. dried apricots
½ cup sugar
3-oz. pkg. orange gelatin
3-oz. pkg. lemon gelatin
3 cups hot water
8 ozs. cream cheese, softened
8-oz. can crushed pineapple,
   drained

1. Cook apricots and drain excess water. Beat in blender until smooth. Stir in sugar. Cool mixture.
2. Dissolve gelatins in hot

water. Chill until partially set. Beat together with apricot purée.

3. Pour ½ of apricot gelatin mixture into greased 8-cup ring mold. Chill until firm.

4. Beat cream cheese and pineapple until well blended. Spread over chilled layer of gelatin. Pour remaining apricot gelatin over cream cheese mixture.

5. Chill until firm.

Cherry Salad Supreme

Florine Plenert
Wichita, KS
Lorraine Avenue Mennonite Church

Makes 24-30 servings

3-oz. pkg. raspberry gelatin
1 cup boiling water
21-oz. can cherry pie filling
3-oz. pkg. lemon gelatin
1 cup boiling water
3-oz. pkg. cream cheese
⅓ cup mayonnaise
1 cup whipped topping
1 cup crushed pineapple
with juice
1 cup tiny marshmallows
2 Tbsp. chopped nuts

1. Dissolve raspberry gelatin in boiling water. Stir in pie filling. Turn into 9" x 13" baking dish. Chill until partially set.

2. Dissolve lemon gelatin in boiling water.

3. Beat cream cheese and mayonnaise together. Fold into lemon gelatin. Also fold

whipped topping, pineapple with juice and marshmallows into lemon gelatin.

4. Spread lemon gelatin mixture over cherry mixture. Top with chopped nuts.

5. Chill until set.

Red Raspberry Salad

Edith Yordy
Hinsdale, IL
Lombard Mennonite Church

Makes 4-6 servings

3-oz. pkg. raspberry gelatin
1 cup boiling water
1 cup applesauce
10-oz. pkg. frozen
raspberries
1 cup sour cream
1 cup miniature
marshmallows

1. Dissolve gelatin in boiling water. Add applesauce and let cool to room temperature.

2. Thaw and drain raspberries. Fold into gelatin and chill until firm.

3. Combine sour cream and marshmallows and let set 1 hour. Whip with mixer. Spread over chilled gelatin.

4. Refrigerate overnight before serving.

Blueberry Salad

Sharon Hartman
Winston-Salem, NC
Oak Hill Mennonite Church

Makes 10-12 servings

8-oz. can crushed pineapple
1 pint frozen blueberries
6-oz. pkg. blueberry gelatin
3 cups hot water
1 cup sour cream
8-oz. pkg. cream cheese,
softened
½ cup sugar
½ tsp. vanilla

1. Drain pineapple and blueberries, reserving juice.

2. Dissolve gelatin in hot water. Add reserved juice, adding water to make 1 cup liquid. Cool mixture.

3. Fold pineapple and blueberries into cooled gelatin mixture.

4. Blend sour cream, cream cheese, sugar and vanilla until smooth. Spread over cooled gelatin.

5. Chill and serve.

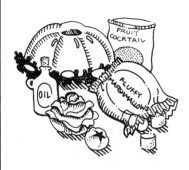

Red Hot Salad

Elsie Regier
Newton, KS

Makes 6-8 servings

⅔ cup red hots
1½ cups applesauce
3-oz. pkg. strawberry gelatin
1 cup boiling water
8 ozs. cream cheese
½ cup mayonnaise
½ cup chopped celery
½ cup pecans

1. Stir red hots, applesauce and gelatin into boiling water. Let cool. Pour ½ of mixture into oblong glass dish. Chill until firm.
2. Combine cream cheese, mayonnaise, celery and pecans and mix until smooth. Pour over firm gelatin.
3. Pour remaining gelatin over cheese mixture. Return to refrigerator and chill until firm.

Applesauce Salad

Agnes Schertz
Goshen, IN
Goshen College Mennonite Church

Makes 10 servings

1 cup hot water
¼ cup red hots
3-oz. pkg. raspberry gelatin
2 cups applesauce
¼ cup pineapple tidbits
¼ cup pecans
Cottage cheese

1. Combine hot water and red hots. Simmer until candies are dissolved. Bring to a boil. Add gelatin, stirring to dissolve.
2. Remove from heat and stir in applesauce, pineapple and pecans. Pour into lightly greased mold or glass dish. Chill until firm.
3. Garnish with cottage cheese and serve.

Applesauce Deluxe

Sharon Lantzer
Galeton, PA
Hebron Tabernacle

Makes 4-6 servings

3-oz. pkg. cherry gelatin
1 cup boiling water
1½ cups applesauce
1 tsp. lemon juice

1. Combine all ingredients. Pour into pretty glass dish.
2. Chill until firm and serve.

Low-Cal Salad

Elaine Jantzen
Hillsboro, KS
First Mennonite Church

Makes 8-10 servings

6-oz. pkg. lemon gelatin
  (aspartame sweetened)
1¼ cups boiling water

1 cup unsweetened
  applesauce
1 cup low-fat cottage cheese
1 cup chopped celery
½ cup chopped pecans
Lettuce leaves

1. Combine gelatin and boiling water. Add all other ingredients. Pour into lightly greased mold.
2. Chill until firm. Unmold onto plate of lettuce leaves and serve.

Sharon Reber's Frozen Fruit Salad

Sharon Reber
Newton, KS

Makes 12-15 servings

8 ozs. cream cheese, softened
¾ cup sugar or less
12-oz. container whipped
  topping
3 bananas, sliced
1½ cups diced strawberries
1 cup crushed pineapple,
  drained

1. Blend together cream cheese and sugar. Add whipped topping and mix until smooth.
2. Fold in bananas, strawberries and pineapple. Spoon into 9" x 13" pan and freeze. Keep frozen until ready to serve.
3. About 3 hours before serving, move from freezer to refrigerator. Cut into squares and serve.

LaVerne Wolfer's Frozen Fruit Salad

LaVerne Wolfer
Hutchinson, KS
South Hutchinson Mennonite
Church

Makes 24 servings

29-oz. can apricot halves
20-oz. can crushed pineapple
3-oz. pkg. unflavored gelatin
1 cup sugar
2 10-oz. pkgs. frozen
　strawberries
2 bananas, sliced

1. Drain apricots and pineapple, reserving juice. Add gelatin and sugar to juice and heat until clear.
2. Remove from heat and fold in apricots, pineapple, strawberries and bananas.
3. Line muffin tins with paper cups. Pour mixture into tins and freeze.
4. Remove from freezer approximately 15 minutes before serving.

Frozen Fruitcake Salad

Ellen Helmuth
Debec, NB
New Brunswick Monthly Meeting,
Society of Friends

Makes 8 servings

1 cup sour cream
½ cup sugar
¼ cup frozen whipped
　topping
2 Tbsp. lemon juice
1 tsp. vanilla
14-oz. can fruit cocktail,
　drained
14-oz. can crushed
　pineapple, drained
2 medium bananas, sliced
½ cup chopped walnuts
Cherries (optional)

1. Blend together sour cream, sugar, whipped topping, lemon juice and vanilla.
2. Fold drained fruit, bananas and walnuts into the mixture. Turn into a serving dish, cover and freeze.
3. Remove from freezer approximately 1 hour before serving. Garnish with cherries if desired.

Frozen Grape Salad

Ethel B. Miller
Landisville, PA
Landisville Mennonite Church

Makes 8-10 servings

2 3-oz. pkgs. cream cheese
2 Tbsp. mayonnaise
2 Tbsp. pineapple juice
24 marshmallows, quartered
2½ cups pineapple tidbits,
　drained
1 cup heavy cream, whipped
2 cups grapes, halved and
　seeded

1. Soften cream cheese. Blend with mayonnaise. Beat in pineapple juice. Add marshmallows and pineapple tidbits.
2. Whip the cream. Fold into salad. Add grapes and mix gently.

3. Spoon into 1-quart refrigerator tray. Freeze until firm.
4. Cut into squares and serve.

Fresh Fruit Salad

Karla Kneif
London, OH
Shalom Community Church

Makes 15-20 servings

1 large watermelon
1 medium cantaloupe
2 cups grapes
2 cups strawberries
2 cups fresh pineapple
　chunks
1 cup blueberries

1. Cut watermelon in half lengthwise. Save other half for future use.
2. Scoop watermelon balls out of half of watermelon.
3. Scoop cantaloupe balls out of cantaloupe.
4. Combine all fruit in a large bowl. Put into hollowed out half of watermelon. Cover with plastic wrap and keep cool in ice chest until ready to serve.

Cool Fruit Salad

Sheri Hartzler
Harrisonburg, VA
Community Mennonite Church

Makes 6-8 servings

2 11-oz. cans mandarin
    oranges
2 20-oz. cans pineapple
    tidbits
16-oz. can pears, cut up
4 large bananas, sliced
2 cups seedless white grapes
2 21-oz. cans peach *or*
    apricot pie filling

1. Drain oranges, pineapple and pears, reserving pineapple juice.
2. Slice bananas into pineapple juice and put in separate container.
3. Combine all other ingredients and chill.
4. Immediately before serving, drain juice from bananas and add to other fruits.

Healthy Fruit Salad

Ida C. Knopp
Salem, OH
Midway Mennonite Church

Makes 6-8 servings

3 tart red apples, chopped
3 oranges, chopped
½ cup chopped celery
⅓ cup raisins
⅓ cup chopped nuts
3 Tbsp. honey
3 Tbsp. lemon juice

1. In a serving bowl toss apples, oranges, celery, raisins and nuts.
2. In a small bowl combine honey and lemon juice. Drizzle over fruit salad and serve.

Fruit Salad Dressing

Marjora Miller
Archbold, OH
West Clinton Mennonite Church

Makes 3 cups dressing

⅓-½ cup sugar
4 Tbsp. clear gel
1 cup cold water
1½ cups hot water
2 Tbsp. margarine
2 Tbsp. vinegar
½ tsp. salt
1 tsp. vanilla

1. In a saucepan mix sugar and clear gel with cold water. Add hot water. Cook until mixture thickens, stirring frequently.
2. Add margarine, vinegar, salt and vanilla.
3. Cool dressing and pour over choice of fruit. (Dressing keeps well in refrigerator for as long as two weeks.)

Main Dishes

Vegetable Main Dishes

Spinach Squares

Ellen S. Peachey
Harpers Ferry, WV
Hyattsville Mennonite Church

Makes 12 servings

3 eggs
1 cup milk
1 cup flour
1 tsp. baking powder
½ lb. Monterey Jack cheese, grated
¼ lb. jalapeño Monterey Jack cheese, grated
12-oz. pkg. frozen, chopped spinach

1. Combine eggs, milk, flour and baking powder into a batter. Stir in cheese and thawed spinach.
2. Spread mixture into a greased 9" x 13" baking pan.
3. Bake at 350° for 35 minutes or until knife comes out clean.

Variation:
Substitute 1 lb. cheddar cheese, grated, for the Monterey Jack cheeses. Add 1 Tbsp. minced onion with cheese.
Bertha Rush
Hatfield, PA

Hearty Spinach and Tofu Risotto

Julie Hurst
Leola, PA
Village Chapel Mennonite Church

Makes 6 servings

8 ozs. tofu, drained
1 medium onion, chopped
1 clove garlic, minced
2 Tbsp. cooking oil
14-oz. can Italian tomatoes
1 tsp. dried oregano
2 cups cooked brown rice
10-oz. pkg. frozen spinach
½ cup shredded Swiss cheese
½ tsp. salt
¼ tsp. pepper
1 Tbsp. sesame seeds

1. Blend tofu until smooth. Set aside.
2. In a large saucepan sauté onion and garlic in hot oil until onion is tender. Add undrained tomatoes and oregano. Bring to a full boil; reduce heat. Simmer, uncovered, about 3 minutes.
3. Stir in tofu and rice.
4. Thaw and drain spinach. Add spinach, ½ of cheese, salt and pepper. Mix gently. Spoon mixture into greased 1½-quart casserole dish.
5. Bake, uncovered, at 350° for 30 minutes. Top with remaining cheese and sesame seeds.

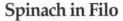

Spinach in Filo

Jeanette Zacharias
Morden, MB
Barn Swallow Quilters

Makes 20 slices

1 medium onion, finely chopped
10-oz. pkg. frozen spinach
1 cup finely chopped mushrooms
1 clove garlic, crushed
1 Tbsp. oregano
2 Tbsp. white wine
1 cup cottage cheese
1 egg
Salt and pepper to taste
12 sheets filo dough
¼ cup melted butter

1. Sauté onion in non-stick skillet until transparent.
2. Thaw and drain spinach. Chop into fine pieces.
3. To onions in skillet add spinach, mushrooms, garlic, oregano and wine. Cook until most of moisture has evaporated. Cool.
4. Combine cottage cheese and egg. Add cooled spinach mixture. Add salt and pepper.
5. Spread filo sheets out and layer one on top of the other, brushing melted butter over each sheet. On last filo sheet put spinach filling. Roll up, being careful to fold in ends. Lay seam side down on greased cookie sheet. Brush filo roll with melted butter.
6. Bake at 350° for 30-35 minutes or until golden brown and crisp.
7. Slice and serve either hot or cold.

Spinach Mushroom Squares

Edith Williams Seibert
Bedford, VA
Main Street Methodist
Friendship Bible Class

Makes 10 servings

2 pkgs. frozen, chopped spinach
1 cup grated sharp cheese
2 eggs, well beaten
1 can cream of mushroom soup
1 cup mayonnaise
1 medium onion, chopped
4-oz. can mushrooms
Dash nutmeg
4 Tbsp. margarine, melted
1 cup bread crumbs

1. Cook spinach and drain. Add cheese, eggs, soup, mayonnaise, onion and mushrooms and mix well. Spoon into large, greased casserole dish. Sprinkle with nutmeg.
2. Combine margarine and bread crumbs. Spread over spinach mixture.
3. Bake at 350° for 1 hour. Serve either hot or cold.

Spinach Casserole

Sharon Lantzer
Galeton, PA
Hebron Tabernacle

Makes 10 servings

3 pkgs. frozen, chopped spinach
1 pkg. dry onion soup mix
1 pint sour cream
Bread cubes
Butter

1. Cook spinach and drain. Combine spinach, onion soup and sour cream and refrigerate overnight or for several hours.
2. Brown bread cubes in butter.
3. Spoon spinach mixture into casserole dish and top with bread cubes.
4. Bake at 350° for ½ hour.

Spinach Potatoes

Naomi Neuenschwander,
Louisville, OH,
Buch Mennonite Church;

Lois Hallman
Goshen, IN,
College Mennonite Church

Makes 6 servings

6-8 large potatoes
¾ cup sour cream
1 tsp. salt
1 tsp. sugar
1 tsp. pepper
4 Tbsp. margarine
2 Tbsp. chopped chives
¼ tsp. dill weed

1 pkg. frozen, chopped
  spinach
1 cup grated cheddar cheese

1. Cook and mash potatoes.
Add sour cream, salt, sugar,
pepper and margarine and
beat well. Add chives and dill
weed and mix well.

2. Cook and drain spinach.
Fold into other ingredients.
Spoon into casserole dish and
sprinkle with cheese. Refrigerate overnight.

3. Bake at 400° for 20 minutes.

Spinach Pie

Sara Fretz-Goering
Silver Spring, MD
Hyattsville Mennonite Church

Makes 6-8 servings

2 pkgs. frozen spinach
1 small onion, minced
½ tsp. salt
¼ tsp. nutmeg
3 Tbsp. margarine
12-15 ozs. cottage *or* ricotta
  cheese
½ cup Parmesan cheese
½ cup milk
3 eggs, beaten
1 9" unbaked pie shell

1. Cook and drain spinach.
2. Sauté onion and spices
in margarine.
3. Combine cheeses, milk
and eggs in a bowl and mix
well. Add spinach and onion
to mixture. Spoon into pie
shell.
4. Bake at 350° for 40-50
minutes.

Broccoli Soufflé

Gail U. Pentz
Sarasota, FL
Bahia Vista Mennonite Church

Makes 6-8 servings

6 eggs
2 lbs. cottage cheese
6 Tbsp. flour
½ lb. cheddar cheese, diced
2 pkgs. frozen, chopped
  broccoli, uncooked
4 Tbsp. butter *or* margarine
2 green onions, chopped

1. Bring all ingredients to
room temperature. Mix to-
gether in following order:
eggs, cottage cheese, flour,
cheddar cheese, broccoli, butter and onions. Spoon into
greased 9" x 12" baking dish.

2. Bake at 350° for 60-70
minutes. Allow to set 10 minutes before serving.

Variation:
*Substitute 1 large head cauli-
flower for the broccoli. Steam
cauliflower before adding to
other ingredients. Bake at 325°
for 45 minutes.*
Helen Rose Pauls
Sardis, BC
Sardis Community Church

Broccoli Squares

Winifred Paul
Scottdale, PA
Kingview Mennonite Church

Makes 6-8 servings

2 bunches fresh broccoli
1 can cream of mushroom
  soup
4 ozs. cheddar cheese, grated
1 medium onion, chopped
¾ cup mayonnaise
Ritz crackers
Butter (optional)

1. Cook broccoli until just
tender. Drain well. Combine
with all other ingredients except Ritz crackers and butter.
Spoon into greased 9" x 13"
baking pan.

2. Crush crackers and
sprinkle over broccoli mixture. Dot with butter if desired.

3. Bake at 350° for 30 minutes.

Variation:
*Add two eggs to broccoli mix-
ture. Substitute crushed corn-
flakes for Ritz crackers. Omit
butter.*
Betty Pellman
Millersville, PA
Rossmere Mennonite Church

Broccoli Casserole

Anne Giesbrecht
Richmond, BC
Richmond Bethel Mennonite
Brethren Church

Makes 6-8 servings

1 clove garlic, minced
1 large onion, chopped
¼ cup margarine
4 cups cooked broccoli
¼ cup chopped almonds
4-oz. can sliced mushrooms,
   drained
1 cup grated cheese
1 can cream of mushroom
   soup
1 cup buttered bread crumbs

1. Sauté garlic and onion
lightly in margarine.
2. Layer ingredients into
9" x 13" baking pan in following order: garlic and onions,
½ of broccoli, ½ of almonds,
mushrooms, ½ of broccoli.
3. Heat cheese and mush-
room soup together until
cheese has melted. Pour over
casserole and top with remaining almonds and bread
crumbs.
4. Bake at 350° for 45 minutes.

Party Walnut Broccoli

Naomi E. Fast
Newton, KS
Goessel Mennonite Church

Makes 8-10 servings

3 10-oz. pkgs. frozen,
   chopped broccoli
6 Tbsp. margarine
4 Tbsp. flour
1 cup chicken broth
2 cups skim milk
⅔ cup water
2 cups herb stuffing
⅔ cup chopped walnuts

1. Cook broccoli until just
barely tender. Drain and
place into greased 2-quart
casserole dish.
2. Melt 2 Tbsp. margarine
in saucepan. Stir in flour and
cook briefly. Add chicken
broth and milk and simmer
until thickened. Set aside.
3. Heat water and melt remaining 4 Tbsp. margarine
in hot water. Combine with
stuffing and walnuts. Toss to
mix evenly.
4. Pour chicken cream
sauce over broccoli. Top with
moistened stuffing and walnuts.
5. Bake at 400° for 20 minutes.

Broccoli Rice Casserole

Marcella Klaassen
Hillsboro, KS
Hillsboro First Mennonite Church

Maxine Bergen
Henderson, NE

Makes 6-8 servings

1 Tbsp. margarine
2 pkgs. frozen, chopped
   broccoli
1 medium onion, finely
   chopped
1 cup boiling water
1 cup minute rice
1 can cream of mushroom
   soup
8 ozs. low-fat cheese, grated
½ cup milk

1. Cook broccoli and on-
ion in margarine until just
tender.
2. Pour boiling water over
rice according to package directions.
3. Combine soup, cheese
and milk.
4. Fold together all ingredients and spoon into
greased 2½-quart casserole
dish.
5. Bake, uncovered, at 350°
for 30-40 minutes.

Baked Fresh Corn

Esther B. Loux
Souderton, PA
Blooming Glen Mennonite Church

Makes 6-10 servings

1 medium onion, chopped
1 green pepper, chopped
3 Tbsp. margarine
3 Tbsp. flour
1-2 cups skim milk
1 cup grated low-cholesterol
   cheese
1 tsp. sugar
1 tsp. salt
Dash pepper
2 cups fresh corn
2 egg beaters
Bread crumbs

1. Sauté onion and green pepper in margarine until tender. Stir in flour. Add milk and bring to a boil, stirring constantly. Remove from heat.
2. Stir in cheese, sugar, salt and pepper. Add corn and egg beaters. Turn into casserole dish and top with bread crumbs.
3. Bake in shallow pan of hot water at 350° for 1 hour.

Baked Corn

Barbara Hershey
Lancaster, PA
Rossmere Mennonite Church

Makes 6 servings

2 cups creamed corn
2 eggs, beaten
1 tsp. salt
⅛ tsp. pepper
1 Tbsp. sugar
2 Tbsp. butter, melted
1 Tbsp. flour
¾ cup milk

1. Combine all ingredients and pour into greased 2-quart baking dish.
2. Bake at 350° for 40-45 minutes or until center is done.

Scalloped Corn

Ruth Weber
Ephrata, PA
Charlotte Street Mennonite Church

Makes 6 servings

2 eggs, beaten
1 cup milk
⅔ cup cracker *or* bread
   crumbs
2 cups cooked corn
1 tsp. minced onion
½ tsp. salt
⅛ tsp. pepper
1 Tbsp. sugar (optional)
3 Tbsp. butter, melted

1. Combine eggs, milk and crumbs. Add corn, onion and seasonings. Mix well

and add melted butter. Pour into greased casserole dish.
2. Bake at 350° for 40 minutes.

Corn Pudding Casserole

Berdella Miller
Millersburg, OH
Berlin Mennonite Church

Makes 6-8 servings

2 Tbsp. margarine
2 Tbsp. flour
1½ cups milk
1 tsp. salt
¼ tsp. dry mustard
1 tsp. white sugar
2 cups corn pulp
1 egg, slightly beaten
1 Tbsp. Worcestershire sauce
1 slice buttered bread

1. Melt margarine in a saucepan. Add flour, stirring until bubbly. Gradually add milk, salt, mustard and sugar, stirring until smooth.
2. Cook corn pulp and drain well.
3. Add corn, egg and Worcestershire sauce to white sauce. Spoon into baking dish.
4. Break slice of bread into tiny pieces. Cover casserole with bread crumbs.
5. Bake at 350° for 25-30 minutes.

Corn Pudding

Ferne Ropp
Tremont, IL
First Mennonite Church

Makes 10-12 servings

3 Tbsp. melted margarine
4 Tbsp. sugar
4 eggs
4 Tbsp. flour
2 16-oz. cans cream-style
   corn
½ lb. Velveeta cheese,
   cubed

1. Combine all ingredients. Spoon into casserole dish.
2. Bake at 350° for 1 hour.

Three Corn Casserole

Ruth Ann Swartzendruber, Hydro, OK; Naomi Headings, West Liberty, OH; Maxine Miller, Wakarusa, IN; Annetta Miller, Berlin, OH

Makes 10-12 servings

16-oz. can whole kernel corn,
   drained
16-oz. can cream-style corn,
   undrained
4 Tbsp. margarine, melted
2 eggs
8-oz. box corn muffin mix
1 cup yogurt *or* sour cream

1. Combine all ingredients with electric mixer and mix until moistened. Spoon into greased 9" x 13" baking pan.
2. Bake at 350° for 1 hour or until golden brown.

Corn Casserole

Pauline Hofstetter
Versailles, MO
Bethel Mennonite Church

Makes 10-12 servings

16-oz. can cream-style corn
16-oz. can whole kernel corn,
   drained
1 cup broken spaghetti pieces
1 cup cubed cheese
4 Tbsp. margarine, melted
Salt and pepper to taste
2 Tbsp. chopped onion

1. Combine all ingredients and spoon into large casserole dish.
2. Cover and bake at 350° for ½ hour. Uncover and bake ½ hour longer.

Baked Corn and Noodle Casserole

Ruth Hershey
Paradise, PA
Paradise Mennonite Church

Makes 6 servings

3 cups noodles
2 cups corn
¾ cup cubed cheese
1 egg, beaten
½ cup butter, melted

1. Cook noodles in salted water. Rinse in cold water and drain.
2. Combine all ingredients in greased baking dish.
3. Bake at 350° for 40 minutes.

Frozen Corn

Lucille Taylor
Hutchinson, KS
First Mennonite Church

Makes 8-10 servings

4 cups raw corn
2 Tbsp. sugar
1 tsp. salt
¾ cup water
1 oz. cream cheese

1. Cut raw corn from cobs.
2. Combine corn, sugar, salt and water and boil for 3 minutes. Freeze.
3. When ready to serve, add cream cheese and reheat in crockpot during church service.

Eggplant Casserole

Betty Rutt
Elizabethtown, PA

Makes 8-10 servings

4 cups diced eggplant
½ tsp. salt
⅓ cup milk
1 can mushroom soup
1 egg, slightly beaten
½ cup chopped onion
1 ¾ cups herb-seasoned
    stuffing
2 Tbsp. butter, melted
1 cup grated sharp cheese

1. Cook eggplant until tender in salted water, about 5-6 minutes.
2. In mixing bowl combine milk and soup. Stir in egg, drained eggplant, onion and ¾ cup stuffing. Toss lightly to mix and spoon into greased baking dish.
3. Crush remaining 1 cup stuffing and toss with melted butter. Sprinkle over casserole. Top with cheese.
4. Bake at 350° for about 25 minutes.

Squash Medley

Ellen Helmuth
Debec, NB
New Brunswick Monthly Meeting
Society of Friends

Makes 4 servings

1 cup uncooked rice
2 cups water
½ tsp. salt

½ cup lentils
1 squash
1 onion, chopped
6 cloves garlic, crushed
2 Tbsp. cooking oil
4 ozs. tofu, diced
1 Tbsp. curry powder
2 tsp. oregano
Salt and pepper to taste
1 pint canned tomatoes
1 cup shredded cheese

1. Cook rice in 2 cups water and ½ tsp. salt.
2. Cook lentils in water to cover. Drain.
3. Peel and cube squash. Cook until tender.
4. Sauté onion and garlic in oil. Add tofu, curry and oregano. Salt and pepper to taste. Add lentils, squash and tomatoes and heat through.
5. Top with shredded cheese and allow to melt slightly. Serve with rice.

If you do not enjoy spicy foods, cut curry powder and oregano in half.

Squash Apple Bake

Ruth Ann Swartzendruber
Hydro, OK
Pleasant View Mennonite Church

Makes 8 servings

4 cups cubed butternut
    squash
3 Tbsp. honey
⅓ cup orange *or* apple juice
2 apples, thinly sliced
¼ cup raisins
Cinnamon
1 Tbsp. margarine

1. Slice butternut squash into ¾" rounds. Peel and remove any seeds. Cut into cubes.
2. Combine honey and juice.
3. In a greased 2-quart casserole dish make 2 layers of squash, apples and raisins. Sprinkle generously with cinnamon and pour juice mixture over layers. Dot with margarine.
4. Cover and bake at 350° for 45-60 minutes or until tender. Serve warm as a vegetable.

Winter Squash Casserole

Christine Guth
Goshen, IN
East Goshen Mennonite Church

Makes 8 servings

1 medium onion, chopped
2 cloves garlic, minced
1 Tbsp. cooking oil
4 cups cubed winter squash
⅓ cup chopped fresh parsley
2 Tbsp. soy sauce
3 eggs
1½ cups milk
1½ cups grated cheese

1. Sauté onion and garlic in oil.
2. Steam winter squash until just tender.
3. Combine all ingredients and mix well. Spoon into greased 9" x 13" baking pan.
4. Bake at 375° for 1 hour or until center is firm.

Mother's Onion Pudding

Vera Kuhns
Harrisonburg, VA
Parkview Mennonite Church

Makes 6 servings

½ lb. saltine crackers
4 large onions, sliced
2½ cups milk
¼ lb. butter *or* margarine
½ tsp. salt
½ tsp. pepper

1. Layer crackers and onions into greased casserole dish. Pour milk over crackers and onions. Dice butter into dish. Add salt and pepper.
2. Bake at 350° for 35-45 minutes.

Onion Chip Casserole

Judy Hall
Molalla, OR
Zion Mennonite Church

Makes 4-6 servings

4 medium, sweet onions
1 cup water
1 can cream of mushroom soup
½ cup milk
9-oz. pkg. potato chips, crushed
1 cup grated cheddar cheese
Paprika

1. Peel onions and slice them thinly. Simmer in water until almost tender, about 5-8 minutes. Drain.
2. Combine mushroom soup with milk.
3. In a greased 2-quart casserole dish arrange ingredients in following order: onions, potato chips, cheese, mushroom soup. Sprinkle with paprika.
4. Bake at 350° for 30 minutes.

Green Bean Casserole

Arlene Wiens
Newton, KS
Goessel Mennonite Church

Makes 8 servings

1 can cream of mushroom soup
½ cup grated American cheese
¾ cup milk
1 quart green beans
½ cup onion rings

1. Heat soup, cheese and milk until it bubbles and cheese melts. Remove from heat.
2. Drain beans and add to soup mixture. Add half the onion rings. Pour into casserole dish and top with remaining onion rings.
3. Bake, uncovered, at 325° until heated through.

Variation:
Substitute 1 can cream of celery soup for the cheese. Combine soups with milk, but do not heat them. Salt and pepper to taste. Substitute ½ cup buttered bread crumbs for the onion rings. Bake at 375° for 30 minutes.

Erma Kauffman
Cochranville, PA,
Media Mennonite Church

Cabbage and Noodle Casserole

Sharon Troyer
Waterford, PA

Makes 15-20 servings

2 large heads cabbage
1 onion, sliced
8 Tbsp. margarine
16-oz. pkg. wide noodles
Salt and pepper to taste

1. Wash and slice cabbage. In large skillet with small amount of water, steam cabbage. When cabbage has cooked down and water is gone, add onion and margarine and brown cabbage slightly. (If you have a small skillet, do in several batches.)
2. Meanwhile, cook noodles according to package directions. Drain and add to cabbage. Salt and pepper to taste. Simmer until heated through.

To make this a non-vegetarian dish add Keilbasa and heat through.

Escalloped Carrots

E.B. Heatwole
Rocky Ford, CO
Rocky Ford Mennonite Church

Makes 8 servings

4 cups sliced carrots
1/4 cup diced green pepper
1/2 cup chopped green onions

4 Tbsp. butter *or* margarine
4 Tbsp. flour
2 cups milk
1/4 tsp. salt
1/8 tsp. pepper
Cornflakes *or* bread crumbs

1. Cook carrots until just tender.
2. Sauté pepper and onions in butter. Add flour, stirring constantly. Add milk, salt and pepper. Cook, stirring until thickened.
3. Place carrots into greased casserole dish. Cover with sauce. Top with cornflakes or bread crumbs.
4. Bake at 350° for 30 minutes or until bubbly.

Sweet and Sour Carrots

Joann Ewert
Modesto, CA
Modesto Church of the Brethren

Makes 8-10 servings

2 lbs. carrots
8-oz. can tomato sauce
1 cup sugar or less
1/4 cup cooking oil or less
1/2 cup vinegar
1 medium bell pepper, chopped
1 tsp. salt
1/2 tsp. pepper
1/2 tsp. Worcestershire sauce
1/2 tsp. dry mustard
1 medium red onion, chopped

1. Slice carrots and cook until tender. Drain.
2. Combine all other ingre-

dients in a saucepan and cook until heated through.
3. Immediately before serving, pour sauce over hot carrots.

Carrot and Cheese Casserole

Carolyn Hartman
Harrisonburg, VA
Parkview Mennonite Church

Makes 10-12 servings

2 lbs. carrots
4 Tbsp. butter *or* margarine
1/2 lb. Velveeta cheese
Toasted bread crumbs

1. Peel, slice and cook carrots until just tender. Place in casserole dish.
2. Melt butter and cheese together. Pour over carrots. Top with toasted bread crumbs.
3. Bake at 350° for 30 minutes.

Variation:
Add 1 small chopped onion to the ingredients. Salt and pepper to taste.

Sue Williams
Gulfport, MS,
Gulfhaven Mennonite Church

Scalloped Rhubarb

Winifred Ewy
Newton, KS
Bethel College Mennonite Church

Makes 6-8 servings

8 Tbsp. butter or margarine
3 cups diced, uncooked
rhubarb
1 cup sugar
3 cups cubed stale bread

1. Put butter in glass 6" x 10" baking pan. Place in 325° oven until butter melts.
2. Combine rhubarb and sugar. Add bread cubes. Spoon into baking pan with melted butter and mix. Pour 1 Tbsp. water into each of the 4 corners in the pan.
3. Bake at 325° for 45 minutes.
4. Serve hot or cold.

Creamed Peas and Mushrooms

Diena Schmidt
Henderson, NE
Bethesda Mennonite Church

Makes 8 servings

20-oz. pkg. frozen peas
½ cup mushroom caps
1 Tbsp. minced onion
2 Tbsp. butter
2 Tbsp. flour
1½ cups half-and-half
3 slices Velveeta cheese
¼ tsp. salt

1. Cook peas in boiling, salted water until tender.
2. Sauté mushrooms and onion in butter until lightly browned. Add to peas.
3. Stir flour into remaining drippings, adding more butter if needed. Add half-and-half gradually, cooking and stirring until slightly thickened. Turn heat to low and add sliced cheese. Stir until dissolved.
4. Pour sauce over peas and heat until bubbly.

Hot Mushroom Turnovers

Sarah Klassen
Winnipeg, MB
River East Mennonite Brethren Church

Makes 50 turnovers

8-oz. pkg. cream cheese,
softened
½ cup softened butter
1½ cups flour
½ lb. mushrooms, chopped
1 large onion, chopped
1 Tbsp. butter
1 tsp. salt
¼ tsp. thyme
2 Tbsp. flour
¼ cup sour cream
1 egg, beaten

1. Beat together cream cheese and ½ cup butter. Add 1½ cups flour and mix until soft dough forms. Wrap dough in wax paper and refrigerate for 1 hour.
2. Sauté mushrooms and onion in 1 Tbsp. butter until tender, about 5 minutes. Stir in salt, thyme, 2 Tbsp. flour and sour cream and mix well.
3. On a floured board roll out half of dough into a thin sheet. Cut into 2"-3" circles. Collect remaining scraps of dough, refrigerate and roll out again until all of dough has been cut. Repeat with other half of dough.
4. Place 1 tsp. mushroom mixture on half of each pastry circle. Brush edges with egg. Fold edges together and seal with a fork. Prick top in 3 places to let out steam. Place on ungreased cookie sheets and brush tops with egg.
5. Bake at 450° for 12-15 minutes or until golden brown.

Tarragon Mushrooms

Willard and Alice Roth
Elkhart, IN
Southside Fellowship

Makes 24 servings

1 lb. small mushrooms
¼ cup olive oil
¼ cup wine vinegar
⅓ cup water
¼ cup sugar
1 Tbsp. soy sauce
1 Tbsp. Worcestershire sauce
1 Tbsp. tarragon
1 tsp. thyme
Hint of hot sauce

1. Clean and dry mushrooms.

2. Combine all ingredients except mushrooms in a jar and shake well.

3. In an airtight plastic container pour liquid over mushrooms. Cover and refrigerate, shaking occasionally.

4. Marinate overnight before serving. This dish will keep up to two weeks.

5. Serve in glass jar or dish with miniature fork.

Artichoke Nibbles

Betty Pellman
Millersville, PA
Rossmere Mennonite Church

Makes 36 servings

2 6-oz. jars marinated
  artichoke hearts
1 small onion, minced
1 clove garlic, minced
1/4 cup fine, dry bread
  crumbs
4 eggs, beaten
1/8 tsp. pepper
1/8 tsp. oregano
1/8 tsp. Tabasco sauce
8 ozs. sharp cheddar cheese,
  grated
2 Tbsp. minced parsley

1. Drain liquid from 1 jar artichoke hearts into a skillet. Sauté onion and garlic until limp. Drain most of liquid from onion and garlic.

2. Drain liquid from other jar artichoke hearts. Chop artichokes and set aside.

3. Combine bread crumbs, eggs, pepper, oregano and Tabasco sauce. Fold in cheese, parsley, onion mix-

ture and artichokes. Turn into 7" x 11" baking pan.

4. Bake at 325° about 30 minutes or until mixture has set. Cool and cut into 1-inch squares.

5. Immediately before serving, reheat 10-12 minutes.

Baked Pineapple

Virginia Moye
New Oxford, PA

Makes 8 servings

1/2 cup butter
1/2-3/4 cup sugar
3 eggs, beaten
20-oz. can crushed pineapple
4 slices white bread, cubed
Dash salt

1. Cream butter and sugar. Add eggs and mix well. Add remaining ingredients, including juice from pineapple, and mix well. Turn into greased 8-inch square casserole dish.

2. Bake at 350° for 50 minutes.

Vegetable Casserole

Helen Ruth Unruh
Hutchinson, KS
First Mennonite Church

Makes 8 servings

16-oz. pkg. frozen Oriental-
  style vegetables
2 cups chopped cauliflower
2 4-oz. jars sliced
  mushrooms
2 cups cooked carrots
1 can cream of mushroom
  soup
1/4 cup milk
1/2 cup grated Swiss cheese
8 slices American cheese,
  cut up
1 Tbsp. parsley flakes
1/2 tsp. tarragon
1/2 cup buttered bread *or*
  cracker crumbs

1. Cook frozen vegetables and cauliflower until just crispy. Drain.

2. Drain liquid from mushrooms and cooked carrots. Arrange all vegetables in 2-quart baking dish.

3. Combine mushroom soup, milk, cheeses, parsley and tarragon. Cook over low heat until cheese has melted. Pour sauce over vegetables. Sprinkle buttered crumbs on top.

4. Bake at 375° for 35-40 minutes until bubbly.

Sweet Potato and Apple Casserole

Anna S. Eby
Lititz, PA
Lititz Mennonite Church

Makes 6-8 servings

⅓ cup brown sugar, firmly packed
½ tsp. ground ginger
⅛ tsp. salt
2 lbs. cooked sweet potatoes, peeled
2 large apples, sliced
3 Tbsp. butter, melted
½ cup shredded coconut
¼ cup chopped pecans

1. In a small bowl combine sugar, ginger and salt. Set aside.
2. Cut sweet potatoes into ½-inch thick slices. Arrange ½ of potatoes in greased, shallow baking dish. Cover with apples.
3. Sprinkle ½ of brown sugar mixture over apples. Top with remaining sweet potato slices. Sprinkle with remaining brown sugar. Spread 2 Tbsp. melted butter over layers.
4. Cover and bake at 375° for 35 minutes. Remove from oven.
5. Combine coconut, pecans and remaining 1 Tbsp. melted butter. Sprinkle over sweet potatoes. Return dish to oven and bake 10 minutes longer or until lightly browned.

Orange-Glazed Sweet Potatoes

Annabelle Kratz
Clarksville, MD
Hyattsville Mennonite Church

Makes 8 servings

8 medium sweet potatoes
½ tsp. salt
1 cup brown sugar, packed
2 Tbsp. cornstarch
½ tsp. shredded orange peel
2 cups orange juice
½ cup raisins
6 Tbsp. margarine
¼ cup chopped walnuts

1. Cook potatoes in boiling, salted water until just tender. Drain. Peel potatoes and cut lengthwise into ½-inch slices. Arrange in 9" x 13" baking dish. Sprinkle with salt.
2. In a saucepan combine brown sugar and cornstarch. Blend in orange peel and juice. Add raisins. Cook and stir over medium heat until thickened and bubbly. Cook 1 minute longer. Add margarine and walnuts, stirring until butter has melted. Pour sauce over sweet potatoes.
3. Bake at 325° for 30 minutes or until sweet potatoes are well glazed. Baste occasionally.

Variation:
Immediately before pouring sauce over sweet potatoes, fold in 2 cups apricot halves.

Dorothy Shank
Goshen, IN
College Mennonite Church

Sweet Potatoes Almondine

Winifred Ewy
Newton, KS
Bethel College Mennonite Church

Makes 8-10 servings

4 large sweet potatoes
4 Tbsp. butter *or* margarine
⅔ cup milk
¼ tsp. salt
½ cup brown sugar
¼ tsp. pumpkin pie spice
½ cup slivered almonds
4 Tbsp. butter *or* margarine

1. Cook, peel and mash sweet potatoes. Add 4 Tbsp. butter, milk and salt. Spoon into greased casserole dish.
2. Cream together brown sugar, pumpkin pie spice, almonds and 4 Tbsp. butter. Spread over sweet potato mixture.
3. Bake at 350° until heated through and topping has melted.

Sweet Potato Pudding

Alice Whitman
Lancaster, PA
South Christian Street Mennonite Church

Makes 6 servings

6 medium sweet potatoes
6 Tbsp. sugar
1 tsp. salt
2 Tbsp. butter *or* margarine, melted
1 cup milk
2 eggs, beaten
½ cup miniature marshmallows

1. Cook, peel and mash sweet potatoes.
2. Add sugar, salt, melted butter and milk to mashed sweet potatoes. Mix well. Stir in eggs and beat well.
3. Spoon into greased 2-quart casserole dish. Top with marshmallows.
4. Bake at 350° for 45 minutes.

Gourmet Cheese Potatoes

Lillian Miller, Leola, PA; Sharon Hartman, Winston-Salem, NC; Jeannine Janzen, Elbing, KS; Alma C. Ranck, Paradise, PA; Maxine Hershberger, Dalton, OH; Helen R. Goering, Moundridge, KS; Ruth Ann Esh, Willow Street, PA; Mabel Neff, Quarryville, PA

Makes 8-10 servings

6 medium potatoes
2 cups shredded cheddar cheese

¼ cup butter
1½ cups sour cream *or* 1 cup milk
⅓ cup finely chopped onion
1 tsp. salt
¼ tsp. pepper
2 Tbsp. butter
Paprika

1. Cook potatoes in their skins. (Do not overcook). Cool, peel and shred coarsely.
2. In a saucepan over low heat combine cheese and ¼ cup butter. Stir until almost melted. Remove from heat and blend in sour cream or milk, onion, salt and pepper. Fold in shredded potatoes.
3. Place in casserole dish and dot with butter. Sprinkle with paprika.
4. Bake at 350° for 30 minutes.

Variation:
Add 2 tsp. dry mustard to sauce before adding potatoes.
Marie Horst
Lititz, PA

Delicious Potato Casserole

Clara L. Hershberger
Goshen, IN
Goshen College Mennonite Church

Makes 8-10 servings

8 unpeeled, medium potatoes
1 bay leaf
1 can cream of chicken soup
¼ cup butter *or* margarine, melted

1½ cups light sour cream
½ tsp. salt
¼ tsp. pepper
3 green onions, chopped
2 cups grated cheese
½ cup crushed cornflakes

1. Cook jacket potatoes in salted water with bay leaf. Cool, peel and grate coarsely.
2. Combine soup with melted butter. Blend in sour cream, salt, pepper, onions and 1½ cups grated cheese. Pour over potatoes.
3. Bake, uncovered, at 350° for 30 minutes. Remove from oven.
4. Combine ½ cup cheese with cornflakes and sprinkle over casserole. Return to oven and bake 10-15 minutes longer.

Variation:
Do not peel potatoes before grating them. Substitute paprika for cornflake and cheese topping. Arrange all ingredients in a crockpot and turn to low or medium. Potato dish will be hot just in time for the noon fellowship meal at church.
Joy Maust
West Jefferson, OH
Shalom Community Church

Very Good Potatoes

Viola Weidner
Allentown, PA
First Mennonite Church

Makes 8-10 servings

5 large potatoes
$\frac{1}{3}$ cup margarine
$\frac{1}{2}$ cup grated sharp cheese
1 tsp. paprika
1$\frac{1}{2}$ tsp. salt
2$\frac{1}{2}$ Tbsp. bread crumbs

1. Peel potatoes and cut into wedges.
2. Melt margarine in a shallow baking pan. Toss potatoes in baking pan until coated with margarine.
3. Combine cheese, paprika, salt and bread crumbs. Sprinkle over potatoes.
4. Bake at 425° for 30-40 minutes.

Irish Potato Casserole

Carolyn Hartman
Harrisonburg, VA
Parkview Mennonite Church

Makes 8-10 servings

8-10 medium potatoes,
**   peeled**
8-oz. pkg. cream cheese
8 ozs. sour cream
$\frac{1}{2}$ cup melted butter *or*
**   margarine**
$\frac{1}{4}$ cup chopped chives
1 clove garlic, minced
2 tsp. salt
Paprika

1. Cook potatoes and mash. (Do not add any liquid).
2. Beat cream cheese with electric mixture until smooth. Add potatoes and all other ingredients except paprika. Beat until all ingredients have combined. Spoon into lightly greased 2-quart casserole dish. Sprinkle with paprika and refrigerate overnight.
3. Uncover and bake at 350° for 30 minutes or until thoroughly heated.

Variations:
   Add $\frac{1}{4}$ cup finely chopped onion to the ingredients before baking.

Carol Sommers
Millersburg, OH,
Martins Creek Mennonite Church

Cheese Potato Puff

Melba Eshleman
Manheim, PA
Chestnut Hill Mennonite Church

Makes 10 servings

12 medium potatoes
6 Tbsp. butter *or* margarine
2$\frac{1}{4}$ cups grated cheddar
**   cheese**
1-1$\frac{1}{4}$ cups milk
$\frac{3}{4}$-1 tsp. salt
2 eggs, beaten

1. Peel potatoes. Cook in salted water until tender. Drain and mash thoroughly. Add butter, cheese, milk and salt. Beat until butter and cheese have melted. Fold in eggs.

2. Spoon into greased baking dish.
3. Bake at 350° for 30-45 minutes or until puffy and golden brown.

Au Gratin Hash Brown Potatoes

Eileen Heintz
Sarasota, FL
Bayshore Mennonite Church

Makes 12-15 servings

2 lbs. hash brown potatoes
1 small onion, diced
1 pint half-and-half
8 Tbsp. margarine
9 ozs. American cheese
12-oz. container cottage
**   cheese**

1. Spread potatoes evenly into greased 9" x 13" baking pan. Layer diced onion over potatoes.
2. In a saucepan heat half-and-half, margarine and cheese. Cook until melted. Stir in cottage cheese. Pour sauce over potatoes. Let stand at least 1 hour or overnight.
3. Bake at 350° for 1-1$\frac{1}{2}$ hours.

Scalloped Potatoes with Cornflake Topping

LaVerna Klippenstein
Winnipeg, MB
Home Street Mennonite Church

Makes 10 servings

8 medium potatoes
½ cup margarine
¼ cup chopped onion
1 can cream of chicken soup
1 cup sour cream
1½ cups grated cheddar cheese
¾ cup crushed cornflakes
2 Tbsp. margarine, melted

1. Cook and slice potatoes.
2. In a saucepan combine margarine, onion, soup, sour cream and cheese. Heat until well blended. Pour sauce over potatoes.
3. Combine cornflakes and melted margarine. Sprinkle over potatoes.
4. Bake at 350° for 25 minutes.

Scalloped Potatoes with Saffron

Martha Landis
Lancaster, PA
Mellinger Mennonite Church

Makes 60 servings

5 lbs. peeled, shredded potatoes
Salt and pepper to taste
1 pkg. saffron
¼-½ lb. butter
2 quarts milk
1 cup dry bread crumbs

1. Layer potatoes in large roasting pan. Sprinkle with salt, pepper and saffron. Dot with butter.
2. Heat milk and pour over potatoes. Milk should come to within about 1½ inches of top of potatoes. Layer bread crumbs over potatoes and milk.
3. Cover and bake at 350° for about 1 hour. Tilt lid and brown for an additional 15 minutes.

I never measure ingredients so I am not exactly sure of measurements. However, these potatoes always turn out and many people say they come to the fellowship meal for my potatoes. I think shredding the potatoes and adding saffron are the two secrets to success in this recipe.

Scalloped Potatoes with Cheese

Colleen Heatwole
Burton, MI
New Life Christian Fellowship

Makes 15 or more servings

12-15 potatoes
½ cup minced onion
6 Tbsp. minced green pepper
1 Tbsp. margarine
½ cup margarine
4 Tbsp. flour
4 Tbsp. cornstarch
½ tsp. black pepper
1½ tsp. salt
6 cups milk
2-3 cups grated sharp cheese

1. Peel and slice potatoes.
2. Sauté onion and green pepper in 1 Tbsp. margarine.
3. Place ½ of potatoes into lightly greased 5-quart rectangular roaster.
4. Prepare a white sauce by melting ½ cup margarine. Add flour, cornstarch, pepper and salt. Stir until heated. Slowly add milk, stirring constantly until thickened.
5. Add sautéed onion and green pepper to white sauce. Pour half the sauce over sliced potatoes. Add ½ of grated cheese. Repeat layers.
6. Bake at 350° for 1 hour or until potatoes are done.

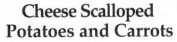

Cheese Scalloped Potatoes and Carrots

Ruth A. Bowman
Salem, OH
Midway Mennonite Church

Makes 6-8 servings

2 cups boiling water
1 tsp. salt or less
2 lbs. potatoes, pared and
  sliced
1½ cups sliced onions
5 medium carrots, sliced
3 Tbsp. butter
2 Tbsp. flour
½ tsp. salt or less
⅛ tsp. pepper
Dash cayenne pepper
1½ cups milk
1½ cups grated sharp
  cheddar cheese

1. Cook potatoes, onions and carrots in boiling, salted water for about 5 minutes or until just tender. Drain and set aside.

2. Make a cheese sauce by melting butter. Stir in flour, salt, pepper and cayenne, stirring constantly for 1 minute. Remove from heat, stir in milk and blend well. Bring mixture to a boil over medium heat, stirring until thick and smooth. Add 1 cup cheese and stir until cheese has melted. Reserve ½ cup cheese.

3. Layer ½ of vegetables in greased 2½-quart casserole dish. Top with ½ of cheese sauce. Repeat. Top with remaining cheese.

4. Cover and bake at 375° for 30 minutes. Uncover and bake 10 minutes longer.

Hash Brown Scalloped Potatoes

Bertha Selzer
Hesston, KS
Whitestone Mennonite Church

Makes 8-10 servings

2 lbs. hash brown potatoes
1 can cheddar cheese soup
1 can cream of celery soup
⅔ cup milk
8-oz. pkg. cream cheese
1 medium onion, chopped
10 ozs. cheddar cheese,
  grated

1. Combine potatoes, soups, milk, cream cheese and onion.

2. Bake at 350° for 1 hour. Remove from oven.

3. Sprinkle grated cheddar cheese over mixture. Return to oven for 15 more minutes.

Mushroom Soup Scalloped Potatoes

Herta Janzen
Coaldale, AB
Coaldale Mennonite Church

Makes 75 servings

12 quarts sliced potatoes
4 cups sliced onions
3 cups margarine
1 cup flour
4 quarts milk
3 scant Tbsp. salt
1½ tsp. pepper
3 cans cream of mushroom
  soup

1. Layer potatoes and onions in large roaster.

2. In a large saucepan make a white sauce. Melt margarine. Add flour and milk, stirring constantly until sauce thickens. Add seasoning. Remove from heat and fold in mushroom soup. Pour over potatoes and onions.

3. Bake at 350° for 2½ hours or until done.

Miriam Weaver's Scalloped Potatoes

Miriam L. Weaver
Harrisonburg, VA
Mt. Clinton Mennonite Church

Makes 12-15 servings

10-12 large potatoes
2 cups grated Longhorn *or*
  Colby cheese

1 medium onion, grated
1 tsp. salt
Dash pepper
Dash garlic powder
2½ cups milk
1-2 Tbsp. margarine

1. Cook potatoes. Peel and grate them. Layer into greased 9" x 13" baking dish. Add a layer of cheese, reserving 1 cup. Add layer of onions and seasonings.

2. Pour milk over ingredients. Dot with margarine. Sprinkle remaining cheese over top.

3. Bake at 350° for 30 minutes or until heated through and cheese has melted.

Hilda Born's Scalloped Potatoes

Hilda J. Born
Matsqui, BC
Central Heights Mennonite Brethren Church

Makes 8 servings

6-8 potatoes
1 medium onion, thinly
  sliced
1 Tbsp. flour
1 tsp. salt
¼ tsp. pepper
¾ cup grated cheese
1 cup milk or more
2 Tbsp. butter
Paprika

1. Peel and thinly slice the potatoes. Arrange ½ of potatoes and onion in greased 1½-quart casserole dish. Sprinkle with flour, salt, pep-

per and ½ of cheese. Cover with remaining potatoes and onions.

2. Pour milk over ingredients, adding enough to almost cover potatoes. Dot with butter.

3. Cover and bake at 350° for 20-30 minutes. Uncover and bake 15-20 minutes longer. Remove from oven.

4. Sprinkle with remaining cheese and paprika. Cover and let stand for 5 minutes. Serve hot.

Mary Zehr's Scalloped Potatoes

Mary Zehr
Mt. Pleasant, PA
Mennonite Church of Scottdale

Makes 6 servings

5 medium potatoes
9 slices American cheese
1 can cream of celery soup
2 Tbsp. flour
¼ cup milk
2 Tbsp. butter *or* margarine

1. Peel potatoes and slice thinly.

2. In a lightly greased deep baking dish layer ⅓ of potatoes, ⅓ of cheese and ⅓ of soup. Repeat twice.

3. Combine milk and flour. Pour over other ingredients. Dot with butter.

4. Cover and bake at 350° for ½ hour. Uncover and bake 1 hour longer.

Lefse

Irene Crosland
Edson, AB
Edson Mennonite Church

Makes 4 servings

2 large potatoes
1 Tbsp. lard, melted
1 tsp. sugar
¼ tsp. salt
½ cup flour
Butter, sugar and cinnamon

1. Cook and peel potatoes. Using a potato ricer, rice potatoes. Measure 1 cup riced potatoes, packed lightly.

2. While potatoes are still hot, add lard, sugar and salt and mix well. Cool overnight.

3. Work in flour. (Amount of flour will seem excessive, but it will work in.) After flour is worked in, bring mixture to room temperature and roll out in an additional generous amount of flour.

4. Heat frying pan or griddle to hot. Bake pancake lightly on both sides. Place between two cloths to cool.

5. When cool, cut into quarters and spread with butter, sugar and cinnamon. Serve.

Curried Rice with Peas

Priscilla Falb and Rosemary Rupp
Dalton, OH
Martins Mennonite Church

Makes 8 servings

2 chicken bouillon cubes
2 cups boiling water
1 cup uncooked long-grain
   rice
2 tsp. curry powder
2 Tbsp. cooking oil
1 cup peas
1 tsp. salt

1. In a casserole dish dissolve bouillon cubes in boiling water. Add all other ingredients and stir until well mixed.
2. Cover and bake at 350° for 1 hour or until rice is tender. Fluff mixture before serving.

Rice for a Crowd

Lorna Sirtoli
Cortland, NY
Nazarene Church of Cortland

Makes 8 cups cooked rice

3 cups uncooked rice
6 cups boiling water
2 tsp. salt
1 Tbsp. butter
1 Tbsp. parsley flakes
1 Tbsp. dehydrated onion

1. Combine all ingredients in large casserole dish.
2. Cover tightly and bake at 350° for 40 minutes.

Wild Rice

Edith von Gunten
Riverton, MB
Native Ministries Fellowship

Makes 8-10 servings

1 cup uncooked wild rice
1/2 cup sliced mushrooms
1/2 cup diced onion
1/2 cup diced green peppers
1/2 cup diced celery
1 Tbsp. cooking oil
1/2 tsp. salt
2 cups chicken broth

1. Stir fry rice and vegetables in cooking oil.
2. Heat chicken broth.
3. In a 2-quart casserole dish combine rice and vegetables, salt and chicken broth.
4. Cover and bake at 350° for 1-1 1/2 hours or until rice is fluffy and broth is aborbed.

Coconut Rice

Ellen S. Peachey
Harpers Ferry, WV
Hyattsville Mennonite Church

Makes 8-10 servings

1 1/2 cups uncooked rice
6-8 ozs. cashews, halved
2 Tbsp. butter
7 ozs. flaked coconut
1 tsp. curry powder

1. Cook rice according to directions.
2. Sauté cashews in butter. Add coconut and curry and stir well. Remove from heat. Add rice and stir until well blended.
3. Serve.

Rice Soufflé

Edith Petri
Wood Dale, IL
Lombard Mennonite Church

Makes 6 servings

2 cups milk
Pinch salt
2/3 cup uncooked rice
4 Tbsp. butter
1/2 cup sugar
3 egg yolks
1 tsp. vanilla
2 tsp. baking powder
3 egg whites
1/2 cup raisins (optional)

1. Bring milk with pinch of salt almost to boiling point. Add rice. Simmer until rice has absorbed the milk.

Cool to lukewarm.

2. Meanwhile, cream together butter, sugar, egg yolks, vanilla and baking powder. Add to cooled rice.

3. Beat egg whites until stiff. Gently fold egg whites into rice mixture. Add raisins. Spoon into well-greased baking dish.

4. Bake at 350° for 40 minutes or until golden brown.

5. Serve as a main dish. May also be served as a dessert with fresh or canned fruit.

Rice Casserole

Irla Martin
North Hollywood, CA
Pasadena Mennonite Church

Makes 8-10 servings

2 cups uncooked long-grain rice
¼ cup cooking oil
1 can sliced mushrooms
3 Tbsp. soy sauce
Salt and pepper to taste
1 pkg. onion soup mix
1 medium green pepper, chopped
4 cups water

1. In a greased 2½-quart casserole dish combine all ingredients.

2. Cover and bake at 350° for 50 minutes. Uncover and bake 10 minutes longer.

Mom's Lentil Loaf

Jane Miller
Minneapolis, MN
St. Paul Mennonite Fellowship

Makes 8-10 servings

2 ⅓ cups uncooked lentils
1½ quarts water
1 lb. cheddar cheese, chopped
½ cup margarine
2 small onions, chopped
1 can cheddar cheese soup
1-2 tsp. salt
½ tsp. pepper
1 tsp. basil
3 eggs
2 cups fine bread crumbs

1. Place lentils in large saucepan and add water. Simmer without cover for 1-1½ hours or until lentils are mushy.

2. While lentil mush is still hot, add cheese and margarine. Stir in all other ingredients in order listed. Mix well. Spoon into 2 greased loaf pans.

3. Bake at 350° for 45-60 minutes or until firm. Serve.

Curried Lentils

Millie Glick
Edmonton, AB
Holyrood Mennonite Church

Makes 12 servings

2 cups uncooked lentils
5 cups water
4 beef bouillon cubes

2 bay leaves
2 tsp. salt
½ cup margarine
2 large onions, chopped
2 cloves garlic, minced
2-3 Tbsp. Malaysian curry powder
2 Tbsp. lemon juice
Chopped parsley

1. Combine lentils, water, bouillon cubes, bay leaves and salt. Bring to a boil. Reduce heat and simmer for 20 minutes.

2. Sauté onions and garlic in margarine. Add curry powder. Fold into cooked lentils. Add lemon juice and chopped parsley.

3. Mix well and serve.

When taking this to a fellowship meal, I cook the lentils the evening before. The next morning I sauté the vegetables, combine all ingredients in a casserole dish, pop it in my oven at 250° and bake it for about 1 hour or until we are ready to leave for church. I wrap the casserole dish in a large bath towel and it stays nice and hot.

Jeanette Harder's Varenika

Jeanette Harder
Garland, TX

Makes 45-50 servings

48 ozs. cottage cheese
1 tsp. pepper
2 tsp. salt
8 egg yolks
8 egg whites
2 Tbsp. salt
¼ cup cooking oil
2 cups milk
8 cups flour
Melted butter

1. Combine cottage cheese, pepper, salt and egg yolks. Beat for 5 minutes or until well mixed. Set aside.

2. Beat egg whites lightly with fork. Add salt, oil, milk and enough flour to make a soft dough. Roll out as thin as possible and cut into circles with a tuna can.

3. Place a heaping tablespoon of cottage cheese mixture on each circle. Fold over into half circle and pinch edges together to seal.

4. Drop the filled Varenika into boiling, salted water. Boil 5-8 minutes or until the Varenika float.

5. Drain on a cooling rack and roll in melted butter.

6. Lay Varenika on cookie sheet and freeze. When Varenika are frozen, stack in plastic bag to store in freezer.

7. Immediately before serving, put frozen Varenika on a hot griddle and fry until golden brown.

8. Serve with sausage or ham gravy or sour cream.

Jessie Penner's Varenika

Jessie Penner
Bakersfield, CA

Makes 15-24 servings

2 cups flour
1 egg white
½ cup sweet *or* sour cream
1 egg yolk
1½ cups cottage cheese
1 Tbsp. butter *or* sour cream
Salt and pepper
Melted butter

1. Combine flour, egg white and cream to make a soft dough. Roll out as thin as possible and cut into squares or circles.

2. Combine egg yolk, cottage cheese, butter, salt and pepper.

3. Add cottage cheese filling to center of each circle or square of dough. Fold over and press edges tightly together. Put into a kettle of rolling, boiling water. Cook until soft, but do not over-boil. Drain carefully.

4. Brush each Varenika with melted butter. (At this point they may be frozen.)

5. Fry on both sides and serve with gravy.

Bohnen Biroggi

Jeanette Friesen
Loveland, CO
Boulder Mennonite Church

Makes 35 single servings

Filling:
2 cups pinto beans
1 tsp. salt
1 cup sugar or less

Dough:
1 pkg. yeast
½ cup warm water
⅔ cup sugar
1½ tsp. salt
⅔ cup lard *or* butter
2 cups hot water
2 eggs, beaten
8 cups flour

Sauce:
2 cups milk
2 cups cream
3 Tbsp. cornstarch *or* flour
1 cup sugar

1. To prepare filling cook pinto beans. Drain and mash. Add salt and sugar. Set aside.

2. To prepare dough dissolve yeast in warm water. Set aside.

3. Combine sugar, salt, lard, hot water and eggs.

Cool mixture. Add yeast and enough flour to make a soft dough. Knead and let rise approximately 1 hour. Knead down.

4. Take small amount of dough and flatten into 3-inch diameter in hand. Place 1 Tbsp. prepared beans in center of each piece of dough. Bring edges together and press tightly to seal. Place on greased cookie sheet. Let rise 20 minutes.

5. Bake at 325° for about 30 minutes or until golden brown.

6. To prepare sauce combine small amount of liquid with cornstarch or flour and make a paste. Combine remaining liquid, sugar and paste. Cook 2-3 minutes or until sauce thickens.

7. Immediately before serving, pour sauce over Biroggi.

This time consuming recipe is well worth the effort! At fellowship meals it is always a conversation piece.

Enilesnika

Johanna Dyck
Coaldale, AB
Coaldale Mennonite Church

Makes 8-10 servings

2 cups flour
4 cups milk
¼ cup melted margarine
5 eggs
1 tsp. salt

1 lb. cottage cheese
½ cup mashed potatoes
½ cup chopped green onions
1 Tbsp. dill weed
1 egg
1 tsp. salt
¼ tsp. pepper
1 cup cream, heated
¾ cup melted butter
Fresh dill (optional)

1. Combine flour, milk, margarine, 5 eggs and 1 tsp. salt. Roll dough out as thin as possible and cut into 3-inch crepes. Cook as you would pancakes. Keep warm.

2. Combine cottage cheese, mashed potatoes, green onions, dill weed, 1 egg, 1 tsp. salt and pepper.

3. Place 1 tsp. filling on each crepe. Roll up and place in greased casserole dish. Pour heated cream and melted butter over crepes. Sprinkle with dill if desired.

4. Bake at 325° for 35 minutes.

Variation:
Make a cream gravy to pour over crepes instead of heated cream and butter.

Chilaquile Casserole

Kirsten L. Zerger
Berkeley, CA
First Mennonite Church of San Francisco

Makes 8-12 servings

12 corn tortillas
2 4-oz. jars diced green chilies
2-3 cups grated Monterey Jack cheese
1 cup chopped onions
2 cloves garlic, minced
1 Tbsp. butter *or* olive oil
⅛ tsp. cumin
⅛ tsp. basil
⅛ tsp. oregano
1-2 cups cooked pinto beans
4 large eggs
2 cups buttermilk
Dash salt and pepper

1. Tear 6 tortillas into bite-sized pieces and spread evenly in greased 2-quart casserole dish.

2. Distribute ½ of chilies and ½ of cheese over tortillas.

3. Sauté onions and garlic in butter or olive oil. Add cumin, basil and oregano.

4. Spread beans over chilies and cheese. Spread onion and garlic sauté over beans.

5. Tear remaining tortillas into bite-sized pieces and spread evenly over top. Follow with remaining chilies and cheese.

6. Beat eggs and buttermilk together with salt and pepper. Slowly, pour this custard over the casserole.

7. Bake, uncovered, at 375° for 35 minutes.

Vegetarian Enchiladas

Betty J. Rosentrater
Nappanee, IN
Iglesia Menonita del Buen Pastor

Makes 12 servings

2 Tbsp. margarine *or*
 cooking oil
2 cups water
¼ cup masa harina
2 Tbsp. cocoa
½ tsp. salt
5 tsp. chili powder
½ tsp. cumin
12 corn tortillas
2 cups chopped onions
2 cups grated cheese

1. Combine margarine, water, masa harina, cocoa, salt, chili powder and cumin. Bring to a boil. Boil gently, stirring until mixture thickens.
2. Put onions and cheese on each tortilla, reserving about ½ cup cheese. Roll up and place in shallow baking pan. Pour sauce over tortillas and top with remaining cheese.
3. Bake at 375° for 15 minutes.

White Tortillas

Mabel E. De Leon
La Junta, CO
Emmanuel Mennonite Church

Makes 8 servings

2 cups white flour
1 tsp. baking powder
1 tsp. salt

¼ cup shortening
¾ cup lukewarm water

1. Combine flour, baking powder and salt. Cut in shortening and mix by hand until crumbly.
2. Slowly add water, mixing until you have a fairly stiff dough. Knead until dough is smooth, approximately 10 minutes.
3. Form dough into small balls, about 1½-2 inches in diameter. Roll out until round and thin.
4. Cook on a hot, dry griddle, browning on both sides. Watch carefully to prevent burning. Wrap in a dish towel to keep tortillas warm and soft.
5. Serve warm with rice and beans.

Pupusas

Rosa Elena Moreno
Eureka, IL
First Mennonite Church

Makes 5 servings

3 cups sliced cabbage
½ of a green chili pepper
1 small onion, sliced
½ cup sliced carrots
2 jalapeño peppers, chopped
1 Tbsp. salt
1 tsp. oregano
1 cup vinegar
2 cups water
2½ cups corn tortilla flour
2 cups water
2 cups sliced mozzarella
 cheese
Lard

1. In a bowl combine cabbage, chili pepper, onion, carrots, peppers, salt, oregano, vinegar and 2 cups water. Let stand in refrigerator overnight.
2. Combine tortilla flour and water into a soft dough. Knead well.
3. Using a portion of dough, make a tortilla. Place small amount of cheese in center of tortilla. Make another thinner tortilla and place on top. Pinch edges of two tortillas together.
4. Fry on a hot, flat griddle lightly greased with lard.
5. After frying, cover tortilla with vegetable mixture and serve.

Italian Pie

Lois Cable
Johnstown, PA
Kaufman Mennonite Church

Makes 12-16 servings

4 cups flour
1 tsp. salt
1 egg
¾ cup shortening
1 cup warm water
1½ cups shredded Swiss
 cheese
1½ cups shredded cheddar
 cheese
1½ cups shredded
 Provolone cheese
½ lb. sliced pepperoni
5 eggs, beaten
1 egg, beaten

1. Combine flour, salt, egg, shortening and warm

water to form dough. Divide into two pieces. Roll out one piece and pat into 9" x 13" baking pan.

2. Layer cheeses and pepperoni on dough. Pour 5 beaten eggs over layers.

3. Roll out remaining piece of dough. Layer over ingredients for a top crust. Brush with 1 beaten egg. Slit in several places.

4. Bake at 350° for 45 minutes.

Chicken Main Dishes

Belizean Whole Baked Chicken

Debbie Rowley and Leanora Harwood
Lancaster, PA
South Christian Street Mennonite Church

Makes 6 servings

1 whole chicken, cleaned
½ cup margarine
2 Tbsp. soy sauce
1 Tbsp. mustard
1½ cups bread crumbs
1 onion, chopped
½ cup chopped celery
Salt and pepper to taste

1. Melt margarine over low heat. Add soy sauce and mustard. Add all other ingredients except chicken and heat through.

2. Stuff mixture into chicken. Sew up opening. Wrap in aluminum foil and put into baking pan with 2 cups water.

3. Bake at 350° for 2 hours.

Chicken Stuffed with Southern Cornbread Dressing

Alice Whitman
Lancaster, PA
South Christian Street Mennonite Church

Makes 12-15 servings

2 whole chickens
1 ¼ cups flour
¾ cup cornmeal
5 tsp. baking powder
1 cup milk
1 egg, well beaten
2 Tbsp. margarine, melted
½ cup chopped onion
1 cup chopped celery
¼ cup margarine
6 cups cubed white bread
1 tsp. poultry seasoning
Pepper to taste
1 tsp. salt
1 egg, well beaten
1½ cups chicken stock

1. Make 1 batch cornbread dressing by combining flour, cornmeal and baking powder. Add milk, egg and margarine. Beat well and spoon into a shallow baking dish.

2. Bake at 375° for 20 min-

utes. Cool. Crumble 4 cups cornbread and set aside.

3. In a frying pan cook onion and celery in ¼ cup margarine until soft and clear. Add crumbled cornbread and white bread. Fry until slightly browned, about 5-10 minutes.

4. Remove from heat and add poultry seasoning, salt and pepper.

5. Combine egg with chicken stock and pour over bread mixture. Stir to mix thoroughly.

6. Stuff carefully cleaned chickens with dressing and place in large roast pan.

7. Bake at 350° for 3 hours.

Oven Barbecued Chicken

Edna Mast
Cochranville, PA
Maple Grove Mennonite Church

Makes 15 servings

1 cup ketchup
¼ cup water
¼ cup vinegar
¼ cup butter *or* margarine
3 Tbsp. brown sugar
2 Tbsp. Worcestershire sauce (optional)
1 Tbsp. prepared mustard
¼ tsp. pepper
½ tsp. salt
Juice of 1 lemon (optional)
1 onion, diced
15 large chicken thighs

1. Combine all ingredients except chicken thighs and bring to a boil. Simmer for 10 minutes.
2. Wash chicken thighs and discard skin. Put ¼ cup water in bottom of 10" x 15" cake pan or similar large baking dish. Pack chicken thighs into dish, getting in as many as possible. Spoon barbecue sauce over chicken.
3. Bake at 350° for 1 hour or until well done.

Occasionally, when I know a fellowship meal is coming up, I pack meat into pan and freeze it, ready for the sauce and oven when I need it.

Inside-Out Stuffed Chicken

Jeanette Harder
Garland, TX

Makes 8-10 servings

8 ozs. cornbread stuffing mix
¼ cup butter, melted
1 can cream of mushroom soup
⅓ cup milk
3-lb. chicken, cut in pieces

1. In large bowl combine stuffing mix and melted butter. Toss well.
2. In medium bowl stir together soup and milk.
3. Dip chicken pieces into soup mixture, then into stuffing mixture, pressing with hands to coat pieces.
4. Place coated chicken pieces in 10" x 15" baking pan.
5. Bake at 375° about 1 hour or until done. Transfer to crockpot before taking to fellowship meal. Plug crockpot in and turn to low.

Crispy Baked Chicken

Thelma P. Plum
Waynesboro, PA
Waynesboro Church of the Brethren

Makes 6 servings

1 ⅓ cups cornflake crumbs
¼ cup Parmesan cheese
Dash of salt and pepper
3-lb. chicken, cut in pieces
¾ cup low-calorie salad dressing

1. Combine cornflake crumbs, Parmesan cheese, salt and pepper.
2. Skin chicken pieces and brush with salad dressing. Coat each piece with crumbs.
3. Place in 9" x 13" baking dish.
4. Bake at 350° for 1 hour or until tender.

Buttermilk Baked Chicken

Lorraine Martin
Dryden, MI
Bethany Mennonite Fellowship

Makes 4-6 servings

½ tsp. thyme
½ tsp. paprika
½ tsp. MSG (optional)
½ tsp. salt
¼ tsp. garlic salt
¼ cup margarine
1 young chicken, cut in pieces
1 cup sour milk *or* buttermilk
1-1½ cup cornflake crumbs

1. Combine all seasonings. Set aside.

2. Melt margarine in 9" x 13" baking dish.

3. Dip chicken pieces in milk, then in cornflake crumbs. Place in baking dish, skin side down.

4. Sprinkle seasonings over chicken pieces.

5. Cover and bake at 350° for 1 to 1½ hours. Turn pieces of chicken and bake, uncovered, 20 minutes longer.

Baked Chicken

Mary Smucker
Goshen, IN
College Mennonite Church

Makes 6-8 servings

1 chicken, cut in pieces
1 small onion, chopped
3 tsp. curry powder
1 apple, diced
1 can cream of mushroom
   soup
1 12-oz can evaporated milk
Salt, pepper and paprika

1. Skin chicken and remove fat. Brown chicken in own fat. Place chicken pieces in casserole dish.

2. Sauté onion and curry powder in chicken fat or cooking oil if needed.

3. Mix onion and curry powder with all other ingredients. Pour over chicken.

4. Bake at 350° for 1½ hours.

Breast of Chicken

Ila Yoder
Hesston, KS
Whitestone Mennonite Church

Makes 8 servings

1 pkg. dried beef
8 strips bacon
8 boned chicken breasts
½ pint sour cream
1 can cream of mushroom
   soup

1. Cover bottom of 9" x 13" baking dish with dried beef.

2. Wrap 1 strip bacon around each chicken breast in spiral fashion. Lay on top of dried beef.

3. Mix sour cream and soup and pour over chicken.

4. Bake at 275-300° for 3 hours, uncovered.

Oven-Fried Chicken Legs

Hazel N. Hassan
Goshen, IN
College Mennonite Church

Makes 12 servings

1 cup bread crumbs
1 tsp. salt or less
1 tsp. paprika
1 tsp. poultry seasoning
½ tsp. onion salt
¼ tsp. pepper
2 Tbsp. cooking oil
12-14 chicken legs

1. Mix bread crumbs, seasoning and cooking oil.

2. Rinse chicken legs under running water and roll each leg in crumb mixture, shaking off excess.

3. Place legs in two rows in greased 9" x 13" baking pan, alternating thick and thin sides of legs.

4. Bake at 350° for 1 hour. Remove from oven and place in clean, hot casserole dish. Wrap well in newspaper for transporting to church.

I first made this dish for the benefit of the children, and was amused to see adults put one leg on child's plate and take one or two for themselves.

Variation:
Use a variety of chicken pieces with this coating recipe.
Margaret Willms
Coaldale, AB
Coaldale Mennonite Church

Chicken Cordon Bleu

Louise T. Cullar
North Lima, OH
Midway Mennonite Church

Makes 6 servings

6 half chicken breasts,
**   boneless**
6 slices ham
6 slices Swiss cheese
Margarine, melted
Bread crumbs

1. Place 1 slice ham and 1 slice Swiss cheese on each chicken breast. Roll up and hold together with toothpick.
2. Roll each piece in melted margarine, then in bread crumbs.
3. Place in casserole dish and bake at 325° until the cheese melts, approximately 40 minutes or less.

Chicken Dijon

Esther B. Loux
Souderton, PA
Blooming Glen Mennonite Church

Makes approximately 6 servings

1 can cream of chicken soup
1 12-oz. can evaporated
**   skim milk**
2 Tbsp. Dijon mustard
1 Tbsp. flour, rounded
½ cup water
2 boneless chicken breasts
1 small onion, chopped
½ cup mushrooms,
**   chopped**
Salt and pepper to taste

1. Heat soup, milk and mustard.
2. Make a paste with flour and water. Thicken soup mixture slightly with this paste. Bring to boiling point.
3. Skin chicken breasts and cut into strips. Brown chicken in skillet. Add onion and mushrooms.
4. Arrange chicken mixture in shallow baking dish. Pour sauce over chicken.
5. Bake at 350° for 30-40 minutes.

Soy Sauce Chicken

Adella Kanagy
Belleville, PA
Allensville Mennonite Church

Makes 8 servings

1 whole chicken, cut in
**   pieces**
⅔ cup soy sauce
½ cup honey
2 cloves garlic
2 cups water
Green onions, chopped

1. Remove skin and fat from chicken.
2. Combine soy sauce, honey, garlic and water. Heat to boiling. Add chicken, cover and simmer until tender, basting occasionally.
3. Garnish with green onions and serve with plain, cooked brown rice.

Chicken in Ginger

Lois Cable
Johnstown, PA
Kaufman Mennonite Church

Makes 4 servings

1 cup soy sauce
5 cups water
8 pieces crystallized ginger
2 bunches green onion,
**   chopped**
2 Tbsp. sugar
¼ cup sherry (optional)
1 whole chicken

1. Mix all ingredients except chicken and bring to a boil. Add chicken and simmer for ½ hour.
2. Cover dish and let stand for ½ hour.
3. Remove chicken from sauce and place on foil-lined pan.
4. Bake chicken at 400° for 30 minutes or until reddish brown. Cool and bone chicken, letting chicken meat in large pieces.
5. Serve chicken either as dippers with soy sauce or serve chicken and sauce with rice.

Couscous with Chicken and Peanut Sauce

Naomi E. Fast
Newton, KS
Goessel Mennonite Church

Makes 6-8 servings

1 whole chicken, cut in
  pieces
1 quart water
Salt to taste
2 Tbsp. olive oil
⅔ cup crunchy peanut
  butter
2 tsp. salt
¼ tsp. black pepper
1 tsp. paprika
½ tsp. nutmeg
1 pkg. couscous

1. Cook chicken in water until just tender. Season with salt.
2. Heat oil in Dutch oven. Add peanut butter, seasonings and 1½ cups chicken broth. Blend well. Add chicken pieces to mixture and cook over low heat 10-15 minutes.
3. Prepare couscous according to package directions. Place in 3½-quart casserole dish. Make a well in couscous and pour chicken pieces with sauce into center of couscous. Serve.

Chicken and Biscuits

Ruth Heatwole
Charlottesville, VA
Charlottesville Mennonite Church

Makes 4-6 servings

3-lb. chicken, cut in pieces
Salt and pepper to taste
2-3 carrots, diced
2 ribs celery, diced
1 small onion, diced
1 clove garlic, finely
  chopped
2-3 mushrooms, sliced
1 can cream of mushroom *or*
  cream of chicken soup
½ cup no-fat milk
2 Tbsp. chopped parsley
½-1 cup peas
1 can biscuits

1. Dip chicken pieces in flour and brown in an electric skillet, using as little fat as possible. Sprinkle lightly with salt and pepper and cook approximately 15 minutes.
2. Add carrots, celery, onion, garlic, mushrooms, and soup which has been diluted with milk.
3. Cover and cook over low heat for about 30 minutes or until chicken is tender. Stir occasionally and add more milk if necessary.
4. Take skillet and all to church. Heat through and add parsley and peas. Arrange biscuits on top. Cover and cook on medium heat until biscuits are done. Serve.

Chicken Briyani

Laverne Nafziger
Hopedale, IL
Hopedale Mennonite Church

Makes 4-6 servings

1 whole chicken
1 clove garlic
1-inch piece fresh ginger
  root
1 small green chili
½ cup cooking oil
1 large onion, diced
4 whole cardamom
6 whole cloves
3 bay leaves
2-3 Tbsp. coriander leaves
1 tsp. turmeric powder
Salt to taste
2 cups uncooked rice
4¾ cups chicken broth
  or water
2 large tomatoes, chopped

1. Cook, cool and bone chicken. Reserve broth.
2. Combine garlic, ginger root and chili into a paste in blender.
3. In large pan sauté onion and spices in cooking oil. Add all remaining ingredients and cook until rice is tender. Serve.

Chicken Pilaf

Joan B. Lange
New Oxford, PA
The Brethren Home
Retirement Village

Makes 6-8 servings

1 can cream of mushroom
    soup
1¼ cups boiling water
¼ cup dry sherry
½ pkg. dry onion soup
1 ⅓ cups uncooked rice
5-6 chicken breasts
Butter *or* margarine, melted
Salt, pepper and paprika

1. Combine mushroom
soup, boiling water, sherry,
onion soup and rice. Pour
into 1½-quart casserole dish.
2. Brush chicken breasts
with melted butter and season
with salt, pepper and paprika.
Lay on top of rice mixture.
3. Cover and bake at 375°
for 1 ¼ hours or until
chicken and rice are tender.

Sunday Dinner Chicken

Grace Krabill
Goshen, IN
College Mennonite Church

Makes 18 servings

3 whole chickens, cut in
    pieces
4 cups uncooked brown rice
4 cans creamed soup*
1⅓ cans water

1 pkg. dried onion soup
Paprika
Parsley
*Use any mixture of the
following soups: cream of
chicken, cream of celery or
cream of mushroom. Or use
4 cups homemade cream
sauce.

1. Skin chicken pieces. Set
aside.
2. In large oval, enamel
roaster mix rice, soups and
water. Lay chicken pieces
over rice.
3. Sprinkle with onion
soup, paprika and parsley.
4. Cover and bake at 300°
for 3 hours.

*I think the dark roasting pan
helps this dish to cook in three
hours at a low temperature.
The chicken always browns
nicely.*

Chicken Rice Casserole

Elaine Gibbel
Lititz, PA
Lititz Church of the Brethren

Makes 8 servings

1 can cream of celery soup
1 can cream of chicken soup
2½ cans milk
1¼ cups uncooked rice
4 chicken breasts, boned
    and halved
¼ cup Parmesan cheese
2 Tbsp. slivered almonds

1. Mix soups with milk.
2. Place rice on bottom of

greased 9" x 13" baking pan.
Pour half of soup mixture
over rice.
3. Lay chicken pieces, skin
side up, over rice. Pour remaining soup over chicken.
4. Sprinkle with Parmesan
cheese and almonds.
5. Cover and bake at 275°
for 2½ hours. Uncover and
bake ½ hour longer.

Chicken with Raisins and Rice

Bonnie Heatwole
Springs, PA
Springs Mennonite Church

Makes 8 servings

3 bouillon cubes
3 cups boiling water
1 cup uncooked rice
¾ cup raisins
½ cup chopped onion
1 whole chicken, cut in pieces
½ cup flour
1 Tbsp. curry
½ tsp. salt
½ cup chopped peanuts

1. Dissolve bouillon cubes
in boiling water.
2. Combine rice, raisins
and onions. Pour dissolved
bouillon cubes over mixture.
Spoon into baking dish.
3. Combine flour, curry and
salt. Add chicken pieces and
coat each piece thoroughly.
Lay chicken pieces over rice.
4. Bake at 350° for ½ hour.
5. Remove from oven and
stir peanuts into rice. Bake ½
hour longer.

Chicken and Rice

Cheri Jantzen
Houston, TX
Houston Mennonite Church

Makes 6 servings

3-lb. chicken, cut in pieces
2 tsp. paprika
2 tsp. garlic salt
2 tsp. celery salt
1 cup uncooked rice
2-oz. can mushrooms,
    drained
2 cups chicken broth and
    mushroom juice
2 tsp. lemon juice
¼ tsp. ground pepper
2 Tbsp. chopped parsley
½ cup sliced ripe olives

1. Season chicken with paprika, garlic salt and celery salt. Place in 9" x 13" casserole dish.
2. Bake at 425° for 20 minutes. Push chicken pieces to one side.
3. Add all remaining ingredients except olives. Arrange chicken over rice mixture.
4. Cover and bake at 425° for 30 minutes or until rice is tender and liquid is absorbed.
5. Sprinkle with olives before serving.

Arroz con Polla

Louise Cullar
North Lima, OH
Midway Mennonite Church

Makes 12 servings

¼ cup cooking oil
1 large onion, chopped
3-lb. chicken, cut up
Dash garlic powder
1 tsp. salt
½ tsp. pepper
1 tsp. paprika
2 bay leaves
6 cups hot water
2 cups uncooked rice
2 cups frozen peas

1. Heat oil in large kettle. Sauté onion until golden brown. Add chicken pieces, garlic, salt, pepper, paprika and bay leaves. Cook until slightly brown, turning chicken several times.
2. Add water and bring mixture to a boil. Add rice and simmer until rice is tender, stirring as needed.
3. Add peas and cook several minutes longer.
4. Remove bay leaves and serve.

Chicken Curry

Mary Dyck
Mission, BC
Cedar Valley Mennonite Church

Makes 6 servings

½ cup shortening
2 cups chopped onions
½ cup chopped green
    pepper
3-lb. chicken, cut in pieces
2 Tbsp. flour
½ Tbsp. curry powder
1½ tsp. salt
½ cup water
¼ cup lemon juice
8-oz. can tomato sauce
1-2 cloves garlic, crushed

1. Melt shortening. Add onion and green pepper and cook until tender. Add chicken pieces and fry until browned.
2. In separate bowl mix flour, curry powder and salt. Slowly stir in water and lemon juice to make a paste. Add tomato sauce and garlic and pour mixture over chicken.
3. Cover and simmer over low heat until tender, about 2 hours. Serve with rice.

I use an electric frying pan to make this and take the prepared dish to church in the frying pan. At church I simply plug it in to quickly heat it up.

Yellow Rice and Chicken

Frances Cortez
Des Allemands, LA

Makes 6-8 servings

1-lb. pkg. yellow Spanish rice
½ cup chopped celery
½ cup chopped green pepper
1 large onion, chopped
3-lb. whole chicken, cut up
1 tsp. garlic powder
Salt and pepper to taste
4 Tbsp. butter

1. Cook rice with celery, green pepper and onion according to directions on package.
2. Lay chicken pieces in a shallow baking dish. Sprinkle with garlic powder, salt and pepper.
3. Bake at 350° for 35-40 minutes or until done.
4. Remove from oven and reserve broth. Cool and bone chicken.
5. In baking dish combine rice mixture, chicken and broth. Stir until fluffy. Dot with butter.
6. Return to oven and heat 10 minutes longer.

Laotian Chicken Curry

Thavone Senevonghachack
Regina, SK
Laotian Fellowship

Makes 6 servings

3 lbs. chicken
2 Tbsp. cooking oil
2 Tbsp. finely chopped onion
2 cloves garlic, minced
1 Tbsp. minced ginger root
1 can coconut milk
1½ tsp. curry powder
1 tsp. chili powder
1 tsp. salt
2 cups water

1. With a sharp knife cut chicken from bones and cut into small pieces.
2. Heat oil in frying pan. Sauté onion, garlic and ginger until browned. Add coconut milk, curry, chili powder and salt. Stir fry for 2-3 minutes on medium heat. Add chicken.
3. Cover pan and let cook for 2-3 minutes. Add water, cover and cook until chicken is tender.

Laotian Chicken Stew

Boulieng Luangviseth
Regina, SK
Laotian Fellowship

Makes 4-6 servings

3 lbs. chicken
1 Tbsp. cooking oil
1 Tbsp. chopped onion
1 tsp. chopped garlic
1 tsp. chili powder
1 tsp. salt
1 tsp. fish sauce
3 cups cold water or less
2 cups green beans
½ cup diced celery
2 tsp. cornstarch

1. With a sharp knife cut chicken from bones. Cut into small pieces.
2. Heat oil in wok. Add onion, garlic and chili powder. Turn heat to low and stir until onion and garlic turn brown. Add chicken, salt and fish sauce. Turn heat to medium and stir. Cover and cook for several minutes.
3. Add cold water and bring to a boil, cooking until chicken is tender. Add green beans and celery. Cook until vegetables are tender.
4. Stir in cornstarch and heat through. Serve immediately.

Tangy Oven-Fried Curried Chicken

Elizabeth Weaver Bonnar
Thorndale, ON
Valleyview Mennonite Church

Makes 6 servings

4-5-lb. chicken, cut in pieces
1 tsp. salt
1 clove garlic, minced
½ cup boiling water
2 chicken bouillon cubes
2 tsp. curry powder
½ tsp. dry mustard
1 Tbsp. water
2 tsp. Worcestershire sauce
1 tsp. oregano
½ tsp. paprika
2-3 dashes hot cayenne
    pepper

1. Salt chicken and place skin side down in shallow baking dish.
2. Combine all remaining ingredients and brush both sides of chicken with mixture.
3. Bake at 350° for 45 minutes, turning and basting often.
4. Immediately before serving, put dish in 400° oven for 10 minutes for crisp chicken.

Almond Chicken

Philene Houmphan
Regina, SK
Chinese Fellowship

Makes 6 servings

2-3 lbs. boneless chicken
    breasts
½ Tbsp. wine *or* sherry
½ tsp. salt
1 tsp. sugar
Dash pepper
1 egg white
1½ Tbsp. cornstarch
1½ cups sliced almonds
6 cups cooking oil

1. Remove skin from chicken. Cut chicken breast into paper-thin slices.
2. Combine wine, salt, sugar, pepper, egg white and cornstarch. Spoon over chicken and marinate for 20 minutes.
3. Place almonds in a dish and coat each slice of chicken with almonds.
4. Heat oil over medium heat in wok or large frying pan. Deep fry chicken for 1½ minutes. Chicken will rise to surface.
5. Remove chicken pieces from oil and serve.

Double Dipped Fried Chicken

Faye Pankratz
Inola, OK
Eden Mennonite Church

Makes 6 servings

2 eggs
1½ cups milk
3 cups flour
1½ tsp. salt
2 cups shortening
1 fryer chicken, cut in pieces

1. Beat the eggs and add milk.
2. In separate bowl combine flour and salt.
3. Heat shortening in large skillet.
4. Dip each piece chicken in egg and milk mixture, then in flour. Repeat.
5. Pan fry over medium flame until brown on both sides. (It is best to remove skillet from burner when turning pieces of chicken).
6. Drain on absorbent paper. Serve.

I like taking this to fellowship meals because it may be served cold. However, I often place it in heated oven a few minutes before serving.

Variation:
I like to pan fry chicken in peanut oil because it is much less greasy.
Linda Sponenburgh
DeLand, FL

Chicken with Lychees

Jixun Chang
Regina, SK
Chinese Fellowship

Makes 4 servings

3 large boneless chicken
    breasts
6 shallots
Corn flour
3 Tbsp. cooking oil
1 red pepper, diced
½ cup water
2 chicken stock cubes
3 Tbsp. tomato sauce
1 tsp. sugar
Salt and pepper to taste
15-oz. can lychees
1 tsp. corn flour
2 tsp. water

1. Cut chicken breasts in
half, lengthwise. Cut each
half into 3 pieces. Set aside.
2. Chop shallots into 2-
inch lengths. Set aside.
3. Coat chicken pieces in
corn flour, shaking off excess.
4. Heat oil in wok. Add
red pepper and chicken
pieces. Cook until chicken
turns light golden brown.
5. In a bowl combine ½
cup water, stock cubes, tomato sauce, sugar, salt and
pepper. Add drained lychees
and mix well. Cover and simmer until chicken is tender,
about 5 minutes.
6. Mix 1 tsp. corn flour
and 2 tsp. water into a
smooth paste. Add to
chicken mixture and stir until boiling. Serve.

Never Fail Chicken

Marcella Klaassen
Hillsboro, KS
Hillsboro First Mennonite Church

Whole chicken, cut in pieces
2-3 cans celery soup

1. Remove excess fat and
skin from chicken if desired.
2. Place in shallow baking
dish in one layer. Cover with
as many cans celery soup as
it takes.
3. Bake at 350° for 1 hour,
uncovered.

Tasty Chicken Wings

Anne Martin
Castorland, NY
First Mennonite Church

Makes 12 servings

2 lbs. chicken wings
Salt to taste
1 cup orange juice
¼ cup brown sugar
1 Tbsp. garlic powder
1 Tbsp. Worcestershire sauce

1. Place chicken in greased
9" x 13" baking dish. Sprinkle
with salt.
2. Mix all other ingredi-
ents and pour over chicken.
3. Bake at 325° for 1 hour
or until done. Stir and baste
several times during baking.

Chicken Wings

Philene Houmphan
Regina, SK
Chinese Fellowship

Makes 6 servings

1½ lbs. chicken wings
10-12 Tbsp. soy sauce
6 cups cooking oil
1½ Tbsp. wine *or* sherry
3 Tbsp. soy sauce
2 tsp. sugar
1½ cups water
¼ lb. spinach
2 tsp. cornstarch
1 Tbsp. water

1. Cut each chicken wing
at joint. Pour 1 Tbsp. soy
sauce over each wing. Marinate for 20 minutes.
2. Heat wok and add cook-
ing oil. Deep fry chicken
wings for 1 minute or until
golden brown. Drain oil.
3. Add wine, 3 Tbsp. soy
sauce, sugar and 1½ cups
water to chicken in wok.
Cover and bring to a boil;
lower heat and cook for 15
minutes.
4. Add spinach and cook
for another 10 minutes.
Sauce should cook down to
about ⅔ cup.
5. Combine cornstarch
and 1 Tbsp. water. Slowly
pour over chicken wing mixture, stirring to thicken
sauce. Serve.

Chicken Pot Pie

Mary Bomberger
Lancaster, PA
Community Mennonite Church of
Lancaster

Makes 8-10 servings

4-6 chicken thighs and
   drumsticks
1½ quarts water
2 cups flour
¼ tsp. salt
2 Tbsp. shortening
¼ cup water
1 large egg, slightly beaten
2-3 potatoes, sliced
1 onion, sliced
2 stalks celery, diced
3 carrots, diced
¼ cup chopped parsley
Salt and pepper to taste

1. Cook chicken in water
until tender. Let chicken cool
and remove from bones.
Skim and save broth.

2. To prepare dough com-
bine flour and salt and cut in
shortening. Add water and
egg. Work together to form a
soft ball. Cover and let stand
while preparing vegetables.

3. Add vegetables to broth
and cook until tender.

4. On floured surface roll
dough as thin as possible.
Cut into 2-inch squares and
drop into boiling broth. Stir
gently to prevent potatoes
and dough from sticking together. Cook about 10-15
minutes more.

5. Return chicken pieces to
broth and heat through.
Serve.

Chicken and Dumplings

Karla Knief
London, OH
Shalom Community Church

Makes 8-10 servings

4 chicken breasts *or* 1 small
   chicken
½ cup diced carrots
¼ cup diced onion
¼ cup diced celery
1 cup peas
2 heaping Tbsp. flour
1 cup water
Salt and pepper to taste
Bisquick dumplings
Paprika

1. Cook chicken. Cool,
skin and bone chicken. Save
broth and skim fat.

2. Chop vegetables and
cook in microwave on high
for 5 minutes.

3. Shake together flour
and water. Add to boiling
chicken broth to make a
gravy. Add enough extra
water to make 4 cups broth.
Salt and pepper to taste.

4. Put gravy, vegetables
and diced chicken into a 3-
quart crockpot.

5. Mix Bisquick dump-
lings as directed on the box.
Place on top of mixture and
sprinkle with paprika.

6. Cook during church
service on high for 3 hours.

Chicken Potato Filling

Ruth K. Nafziger
Bally, PA
Boyertown Mennonite Fellowship

Makes 15 servings

6 potatoes, diced
2½ cups water
2 cans cream of chicken soup
3 eggs, beaten
1 small bunch parsley
1 onion, chopped
Salt and pepper to taste
¾ loaf bread, cubed
2 cups diced, cooked chicken

1. Cook potatoes with
water. Drain, reserving potato water.

2. Combine potato water,
soup, eggs, parsley, onion,
salt and pepper. Fold in
bread cubes, chicken and
diced potatoes. Spoon into
greased 9" x 13" baking pan.

3. Bake at 300° for 1 hour.

Main Dishes

Amish Filling

Miriam M. Witmer
Manheim, PA
Erisman Mennonite Church

Makes 15-20 servings

4 cups diced, cooked chicken
12-16 Tbsp. butter *or*
**   margarine**
1 medium onion, minced
1 cup diced celery
4 eggs, beaten
3 cups milk
18-20 slices bread, cubed
Salt and pepper to taste

1. Cook, bone and dice chicken. Reserve chicken broth.

2. Melt butter in saucepan. Sauté onion and celery.

3. Pour eggs and milk over bread cubes and toss until completely moistened. Add mixture to celery and onion and fry until lightly browned.

4. Put into large crockpot, layering filling and chicken. Pour approximately ½ cup chicken broth across top of filling when crockpot is full. Add more broth while cooking to keep mixture moist.

5. Cook on low for several hours.

Chicken Dressing

Mary Vaughn Warye
West Liberty, OH
Oak Grove Mennonite Church

Makes 25-30 servings

¾ cup margarine *or* butter
2 cups chopped onion
2 cups chopped celery
¼ cup parsley sprigs
8-oz. can mushrooms,
**   drained**
12-13 cups bread cubes
1 tsp. poultry seasoning
1½ tsp. salt
1 tsp. thyme
½ tsp. pepper
½ tsp. marjoram
3½-4 ½ cups chicken broth
4 cups diced, cooked chicken
2 eggs, beaten
1 tsp. baking powder

1. Melt margarine in skillet and sauté onion, celery, parsley and mushrooms.

2. Put bread cubes in large mixing bowl. Add all seasonings and toss well. Pour in broth to make mixture quite moist. Fold in diced chicken.

3. Add eggs and toss together well. Add the baking powder and mix well. Pack lightly into large crockpot.

4. Cook on medium heat for 3-4 hours.

Chicken Loaf

Katie Troyer
Mio, MI
Fairview Mennonite Church

Makes 15 servings

6 cups cooked chicken
1½ cups chopped celery
½ cup chopped onion
½ cup chopped green
**   pepper**
1 cup sliced mushrooms
2 Tbsp. margarine
2½ quarts bread cubes
2 cups cubed cheese
1 tsp. salt
2 tsp. poultry seasoning
6 eggs
3 cups chicken broth

1. Cook, bone and dice chicken. Reserve chicken broth.

2. Sauté vegetables in margarine.

3. In large bowl mix bread cubes, cheese, chicken, vegetables and seasonings. Add slightly beaten eggs and chicken broth. Mix well. Spoon into large roasting pan.

4. Cover and bake at 350° for 1 hour. Uncover and bake 15 minutes longer until slightly browned.

La Junta Chicken Enchilada Casserole

Marlene Smucker
Arvada, CO

Makes 12 servings

1 whole chicken
2 Tbsp. margarine
1 medium onion, chopped
4 Tbsp. flour
2 cups chicken broth
1 can cream of chicken soup
1 can green chilies
2 jalapeño peppers
  (optional)
1 pkg. soft corn tortillas
1 lb. longhorn cheese, grated

1. Cook, bone and dice chicken. Reserve at least 2 cups broth.
2. Sauté onion in margarine. Add flour and stir until well mixed. Add broth and heat, stirring constantly. Add soup, chicken, chilies and peppers if desired.
3. In large casserole dish layer 3-4 tortillas, ¼ of cheese and ¼ of chicken mixture. Repeat until all ingredients are used and top with cheese.
4. Bake at 350° for 30 minutes.

Chicken Sopa

Laverne Nafziger
Hopedale, IL
Hopedale Mennonite Church

Makes 6 servings

1 whole chicken
1 onion, chopped
1 green chili
1 jalapeño pepper (optional)
1 Tbsp. cooking oil
1 cup chicken broth
1 can cream of chicken soup
1 can cream of mushroom
  soup
½ cup plain yogurt
1 jar red pimento (optional)
1 pkg. corn tortillas
1 lb. longhorn cheese, grated

1. Cook chicken. Cool and debone it. Reserve 1 cup chicken broth.
2. Brown onion, chili and pepper in cooking oil.
3. Combine sautéed vegetables with chicken, chicken broth, soups, yogurt and pimento.
4. In large baking dish, electric skillet *or* crockpot layer tortillas, soup mixture and cheese. Repeat layers until all ingredients have been used. Top with cheese.
5. In the oven bake at 350° for 45-50 minutes. In crockpot cook for 2 hours on high. In electric skillet cook at 200° for 2-3 hours.

Sour Cream Chicken Enchiladas

Edna Otto
Glenwood Springs, CO
Glenwood Mennonite Church

Makes 8 servings

Filling:
2 cups grated cheddar cheese
2 cups diced chicken
½ cup diced mild onion
1 dozen flour tortillas

Sauce:
3 cans cream of chicken soup
¾ cup sour cream
2 cans diced green chilies
¾ tsp. salt

1. Combine all sauce ingredients and heat until mixture is smooth.
2. Mix cheese, chicken and onion together.
3. Place a spoonful of sauce on each tortilla. Add a spoonful of filling mixture.
4. Roll tortillas and place side by side in 9" x 13" baking dish. Pour any remaining sauce over enchiladas.
5. Bake at 350° for 30 minutes or until heated through.

Chicken Enchilada Casserole

Freda Friesen
Hillsboro, KS
Hillsboro Mennonite Brethren Church

Makes 10-12 servings

2-3 large chicken breasts
1 cup uncooked rice
1 can cream of mushroom
  soup
1 can cream of chicken soup
1 can tomatoes, diced
1½ cups chicken broth
1 tsp. chili powder
4 tsp. minced onion
¼ tsp. garlic powder
¼ tsp. black pepper
8 ozs. cheese, grated
4-6 cups crushed nacho
  chips

1. Cook and bone chicken. Reserve broth for later use.

2. Prepare rice according to directions. Add all other ingredients except cheese and nacho chips.

3. Layer ingredients into 3-quart casserole in following order: ½ of nacho chips, ½ of chicken, ½ of sauce and ½ of cheese. Repeat layers.

4. Bake at 350° for 30 minutes or until cheese melts.

Chicken Pie with Celery Seed Crust

Kathy Hertzler
Lancaster, PA
Charlotte Street Mennonite Church

Makes 10-15 servings

Filling:
⅓ cup butter
⅓ cup flour
⅓ cup chopped onion
½ tsp. salt
¼ tsp. pepper
1 ¾ cups chicken broth
⅔ cup milk
2½ cups diced, cooked
  chicken
10-oz. pkg. peas and carrots

Pastry:
3 cups flour
1 Tbsp. celery seed
1 tsp. salt
1 cup + 3 Tbsp. margarine *or*
  shortening
6-7 Tbsp. ice water

1. To prepare filling melt butter over low heat in saucepan. Blend in flour, onion and seasonings, stirring until mixture is bubbly.

2. Remove from heat and stir in chicken broth and milk. Return to heat and bring to a boil, stirring constantly. Boil and stir for 1 minute. Gently add chicken and vegetables. Set aside.

3. To prepare pastry measure flour, celery seed and salt into a bowl. Cut in margarine or shortening until mixture becomes crumbly. Sprinkle with water, 1 Tbsp. at a time, mixing until all flour is moistened and

dough almost cleans sides of bowl. Gather dough into ball.

4. On lightly floured surface roll ⅔ of dough into a rectangle, approximately 13" x 17".

5. Ease pastry into 9" x 13" baking dish. Pour filling over pastry.

6. Roll remaining dough into 9" x 13" rectangle and place over filling. Seal edges. Cut slits in center to allow steam to escape.

7. Bake at 425° for 30-35 minutes.

Chicken a la King

Topeka, KS
Southern Hills Mennonite Church

Makes 12 or more servings

4-oz. can mushrooms
½ cup chopped green
  pepper
½ cup butter
½ cup flour
1 tsp. salt
¼ tsp. pepper
2 cups chicken broth
2 cups cream
2 cups diced, cooked chicken
½ cup chopped pimento

1. Sauté mushrooms and green pepper in butter. Blend in flour and seasonings. Cook over low heat, stirring until mixture is smooth and bubbly. Remove from heat.

2. Slowly add broth and cream. Return to heat and bring to a boil over low heat,

stirring constantly. Boil 1 minute.

3. Add chicken and pimento. Continue cooking until chicken is heated through. Serve over baked potatoes.

Once a year we have a supper with a set menu. We used this particular recipe with a baked potato supper. We took this recipe times four and also served grated cheese, bacon bits, sour cream, butter, mushrooms, cheese and broccoli. It was a hit!

Chicken Gumbo

Lois Martin
Robesonia, PA
Hampden Mennonite Church

Makes 8-10 servings

¼ **cup margarine, melted**
½ **cup salad dressing**
4 eggs
1 cup milk
1 cup chicken broth
1 tsp. salt or less
9 slices bread
4 cups cubed, cooked chicken
9 slices cheese
2 cans cream of celery or
** cream of mushroom soup**
Bread crumbs

1. Combine margarine, salad dressing, eggs, milk, chicken broth and salt.
2. Layer slices of bread and chicken into 9" x 13" baking dish. Pour chicken broth mixture over chicken. Layer cheese over chicken. Pour soup over cheese. Top with bread crumbs.

3. Bake at 350° for 1½ hours.

Hot Chicken Casserole

Edith Williams Seibert
Bedford, VA
Main Street Methodist Friendship Bible Class

Makes 6 servings

4 chicken breasts or 2 lbs.
** chicken pieces**
Water to cover
8 Tbsp. margarine or butter
16-oz. pkg. Pepperidge Farm
** cornbread crumbs**
1 can cream of mushroom
** soup**
1 can cream of celery soup
2 cans chicken broth

1. Cook chicken in water until skin comes off easily. Cool, skin and bone chicken. Reserve broth.
2. Melt margarine and stir in crumbs. Set aside.
3. Mix soups with broth. Set aside.
4. In greased baking dish put layer of crumbs. Alternate layers of soup with layers of chicken. Top with crumbs.
5. Bake at 350° for 45 minutes to 1 hour. Serve with cranberry sauce.

Sour Cream Chicken Casserole

Edith M. Weaver
College Park, MD
Hyattsville Mennonite Church

Makes 6-8 servings

4-6 chicken breasts or
1 whole fryer
8-oz. pkg. Pepperidge Farm
** stuffing mix**
8 Tbsp. butter or margarine,
** melted**
8-oz. container sour cream
1 can cream of chicken soup
1 can cream of celery soup

1. Cook chicken. Cool, skin, bone and cube chicken.
2. Layer ½ of stuffing mix with ½ of butter in casserole or baking dish.
3. In medium bowl mix sour cream, soups and chicken. Spoon over stuffing.
4. Mix together remaining stuffing and butter and spread over top of chicken.
5. Bake at 350° for 45 minutes.

Essex Chicken Casserole

Phyllis Eller
La Verne, CA

Sheri Hartzler
Harrisonburg, VA
Community Mennonite Church

Makes 10 servings

2 cups diced, cooked chicken
2 cups uncooked macaroni
2 cans cream of mushroom
**   or cream of chicken soup**
1 cup milk
1½ cups chicken broth
1 small onion, finely
**   chopped**
2-oz. jar diced pimentos
5-oz. can water chestnuts
½ tsp. salt
½ lb. cheddar cheese, grated

1. Combine all ingredients except grated cheese in 9" x 13" baking dish. Sprinkle cheese over top.
2. Cover and refrigerate at least 12 hours or overnight.
3. Bake, uncovered, at 350° for 1 hour.

Chicken Macaroni Casserole

Anita Falk
Mountain Lake, MN
Bethel Mennonite Church

Makes 12 servings

2 cups uncooked macaroni
½ lb. cheddar cheese, grated

2 cans cream of mushroom
**   soup**
1 cup milk
1 cup chicken broth
2 cups diced, cooked chicken
Grated onion to taste
Salt and pepper to taste

1. Mix all ingredients together. Refrigerate overnight.
2. Bake at 350° for 1 hour or until heated through.

Variations:
Substitute ½ lb. mild cheese, cubed ,for cheddar cheese and add 4 diced, hard-boiled eggs.
Kathy Falk
Champaign, IL

Catherine Bechtel
Oley, PA

Noodle and Chicken Casserole

Ruth Hershey
Paradise, PA
Paradise Mennonite Church

Makes 12 servings

4 cups diced, cooked chicken
16-oz. pkg. medium noodles
2 cups chopped celery
2 tsp. salt
2 cans cream of mushroom
**   soup**
1½ cups milk
1 cup grated white American
**   cheese**

1. Reserve chicken stock from cooking chicken. Cook noodles, celery and salt in stock for 8 minutes. Drain liquid from noodles. Add chicken to mixture.
2. Blend soup and milk to-

gether. Add along with cheese to other ingredients. Pour into greased baking dish.
3. Bake at 350° for 40 minutes.

Variation:
Add 1 can corn to ingredients.
Anna Marie Ramer
New Paris, IN

Chicken Tetrazzini

Viola Stauffer
Milford, NE
Bellwood Mennonite Church

Makes 8-10 servings

1 whole chicken
8-oz. pkg. noodles
1 onion, chopped
⅓ cup chopped celery
⅓ cup chopped green
**   pepper**
3 Tbsp. butter
3 Tbsp. flour
1 tsp. salt
Pepper to taste
1 cup milk
2 cups chicken broth
1 cup shredded cheddar
**   cheese**
1 cup bread crumbs,
**   buttered**

1. Cook, bone and dice chicken. Reserve 2 cups broth.
2. Cook noodles according to package directions. Drain.
3. Sauté onion, celery and green pepper in butter. Add flour, salt and pepper. Add milk and chicken broth and cook until thickened. Stir in cheddar cheese. Add noodles

and chicken to this mixture.

4. Spoon into greased casserole dish and cover with bread crumbs.

5. Bake at 350° for 30-45 minutes or until bubbly.

Chicken Spectacular

Ruth Brunk
Sarasota, FL
Bahia Vista Mennonite Church

Makes 8-10 servings

3 cups diced, cooked chicken
1 can cream of celery soup
1½-2 cups cooked rice
2 cups French-style green
  beans
1 small onion, diced
7-oz. jar chopped pimento
8-oz. jar water chestnuts
1 cup mayonnaise
3-oz. can mushrooms
Salt and pepper to taste

1. Drain green beans, pimento, water chestnuts and mushrooms of liquid. Do not reserve.

2. In large bowl mix all ingredients.

3. Spoon into 2-quart baking dish.

4. Bake at 350° for 45 minutes or until done.

Chicken Supreme

Verna Birky
Albany, OR
Albany Mennonite Church

Makes 8 servings

3 cups cooked chicken,
  coarsely chopped
2 cups chicken broth
3 cups cooked rice
1½ cups milk
4-oz. jar mushroom pieces
6 Tbsp. flour
1 tsp. salt
Pepper to taste
2 Tbsp. margarine
½ cup blanched and
  slivered almonds
1 jar pimentos (optional)
Buttered bread crumbs
Paprika

1. Mix ½ cup chicken broth with rice. Set aside.

2. In a saucepan combine remaining broth and milk.

3. Drain liquid from mushroom pieces and shake well with flour. Use this combination to thicken broth and milk mixture. Add salt and pepper.

4. In separate saucepan fry mushrooms in margarine until lightly browned. Set aside.

5. Cover bottom of greased 9" x 13" baking dish with ½ of rice. Cover with ½ of chicken. Cover with ½ of gravy. Dot with almonds, pimentos and mushrooms. Add remaining rice, chicken and gravy. Sprinkle with bread crumbs and paprika.

6. Bake, uncovered, at 350° for 45 minutes.

Chicken Salad Casserole

Mary Grieser
Jefferson, OR
Bethany Mennonite Church

Makes 8-10 servings

2 cups diced, cooked chicken
1 can cream of celery soup
1 cup cooked rice
5-oz. can water chestnuts
1 Tbsp. lemon juice
½ tsp. salt
¾ cup mayonnaise
1 cup shredded cheese
2 cups crushed potato chips

1. Combine all ingredients except potato chips.

2. Pour into 9" x 13" baking dish. Cover with crushed potato chips.

3. Bake at 375° for 45 minutes to 1 hour.

Variation:

Substitute 1 cup diced celery and ½ cup almonds for the cooked rice.

Lorraine J. Kaufman
Moundridge, KS
West Zion Mennonite Church

Wild Rice Casserole

Samay Phommalee
Toledo, OH

Makes 8 servings

4 cups cooked wild rice
1 can cream of mushroom
  soup
½ cup chicken gravy
2 cups diced, cooked chicken
1 cup soft bread crumbs
2 Tbsp. margarine, melted

1. Combine rice, soup, chicken gravy and chicken. Turn into greased 2-quart casserole dish.
2. Toss together bread crumbs and margarine. Sprinkle over casserole.
3. Bake at 350° for 50-60 minutes.

Chicken Fried Rice

Hmong Christian Church
Kitchener, ON

Makes 4 servings

1 oz. dried mushrooms
Water
4 eggs, beaten
1 tsp. cooking oil
7 ozs. diced ham
3 tsp. cooking oil
3½ ozs. green onion,
  sliced
4 cups steamed rice
½ can bamboo shoots, sliced
4 Tbsp. green beans or more
7 ozs. diced, cooked chicken
Salt and pepper to taste

1. Boil mushrooms in water for 3-5 minutes until softened. Drain water and slice mushrooms.
2. Stir fry eggs in 1 tsp. oil. Add ham and cook until heated through. Set aside.
3. Stir fry onion in 3 tsp. oil. Add rice, mushrooms, bamboo shoots, green beans, chicken, eggs and ham. Stir fry at least 5 minutes. Salt and pepper to taste before serving.

Chicken Casserole

Sheri Hartzler
Harrisonburg, VA
Community Mennonite Church

Makes 6-8 servings

6-oz. pkg. long-grain wild
  rice, cooked
2 cups diced, cooked chicken
¼ lb. mushrooms
1 can cream of mushroom
  soup
½ cup milk
4-oz. can black olives,
  chopped
2 cups grated cheddar
  cheese
⅓ cup slivered almonds

1. Spread cooked rice in greased 3-quart casserole dish. Top with cooked chicken and mushrooms.
2. Combine soup and milk and pour over other ingredients. Add layer of olives and cheese. Sprinkle with almonds.
3. Bake at 350° for 45 minutes.

Curry Chicken Divan

Ferne Burkhardt
Petersburg, ON
Mannheim Mennonite Church

Makes 10 servings

3 chicken breasts
1 carrot, sliced
1 small onion, chopped
1 tsp. salt or less
2 10-oz. pkgs. frozen broccoli
1 can cream of chicken soup
⅔ cup salad dressing
1 cup evaporated milk
½ cup grated cheese
1 tsp. lemon juice
1 tsp. curry powder or more
1 Tbsp. butter *or* margarine,
  melted
½ cup dried bread crumbs

1. Cook chicken, carrot, onion and salt until tender (about 45 minutes). Drain and save broth for another time. Bone chicken and cut into bite-sized pieces.
2. Cook broccoli according to directions and drain.
3. Combine soup, salad dressing, milk, cheese, lemon juice and curry to make sauce.
4. Toss melted butter with bread crumbs.
5. To assemble place chicken, carrot, onion and broccoli in greased 2-quart casserole dish. Pour sauce over chicken and broccoli. Sprinkle bread crumbs on top.
6. Bake at 350° for 30 minutes.

I often prepare this dish ahead of time, refrigerate it and bring to room temperature before baking. I like to bake it in the church oven if possible.

Chicken Divan

Beryl H. Brubaker
Harrisonburg, VA
Parkview Mennonite Church
Edith Branner
Harrisonburg, VA

Makes 8 servings

2 bunches fresh broccoli
2 cups diced, cooked white
   chicken
2 cans cream of chicken soup
1 cup mayonnaise
1 tsp. lemon juice
½ tsp. curry powder
½ cup grated cheddar
   cheese
½ cup bread crumbs
1 Tbsp. margarine, melted

1. Cook broccoli and drain.
2. Arrange broccoli in greased, rectangular baking dish. Put chicken on top of broccoli.
3. Combine chicken soup, mayonnaise, lemon juice and curry. Pour over chicken. Sprinkle with cheese.
4. Combine bread crumbs and margarine. Layer over cheese.
5. Bake at 350° for 30 minutes.

Variation:
Substitute 2 cups chow mein noodles for bread crumbs and margarine.
Mary Dyck
Mission, BC
Cedar Valley Mennonite Church

Chicken Rice Broccoli Casserole

Marcella Stalter
Flanagan, IL
Waldo Mennonite Church

Makes 8-10 servings

6 cups cooked rice
2 cups cooked chicken, cut
   in bite-sized pieces
2 cans cream of chicken soup
1 cup light mayonnaise
⅓ cup milk
1 tsp. lemon juice
½ tsp. curry powder
1 large bunch fresh broccoli
½ cup bread crumbs,
   buttered
½ cup grated American
   cheese

1. Spread cooked rice into bottom of 9" x 13" casserole dish. Spread chicken over rice.
2. Combine soup, mayonnaise, milk, lemon juice and curry powder. Pour over chicken and rice.
3. Cook broccoli until just tender and drain well. Spread into casserole. Top with bread crumbs and cheese.
4. Bake at 375° for 25 minutes.

Chicken Broccoli Casserole

Violet Jantzi
Medina, NY
Harris Hill Mennonite Fellowship

Makes 6-8 servings

1 bunch fresh broccoli
1 can cream of mushroom
   soup
1½ cups water
1 pkg. dry onion soup
1 cup uncooked rice
1 whole chicken, cut in
   pieces

1. Place uncooked broccoli on bottom of casserole.
2. Mix mushroom soup, water, onion soup and rice and pour over broccoli.
3. Lay chicken pieces over top.
4. Cover and bake at 325° for 2 hours or more.

Chicken Broccoli Casserole with Macaroni

Lillian F. Gardner
Crystal, MN
New Hope Mennonite Brethren Church

Makes 10 servings

1 cup elbow macaroni
6 small green onions, chopped
4 Tbsp. butter
6-8 slices American cheese
2 10-oz. pkgs. frozen broccoli
2 cups cubed, cooked chicken
½ tsp. salt
½ cup milk
1 can cream of chicken soup
½ cup grated cheese

1. Cook macaroni according to directions.
2. Sauté onions in butter and mix with cooked macaroni. Spoon into greased 9" x 13" baking dish. Cover with slices of American cheese. Break up uncooked broccoli and place over cheese. Cover with cubed chicken.
3. Combine salt, milk and soup. Pour over other ingredients. Add grated cheese.
4. Cover and bake at 375° for 30 minutes. Uncover and bake 5-10 minutes longer.

Chicken Vegetable Casserole

Mary E. Martin
Goshen, IN
Benton Mennonite Church

Makes 50 servings

4 whole chickens
12 medium potatoes, cubed
1 bunch celery, chopped
4 onions, chopped
4 loaves bread
½ lb. margarine, melted
1 dozen eggs
4 cups peas
4 cups corn
Salt to taste

1. Stew chickens in water until tender. Cool and bone chickens. Put chicken meat back into broth. Set aside.
2. Cook potatoes until almost tender. Add celery and onions and cook several minutes longer. Drain and set aside.
3. Melt margarine in large saucepan. Cube bread and add to margarine. Stir over low heat until bread is toasted.
4. Beat eggs in large bowl. Add chicken and broth, potatoes, celery, onions, bread, eggs, peas and corn. Salt to taste. Pour mixture into large roaster.
5. Bake at 325° for 1-1½ hours.

We have frequently used this recipe for funeral meals, and find it is appreciated.

Chicken Asparagus Casserole

Miriam Christophel
Battle Creek, MI
Pine Grove Mennonite Church

Makes 4-6 servings

4 medium-sized boneless chicken breasts
2 Tbsp. cooking oil
1 can cream of chicken soup
⅓ cup mayonnaise *or* plain yogurt
1 tsp. lemon juice
½ tsp. curry powder
⅛ tsp. pepper
10-oz. pkg. frozen asparagus spears
¼ cup grated cheddar cheese

1. Cut each chicken breast crosswise into 1-inch strips.
2. Heat cooking oil in 12-inch skillet. Over high heat sauté chicken pieces until lightly browned. Drain chicken pieces.
3. In small bowl combine chicken soup, mayonnaise, lemon juice, curry powder and pepper.
4. Place half of asparagus spears in bottom of shallow 1½-quart casserole dish. Top with ½ of chicken soup mixture and all of chicken pieces. Tuck remaining asparagus into casserole and top with remaining soup mixture. Sprinkle with cheddar cheese.
5. Cover and bake at 375° for 30-35 minutes until sauce is hot and bubbly and chicken is tender.

Chicken Casserole with Eggs

Anne Giesbrecht
Richmond, BC
Richmond Bethel Mennonite
Brethren Church

Makes 4-6 servings

2 cups diced, cooked chicken
1 can cream of mushroom
  soup
1 cup milk
¼ tsp. salt
½ cup peas
2 hard-boiled eggs, chopped
3 cups crushed potato chips
¼ cup grated cheese
Paprika

1. Combine chicken, soup, milk, salt and peas. Heat until blended. Remove from heat and stir in eggs.
2. Spread ½ of chips in bottom of 2-quart casserole dish. Pour in the chicken mixture. Top with remaining chips. Sprinkle with cheese and paprika.
3. Bake at 350° for 25-30 minutes.

Chicken Strata Casserole

Mrs. Lewis L. Beachy
Sarasota, FL
Bahia Vista Mennonite Church

Mary Vaughn Warye
West Liberty, OH,
Oak Grove Mennonite Church

Makes 6-8 servings

2 cups cubed, cooked
  chicken
½ cup chopped celery
½ cup chopped onion
½ cup chopped green
  pepper
½ cup mayonnaise
½ tsp. salt
¼ tsp. pepper
4 slices bread, cubed
1½ cups milk
2 eggs, beaten
1 can cream of mushroom
  soup
½ cup grated yellow cheese

1. Combine chicken, celery, onion, green pepper, mayonnaise, salt and pepper.
2. Put ½ bread into well-greased casserole. Top with chicken mixture and remaining bread.
3. Combine milk and eggs and pour over other ingredients. Top with mushroom soup and cheese.
4. Bake at 350° for 1 hour.

Chicken Green Bean Casserole

Donna Horst
Leola, PA
Groffdale Mennonite Church

Makes 4-6 servings

2 cups cubed, cooked
  chicken
1 can green beans
1 can cream of chicken soup
¼ can chicken broth *or*
  water
Salt and pepper to taste
2 cups bread cubes
¼ cup butter, melted
¼ cup grated cheese

1. Combine chicken and green beans.
2. Combine soup and broth and bring to a boil. Add to chicken and green beans. Salt and pepper to taste.
3. Spoon into greased casserole dish.
4. Combine bread cubes, melted butter and grated cheese. Pour over casserole ingredients.
5. Bake at 350° for 30 minutes.

Hot Chicken Salad

Mary Jane Miller
Wellman, IA
Kalona Mennonite Church

Makes 4-6 servings

1 can cream of chicken soup
¾ cup mayonnaise
¼ cup diced onion
1 cup chopped celery
1 Tbsp. lemon juice
2 cups diced, cooked chicken
1 cup cooked rice
1 cup crushed cornflakes
3 Tbsp. margarine, melted

1. In a large bowl combine soup, mayonnaise, onion, celery and lemon juice. Fold in chicken and rice. Turn into greased casserole dish.
2. Combine cornflakes and melted margarine. Sprinkle over chicken salad.
3. Bake at 350° for 30 minutes.

Variation:
Add 1 cup chopped nuts to the cornflake topping mixture.
Rosetta Martin
Columbiana, OH,
Midway Mennonite Church

Hot Chicken Salad Soufflé

Annabelle Kratz
Clarksville, MD
Hyattsville Mennonite Church

Makes 10 servings

6 slices bread
2 eggs
1½ cups milk
2 cups diced, cooked chicken
½ cup chopped onion
½ cup chopped celery
½ cup chopped green pepper
½ cup mayonnaise
1 can cream of mushroom soup
½ cup shredded cheese

1. Remove crusts from bread. Cut slices in half and spread with butter. Grease an oblong baking dish and place half the bread on the bottom of the dish.
2. In a small bowl beat the eggs. Add milk and set aside.
3. In a medium bowl combine chicken, onion, celery, green pepper and mayonnaise. Spread this mixture over the buttered bread. Layer remaining bread over chicken mixture.
4. Pour egg and milk mixture over bread layer. Cover and refrigerate several hours or overnight.
5. Immediately before baking, pour mushroom soup over casserole.
6. Bake at 325° for 55 minutes. Remove from oven and top with cheese. Return to oven for 5 minutes longer.

Oven Chicken Salad

Mrs. John D. Hartzler
Eureka, IL

Makes 10-12 servings

2 cups cubed, cooked chicken
2 cups thinly sliced celery
1 cup toasted bread cubes
1 cup mayonnaise
½ cup toasted, slivered almonds
2 Tbsp. lemon juice
2 tsp. minced onion
½ tsp. salt
½ cup grated cheese
1 cup toasted bread cubes

1. Combine all ingredients except cheese and 1 cup bread cubes.
2. Bake at 450° for 10-15 minutes or until bubbly. Remove from oven and spread cheese and remaining bread cubes over top. Return to oven and bake until cheese is melted and bread cubes are browned.

Baked Chicken Salad

Helen Wiebe
Selkirk, MB
Selkirk Christian Fellowship Ladies

Makes 8 servings

1 cup uncooked macaroni
1 Tbsp. margarine
2 Tbsp. chopped onion
¼ cup chopped green pepper
1 cup diced celery

2 cups diced, cooked chicken
1 can cream of chicken soup
¾ cup mayonnaise
1 Tbsp. lemon juice
4-oz. can mushrooms
½ cup sliced almonds
2 cups crushed potato chips

1. Cook macaroni according to directions. Drain and rinse.
2. Sauté onion, green pepper and celery in margarine.
3. Combine all ingredients except potato chips in a shallow baking pan. Cover with potato chips.
4. Bake at 350° for 30 minutes.

Spanish Paella

Melodie Davis
Harrisonburg, VA
Trinity Presbyterian Church

Makes 8-10 servings

1 whole chicken, cut up
¼ cup olive oil
¼ lb. pork
¼ lb. bulk sausage
8 slices onion
4 medium tomatoes, diced
1 green pepper, chopped
2 cups uncooked rice
3 cups chicken broth
2 Tbsp. paprika
2 Tbsp. salt
½ tsp. pepper
¼ tsp. red pepper
⅛ tsp. saffron
Pinch of minced garlic
2 cups shrimp
10-oz. pkg. green peas
4 ozs. sliced pimento,
    drained

1. Wash chicken pieces and dry. In Dutch oven or heavy kettle brown chicken in oil. Remove chicken and drain excess fat.
2. Brown pork and sausage. Remove and drain excess fat.
3. Sauté onions, tomatoes and green pepper, stirring until onion is tender. Stir in rice, chicken broth and seasonings. Add chicken.
4. Cover tightly and simmer for 20 minutes.
5. Gently fold in shrimp, pork, sausage and peas. Cover and simmer another 15 minutes. Add pimento, heat through and serve.

Pastel de Choelo

Mary Hochstedler
Kokomo, IN
Parkview Mennonite Church

Makes 20 servings

10 ears fresh corn
1 Tbsp. salt
1 Tbsp. fresh basil
3 Tbsp. sugar
3-lb. chicken
1 lb. ground beef
2 onions, diced
¾ cup raisins
½ tsp. salt
½ tsp. pepper
¼ tsp. cumin
¼ tsp. cayenne pepper
¼ tsp. oregano
¼ tsp. paprika
1 cup chicken broth
10-12 olives
2 hard-boiled eggs, sliced
½ cup brown sugar

1. Cut corn from ears. Run through blender with 1 Tbsp. salt, basil and 3 Tbsp. sugar. Set aside.
2. Cook chicken until tender. Cool, bone and chop chicken.
3. Brown ground beef and onions. Drain excess fat. Add chicken, raisins, seasonings and chicken broth. Set aside.
4. Using two 9" x 13" baking pans layer ¼ of corn mixture into each pan. Cover with chicken and ground beef mixture. Top with remaining corn.
5. Garnish with olives and hard-boiled eggs. Press down into corn mixture to prevent drying out. Sprinkle with brown sugar.
6. Bake at 350° for 40-45 minutes or until bubbly and browned on top.

Beef Main Dishes

Salisbury Steak

Fannie Bender
Accident, MD
Cherry Glade Mennonite Church

Makes 30 medium servings

4 lbs. ground beef
4 cups bread crumbs
4 eggs
2 cups milk
2 medium onions, diced
Salt and pepper to taste
2-3 cans cream of mushroom
   soup

1. Mix all ingredients except mushroom soup. Form into patties and place on cookie sheets.
2. Bake at 350° just long enough to brown, 10-15 minutes.
3. Place meat patties in roaster and pour soup over meat.
4. Bake at 225° for 1 hour.

Microwave Meat Loaf

Elaine Unruh
Moundridge, KS
First Mennonite Church

Makes 6-8 servings

Meat Loaf:
1½ lbs. ground beef
¾ cup tomato sauce
1 egg, slightly beaten
½ cup bread crumbs
1 Tbsp. minced onion
¼ tsp. minced garlic
½ tsp. salt
¼ tsp. pepper

Sauce:
⅓ cup ketchup
1 tsp. Worcestershire sauce
1 Tbsp. brown sugar
1 Tbsp. prepared mustard

1. Combine all ingredients for meat loaf in large bowl. Mix well. Pat into 5" x 9" loaf pan. Cook on full power for 6 minutes.
2. Meanwhile, combine all sauce ingredients in small bowl. Pour sauce over meat loaf. Continue cooking on level 3 (defrost) for 25-30 minutes. If your microwave has temperature probe, heat to 160°.

Pita Burgers

Willard and Alice Roth
Elkhart, IN
Southside Fellowship

Makes 12 servings

2 lbs. lean ground chuck
1 cup oatmeal
1 egg
1 medium onion, finely
   chopped
15-oz. can tomato sauce
2 Tbsp. brown sugar
2 Tbsp. cider vinegar
1 Tbsp. Worcestershire sauce
1 Tbsp. soy sauce
12-slice pkg. pita bread

1. Combine ground chuck, oatmeal, egg and onion. Shape mixture into 12 burgers.
2. Combine tomato sauce, brown sugar, vinegar, Worcestershire sauce and soy sauce. Coat each burger with sauce.
3. Place burgers with any remaining sauce in crockpot. Cover and cook on low 6 hours (or high 4 hours).
4. Invite diners to lift a burger with tongs from crockpot and put into pita pocket.

Meatballs

Bertha Selzer, Hesston, KS;
Carol Friesen, Wallace, NE;
Betty Hartzler, Toano, VA;
Doris Risser, Orrville, OH

Makes 20-24 servings

13-oz. can evaporated milk
3 lbs. lean ground beef
2 cups quick oatmeal
½ tsp. garlic powder
½ tsp. pepper
2 eggs
1 cup chopped onions
2 tsp. salt
2 tsp. chili powder

1. Combine all ingredients and shape into balls.
2. Choose one of the sauce variations which follow this recipe and pour over meatballs.
3. Bake according to directions in each sauce recipe.

Variations:
Substitute 1½ cups dry bread crumbs for 2 cups oatmeal. Add ¾ cup ketchup or tomato sauce.

Helen Classsen
Elkhart, IN

Substitute ground turkey for half of the ground beef. Substitute 1 cup cracker crumbs for 1 cup oatmeal.

Rhoda H. Sauder
York, PA

Meat Kebabs

Annie Mathew
Goshen, IN
Belmont Mennonite Church

Makes 12 servings

2 lbs. lean ground beef
¼ tsp. ground cloves
¼ tsp. ground cardamom
¼ tsp. ground black pepper
¼ tsp. ground cumin
¼ tsp. ground ginger
¼ tsp. red pepper (optional)
1 Tbsp. plain yogurt
1 large onion, chopped
Salt to taste

1. Mix all ingredients thoroughly. Form into small balls or flatten into 3-inch patties. Arrange on cookie sheet.
2. Broil 5 minutes on each side. Delicious when served with green salads.

Barbecue Sauce

Bertha Selzer, Hesston, KS; Carol
Friesen, Wallace, NE; Betty
Hartzler, Toano, VA; Doris Risser,
Orrville, OH

2 cups ketchup
1½ cups brown sugar
½ cup chopped onions
½ tsp. garlic powder
2 Tbsp. liquid smoke

1. Prepare meatball recipe immediately preceding this recipe. Place meat in flat pans, only one layer to each pan.
2. Mix all sauce ingredients and pour over meatballs.

3. Bake meatballs and sauce at 350° for 1 hour.

Sweet and Sour Sauce

Melanie Frayle
Ridgeway, ON
Riverside Chapel

1¾ cups sugar
2 cups water
1 cup ketchup
¼ cup vinegar
2-3 Tbsp. cornstarch water

1. Prepare meatball recipe according to directions. Bake meatballs at 350° for 30-35 minutes. Drain excess fat.
2. Dissolve sugar in water over medium heat. Add ketchup and vinegar. Bring to a boil, stirring constantly. Thicken sauce by adding cornstarch water. Stir.
3. Remove meatballs from oven and pour sauce over meatballs.
4. Bake meatballs and sauce at 350° for 15-20 minutes or until heated through.

Mushroom Sauce

Bruni Winter
Winnipeg, MB
Sargent Avenue Mennonite Church

2 cans cream of mushroom
soup
1 can tomato soup
2 cans water
2 8-oz. jars mushrooms
Parsley

1. Prepare meatball recipe on page 129. Brown meatballs on both sides in large skillet.

2. To prepare sauce combine soups, water and mushrooms with liquid. Pour over meatballs.

3. Simmer for 1/2-3/4 hour on low heat. If sauce is too thick, add a little water. If it is too thin, simmer 10 minutes longer, uncovered.

4. Immediately before serving, sprinkle with parsley.

Creamy Sauce

Barbara Hershey
Lancaster, PA
Rossmere Mennonite Church

3 cans cream of chicken soup
1 cup milk
1/2 tsp. nutmeg
1/2 tsp. dry dill weed
1 1/2 cups sour cream
Parsley

1. Prepare meatball recipe on page 129. Bake, uncovered, at 400° for 20 minutes.

2. In large skillet combine cooked meatballs, soup,

milk, nutmeg and dill weed. Heat to boiling, stirring occasionally.

3. Reduce heat and simmer for 15 minutes. Stir in sour cream. Cover and heat 2-3 minutes.

4. Immediately before serving, sprinkle with parsley.

Cranberry Meatballs

Marjorie Anderson
Lima, OH

Makes 20-25 servings

Meatballs:
2 lbs. lean ground beef
2 Tbsp. soy sauce
2 Tbsp. minced onion
2 eggs
1/3 cup dried parsley flakes
2 cloves garlic, minced
1 cup bread crumbs
2 tsp. salt
1/4 tsp. pepper
1 cup milk *or* water

Sauce:
1 lb. cranberry sauce, jellied
or whole berry
1/3 cup ketchup
2 Tbsp. brown sugar
12 ozs. chili sauce
1 Tbsp. lemon juice

1. In a large bowl combine all meatball ingredients. Divide meat into four sections and make 15 meatballs from each section.

2. Place in large casserole dish.

3. Combine all sauce ingredients and pour over meatballs.

4. Bake at 350° for 50 minutes to 1 hour.

Waikiki Meatballs

Sharon L. Spicher
Huntingdon, PA
Allensville Mennonite Church

Tena Neufeld
Delta, BC
Peace Mennonite Church

Makes 10-12 servings

1 1/2 lbs. ground beef
or ground turkey
2/3 cup cracker crumbs
1/3 cup minced onion
1 egg
1 1/2 tsp. salt
1/4 tsp. ginger
1/4 cup milk
2 Tbsp. cornstarch
1/2 cup brown sugar
20-oz. can pineapple tidbits
1/3 cup vinegar
1 Tbsp. soy sauce
1/3 cup chopped green
pepper

1. Thoroughly mix ground beef, cracker crumbs, onion, egg, salt, ginger and milk. Shape into small balls and brown in a skillet. Set meatballs aside in a bowl.

2. In skillet combine cornstarch and sugar. Stir in pineapple juice, vinegar and soy sauce until smooth. Cook over medium heat, stirring constantly until mixture thickens. Add meatballs, pineapple tidbits and green pepper. Heat through.

3. Serve with steamed rice.

Sweet and Sour Meatballs with Pineapple and Peppers

Ethel O. Yoder
Goshen, IN
College Mennonite Church

Makes 6-8 servings

1 lb. ground beef
1 egg
1 Tbsp. cornstarch
1 tsp. salt
Dash pepper
2 Tbsp. chopped onion
1 cup pineapple juice
3 Tbsp. cornstarch
1 Tbsp. soy sauce
3 Tbsp. vinegar
6 Tbsp. water
$\frac{1}{2}$ cup sugar
4 slices pineapple, cut up
1 large green pepper, cut in strips

1. Combine ground beef, egg, cornstarch, salt, pepper and onion. Form into 18 or more meatballs. Brown in large skillet and drain.
2. In separate saucepan bring pineapple juice almost to boiling point over low heat.
3. Combine cornstarch, soy sauce, vinegar, water and sugar. Add to pineapple juice and cook until sauce thickens, stirring constantly. Pour over meatballs.
4. Add pineapple and peppers. Heat thoroughly. Serve hot.

Savory Meatball Casserole

Miriam Showalter
Salem, OR
Salem Mennonite Church

Makes 8-10 servings

1$\frac{1}{2}$ lbs. lean ground beef
$\frac{1}{2}$ cup dry bread crumbs
$\frac{1}{3}$ cup evaporated milk
2 Tbsp. chopped onion
1 tsp. chili powder
$\frac{1}{8}$ tsp. pepper
4-6 ozs. noodles
1 can cream of mushroom soup
1 cup evaporated milk
$\frac{1}{4}$ cup water
Paprika

1. Combine ground beef, bread crumbs, milk, onion, chili powder and pepper. Shape into meatballs about the size of a tablespoon. Brown under broiler, turn once and drain.
2. Cook noodles until just cooked. Drain.
3. In large bowl combine mushroom soup and milk and mix well. Add water. Fold in noodles and meatballs. Spoon into greased 1$\frac{1}{2}$-quart casserole dish.
4. Cover and bake at 375° for 20-25 minutes. Sprinkle with paprika.

Meatballs Stroganoff

Lorna Sirtoli
Cortland, NY
Nazarene Church of Cortland

Makes 25-30 servings

Meatballs:
5 lbs. ground beef
2 cups cooked rice
4 eggs
2 4-oz. cans tomato sauce
2 medium onions, chopped
$\frac{3}{4}$ tsp. garlic salt
1 tsp. salt
Dash pepper
$\frac{1}{4}$ tsp. allspice
2 tsp. parsley flakes

Sauce:
2 8-oz. jars sliced mushrooms
2 cans cream of mushroom soup
1 can cream of celery soup
2 cans cream of chicken soup
2 cans milk
$\frac{1}{2}$ cup chicken stock
$\frac{1}{2}$ tsp. garlic powder *or* salt
3 Tbsp. parsley
2 Tbsp. Parmesan cheese
$\frac{1}{4}$ cup white wine
1 cup sour cream
2 Tbsp. dehydrated onion
Salt and pepper to taste

1. Combine all meatball ingredients and form into tiny meatballs. Bake at 350° for 15-20 minutes. Drain excess fat.
2. Combine all sauce ingredients and heat. Add meatballs to mixture and serve with rice.

Beef Stroganoff

Elda Martens
Fairview, OK
Fairview Mennonite Brethren
Church

Makes 200 servings

36 lbs. ground chuck
4½ cups flour
3¾ cups dehydrated onion
2 Tbsp. garlic powder
1½ cups parsley
1½ Tbsp. pepper
16 ½ cups instant dry milk
9 3-lb. cans cream of
   mushroom soup
9 quarts water
20 lbs. uncooked rice
26¼ quarts water
14 Tbsp. salt
14 Tbsp. cooking oil

1. At our church we make this recipe in three separate electric roasters. Following are the directions for each roaster.

2. Brown and drain 12 lbs. ground chuck. Add 1½ cups flour, 1 ¼ cups dehydrated onion, 2 tsp. garlic powder, ½ cup parsley, 1½ tsp. pepper, 5 ½ cups dry milk and 3 cans mushroom soup. Add approximately 3 quarts water.

3. Meanwhile, prepare rice by oven method. In seven different 12" x 20" pans combine 3 lbs. rice, 3 ¾ quarts water, 2 Tbsp. salt and 2 Tbsp. cooking oil. Cover pans.

4. Bake rice at 350° for 30 minutes.

Serve rice and meat sauce separately with green beans, French bread, cake and peaches.

Barbecue

Elsie Miller
Glendive, MT
White Chapel Mennonite Church

Makes 50 servings

8 lbs. ground beef
1 lb. onions, chopped
Salt and pepper to taste
2 cups diced celery
2 quarts ketchup *or* tomato
   sauce
¼ cup lemon juice
½ cup brown sugar
1 cup water
2 tsp. dry mustard
2 cups diced green peppers
Dash of Worcestershire
   sauce

1. Brown ground beef and chopped onions. Salt and pepper to taste. Drain excess fat.

2. Add all remaining ingredients and simmer for 1-2 hours.

3. Put ¼ cup barbecue on each hamburger bun.

Sloppy Joes for a Crowd

Mary Alice Miller
Elkhart, IN
Prairie Street Mennonite Church

To Serve 40-50

6¼ lbs. ground beef
1 cup onion
3¾ cups celery
2 Tbsp. mustard

1½ Tbsp. salt
½ cup brown sugar
4½ cups ketchup
½ cup vinegar
3 cups water

To Serve 100

12½ lbs. ground beef
2 cups onion
7 ½ cups celery
¼ cup mustard
3 Tbsp. salt
1 cup brown sugar
2¼ quarts ketchup
1¼ cups vinegar
1½ quarts water

To Serve 200

25 lbs. ground beef
4 cups onion
3¾ quarts celery
½ cup mustard
6 Tbsp. salt
2 cups brown sugar
4½ quarts ketchup
2½ cups vinegar
3 quarts water

1. Brown ground beef with chopped onion and celery. Drain excess fat. Combine all ingredients except water. Begin simmering. Add water, 1 cup at a time.

2. Simmer several hours.

Variations:
Substitute chicken, turkey, lamb or pork for ground beef.
Use meat broth instead of water when using chicken or turkey.

Barbecued Hamburger

Erma Kauffman
Cochranville, PA
Media Mennonite Church

Makes 8 servings

2 lbs. ground beef
1 small onion
½ cup ketchup
2 Tbsp. brown sugar
2 tsp. mustard
1 cup tomato juice
1 tsp. Worcestershire sauce
  (optional)

1. Brown ground beef with onion. Drain excess fat. Add all remaining ingredients.
2. Simmer about 20 minutes. Add extra tomato juice if mixture appears too dry.
3. Serve with hamburger rolls.

Variation:
Substitute chicken or turkey for ground beef.
Alta M. Ranck
Lancaster, PA

Sloppy Joes

Carolyn Hartman
Harrisonburg, VA
Park View Mennonite Church

Makes 10 servings

1 lb. ground beef
1 cup onion, finely chopped
1 cup celery, finely chopped
1 Tbsp. brown sugar

1 Tbsp. prepared mustard
1 Tbsp. Worcestershire sauce
1 Tbsp. vinegar
1 tsp. salt
1 cup ketchup

1. Brown ground beef and drain excess fat. Add all remaining ingredients.
2. Cover and simmer for 30 minutes.

Carry-In Casserole

LaVerna Klippenstein
Winnipeg, MB
Home Street Mennonite Church

Makes 6-8 servings

1 lb. ground beef
2 cups diced celery
1 cup chopped onions
1 can Chinese vegetables
2 cans cream of mushroom
  soup
2 Tbsp. soy sauce
3-4 cups cooked rice

1. Brown ground beef, celery and onions. Add all remaining ingredients.
2. Bake at 350° for 30-40 minutes or until heated through.

Six Layer Casserole

Mrs. Frank Neufeld
Didsbury, AB
Bergthal Mennonite Church

Makes about 8 servings

2 medium potatoes, sliced
2 medium onions, chopped
1 lb. ground beef
2 cups chopped carrots
1 cup cooked rice
1 quart canned tomatoes
Salt and pepper

1. Layer ingredients in greased casserole dish in following order: potatoes, onions, ground beef, carrots, rice, tomatoes. Salt and pepper to taste.
2. Bake at 300° for at least 2 hours. As this bakes, you may need to add more tomatoes.

Variations:
Brown ground beef and drain excess fat before putting into casserole. Sprinkle 1 Tbsp. brown sugar over dish before baking.
Hettie Conrad
Colorado Springs, CO

At our chuch we have each family bring this same dish. We then pour all dishes together into our electric roasters. This saves oven space and keeps meal warm until time for serving.
Virginia Graber
Freeman, SD
Salem Zion Mennonite Church

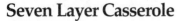

Seven Layer Casserole

Irma Bowman
Akron, PA
Akron Mennonite Church

Makes 12-15 servings

1 cup uncooked rice
Salt and pepper to taste
1 12-oz. can whole kernel
   corn
2 8-oz. cans tomato sauce
1 cup water
1/2 cup chopped onion
1/2 cup chopped green
   pepper
2 lbs. ground beef
6-8 slices lean bacon

1. In ungreased shallow casserole dish spread uncooked rice. Salt and pepper to taste. Add corn.
2. Mix 1/2 cup water with 1 can tomato sauce. Spoon over corn. Sprinkle with onion and green pepper.
3. Crumble uncooked ground beef over dish. Salt and pepper to taste.
4. Combine remaining can tomato sauce with 1/2 cup water. Spoon over meat.
5. Cut bacon slices into fourths and arrange over top.
6. Cover and bake at 375° for about 1 hour. Uncover last 15 minutes to brown.

Hamburger and Rice for Crockpot

Reta Martin
Waterloo, ON
St. Jacobs Mennonite Church

Makes 8-10 servings

1 lb. ground beef
1 small onion, chopped
1/2 cup chopped celery
1/2 cup chopped peppers
2 cups uncooked rice
5 cups tomato juice
1 1/2 tsp. salt
1 tsp. chili powder
1/2 tsp. oregano

1. Brown meat along with onion, celery and peppers. Add rice, tomato juice and seasonings. Bring to a full boil.
2. Put into crockpot and cook on low for 2-4 hours.

Hearty Skillet Meal

Elva Evers
North English, IA
Wellman Mennonite Church

Makes 4 servings

1 lb. ground beef
1/4 cup chopped onion
1/2 cup uncooked rice
1 cup diced carrots
1 cup diced potatoes
1/2 tsp. garlic salt
1-1 1/2 cups water
2 Tbsp. soy sauce (optional)
1 tsp. salt or less
1/4 tsp. pepper

1. Sauté ground beef and onion. Drain excess fat. Stir in rice, carrots, potatoes and garlic salt. Add water, cover and simmer 40 minutes.
2. Immediately before serving, stir in soy sauce, salt and pepper.

I always prepare this meal in my electric skillet which can be plugged in at church.

Hamburger Casserole

Selma Sauder
Pettisville, OH
Tedrow Mennonite Church

Makes 6-8 servings

1 lb. ground beef
1 large onion, diced
1 cup diced celery
1 cup diced carrots
1 cup rice
3 beef bouillon cubes
3 cups hot water
1 pkg. frozen peas
1 can cream of mushroom
   soup

1. Brown ground beef and onion together. Drain off excess juice and fat.
2. Combine bouillon cubes and hot water.
3. Combine all ingredients in a casserole dish. Mix well.
4. Bake at 350° for 1 1/2 hours.

Ground Beef Soup Casserole

Wilma Roeschley
Hinsdale, IL
Lombard Mennonite Church

Makes 4-6 servings

1 lb. ground beef
¼ cup chopped onion
1 can cream of mushroom
  soup
1 can chicken noodle soup
½ cup uncooked rice
2 cups water

1. Brown ground beef and onion and drain off excess fat. Place in baking dish.
2. Add all remaining ingredients and mix thoroughly.
3. Cover and bake at 350° for 1½ hours. Add extra water during baking if dish appears dry.

Ground Beef and Wild Rice Casserole

Lillian F. Gardner
Crystal, MN
New Hope Mennonite Brethren Church

Makes 10 servings

½ cup chopped celery
1 large onion, chopped
1⅓ lbs. ground beef
⅔ cup wild rice, prepared
1 can cream of mushroom
  soup
1 can cream of chicken soup

8-oz. jar mushroom pieces
4-oz. can sliced water
  chestnuts
2 tsp. soy sauce
2 tsp. Worcestershire sauce
Sliced almonds

1. Sauté celery, onion and ground beef in skillet. Drain excess fat. Add all ingredients except almonds and mix thoroughly.
2. Pour into greased 9" x 13" baking dish.
3. Bake at 350° for 30 minutes. Cover with sliced almonds. Bake an additional 30 minutes.

Ground Meat Jambalaya

Herman Cortez Jr.
Des Allemands, LA

Makes 6 servings

1 lb. ground beef
1 Tbsp. steak sauce
1 egg
8-oz. can tomato sauce
¼ cup barbecue sauce
¼ cup mustard
1 Tbsp. cayenne pepper
1 tsp. garlic salt
1 cup water
Salt and pepper to taste
1 cup uncooked rice

1. Combine ground beef, steak sauce and egg. Brown in skillet. Add all remaining ingredients except rice. Bring to a boil.
2. Add rice and bring to a boil again. Reduce heat to simmer.

3. Cover and simmer for 20 minutes. Remove lid and simmer several minutes longer.

Spanish Rice

Ruth Ann Zeiset
Mohnton, PA
Hampden Mennonite Church

Makes 6-8 servings

1 lb. ground beef
2 small onions, chopped
1 green pepper, chopped
1½ tsp. salt or less
¼ tsp. pepper
1 tsp. chili powder
4 cups cooked rice
2 cups cooked tomatoes

1. Brown ground beef, onions and green pepper. Drain excess fat and add salt, pepper and chili powder. Add rice.
2. Place in crockpot and pour tomatoes over rice and meat.
3. Cook on high for several hours or bake at 375° for 50 minutes.

Variation:
Add 1 tsp. Worcestershire sauce to ingredients. Add water if dish appears too dry.
         Loretta Krahn
      Mountain Lake, MN
    Bethel Mennonite Church

Chinese Hamburger Casserole

Bernita Martin Boyts
Shawnee Mission, KS

Makes 8 servings

1½ lbs. ground beef
2 medium onions, chopped
1 cup chopped celery
1 can cream of mushroom
  soup
1 can cream of chicken soup
1 cup bean sprouts, drained
1½ cups warm water
½ cup uncooked rice
¼ cup soy sauce
¼ tsp. pepper
10-oz. can chow mein
  noodles

1. Brown ground beef.
Add onions, celery, soups,
bean sprouts and water. Stir
in rice, soy sauce and pepper. Turn into greased 9" x
13" pan.
2. Cover and bake at 350°
for 30 minutes. Uncover and
bake 30 minutes longer. Top
with chow mein noodles and
bake another 15 minutes.

Variations:

*Substitute 1 ¼ cups un-
cooked minute rice and 1 can
Chinese vegetables for rice and
bean sprouts.*

Doris Schrock
Goshen IN
Yellow Creek Mennonite Church

*Substitute 1½ lbs. ground
turkey browned in 2 Tbsp. cooking oil for ground beef.*

Bernita Martin Boyts
Shawnee Mission, KS

Chinese Stir-Fry Rice

Eileen Lehman
Kidron, OH
Sonnenberg Mennonite Church

Makes 10 servings

2-3 cups uncooked rice
½ lb. ground beef
1 green pepper, chopped
1 onion, chopped
2 carrots, finely cut
2-3 Tbsp. cooking oil
1 cup peas, lightly cooked
Water chestnuts (optional)
Soy sauce

1. Prepare rice and cool.
2. Brown ground beef and
drain excess fat.
3. Heat 1½ Tbsp. cooking
oil in wok. Add ½ of each of
following ingredients: rice,
ground beef, green pepper,
onion and carrots. Stir fry.
Add ½ of peas and ½ of
water chestnuts and heat
through.
4. Repeat step 3 with re-
maining ingredients.
5. Serve with soy sauce.

Curried Rice

Erma J. Sider
Fort Erie, ON
Riverside Chapel Brethren in Christ

Makes 6-8 servings

2 cups uncooked rice
1 medium onion, chopped
1 Tbsp. cooking oil
2-3 tsp. curry powder
1 tsp. ground coriander

1 tsp. ground cumin
½ tsp. cinnamon
¼ tsp. black pepper
1 tsp. salt
2 Tbsp. lemon juice *or*
  vinegar
1 lb. lean ground beef
1 cup tomato juice

1. Prepare rice according
to directions.
2. While rice cooks, sauté
onion in cooking oil until
golden brown.
3. Mix together all spices
and lemon juice or vinegar.
Add mixture to onions. Stir
fry lightly. Add ground beef
and allow to brown slightly.
Add tomato juice and sim-
mer for 15 minutes. If necessary, add water.
4. Pour mixture into baking
dish; add rice and toss lightly.
5. Bake at 325° for 20 minutes.

Pizza Rice Casserole

Gladys Sprunger
Berne, IN
First Mennonite Church of Berne

Makes 6 servings

2 cups cooked rice
2 cups cottage cheese
¾ lb. ground beef *or* turkey
1 onion, chopped
2 cups tomato sauce
¼ tsp. garlic salt
1 tsp. brown sugar
1 tsp. salt
Pepper
½ tsp. oregano
1 tsp. parsley flakes
1 cup shredded cheese

1. Combine rice with cottage cheese.

2. Brown ground beef or turkey and onion in large skillet. Add tomato sauce, garlic salt, brown sugar, salt, pepper, oregano and parsley flakes. Cover and simmer 15 minutes.

3. Layer into greased 2-quart casserole in following order: 1/3 of rice mixture, 1/3 of meat sauce. Repeat two times and top with shredded cheese.

4. Bake at 325° for 30-40 minutes or until hot and bubbly.

Pizza Casserole

Carolyn Slaubaugh Yoder
Wellman, IA
West Union Mennonite Church

Makes 10-12 servings

1 lb. ground beef
1 medium onion, diced
Salt and pepper to taste
1 can cream of mushroom soup
1 can tomato soup
1/4 tsp. thyme
1/4 tsp. oregano
1/4 tsp. garlic powder
1 cup minute rice
Grated cheese

1. Brown ground beef and onion. Salt and pepper to taste.

2. Mix soups, seasonings and rice and simmer for 5 minutes. Combine two mixtures.

3. Pour into casserole dish and top with grated cheese.

4. Bake at 350° for 30 minutes.

Mossetti

Annalee Yordy
Morton, IL

Makes 12 or more servings

1 small bunch celery, chopped
2 large red onions, chopped
1 large green pepper, chopped
2 Tbsp. cooking oil
2 lbs. ground chuck
6 ozs. wide noodles
3/4 cup stuffed olives
8-oz. can mushrooms
16-oz. can tomato sauce
1 can tomato soup
6-oz. can tomato paste
Salt and pepper to taste
Dash Tabasco sauce
1/2 tsp. garlic powder
3 cups grated cheddar cheese

1. Brown celery, onions and pepper in oil. Remove vegetables from oil.

2. Brown ground chuck slowly. Drain excess fat and mix with vegetables.

3. Cook noodles according to package directions. Drain. Add noodles to meat and vegetables. Add olives, mushrooms with juice, tomato sauce, tomato soup and tomato paste. Mix thoroughly. Add seasonings and adjust to taste. Add grated cheese and mix well. Spoon into large, greased casserole dish.

4. Bake at 300° for 1 hour or until thoroughly heated.

Overnight Casserole

Velma Esch
Mio, MI
Fairview Mennonite Church

Makes 12-15 servings

2 cups cooked macaroni
2 1/2 cups milk
2 cans creamed soup*
1 onion, chopped
4 hard-boiled eggs
1 cup shredded cheese
1 lb. meat**

*Choose from cream of mushroom, cream of celery or cream of chicken, according to what is available.

**Choose from chopped ham, chopped chicken, ground beef or canned beef, according to what is available.

1. Prepare evening before fellowship meal. Brown choice of meat. Mix all ingredients. Pour into casserole dish and refrigerate until next morning.

2. Bake at 375° for 1 hour.

Grandma's Casserole

Diana Yaeger
Carlock, IL
Carlock Mennonite Church

Makes 8-10 servings

1 lb. ground beef
1 small onion, diced
Salt and pepper to taste
6 ozs. noodles
2 cups frozen peas
1 cup cream of mushroom
   soup
1 small can mushrooms
4 ozs. cream cheese

1. Brown ground beef with onion and salt and pepper. Drain excess fat.
2. Cook noodles. Add peas for last 5 minutes of cooking time. Drain.
3. Mix together all ingredients except cream cheese and heat through.
4. Add cream cheese and let melt. Serve

Yum-e-setti

Retha Schlabach
Millersburg, OH
Longenecker Mennonite Church

Makes 6-8 servings

1 lb. ground beef
1 cup chopped celery
1 can cream of tomato soup
1 pkg. wide noodles
Salt to taste
1 can cream of chicken soup
1 lb. Velveeta cheese,
   grated

1. Brown ground beef and celery in skillet, stirring occasionally. Drain excess fat. Add tomato soup.
2. Cook noodles, salted to taste, until tender. Drain. Add chicken soup.
3. Layer ground beef and noodle mixtures into casserole dish. Cover with Velveeta cheese.
4. Bake at 300° for 1 hour.

Variations:
Layer into crockpot and plug in at church on low heat. There are always plenty of outlets and it saves oven space.
Priscilla Falb
Dalton, OH
Martins Mennonite Church

Add 1 lb. peas to mixture about 10 minutes before serving.
Mary Hochstedler
Kokomo, IN
Sonnenberg Mennonite Church

Add 1 cup chopped green peppers and 1 can cream of mushroom soup to ground beef before heating.
Janet J. Sprunger
Kidron, OH
Salem Mennonite Church

Hamburger Noodle Casserole

Mary Grieser
Jefferson, OR
Bethany Mennonite Church

Makes 8-10 servings

1 lb. ground beef
1 small onion, chopped
1 Tbsp. diced green pepper

6 ozs. noodles
1/4 tsp. salt
1/2 lb. mozzarella cheese,
   grated
1 can cream of mushroom
   soup
1/2 soup can milk

1. Brown ground beef, onion and pepper together. Drain excess fat.
2. Cook noodles in salted water. Drain and rinse.
3. Arrange ground beef mixture, noodles and grated cheese in layers in casserole dish, reserving some cheese for top. Thin mushroom soup with milk and pour over each layer. Top with grated cheese.
4. Bake at 350° for 1/2 hour.

Meat and Noodle Casserole

Lois Brubacher
Waterloo, ON
Rockway Mennonite Church

Makes 15-20 servings

1 1/2 lbs. ground beef
4 1/2 cups chopped onions
1 green pepper, chopped
28-oz. can tomato sauce
1 tsp. garlic powder
1 tsp. paprika
1 tsp. oregano
1 tsp. sweet basil
1/4 tsp. salt
1/8 tsp. pepper
8-oz. pkg. noodles
1/2 lb. mozzarella cheese,
   grated
1/8 cup butter
1/2 cup Parmesan cheese

1. Brown meat, add onions and green pepper and continue cooking until vegetables are barely tender. Drain excess fat.

2. Add tomato sauce, garlic powder, paprika, oregano, basil, salt and pepper. Simmer while noodles are cooking.

3. In large kettle cook noodles in boiling, salted water for 6 minutes. Drain well. Add to meat mixture. Place in 3-quart casserole dish or 9" x 13" baking pan. Dot with mozzarella cheese and butter.

4. Bake at 350° for 30 minutes. Sprinkle with Parmesan cheese and return to oven for another 15 minutes or until hot and bubbly.

I often mix this dish ahead of time and freeze it. It will keep as long as three months. I let it thaw and bake it while we are preparing for church on Sunday morning.

Macaroni Beef Bake

Frances Schrag
Newton, KS
First Mennonite Church

Makes 10 servings

2 cups macaroni
1 lb. ground beef
½ cup chopped onion
½ cup chopped green
**   pepper**
2 cups cooked tomatoes
¼ tsp. oregano
¼ tsp. crushed sweet basil

1½ tsp. salt
¼ tsp. pepper
1 cup shredded cheddar
**   cheese**

1. Cook macaroni according to directions. Drain.

2. Brown ground beef, onion and green pepper. Drain excess fat. Add macaroni, tomatoes and seasonings. Spoon into greased 9" x 13" baking dish.

3. Bake at 350° for 20-25 minutes or until bubbly. Spread cheese over top for the last few minutes of baking time.

Pizza Macaroni Casserole

Gladys Thiessen
Hillsboro, KS
Hillsboro Mennonite Church

Makes 12 servings

1½ lbs. ground beef
15-oz. jar pizza sauce
4-oz. can sliced mushrooms
1 Tbsp. oregano
1 tsp. garlic salt
1¾ cups macaroni
½ cup milk
2 cups shredded mozzarella
**   cheese**

1. Brown ground beef and drain excess fat. Stir in pizza sauce, undrained mushrooms, oregano and garlic salt.

2. Meanwhile, cook macaroni. Drain and mix with milk.

3. In large casserole dish

arrange several layers of meat, macaroni and cheese. Top with cheese.

4. Cover and bake at 350° for 30 minutes.

Variation:

Add ¼ cup chopped green olives and 1 cup sliced pepperoni to the ground beef mixture.

Darlene Janzen
Butterfield, MN
Evangelical Mennonite Church

Hamburger Macaroni Goulash

Sharon Lantzer
Galeton, PA
Hebron Tabernacle

Makes 16-18 servings

½ cup diced onion
½ cup diced green pepper
1½ lbs. ground beef
1 cup tomato soup
½ can water
8-oz. can tomato sauce
16-oz. whole tomatoes
½ lb. elbow macaroni

1. Sauté onions, green pepper and ground beef until browned. Drain excess fat. Add all other ingredients except macaroni. Simmer for about ½ hour.

2. Meanwhile, cook macaroni lightly. Drain and rinse.

3. Add macaroni to meat mixture and heat through. Keep warm at church in a crockpot.

Beef Chow Mein Noodle Casserole

Helen Rose Pauls
Sardis, BC
Sardis Community Church

Makes 8 servings

1½ lbs. ground beef
½ cup chopped celery
½ cup chopped onion
1 can cream of mushroom
  soup
½ cup milk
1 cup peas
Salt and pepper to taste
10 ozs. chow mein noodles

1. Stir fry ground beef, onions and celery. Drain excess fat.
2. Add mushroom soup, milk and peas. Salt and pepper to taste.
3. Fold in chow mein noodles. Spoon into 2-quart casserole dish.
4. Bake at 350° for 30 minutes.

Variation:
Substitute 2 7-oz. cans tuna, drained and ¼ lb. salted cashew nuts for 1½ lb. hamburger, 1 cup peas and salt.

Jessie Penner
Bakersfield, CA

Norma's Noodle Casserole

Gladys Stoesz
Akron, PA
Akron Mennonite Church

Makes 6-8 servings

8 ozs. noodles
8-oz. pkg. cream cheese
1 cup cottage cheese
½ cup sour cream
3 Tbsp. butter, melted
1½ lbs. ground beef
⅓ cup chopped onion
1 Tbsp. chopped green
  pepper
2 cups canned tomatoes
½ cup tomato soup
1 tsp. Worcestershire sauce

1. Cook noodles according to directions. Drain and set aside.
2. Mix together cream cheese, cottage cheese, sour cream and butter. Set aside.
3. Brown ground beef and drain excess fat. Add all remaining ingredients and stir until heated through.
4. In greased casserole dish layer ½ of noodles, all of cheese mixture and ½ of noodles. Top with meat and tomato sauce.
5. Bake at 350° for 30-45 minutes.

Chinese Dumplings

Jean Yan
Regina, SK
Chinese Fellowship

Makes 20-25 dumplings

1 lb. ground beef and pork
2 small onions, finely
  chopped
1 Tbsp. finely chopped
  ginger root
3 cloves garlic, minced
½ tsp. salt
1 Tbsp. soy sauce
1 large egg
½ tsp. sugar
½ Tbsp. sesame oil
2 green onions, finely
  chopped
3 cups flour
1¼ cups water, room
  temperature

1. Combine ground beef, onions, ginger root, garlic, salt, soy sauce, egg, sugar, oil and green onions. Set aside.
2. Put flour in a deep bowl. Make a well and gradually add water, working it into the flour to make a soft dough. Knead until smooth, about 10 minutes. Cover with a wet towel and set aside for 1 hour.
3. Divide dough into two pieces. With palm of hand roll dough into long, narrow roll, about 1½ inches in diameter. Cut into ½-inch lengths. Roll each piece into a 3-inch round.
4. Place 1 Tbsp. meat mixture in center of each round of dough. Pinch edges together, sealing the dumpling.
5. Boil in deep water for 7 minutes. Serve.

Lazy Man's Cabbage Rolls

Verla Fae Haas
Bluesky, AB

Makes 14 servings

¾ large head cabbage
4 cups uncooked rice
3 onions, chopped
2 lbs. ground beef
2 tsp. salt
1½ tsp. pepper
Garlic powder or garlic salt
¼ cup brown sugar
2 quarts tomato juice
4 cups water

1. In a large roaster spread cabbage leaves across bottom of pan. Shred remaining cabbage. Add layer of rice, onions and ground beef. Repeat layers, starting with shredded cabbage.

2. Sprinkle with seasonings and brown sugar. Pour tomato juice and water over everything.

3. Cover tightly and bake at 325° for 2½-3 hours. Or start at 350 f. for ½ hour and finish at 300° for 2 hours.

Variation:
Dissolve ¼ cup beef base with water and tomato juice.

Jean E. Bender
Williamsville, NY
Harris Hill Mennonite Church

Minnesota Michigan Hamburger Casserole

Melba Handrich
Fairview, MI

Makes 6-8 servings

4-5 potatoes, sliced
1 lb. ground beef
1 can vegetable soup
1 can cream of mushroom soup
Salt and pepper to taste

1. Layer potatoes in bottom of greased 2-quart casserole dish.

2. Brown ground beef and spread over potato layer. Add vegetable soup and mushroom soup. Season to taste.

3. Cover and bake at 325° for 1½ hours or at 400° for 1 hour.

Peasant's Offering

Naomi E. Fast
Newton, KS
Goessel Mennonite Church

Makes 10-12 servings

2 Tbsp. cooking oil
1 medium onion, diced
1 lb. lean ground beef
1 medium head cabbage, grated
2½ tsp. salt
½ tsp. black pepper
1 tsp. paprika
1 cup sour cream
5-6 large potatoes
1 cup milk or less
1 Tbsp. margarine
Chopped parsley *or* chives

1. Heat cooking oil in very large skillet. Add onion and sauté lightly. Add ground beef and stir to keep meat loose and fine. Cook just until pink disappears.

2. Gradually add grated cabbage, stirring until all cabbage is well cooked. Add seasonings, adjusting to taste. Remove from heat.

3. Stir in sour cream. Spoon into rectangular baking dish and spread evenly over bottom. Keep hot in oven.

4. Dice and cook potatoes. Mash with milk and margarine until desired consistency. Layer mashed potatoes over cabbage mixture.

5. Garnish with chopped parsley or chives and serve.

Hamburger Green Bean Pie

Joyce Hofer
Morton, IL
Trinity Mennonite Church

Makes 8 servings

1 lb. ground beef
½ lb. sausage
1 medium onion, chopped
¼ tsp. basil
¼ tsp. savory
¼ tsp. thyme
¼ tsp. marjoram
Salt and pepper to taste
2½ cups green beans, drained
1 can condensed tomato soup
3 cups mashed potatoes

1. Brown meats and onion. Drain excess fat. Add seasonings, adjusting to personal taste. Add green beans and soup. Spoon into greased 2-quart casserole.
2. Prepare mashed potatoes. Spoon in mounds over meat and green bean mixture.
3. Bake at 350° for 40 minutes.

Hamburger Green Bean Casserole

Maxine Hershberger
Dalton, OH
Salem Mennonite Church

Makes 6 servings

1 lb. ground chuck
1 small onion, chopped
½ tsp. salt
Dash pepper
1 tsp. Worcestershire sauce
4 medium potatoes, sliced
1 quart green beans, drained
1 can cream of chicken soup
1 cup milk

1. Brown meat and onion in skillet. Drain excess fat. Season with salt, pepper and Worcestershire sauce.
2. Layer meat, raw potatoes, green beans, soup and milk in 2½-quart casserole dish.
3. Cover and bake at 350° for 1 hour or until potatoes are done.

Variation:
Substitute 1 cup white sauce seasoned with chicken soup base for canned chicken soup.

Hamburger Corn Bake

Loretta Good, Greensboro, NC;
Lanae Waltner, Freeman, SD;
Verda Schrag, Freeman, SD

Makes 10-15 servings

2 lbs. ground beef
½ cup chopped onion
12-oz. can whole kernel corn or 2 pints frozen corn
1 can cream of chicken soup
1 can cream of mushroom soup
1 cup sour cream
¼ cup chopped pimento
¾ tsp. salt or less
¼ tsp. pepper
3 cups noodles
1 cup soft bread crumbs
2 Tbsp. butter, melted

1. Brown ground beef and onion. Drain excess fat. Stir in corn, soups, sour cream, pimento, salt and pepper. Mix well.
2. Meanwhile, cook noodles and drain. Stir noodles into meat mixture. Spoon into 3-quart casserole dish.
3. Combine bread crumbs and melted butter and sprinkle over mixture.
4. Bake at 350° for 30-40 minutes or until heated through.

Stuffed Zucchini

Mrs. Loyal D. Gerber
Archbold, OH
Zion Mennonite Church

Makes 12 or more servings

2-3 large zucchini
1 lb. lean ground beef
1 medium onion, chopped
2 tomatoes, peeled and
    chopped
Salt and pepper to taste
2 eggs, beaten
2 Tbsp. Parmesan cheese
½ cup bread crumbs
Parsley, chopped fine
½ cup uncooked rice
    (optional)
1½ cups tomato sauce

1. Cut off both ends of zucchini, core, rinse and drain.
2. Sauté ground beef and onion. Add tomatoes, salt and pepper. Cook on low heat for 30 minutes. Cool.
3. Add eggs, cheese, bread crumbs, parsley and rice, if desired. Mix lightly and stuff zucchini. (If using rice, allow for expansion.)
4. Place stuffed zucchini in greased baking dish. Pour tomato sauce over zucchini.
5. Cover and bake at 350° for 1½-2 hours.

Zucchini Casserole

Elva Evers
North English, IA
Wellman Mennonite Church

Makes 6 servings

3 cups sliced zucchini
    squash
1 cup water
1 lb. ground beef
1 medium onion, chopped
½ green pepper, chopped
    (optional)
2 Tbsp. uncooked rice
½ cup water
⅛ tsp. paprika
1 can condensed tomato
    soup
⅛ tsp. pepper
1 cup cheese, grated
2 cups toasted bread cubes

1. Boil unpeeled and sliced squash in water.
2. Brown ground beef, onion and green pepper in electric skillet. Drain excess fat.
3. Add squash and all remaining ingredients except bread cubes to electric skillet. Cook at 225° for 1 hour with vent closed. Immediately before serving, top with bread cubes and steam several minutes.

I usually mix everything at home, take skillet to church and finish the 1 hour of cooking time during Sunday school.

Beef Zucchini

Ruth Heatwole
Charlottesville, VA
Charlottesville Mennonite Church

Makes 6 servings

1 lb. ground beef
½ cup chopped onion
1 small clove garlic
5-6 zucchini, sliced
½ cup cracker crumbs
1 tsp. salt
¼ tsp. pepper
⅛ tsp. oregano
¼ cup flour
¼ tsp. pepper
2 cups milk
1 cup grated cheddar cheese

1. Brown ground beef and onion in electric skillet. Drain drippings and reserve.
2. Add garlic, zucchini, cracker crumbs, salt, ¼ tsp. pepper and oregano. Stir well and add a little water if needed. Cover and steam about 5-10 minutes or until zucchini is tender.
3. Meanwhile, prepare a cheese sauce in 1-quart saucepan. To reserved beef drippings add flour and ¼ tsp. pepper, stirring until bubbly. Add 2 cups milk and heat, stirring constantly, until mixture begins to thicken. Turn heat very low and add cheddar cheese. Stir until cheese has melted.
4. Add cheese sauce to zucchini mixture in skillet.
5. Reheat in electric skillet immediately before serving.

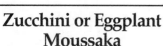

Zucchini or Eggplant Moussaka

Jewel Showalter
Irwin, OH
Mechanicsburg Christian Fellowship

Makes 6-8 servings

4 medium zucchini *or*
  2 large eggplant
1 cup cooking oil
1 lb. ground beef
1 onion, chopped
1 green pepper, chopped
1 tsp. salt
¼ tsp. pepper
3 cups homemade tomato
  sauce
Yogurt *or* sour cream

1. Cut zucchini or eggplant into ¼-inch rounds.
2. In saucepan heat cooking oil. Deep fry vegetable. Drain and spread across bottom of 9" x 13" baking pan.
3. Brown ground beef, onion and green pepper. Drain excess fat. Add salt, pepper and tomato sauce. Simmer 10-15 minutes. Spoon meat mixture over deep fried zucchini or eggplant.
4. Immediately before serving, warm at 350° for about 30 minutes. Serve alone or with rice, noodles or macaroni. Top with a dollop of yogurt or sour cream.

Zesty Italian Casserole

Barbara A. Yoder
Indianapolis, IN
First Mennonite Church

Makes 8-10 servings

2 lbs. ground beef
¼ cup chopped onion
1 pkg. spaghetti sauce mix
8-oz. can tomato sauce
1½ cups mozzarella cheese,
  shredded
½ cup sour cream
8-oz. can crescent dinner
  rolls
2 Tbsp. butter
⅓ cup Parmesan cheese

1. Brown ground beef and onions. Drain excess fat. Stir in spaghetti mix and tomato sauce. Remove from heat and spoon into ungreased 9" x 13" baking dish.
2. Combine mozzarella cheese and sour cream. Spoon over meat sauce.
3. Separate crescent rolls and place rectangles over cheese.
4. Melt butter and combine with Parmesan cheese. Spread over dough.
5. Bake at 375° for 18-25 minutes or until deep golden brown.

Sweet and Sour Lentil Bake

Helene Funk
Laird, SK
Tiefengrund Rosenort Mennonite
Church

Makes 6-8 servings

½ lb. ground beef *or* pork
  sausage
4 cups cooked lentils
2 Tbsp. margarine
1 tsp. curry powder
¼ tsp. cayenne pepper
1 tsp. salt
1 large onion, chopped
1 large carrot, grated
1-2 cloves garlic (optional)
1 tart apple, chopped
1 Tbsp. cornstarch
¼ cup brown sugar
¼ cup vinegar
2 tsp. Worcestershire sauce
½ cup chicken stock

1. Brown ground beef or sausage, breaking it up. Drain and add cooked lentils.
2. In separate skillet melt margarine and sauté curry, cayenne, salt, onion, carrot, garlic and apple for 5 minutes.
3. In small bowl combine cornstarch and brown sugar. Slowly add vinegar, mixing until smooth. Add Worcestershire sauce and chicken stock.
4. Combine all ingredients. Spoon into greased casserole dish.
5. Cover and bake at 325° for 45 minutes or until bubbly. If mixture seems too dry, add more chicken stock.

Beef and Nacho Casserole

Ruth Brunk
Sarasota, FL
Bahia Vista Mennonite Church

Makes 10 servings

1½ lbs. lean ground beef
½ lb. pork sausage
1 ¼ cups chopped onions
2 cloves garlic, minced
1 cup sour cream
8-oz. can tomato sauce
7-oz. can chopped green chilies
6-oz. can tomato paste
4.2-oz. can chopped ripe olives, drained
8-oz. pkg. tortilla chips, crumbled coarsely
12 ozs. Monterey Jack cheese, shredded
Paprika

1. In large skillet sauté beef and sausage. Drain excess fat. Add onions and garlic and sauté. Reduce heat. Stir in sour cream, tomato sauce, green chilies, tomato paste and olives. Heat through, but do not boil.
2. In greased, oblong 3-quart baking dish layer ⅔ of tortilla chips, all of meat mixture, remaining chips and cheese. Sprinkle top with paprika.
3. Bake, uncovered, at 375° for 20-25 minutes.

Soybean Hamburger Casserole

Mary E. Martin
Goshen, IN
Benton Mennonite Church

Makes 6-8 servings

2 Tbsp. cooking oil
½ cup chopped onion
1 cup chopped celery
¼ cup chopped green peppers
¼-½ lb. ground beef
1 tsp. salt
⅛ tsp. pepper
½ tsp. seasoned salt
2½ cups cooked soybeans
1¼ cups tomato soup
1 beef bouillon cube dissolved in 1 cup hot water
2 cups cooked rice
½ cup cheese, grated

1. Heat cooking oil in large skillet. Sauté onion, celery, green peppers and ground beef.
2. When meat has browned, add all other ingredients except cheese. Simmer a few minutes. Spoon into greased casserole dish.
3. Bake at 350° for 45 minutes. Remove from oven and top with grated cheese. Return to oven only long enough to melt cheese.

Easy Enchilada Casserole

Betty Kauffman, Lake Odessa, MI;
Elaine Jantzen, Hillsboro, KS

Makes 10-12 servings

2 lbs. ground beef
1 medium onion, chopped
1 can cream of chicken soup
1 can cream of mushroom soup
8-oz. can taco sauce
8-oz. can enchilada sauce
2 7-oz. cans green chilies
10 tortillas
8 ozs. cheddar cheese, grated

1. Brown ground beef and onion and drain. Add undiluted soups, taco sauce, enchilada sauce and green chilies.
2. In 9" x 13" baking dish layer 5 tortillas, thin layer of meat sauce, 5 tortillas and remaining meat sauce. Top with grated cheese.
3. Bake at 350° for 25-30 minutes.

Beef Enchiladas

Jeanette Zacharias
Morden, MB
Barn Swallow Quilters

Makes 6 servings

1 onion, sliced
1 green pepper, sliced
1 red pepper, sliced
1 clove garlic, minced
2 cups ground beef
1½ cups taco sauce
1 tsp. ground cumin
Pepper
6 flour tortillas
1 cup grated cheddar cheese
½ cup sour cream
2 Tbsp. chopped green
   onions

1. Sauté onion, peppers, garlic and ground beef until beef is browned. Drain excess fat. Add taco sauce, cumin and pepper. Heat thoroughly.
2. Place ¼ cup meat mixture in center of each tortilla. Sprinkle with 1 Tbsp. cheddar cheese. Bring edges of tortilla together, overlapping slightly to enclose filling. Arrange, seam side down, in 7" x 11" baking dish.
3. Spoon remaining meat sauce over tortillas. Spoon sour cream down center of dish. Sprinkle with remaining cheese.
4. Bake at 350° for about 30 minutes. Sprinkle with green onions and serve.

Crockpot Tamale Pie

Jeanne Heyerly
Reedley, CA
Reedley First Mennonite Church

Makes 12 servings

Taco Seasoning Mix:
¼ cup dried onion flakes
4 tsp. cornstarch
1 Tbsp. salt
1 Tbsp. chili powder
1 Tbsp. cumin
1 Tbsp. garlic powder
1 Tbsp. hot pepper
1½ tsp. oregano
2 tsp. beef bouillon

Tamale Pie Ingredients:
2 lbs. ground beef
2 Tbsp. Taco Seasoning Mix
1½ cups yellow cornmeal
3 cups milk
2 eggs, beaten
2 16-oz. cans corn
2 16-oz. cans whole tomatoes
2 cups grated cheese

1. To prepare taco seasoning, mix together all ingredients. Store in airtight container.
2. Brown ground beef and drain. Set aside.
3. Mix cornmeal, milk and eggs. Add ground beef, Taco Seasoning Mix, corn and tomatoes. Stir and pour into 5-quart crockpot. (Reduce recipe if crockpot is smaller.)
4. Cover and cook on high for 1 hour or on low for 3½-4 hours.
5. Sprinkle with cheese 10 minutes before serving.

Taco Rice Casserole

Bonnie Heatwole
Springs, PA
Springs Mennonite Church

Makes 8 servings

1 lb. ground beef
½ cup chopped onion
¼ cup chopped green
   pepper
1 pkg. taco seasoning
1½ cups water
8-oz. can tomato sauce
3 cups cooked rice
Velveeta cheese
Taco chips

1. Brown ground beef, onion and green pepper. Drain excess fat. Add taco seasoning and water and cook at least 5 minutes. Add tomato sauce and cooked rice and spoon into baking dish.
2. Top with slices of Velveeta cheese.
3. Bake at 350° until it bubbles.
4. Immediately before serving, add broken taco chips to top of casserole.

Variation:
Serve with chopped lettuce, chopped tomatoes and taco sauce.

B.J. Eberly
East Earl, PA
Christian Fellowship

Tostado Casserole

Annabelle Kratz
Clarksville, MD
Hyattsville Mennonite Church

Makes 8 servings

1 lb. ground beef
15-oz. can tomato sauce
1 pkg. taco seasoning mix
2½ cups corn chips
15 ½-oz. can refried beans
½ cup cheddar cheese,
shredded

1. Brown beef in skillet. Drain. Add 1½ cups tomato sauce and the taco mix, stirring to mix well.
2. Line the bottom of a 7" x 11" baking dish with 2 cups corn chips. Crush remaining chips and set aside.
3. Spoon meat sauce over chips in baking dish.
4. Combine remaining tomato sauce and refried beans and spread over meat sauce.
5. Bake at 375° for 25 minutes. Sprinkle with cheese and crushed chips and bake 5 more minutes or until cheese has melted.

Tacocitas

Doris Ebersole
Archbold, OH
Zion Mennonite Church

Makes 12 servings

16-oz. can refried beans
¼ tsp. salt
½ tsp. cumin
1 cup grated Monterey Jack
cheese
1½ lbs. ground beef
3 7-oz. cans green
chili salsa
12 flour tortillas
2 cups grated cheddar cheese
Chopped tomatoes and
onions (optional)

1. Combine refried beans, salt, cumin and Monterey Jack cheese. Heat on low, stirring frequently.
2. Sauté ground beef and drain excess fat. Add half of chili salsa. Simmer until juice evaporates.
3. Spread each tortilla with hot bean mixture. Place meat mixture across center of each tortilla. Roll up.
4. Place seam side down in greased baking dish. Pour remaining chili salsa over rolled tortillas. Sprinkle with cheddar cheese. Sprinkle with tomatoes and onions if desired.
5. Bake at 350° for 20-30 minutes.

Chimichangas

Lorene Good
Armington, IL
Hopedale Mennonite Church

Makes 6 servings

1 lb. ground beef
2 Tbsp. diced onion
2 Tbsp. chopped green
pepper
8-oz. can tomato sauce
2 Tbsp. chopped garlic
Salt and pepper
16-oz. can pinto beans
1 dozen flour tortillas

1. Brown ground beef. Add onion and green pepper. Add tomato sauce, garlic, salt and pepper. Simmer.
2. Drain and mash pinto beans. Add to beef mixture. Continue cooking on low heat.
3. Microwave prepared tortillas, one at a time, between 2 paper towels for 20 seconds each.
4. Fill each tortilla with about ⅓-½ cup sauce. Roll up and serve warm or chill and serve later.

Hot Tofu

Jean Yan
Regina, SK
Chinese Fellowship

Makes 6 servings

4 Tbsp. cooking oil
2 tsp. Chinese peppers
½ lb. ground beef *or*
    ground pork
1 Tbsp. chopped ginger root
4 hot chilies, crushed
6 pieces tofu, cut in pieces
½ cup soy sauce
4 green onions, chopped
¼ tsp. salt
½ tsp. sugar
2 tsp. cornstarch

1. In a wok heat oil on medium heat. Add Chinese peppers and cook until dark, dark brown. Remove peppers from oil and discard.
2. Add ground beef, ginger and chilies. Stir fry until browned.
3. Turn heat to high and add tofu, stirring constantly. Add soy sauce, green onions, salt and sugar and stir again.
4. Combine cornstarch with a bit of water. Stir cornstarch paste into tofu mixture. Bring to a boil, stirring constantly.
5. Serve with rice.

Meat Pasties

Jeanette Zacharias
Morden, MB
Barn Swallow Quilters

Makes 12 servings

Dough:
2 cups all-purpose flour
½ cup butter
½ tsp. salt
6-7 Tbsp. milk or more

Filling:
¾ lb. ground beef
2 Tbsp. chopped onion
1 Tbsp. chopped bell
    pepper
1 Tbsp. chopped celery
1 tsp. oregano
1 tsp. basil
2 Tbsp. barbecue sauce

1. Combine all ingredients for dough and mix well. Add as much milk as needed to make a soft dough.
2. Divide dough into four parts. Roll each part out thin and cut into 6-inch circles.
3. Combine all filling ingredients. Heat until meat has browned.
4. Place 1 Tbsp. meat on each circle. Moisten edges of dough with water and fold in half to make a turnover. Seal edges well with fork. Prick top to allow steam to escape. Place on ungreased cookie sheet.
5. Bake at 375° for 40 minutes. Serve hot or cold.

Variation:
Add a bit of shredded mozzarella cheese to each circle before sealing.

Pastelon

Carol Glick
Levittown, PR

Makes 6 servings

3 plantains
1 cup milk
⅓ cup butter
½ lb. ground meat
¼ cup minced onion
¼ cup minced green pepper
2 hard-boiled eggs, sliced
12 olives (optional)
2 Tbsp. raisins
½ tsp. salt
Pepper to taste

1. Boil the plantains until soft. Mash them, adding milk and butter. Set aside.
2. In a skillet fry ground meat lightly. Add onion, green pepper, eggs, olives, raisins, salt and pepper. Cook for 5 more minutes.
3. Spread ½ of mashed plantains into greased 9-inch baking dish. Spoon meat mixture over plantains. Spread remaining plantains over meat mixture.
4. Bake, uncovered, at 350° for 20 minutes.

French Canadian Tortiere

Helene Funk
Laird, SK
Tiefengrund Rosenort Mennonite
Church

Makes 6-8 servings

1 lb. lean ground beef
1 lb. lean ground pork
2 medium onions, chopped
¼ tsp. nutmeg
¼ tsp. allspice
½ tsp. sage
½ tsp. salt
½ tsp. pepper
1 cup water
3 Tbsp. flour
¼ cup water
2 9" unbaked pie shells

1. In large saucepan combine beef, pork, onions, seasonings and 1 cup water. Bring to a gentle boil, stirring occasionally.
2. Dissolve flour in ¼ cup water. Stir into meat mixture. Boil, stirring until thickened.
3. Spoon filling into pie shell. Cover with remaining shell. Prick top of crust.
4. Bake at 350° for 30 minutes or until golden brown.

Bierocks

Agnes Schertz
Goshen, IN
Goshen College Mennonite Church

Makes 25-30 servings

½ cup warm water
2 pkgs. yeast
1½ cups lukewarm milk
½ cup sugar
2 tsp. salt
2 eggs
½ cup shortening, softened
7-7½ cups flour
2 lbs. ground beef
Onion to taste
½ cup butter
1 medium head cabbage

1. Dissolve yeast in warm water.
2. Combine milk, sugar, salt, eggs, shortening and yeast mixture. Add flour until dough handles easily.
3. Turn onto lightly floured board. Knead until smooth and elastic. Place in greased bowl, turning to grease top of dough.
4. Cover with damp cloth and let rise until double, about 1½ hours. Punch down and let rise again until double, about 30 minutes.
5. Brown ground beef and add onion to taste. Drain.
6. In separate skillet, melt butter. Shred cabbage into skillet and cook until cabbage has wilted. Drain. Mix with ground beef.
7. Divide dough in half and roll out. Cut dough into 4-inch squares.
8. Fill each square with about ¼ cup cabbage and

meat mixture. Fold up corners and pinch together. Seal well and turn upside down on a greased pan. Let rise 15 minutes.
9. Bake at 350° for 15 minutes or until a nice brown.

An attractive sandwich! Today I always reheat mine in the microwave. When we took them in our school lunch pails as children, we ate them cold.

Variation:
Add the following ingredients to the hamburger and cabbage mixture: 1 cup tomato juice, ¼-½ cup ketchup and 2-3 tsp. mustard.

Jessie Penner
Bakersfield, CA

Turkey Main Dishes

Turkey Burgers

Irene Epp
Kindersley, SK
Superb Mennonite Church

Makes 8 servings

2 cups ground turkey
¾ lb. ground beef
2 Tbsp. grated onion
¼ tsp. poultry seasoning
1 can cream of mushroom
  soup
1 egg, beaten
Salt and pepper to taste
Dry bread crumbs
½ cup milk

1. Combine turkey, beef, onion and poultry seasoning. Add ¼ cup undiluted mushroom soup. Reserve remaining soup.
2. Add egg, salt and pepper to meat mixture.
3. Shape into patties and roll each patty in dry bread crumbs. Place in shallow baking dish.
4. Bake at 375° for 20 minutes or until golden brown.
5. Combine milk with remaining mushroom soup. Pour over turkey burgers and heat through.

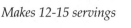

Hot Turkey Salad

Mary Herr and Elsie Lehman
Three Rivers, MI
The Hermitage Community Retreat
Center

Makes 12-15 servings

4 cups cubed, cooked turkey
4 cups chopped celery
1 cup chopped almonds,
  blanched
¾ cup chopped green
  pepper
¼ cup chopped pimento
¼ cup chopped onion
2 tsp. salt
¼ cup lemon juice
1 cup mayonnaise
8 ozs. Swiss cheese, sliced
¼ lb. butter, melted
2 cups cracker crumbs

1. In a large bowl combine turkey, celery, almonds, green pepper, pimento, onion, salt, lemon juice and mayonnaise. Spoon into greased 9" x 13" baking pan. Top with slices of cheese.
2. In small bowl combine melted butter and cracker crumbs. Sprinkle over turkey salad.
3. Bake at 350° for about 45 minutes.

Turkey Meat Loaf

Thelma Harley
Goshen, IN
North Goshen Mennonite Church

Makes 10-12 servings

1½ lbs. ground turkey
1 cup tomato juice
1 cup oatmeal
1 egg, beaten
½ cup chopped onion
⅓ cup grated carrot
2 beef bouillon cubes
¼ cup water
½ tsp. salt
¼ tsp. pepper

1. Dissolve bouillon cubes in ¼ cup water.
2. Combine all ingredients and mix well.
3. Bake in loaf pan at 350° for 1 hour and 10 minutes.

Turkey Potato Surprise

Anna Weber
Atmore, AL
Mennonite Christian Fellowship

Makes 8-10 servings

8 cups boiled, shredded
  potatoes
3 medium onions, chopped
4 Tbsp. butter
4 Tbsp. flour
1 tsp. dried thyme
1 tsp. salt
¼ tsp. black pepper
2 cups evaporated milk
2 cups diced turkey ham
1 cup mayonnaise
2 tsp. Dijon mustard
8 slices bacon *or*
  1 cup bacon bits

1. Prepare potatoes.
2. Sauté onions in butter until soft. Stir in flour, thyme, salt and pepper, stirring until bubbly. Gradually add milk, stirring constantly until thickened. Remove from heat.
3. Fold in turkey ham, mayonnaise, mustard and potatoes. Spoon into greased 2½-quart casserole dish.
4. Bake at 350° for 30 minutes.
5. If using sliced bacon, fry and crumble the pieces.
6. Immediately before serving, sprinkle with crumbled bacon or bacon bits.

Turkey Supreme

Janet Suderman
Indianapolis, IN

Makes 6 servings

2 cups sliced fresh
  mushrooms
1 small onion, chopped
1 cup thinly sliced celery
1 can cream of chicken soup
1 cup milk
2 cups cubed, cooked turkey
2 cups herb-flavored
  stuffing
½ cup sour cream
¼-½ tsp. pepper
¼ cup sliced almonds

1. Combine mushrooms, onion and celery in 2-quart microwave-safe casserole dish.
2. Microwave on high, uncovered, 5-6 minutes or until vegetables are tender, stirring once.
3. Remove from microwave and add soup, milk, turkey, stuffing, sour cream and pepper. Top with sliced almonds.
4. Cover and microwave on high 10-12 minutes or until heated through. Let stand about 5 minutes before serving.

Turkey Casserole

LaVerne Wolfer
Hutchinson, KS
South Hutchinson Mennonite
Church

Makes 12-14 servings

3-4 cups diced, cooked
  turkey
1 lb. hot sausage, cooked
  and drained
1 cup diced onion
1 cup diced green pepper
1 cup diced celery
1 Tbsp. butter
2 4-oz. cans mushrooms
1 cup turkey broth
2 pkgs. slivered almonds
1 lb. cheddar cheese, grated

1. Prepare turkey and sausage. Reserve 1 cup turkey broth.
2. Sauté onion, green pepper and celery in butter. Add mushrooms. Remove from heat.
3. Add turkey, sausage, turkey broth and almonds. Mix well in a large bowl and refrigerate overnight. Spoon into 9" x 13" baking pan.
4. Bake at 350° for 45 minutes. Remove from oven and grate cheese over top. Bake 15 minutes longer.

Turkey Enchilada Casserole

Susan Ortman Goering
Boulder, CO
Boulder Mennonite Church

Makes 10-12 servings

8-oz. pkg. tortilla chips
1½ lbs. ground turkey
1 medium onion, chopped
10-oz. can enchilada sauce
2 cups tomatoes
12-oz. carton cottage cheese
1 egg
8 ozs. cheddar cheese,
   shredded

1. Break tortilla chips into small pieces. Set aside.
2. Brown ground turkey with onion. Add enchilada sauce and tomatoes and mix. Set aside.
3. Combine cottage cheese and egg. Set aside.
4. Layer into casserole dish in following order: tortilla chips, meat mixture, cottage cheese, cheddar cheese. Repeat the layers at least once, ending with cheddar cheese.
5. Bake at 350° for 40 minutes.

When I take this dish to a fellowship meal, I assemble everything the night before and store in the refrigerator until church starts. Since it has been refrigerated, it needs to bake for 1 hour at 350° in order to be warmed through. This makes Sunday morning much less hectic for me.

Jumbulias

Lilli Unrau
Selkirk, MB
Selkirk Christian Fellowship

Makes 4-6 servings

2 Tbsp. margarine
⅓ cup chopped green
   pepper
½ cup chopped onion
1 clove garlic, minced
3 cups water
1½ cups uncooked rice
2 cups cubed, cooked turkey
2 tsp. salt
Dash pepper
2 tsp. Worcestershire sauce
4-oz. can mushroom
   pieces

1. Melt margarine in large saucepan. Add green pepper, onion and garlic. Cook about 10 minutes or until tender. Add water and bring to a boil.
2. Add rice and cover saucepan. Reduce heat to simmer. Cook about 25 minutes or until rice is done.

3. Add meat, salt, pepper, Worcestershire sauce and mushrooms. Simmer over low heat until flavors are blended. Serve.

Ham Main Dishes

Ham Loaf

Beth Selzer
Hesston, KS
Whitestone Mennonite Church

Ruth R. Nissley
Mount Joy, PA
Bethel Mennonite Church

Makes 10-12 servings

Ham Loaf:
1½ lbs. ground ham
1½ lbs. ground beef
2 eggs
1 cup graham cracker
   crumbs
1 cup milk

Sauce:
1 can tomato soup
½ cup water
½ cup vinegar
1 cup brown sugar
1 tsp. prepared mustard

1. Combine all ham loaf ingredients. Form into a loaf and put into baking dish.
2. In a saucepan combine all sauce ingredients and bring to a boil. Pour sauce over ham loaf.
3. Bake at 275° for 2 hours.

Variation:
Substitute 1 cup fine bread crumbs for graham cracker crumbs. Add 2 Tbsp. chopped onion, 2 Tbsp. chopped celery

and 2 Tbsp. chopped green pepper to ham loaf ingredients.

Helen R. Goering
Moundridge, KS
Eden Mennonite
of Rural Moundridge

Ham Balls

Ila Yoder
Hesston, KS
Whitestone Mennonite Church

Makes 30 balls

Meatballs:
1 lb. ground ham
1½ lbs. ground pork
2 cups bread crumbs
2 eggs
1 cup milk

Sauce:
1 cup brown sugar
½ cup water
½ cup vinegar
1 tsp. dry mustard

1. Combine all meatball ingredients and shape into 30 balls. Place ham balls in baking pan or chafing dish.
2. Combine all sauce ingredients and simmer until heated through. Pour sauce over ham balls.
3. Bake or simmer at 300°-325° for 2 hours.

Variations:
Add 2 Tbsp. chopped onion, 2 Tbsp. chopped green pepper and 1 tsp. black pepper to ham ball ingredients.

Wilma Musser
Mechanicsburg, PA

Reduce water measurement in sauce to ⅓ cup and add 4 ozs. crushed pineapple with juice to the ingredients.

Grace A. Zimmerman
Reinholds, PA
Bowmansville Mennonite Church

Ham Rolls Elegante

A. Catharine Boshart
Lebanon, PA
Hereford Mennonite Home Church

Makes 6-8 servings

2 pkgs. frozen broccoli spears
8 slices Swiss cheese
8 slices ham
1 can cream of mushroom soup
½ cup sour cream
1 tsp. mustard

1. Cook broccoli according to package directions and allow to cool. Divide into 8 portions.
2. Place a slice of cheese on each slice of ham. Place 1 portion broccoli on each ham and cheese stack. Roll up securely and place in shallow baking dish, seam side down.
3. Thoroughly blend soup, sour cream and mustard. Pour sauce over ham rolls.
4. Bake, uncovered, at 350° for 20 minutes.

We used this basic recipe to serve 250 women and children at a Mother Daughter Social Dinner. We substituted whole green beans for broccoli spears.

Scalloped Potatoes and Ham

Lydia Yoder
London, OH
Shiloh Mennonite Church

Makes 60-70 servings

20 lbs. potatoes, peeled and diced
10 lbs. ham, cut up
1 gallon milk
1½ cups flour
4 Tbsp. salt
1 tsp. pepper
1½ cups butter *or* margarine
1 lb. Velveeta cheese

1. Prepare potatoes and ham. Place in a large roaster.
2. Take part of the milk and make a thick paste with the flour. Set aside.
3. Bring remaining milk almost to boiling point. Add flour paste, salt and pepper and bring to a full boil. Add butter and cheese and stir until melted.
4. Pour cheese sauce over ham and potatoes in roaster.
5. Bake at 450° for 30 minutes, reduce heat to 350° and bake 30 minutes longer or until done.

Potatoes Au Gratin

Lillian Miller
Leola, PA
Paradise Mennonite Church

Makes 40-50 servings

20 lbs. potatoes, cooked
  and diced
8-10 lbs. ham, diced
3 cans cream of celery soup
5 cans cream of mushroom
  soup
2 lbs. Velveeta cheese, cubed
2 cans evaporated milk
1 pkg. dry taco seasoning

1. Prepare potatoes and
ham. Spoon into large
roaster.
2. Mix all other ingredi-
ents and pour over ham and
potatoes.
3. Bake at 350° until
heated through.

Ham and Scalloped
Potatoes in Crockpot

**Janice Crist, Quinter, KS; Josie Boll-
man, Maumee, OH; Winifred Paul,
Scottdale, PA**

Makes 12 servings

6-8 slices ham, diced
8-10 medium potatoes,
  peeled and thinly sliced
1 large onion, sliced
Salt and pepper to taste
1 cup grated cheddar cheese
1 can cream of mushroom
  soup
Paprika

1. Put ½ of ham, ½ of po-
tatoes and ½ of onion in
crockpot. Sprinkle with salt,
pepper and ½ of grated
cheese. Repeat with remaining ingredients.
2. Spoon soup over top.
3. Cover and cook on low
8-10 hours or on high 4
hours. Immediately before
serving, sprinkle with paprika.

Ham, Carrot and
Potato Casserole

Ferne Miller
Landisville, PA
Landisville Mennonite Church

Makes 6-8 servings

3 cups chopped carrots
3 cups chopped potatoes
1 small onion, diced
4 cups cubed ham
6 ozs. cheese, shredded
1 can cream of mushroom
  soup
Buttered bread crumbs

1. Prepare carrots and put
into large kettle. Add 1 cup
water and begin boiling.
2. Prepare potatoes and
onion and add to carrots. Stir
to mix. Add chunks of ham
and stir again. Cook until
well heated, but not soft.
Add cheese and soup and
stir well. Turn into large casserole dish. Top with buttered bread crumbs.
3. Cover with aluminum
foil and bake at 350° for 1½
hours.

Summertime Potato
and Ham Casserole

Mary Klassen
Winnipeg, MB
Hillsboro Mennonite Church

Makes 4-6 servings

½ cup chopped onion
½ cup chopped green
  pepper
2 Tbsp. butter
1 can cream of celery soup
¼ tsp. pepper
¾ cup milk
4 cups cooked, diced
  potatoes
2 cups cooked, diced ham
½ cup grated cheddar cheese

1. Sauté onion and green
pepper in butter until onion
is transparent. Add soup and
pepper. Gradually add milk,
stirring until smooth.
2. Mix potatoes and ham
in greased casserole dish.
Pour soup mixture over potatoes and ham. Sprinkle with
grated cheese.
3. Bake at 350° for 25-30
minutes or until heated
through.

Soybeans and Ham

Mary Ellen Musser
Reinholds, PA
Gehmans Mennonite Church

Makes 20 servings

2 quarts soybeans
10-12 cups water

½ tsp. salt
1 lb. ham, cubed

1. In a large saucepan bring soybeans and water to a boil. Boil for 2 minutes. Cover, remove from heat and let stand for 1 hour. Add salt and ham.

2. Spoon mixture into large crockpot. Cook on low for 3-4 hours.

Variation:

Substitute 2 Tbsp. butter or margarine for the ham and you have a vegetarian dish.

Asparagus Ham Bake

Elaine Unruh
Moundridge, KS
First Mennonite Church

Makes 6-8 servings

1 can cream of mushroom
  soup
¾ cup milk
2 cups cooked rice
3 cups cubed ham
3 Tbsp. minced onion
½ cup grated cheddar cheese
1 pkg. frozen asparagus
½ cup bread crumbs
2 Tbsp. margarine, melted
Peach slices
Whole cloves

1. Combine soup and milk. Add rice, ham, onion and cheese. Spoon ½ of mixture into 9" x 13" casserole dish. Top with asparagus. Add remaining ham mixture.

2. Combine bread crumbs and melted margarine. Sprin-

---

kle over casserole.

3. Garnish with peach slices and whole cloves.

4. Bake at 375° for 45 minutes. Remove cloves before serving.

Ham Noodle Casserole

Katherine Beachy
Glendive, MT
White Chapel Mennonite Church

Makes 10 servings

8-oz. pkg. noodles
1 cup milk
1 can cream of chicken soup
3 cups cubed ham
¼ cup grated American
  cheese
2 Tbsp. butter
Salt to taste (optional)

1. Cook noodles according to directions and drain.

2. Combine milk and soup.

3. Layer into greased casserole dish: noodles, ham, ½ of grated cheese. Pour soup mixture over other ingredients. Dot with remaining cheese and butter.

4. Bake at 350° for 30 minutes.

Variation:

Combine 2 Tbsp. butter with bread crumbs and top dish with bread crumbs. Bake at 375° for 20-30 minutes.

Wilma Yoder
West Liberty, OH
South Union Mennonite Church

Ham, Macaroni and Cheese Surprise

Jeanette Harder
Garland, TX

Makes 6 servings

2 cups elbow macaroni
3 Tbsp. butter
3 Tbsp. flour
⅛ tsp. pepper
1 cup milk
2 cups grated American
  cheese
2 cups cubed, cooked ham
3-oz. jar mushrooms,
  drained
2 tsp. chopped pimento
¼ cup halved cashews

1. Cook macaroni according to directions. Drain, rinse and set aside.

2. In a saucepan melt butter. Blend in flour and pepper, cooking over low heat until smooth and bubbly. Remove from heat. Stir in milk. Return to heat and bring to a boil, stirring constantly. Boil and stir 1 minute. Add grated cheese and stir until melted.

3. Add macaroni, ham, mushrooms and pimento to white sauce and heat through. Immediately before serving, sprinkle with cashews.

Cheesy Ham Casserole

Hazel L. Miller
Hudson, IL
Carlock Mennonite Church

Makes 4-6 servings

1½ cups corkscrew noodles
½ cup salad dressing
2 cups fresh *or* frozen
  broccoli
1½ cups chopped ham
½ cup chopped peppers
¼ cup milk
1½ cups shredded cheese
¾ cup seasoned croutons

1. Cook noodles according to directions and drain.
2. Combine all ingredients except ½ cup cheese and croutons. Spoon into 1½-quart casserole dish. Sprinkle with remaining cheese and croutons.
3. Bake at 350° for 30 minutes or until heated through.

Ham and Rice Casserole

Mary L. Gaeddert
North Newton, KS
Bethel College Mennonite Church

Makes 8 servings

2 cups cooked rice, unsalted
2 cups cubed ham
½ cup grated cheddar cheese
½ cup evaporated milk
1 can cream of chicken soup
2-4 Tbsp. chopped onion

10-oz. pkg. frozen, chopped
  broccoli
3 Tbsp. butter, melted
¾ cup crushed cornflakes

1. Combine all ingredients except butter and cornflakes. Spoon into greased casserole dish.
2. Combine butter and cornflakes. Top dish with cornflake mixture.
3. Bake at 375° for 40 minutes.

Ham Hocks and Pinto Beans

Joyce M. Marable
Lancaster, PA
South Christian Street Mennonite Church

Makes 8-10 servings

2-3 ham hocks
Water to cover
1 lb. pinto beans
1 large potato, cubed
⅓ cup sugar
Salt
Oregano
Garlic powder

1. In a large saucepan cover ham hocks with water and bring to a boil. Reduce heat and cook slowly for 1 hour.
2. Rinse and sort beans. Add beans and potato to ham hocks. Cook slowly for 2 more hours.
3. Add sugar and season to taste. Cook 1-1½ hours longer or until beans are tender, constantly keeping

water level above meat and stirring occasionally.
4. Serve with rice.

Varenika Casserole

Sharon Reber
Newton, KS

Makes 6-8 servings

10 ozs. noodles
1 lb. cubed ham
1 small onion, chopped
1 cup sour cream
3 cups cottage cheese
1 tsp. salt
1 tsp. pepper

1. Cook noodles according to directions. Drain and set aside.
2. Brown onions and ham. Drain.
3. Combine all ingredients and blend well. Spoon into 2-quart casserole dish.
4. Bake at 350° for 45 minutes to 1 hour.

Curried Fried Rice

Philene Houmphan
Regina, SK
Chinese Fellowship

Makes 4 servings

3 Tbsp. cooking oil
½ Tbsp. curry powder
½ cup shredded onion
½ cup shredded ham
¼ cup shredded carrot

½ tsp. salt
2½ cups cooked rice

1. Heat wok and add cooking oil. Brown curry powder.
2. Sauté onion in curry powder and oil. Add ham and carrot and stir fry lightly. Add salt and rice and stir fry until rice is fried.

Vietnam Fried Rice

Nancy Roth
Colorado Springs, CO
Remnant of Israel Congregation

Mary Jane Miller
Wellman, IA
Kalona Mennonite Church

Makes 4 servings

4 Tbsp. cooking oil
¼-½ lb. cooked or raw meat, cut into strips
3 cloves garlic, minced
1 large onion, chopped
1 tsp. salt
1 tsp. pepper
1 tsp. sugar
1 Tbsp. soy sauce
3 cups cooked rice
1 cup leftover vegetables
2 eggs, beaten

1. Heat cooking oil. Stir fry meat, garlic, onion, salt, pepper, sugar and soy sauce until meat is tender, about 1-2 minutes.
2. Add cooked rice and stir fry an additional 5 minutes.
3. Add any leftover vegetables (peas, green beans, carrots) and stir well into rice mixture.
4. Immediately before serving, add eggs. Over medium heat stir eggs through rice until eggs are cooked.

Korean Fried Rice

Kum Smith
Morton, IL
First Mennonite Church

Makes 6 servings

1 cup long-grain rice
1½ cups water
1 Tbsp. shortening
1 medium white onion, finely chopped
2 large mushrooms, finely chopped
1 medium green pepper, finely chopped *or* 1 cup peas
1 carrot, finely chopped
1 lb. chicken breast *or* 1 lb. steak, finely chopped
Salt and pepper to taste
1 Tbsp. shortening

1. Soak rice in water for 5 minutes. Cover and bring to boil. Cook over medium high heat for 5 minutes. Cover and simmer for 15-20 minutes.
2. Meanwhile, heat 1 Tbsp. shortening in skillet and sauté one vegetable at a time. Clean skillet after each vegetable. Set each vegetable aside.
3. Fry choice of meat and season to taste. Set aside.
4. Stir fry cooked rice in 1 Tbsp. shortening until light brown. Add salt and pepper to taste.
5. Combine all ingredients with small amount of shortening in large skillet and cook until heated.

Fried Rice with Bacon

Millie Glick
Edmonton, AB
Holyrood Mennonite Church

Makes 10-12 servings

2 cups uncooked brown rice
6 slices bacon
1 large onion, diced
8-oz. jar mushrooms, drained
8-oz. jar sliced water chestnuts
2-3 Tbsp. soy sauce

1. Cook the rice according to directions. Do not add salt.
2. Cut bacon into small pieces and fry in an electric skillet. When nearly done, add onion and saute. Add mushrooms and water chestnuts and stir together with bacon and onion.
3. Add cooked rice to skillet and mix thoroughly. Add soy sauce and continue to stir until all ingredients have blended.
4. Put in covered casserole dish to take to fellowship meal.

Savory Rice with Bacon

Grace E. Hess
Lititz, PA
Millport Mennonite Church

Makes 6 servings

½ lb. bacon, diced
¼ cup bacon drippings
⅔ cup uncooked rice
3 Tbsp. minced onion
3 Tbsp. chopped green
   pepper
1 tsp. salt
3 ¼ cups strained tomatoes
   or tomato juice

1. Fry bacon until nearly crisp. Pour off bacon drippings, reserving ¼ cup.
2. To bacon pieces add ¼ cup bacon drippings, rice, onion, pepper and salt. Sauté until rice is light brown.
3. Add tomatoes. Cover and steam for 45 minutes.

Bacon and Noodle Casserole

Elsie Neufeldt
Saskatoon, SK
Nutana Park Mennonite Church

Makes 4-6 servings

2 cups noodles
½ lb. bacon
¼ cup bacon drippings
½ cup chopped onion
28-oz. can tomatoes
1¼ tsp. salt
1 cup bread crumbs
1 tsp. sugar
¼ cup grated cheese

1. Cook noodles according to directions and drain.
2. Fry bacon and drain off bacon drippings, reserving ¼ cup. Break bacon into small pieces.
3. In a skillet brown onion in bacon drippings. Add tomatoes, salt, bread crumbs, sugar and cheese. Cook 8-10 minutes.
4. Pour ingredients into casserole dish. Fold in noodles and bacon. Toss well.
5. Bake at 350° for 30 minutes.

Baked Kraut with Bacon

Elaine Unruh
Moundridge, KS
First Mennonite Church

Makes 6 servings

16-oz. can sauerkraut,
   rinsed and drained
16-oz. can can chopped
   tomatoes
1 cup brown sugar
4 slices bacon, browned and
   crumbled
½ cup chopped onion

1. Combine all ingredients in a casserole dish.
2. Bake at 350° for 2 hours.

Baked German Potato Salad

Bernice Hertzler
Phoenix, AZ
Sunnyslope Mennonite Church

Makes 10-12 servings

8 strips bacon
1 cup chopped celery
1 cup chopped onion
3 Tbsp. flour
1⅓ cups water
1 cup cider vinegar
⅔ cup sugar
1 tsp. salt
¼ tsp. pepper
8 cups cooked potatoes, cubed
1 cup sliced radishes
   (optional)

1. Fry, drain and crumble bacon. Drain all bacon drip-

pings from skillet, reserving ¼ cup. Set bacon pieces aside.

2. Sauté celery and onion in ¼ cup bacon drippings for 1 minute. Blend in flour, stirring until bubbly. Add water and vinegar, stirring constantly until mixture is thick and bubbly. Stir in sugar, salt and pepper, cooking until sugar dissolves.

3. Cube cooked potatoes into greased 3-quart casserole dish. Pour sauce over potatoes and mix lightly. Fold in bacon pieces.

4. Cover and bake at 350° for 30 minutes.

5. Remove from oven and stir in radishes. Serve immediately.

Green Beans and Bacon

Millie Glick
Edmonton, AB
Holyrood Mennonite Church

Makes 6-8 servings

2 quarts green beans
5-6 slices bacon

1. In large skillet fry bacon pieces. Drain off most of bacon drippings. Add green beans and stir occasionally until beans are heated through.

2. Put in covered casserole dish and keep in warm oven until time to leave for church.

Variation:

Substitute 1 lb. smoked turkey sausage for bacon. Cut smoked sausage into ½-inch slices and put into crockpot in alternating layers with green beans. Heat 30-45 minutes on high.

Eva Blosser
Dayton, OH
Huber Mennonite Church

Barbecued Green Beans with Bacon

Sally Longacre
Fairview, MI
Fairview Mennonite Church

Makes 8-10 servings

1 medium onion, chopped
4 slices Canadian bacon, chopped
2 quarts green beans
¾ cup ketchup
⅓ cup brown sugar
1½ Tbsp. mustard
Salt and pepper to taste
Cooked ham (optional)

1. Sauté onion with bacon. Remove from heat and add all other ingredients, including the liquid from 1 quart green beans. Pour into covered casserole dish.

2. Bake at 350° for 1 hour.

Sausage Main Dishes

Pork Sausage Meat Loaf

Iona S. Weaver
Lansdale, PA
Norristown New Life Mennonite Church

Makes 8 servings

¾ cup milk
⅓ cup ketchup
1 Tbsp. Worcestershire sauce
1½ lbs. ground beef
½ lb. pork sausage
⅔ cup oatmeal *or* bread crumbs
⅓ cup chopped onion
¼ cup chopped green pepper
2 tsp. salt
½ tsp. pepper
2 eggs, beaten

1. Blend milk, ketchup and Worcestershire sauce. Mix all ingredients thoroughly.

2. Form into loaf.

3. Bake at 350° for 1½ hours. Drain excess fat before serving.

Sweet and Sour Farmer's Sausage

Sarah Klassen
Winnipeg, MB
River East Mennonite Brethren
Church

Makes 12-15 servings

2 double-link farmer's
  sausages
½ cup diced onion
4 Tbsp. mustard
½ tsp. garlic salt
1 tsp. soy sauce
25-oz. can tomato juice
¾ cup ketchup
¼ cup brown sugar
¼ cup white sugar
½ cup vinegar
Cornstarch (optional)

1. Peel farmer's sausages.
(Easiest to peel when partially frozen.) Bake or boil off
fat. Drain.
2. Sauté onion in small
amount of sausage drippings.
3. In a saucepan combine
onion, mustard, garlic salt,
soy sauce, tomato juice,
ketchup, sugars and vinegar.
Bring to a boil. Add small
amount of cornstarch if
sauce is too thin.
4. Pour over sausage in
casserole dish. Simmer on
top of stove approximately
30-45 minutes. Serve.

Hilda Born's Sausage Casserole

Hilda J. Born
Matsqui, BC
Central Heights Mennonite Brethren
Church

Makes 10 servings

1 lb. link farmer's sausages
1 pkg. flat noodles
1 tsp. salt
1 medium onion, chopped
1 can cream of mushroom
  soup
1 heaping Tbsp. sour cream
1 cup buttered bread crumbs

1. Bake sausages at 350°
for 25-30 minutes. Cool and
cut into thin slices.
2. Cook noodles with salt
according to directions. Drain.
3. Combine all ingredients
except bread crumbs and
spoon into casserole dish.
Top with buttered bread
crumbs.
4. Bake at 350° for 25-30
minutes or until heated
through.

Sauerkraut Casserole

Gladwin and Lois Bartel
La Junta, CO
Emmanuel Mennonite Church

Makes 8 servings

1 lb. Polish *or* German
  sausage
2 lbs. sauerkraut
3 medium potatoes, chopped
Coarse pepper to taste

1. Cut sausage into
chunks and brown.
2. Combine all ingredients
in a crockpot. Cook on high
for 6 or more hours.

Kapuzta

Kathy Hertzler
Lancaster, PA
Charlotte Street Mennonite Church

Makes 6-8 servings

1 lb. fresh pork
1 lb. pork sausage, freshly
  ground
1 medium onion, chopped
1 lb. Polish sausage, sliced
1 quart sauerkraut, drained
¼ head fresh cabbage,
  coarsely chopped
1 Tbsp. caraway seed
1 can cream of mushroom
  soup
Pepper to taste

1. Trim fresh pork and cut
into bite-sized pieces.
2. Brown pork, pork sau-
sage and onion together until
all are cooked thoroughly.
Combine with all other ingredients.
3. Spoon into 5-quart
crockpot. Simmer on low all
day. When taking this to a
lunch potluck, cook on low
for first 2 hours, then turn on
high for 2 more hours.

Suzette Wedel's Sausage Casserole

Suzette Wedel
Topeka, KS
Southern Hills Mennonite Church

Makes 10-15 servings

2 lbs. bulk sausage
8 slices bread, cubed
1 can cream of mushroom
  soup
1 cup milk
2 eggs
1 lb. cheddar cheese, grated

1. Brown and drain sausage. Combine all ingredients and place into greased 9" x 13" pan.
2. Cover and bake at 350° for 1 hour.

Sausage Kraut Casserole

Anne Martin
Castorland, NY
First Mennonite Church

Makes 8 servings

2 cups sauerkraut, drained
2 cups boiled noodles,
  drained
1 lb. turkey kielbasa
2 cups mashed potatoes

1. Parboil kielbasa in water for about 15 minutes.
1. In greased 9-inch square baking dish put layer of drained sauerkraut, layer of noodles and layer of cooked sausage which has been cut into pieces.
2. Bake at 375° for 45 minutes. Top with mashed potatoes and bake 15 more minutes.

Sauerkraut and Kielbasa

Lorna Sirtoli
Cortland, NY
Nazarene Church of Cortland

Makes 15 servings

4 lbs. sauerkraut
10 slices bacon
2 medium onions, sliced
3 Tbsp. light brown sugar
1-2 lbs. kielbasa

1. Thoroughly wash and drain sauerkraut.
2. Sauté bacon to crisp. Remove bacon pieces from skillet. Crumble bacon.
3. Add onions to skillet and saute in bacon fat until onion looks transparent. Remove onion from skillet.
4. Add sauerkraut to skillet. Cover and simmer in bacon fat approximately ¾ hour or until tender. Add water if needed.
5. Add bacon, onion and brown sugar to sauerkraut. (This mixture may be refrigerated 2-3 days as this helps flavors to blend.) Heat through.
6. Parboil kielbasa in water for approximately 15 minutes. Slice kielbasa and add to sauerkraut. Serve.

Sausage Sweet Potato Bake

Mary Hochstedler
Kokomo, IN
Parkview Mennonite Church

Cindy Gingerich
Jackson, MS

Makes 4-6 servings

1 lb. bulk sausage
2 medium raw sweet
  potatoes
3 medium apples
2 Tbsp. brown sugar
1 Tbsp. flour
¼ tsp. ground cinnamon
¼ tsp. salt
½ cup water

1. Brown sausage and drain excess fat.
2. Peel and slice potatoes and apples. Layer sausage, sweet potatoes and apples into 2-quart casserole dish.
3. Combine all other ingredients and pour over layers.
4. Cover and bake at 375° for 50-60 minutes or until done.

Sausage and Creamed Potatoes

Betty Pellman
Millersville, PA
Rossmere Mennonite Church

Makes 8-10 servings

1 lb. link sausage
1 medium onion, finely
diced
6-8 small potatoes, quartered
1 tsp. salt
¼ tsp. pepper
2 Tbsp. flour
1 cup milk

1. Cut sausage links into ½-inch lengths. Combine sausage and onion and fry until slightly brown. Add water to cover and cook 10 minutes.
2. Add potatoes and seasonings. Cover and cook until potatoes are tender.
3. Make a paste with flour and milk. Add to mixture and cook until thickened. Serve.

This is handy dish to reheat on top of stove if ovens are full.

Zucchini Sausage Casserole Supreme

Louise A. Bartel
North Newton, KS
Bethel College Mennonite Church

Makes 6 servings

1 lb. bulk sausage
1 Tbsp. cooking oil
½ cup chopped onion
1 can cream of chicken soup
8-oz. jar cheese spread
¾ cup milk
1 cup quick-cooking rice
2 medium zucchini, grated

1. Crumble sausage. Brown and drain excess fat. Set aside.
2. Sauté onion in cooking oil. Add soup, cheese spread, milk, rice and zucchini. Cook until zucchini is tender crisp. Add sausage and mix well. Spoon into 2-quart baking dish.
3. Bake at 350° for 15-20 minutes or until mixture is bubbly and thickened.

Sausage, Rice and Carrot Casserole

Maxine Hershberger
Dalton, OH
Salem Mennonite Church

Makes 6 servings

⅔ cup uncooked rice
1 cup chopped carrots
½ cup chopped onion
⅓ cup chopped celery

1 ¼ cups chicken broth
¾ lb. bulk sausage

1. Spread rice evenly into 2-quart casserole dish. Layer vegetables over rice. Top with chicken broth.
2. Brown sausage and drain well. Spoon sausage over vegetables.
3. Cover and bake at 350° for 30 minutes. Remove from oven and stir well. Cover and bake an additional 30 minutes.

Sausage Vegetable Casserole

Genie Kehr
Goshen, IN
Berkey Avenue Mennonite Fellowship

Makes 8-10 servings

6 potatoes, sliced
1 lb. fresh carrots, sliced
⅛ cup chopped onion
1 lb. Italian sausage
½ cup flour
1 quart milk
Salt and pepper to taste

1. Prepare vegetables. Set aside.
2. Brown sausage and remove from skillet.
3. Add flour to sausage drippings, stirring until bubbly. Slowly add milk, stirring until thickened. Season with salt and pepper.
4. Combine all ingredients and spoon into 3-quart casserole dish.
5. Bake at 325° for 2 hours.

Crockpot Moosh

Kate Emerson
Strasburg, PA

Makes 8 servings

Various kinds of sausage

1. Cook sausages in boiling water for 10 minutes. Remove from water and cut into bite-sized pieces. Place in crockpot.

2. Take dish to fellowship event and plug in crockpot. Cook on high for 30-45 minutes, stirring occasionally.

3. Transfer sausages to chafing dish and allow people to serve themselves.

Seafood Main Dishes

Red Snapper Creole

Dorothy L. Ealy
Los Angeles, CA
Calvary Christian Fellowship

Makes 6 servings

6 red snapper filets
Salt and pepper to taste
1 Tbsp. butter
1-2 Tbsp. flour
6 slices bacon
2 large onions, chopped

1 clove garlic, minced
2 16-oz. cans tomatoes
1 cup water
1 Tbsp. chopped parsley
1/2 tsp. thyme
2 bay leaves
Lemon wedges

1. Wash fish thoroughly. Rub with salt and pepper. Lay into baking pan, dot with butter and sprinkle with flour.

2. Bake at 350° for 15 minutes.

3. Fry and drain bacon. Set aside.

4. Brown onions and garlic in small amount of bacon drippings. Add tomatoes, water and seasonings. Cook until sauce is thickened.

5. Pour sauce over fish and bake 30 minutes longer. Remove bay leaves.

6. Garnish with bacon slices and lemon wedges. Serve.

Squid with Shallots

Jixun Chang
Regina, SK
Chinese Fellowship

Makes 4 servings

2 lbs. cleaned squid
1/2 cup cooking oil
2 medium onions, quartered
2 tsp. grated green ginger
1 Tbsp. corn flour
1/2 cup water
2 chicken stock cubes,
  crumbled
2 Tbsp. dry sherry
2 Tbsp. oyster sauce
1 Tbsp. soy sauce
1/2 tsp. sesame oil

1/2 tsp. sugar
1/2 tsp. salt
4 shallots, sliced diagonally

1. Cut squid lengthwise down center. Spread them out flat with inside facing upward. With a sharp knife make shallow cuts across squid in a diamond shape.

2. Heat oil in pan or wok. Add squid, cooking until they curl. Remove from pan and drain on absorbent paper.

3. Place onions and ginger in wok and sauté for 3 minutes.

4. In a small bowl blend corn flour with a small amount of water. Add remaining water, crumbled stock cubes, dry sherry, oyster sauce, soy sauce, sesame oil, sugar and salt. Mix well.

5. Add sauce to onions in wok, stirring until sauce boils. Return squid to pan and cook until heated through.

6. Spoon into serving dish, top with shallots and serve with rice.

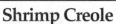

Shrimp Creole

Ethel Camardelle
Des Allemands, LA

Makes 8 servings

2 lbs. shrimp, peeled
Salt and pepper to taste
½ cup cooking oil
1 cup chopped onions
1 cup chopped celery
½ cup chopped bell peppers
8-oz. can tomato paste
8-oz. can tomato sauce
1 Tbsp. Louisiana hot sauce
2½ cups water
3 cloves garlic, minced
1 cup green onions, chopped
Parsley

1. Peel shrimp. Salt and pepper to taste and set aside.
2. In a heavy saucepan heat cooking oil. Sauté onions, celery and peppers until wilted. Add tomato paste and cook 5 minutes over low heat, stirring constantly. Add tomato sauce, hot sauce and water. Cook for 1 hour, stirring occasionally.
3. Stir in shrimp and garlic. Cook another 30-35 minutes.
4. Sprinkle with green onions and parsley. Cook 5 more minutes.
5. Serve with rice.

Braised Prawns with Vegetables

Jixun Chang
Regina, SK
Chinese Fellowship

Makes 4 servings

1 lb. green king prawns
1 Tbsp. cooking oil
8-oz. can bamboo shoots, drained and thinly sliced
8-oz. can mushrooms, drained
1 cucumber, sliced
1 tsp. corn flour
½ cup chicken stock
1 tsp. oyster sauce
Salt and pepper to taste
Pinch of sugar
½ tsp. grated green ginger

1. Shell prawns. Using a sharp knife, cut down back and remove back vein.
2. Heat oil in wok. Add prawns and sauté quickly until tender and light pink in color, approximately 3 minutes.
3. Add bamboo shoots, mushrooms and cucumber and toss well.
4. In a small bowl blend corn flour with chicken stock. Stir in all remaining ingredients.
5. Add sauce to wok and bring mixture to a boil. Cook 1 minute, stirring constantly. Serve.

Shrimp Fried Rice with Egg

Philene Houmphan
Regina, SK
Chinese Fellowship

Makes 2-4 servings

3 Tbsp. cooking oil
1 egg
2 Tbsp. chopped green onions
⅓ cup diced mushrooms
3 Tbsp. peas
6 shrimp, shelled
2½ cups cooked rice
½ tsp. salt
Dash of pepper

1. Heat wok and add oil. Stir fry egg until it solidifies.
2. Add onions, mushrooms, peas and shrimp. Stir fry lightly.
3. Add rice, salt and pepper. Stir fry until rice is brown. Serve.

Shrimp and Chicken Fried Noodles

Thavone Senevonghachack
Regina, SK
Laotian Fellowship

Makes 2-4 servings

1 pkg. rice noodles
Warm water to cover
3 Tbsp. cooking oil
1 Tbsp. white sugar
1 clove garlic, minced
1 cup diced, cooked chicken
½ cup small shrimp
1 Tbsp. soy sauce
½ cup water

1. Soak rice noodles in warm water for 15-20 minutes. Drain thoroughly.

2. Heat oil. Add sugar and heat until sugar turns brown, stirring constantly.

3. Add garlic, chicken, shrimp and soy sauce. Add water and let mixture boil for a few minutes.

4. Reduce heat and add noodles. Cook until noodles are brown and soft, stirring constantly. Serve.

Oyster-Flavored Beef with Rice

Philene Houmphan
Regina, SK
Chinese Fellowship

Makes 4 servings

1 Tbsp. soy sauce
1 Tbsp. cooking wine
1 Tbsp. cornstarch
½ lb. lean beef, cubed
3 Tbsp. cooking oil
1 green onion, sliced
6 slices ginger root, peeled
1 tsp. cooking oil
½ cup water
1½ Tbsp. oyster sauce
1½ Tbsp. soy sauce
½ Tbsp. cooking wine
2 tsp. cornstarch
2 tsp. sugar
Few drops sesame oil
Pinch pepper
1 cup sliced mushrooms
1 cup chopped broccoli, lightly blanched
3 medium carrots, sliced and blanched
2 cups cooked rice

1. Combine 1 Tbsp. soy sauce, 1 Tbsp. cooking wine and 1 Tbsp. cornstarch. Add cubed beef and marinate. Add water if mixture is too dry.

2. Heat wok. Add 3 Tbsp. cooking oil and heat. Stir fry onion and ginger.

3. Stir 1 tsp. cooking oil into meat mixture. Add to wok and stir fry until meat just changes color. Add water, oyster sauce, 1½ Tbsp. soy sauce, ½ Tbsp. cooking wine, 2 tsp. cornstarch, sugar, sesame oil and pepper. Heat until bubbly.

4. Add mushrooms, broccoli and carrots. Stir fry quickly over high heat, making sure the meat and vegetables are evenly coated with the sauce. Serve with rice.

Crab and Zucchini Casserole

Virginia Bender
Dover, DE
Presbyterian Church of Dover

Makes 6 servings

2 medium zucchini, sliced
½ cup chopped onion
2 cloves garlic, crushed
½ cup butter *or* margarine
⅛ tsp. pepper
1 tsp. basil
1 lb. crab meat
1½ cups grated Swiss cheese
1 cup soft bread crumbs
3 medium tomatoes

1. Cook zucchini, onion and garlic in butter about 5 minutes or until tender. Remove from skillet and add seasonings, crab meat, cheese and bread crumbs.

2. Chop tomatoes, removing seeds. Add tomatoes and toss lightly. Place in glass casserole dish.

3. Bake at 375° for 30-35 minutes or until heated through.

Nautical Noodles

Helen Rose Pauls
Sardis, BC
Sardis Community Church

Makes 8 servings

10-oz. pkg. broad noodles
2 7-oz. cans tuna, shrimp or salmon
½ cup milk
Celery salt to taste
Salt and pepper to taste
2 Tbsp. dry onion soup mix

1. Cook noodles according to directions and drain.
2. Drain seafood of liquid.
3. Combine all ingredients and spoon into 2-quart baking dish.
4. Bake at 350° for 30 minutes.

Tuna Casserole

Helen M. Peachey
Harrisonburg, VA
Lindale Mennonite Church

Makes 8 servings

1 can cream of celery soup
⅓ cup milk
7-oz. can tuna, drained
1½ cups cooked noodles
½ cup frozen peas
2 Tbsp. grated American cheese

1. Combine soup and milk to make sauce. Add tuna, noodles and peas. Spoon into casserole dish and sprinkle cheese on top.

2. Bake at 350° for 20-25 minutes.

Variation:

Instead of 1½ cups cooked noodles, use 1 cup uncooked macaroni. Cook macaroni in boiling water and drain before adding to casserole dish. Substitute 1 can cream of mushroom soup for cream of celery soup.

Ellen Helmuth
Debec, NB
New Brunswick Monthly Meeting,
Society of Friends

Add ½ cup peas to ingredients and cook dish in microwave on full power for 7-10 minutes.

Elva Evers
North English, IA
Wellman Mennonite Church

Other Meat Main Dishes

Sweet and Sour Pork

Philene Houmphan
Regina, SK
Chinese Fellowship

Makes 4-6 servings

⅔ lb. pork, cut in bite-sized pieces
1 Tbsp. soy sauce
1 egg yolk
7 Tbsp. cornstarch
6 cups cooking oil

1 small green pepper, sliced
1 Tbsp. water
½ tsp. chopped garlic
½ onion, diced
½ cup pineapple pieces
2 Tbsp. pineapple juice
2 Tbsp. vinegar
3 Tbsp. sugar
3 Tbsp. water
3 Tbsp. ketchup
½ tsp. salt
1½ tsp. cornstarch
1 Tbsp. water

1. Combine soy sauce, egg yolk and 1 Tbsp. cornstarch. Stir in meat pieces and marinate for 20 minutes.
2. Heat 6 cups oil in wok. Stir 6 Tbsp. cornstarch into meat marinade. Spoon into hot oil and deep fry over medium heat for 3 minutes. Remove meat and reheat oil until very hot, but not smoking.
3. Return meat to wok and deep fry another 30 seconds. Remove and drain. Discard oil.
4. Reheat wok with 1 Tbsp. fresh oil. Stir fry green pepper with 1 Tbsp. water. Remove and drain.
5. Add 3 Tbsp. oil and stir fry garlic until it imparts its fragrance. Add onion and pineapple and stir fry briefly. Add green pepper, pineapple juice, vinegar, sugar, water, ketchup and salt. Bring mixture to a boil.
6. Combine 1½ tsp. cornstarch and 1 Tbsp. water. Stir into mixture to thicken. Add meat and toss lightly. Serve.

Pork Loin with Fruit Stuffing

Jeanette Zacharias
Morden, MB
Barn Swallow Quilters

Makes 10-12 servings

1 cup finely chopped dried
   apricots
2 Tbsp. brandy *or* apple juice
6 strips bacon
1 medium onion, finely
   chopped
2 cups French bread crumbs
1 cup chicken broth
4-5-lb. boneless pork loin
Salt and pepper

   1. Soak apricots in brandy or apple juice for 1 hour.

   2. In the meantime fry bacon strips, reserving drippings.

   3. Sauté onion in the bacon drippings.

   4. In a medium bowl combine onion with apricots, bacon, bread crumbs and chicken broth.

   5. Slice pork loin open so it may be stuffed. Spread stuffing along inside of pork. Roll snugly and tie securely in 3 or 4 places. Place fat side up in roasting pan. Sprinkle with salt and pepper.

   6. Roast, uncovered, at 325° for 2½-3 hours. Cover and bake an additional 30-45 minutes. Let stand at least 20 minutes before slicing.

This roast improves in flavor and texture if it is made ahead of time and chilled before slicing. It may be served cold or reheated.

Pork Chops with Rice and Limas

Sandy Tinsler
Wauseon, OH
Central Mennonite Church

Makes 4-6 servings

1 cup uncooked rice
16-oz. pkg. frozen limas
1½ cans mushroom soup
6 pork chops

   1. Combine rice and limas with ½ can soup. Spoon into 8-inch baking pan. Top with uncooked pork chops and remaining soup.

   2. Cover and bake at 325° for 1 ¼ hours or 275° for 2½ hours.

Pork in Ketchup Sauce over Rice

Philene Houmphan
Regina, SK
Chinese Fellowship

Makes 4-6 servings

½ lb. pork, sliced
1 Tbsp. cornstarch
1 Tbsp. water
1 Tbsp. soy sauce
½ Tbsp. cooking wine
   or sherry
5 Tbsp. cooking oil
1 cup diced green pepper
1 cup chopped tomatoes
½ cup chopped onions
½ cup sliced mushrooms
2 cups cooked rice

Sauce:
1 cup water
2 Tbsp. ketchup
1 Tbsp. sugar
½ tsp. salt
Pinch pepper
1 Tbsp. cornstarch

   1. Combine 1 Tbsp. cornstarch, 1 Tbsp. water, soy sauce and wine. Stir pork into mixture and marinate at least 20 minutes.

   2. Heat 1 Tbsp. cooking oil in wok. Stir fry green pepper briefly and remove.

   3. Heat 2 Tbsp. oil and stir fry meat until tender. Remove.

   4. Heat 2 Tbsp. oil in wok. Add onion, tomato and mushrooms and stir fry briefly. Add all sauce ingredients and bring to a boil. Add meat and green pepper and heat through.

   5. Spoon over rice to serve.

Sweet and Sour Ribs

Thavone Senevonghachack
Regina, SK
Laotian Fellowship

Makes 4-6 servings

1/2 cup ketchup
1 cup pineapple juice
5 Tbsp. vinegar
1 tsp. salt
1 tsp. pepper
1 1/2 Tbsp. cornstarch
1 Tbsp. soy sauce
1/2 cup white sugar
1 Tbsp. brown sugar
2 cups water
3 lbs. spareribs

1. Combine all ingredients except spareribs and bring to a boil.
2. Fry spareribs for 5-10 minutes or until they are nicely browned. Place ribs in roaster. Cover with sauce.
3. Cover and bake at 350° for 1 hour or until spareribs are done. Serve.

Barbecued Ribs on Grill

Kenneth F. Hudson
Lancaster, PA
South Christian Street Mennonite
Church

Makes 10-15 servings

8 lbs. pork or beef ribs
4 bay leaves
1 Tbsp. garlic salt
1/2 tsp. lemon pepper
1 Tbsp. seasoned salt

2 Tbsp. meat tenderizer
1 tsp. onion salt
1 cup vinegar
2 gallons barbecue sauce
1 lb. honey
1 cup sugar
1/2 cup water

1. Wash ribs with warm water and cut into 2-3 sections.
2. Fill a large roast pan about 1/3 full of water. Bring water to a boil. Add bay leaves, garlic salt, lemon pepper, seasoned salt, tenderizer, onion salt and vinegar. Bring to a boil and boil for 1 minute. Place ribs into boiling water and simmer for 1 hour.
3. Pour 2 gallons barbecue sauce into a large, high kettle. Bring to a slow boil and turn heat off. Stir in honey.
4. Combine sugar with 1/2 cup water and stir into barbecue sauce. Bring mixture to a slow boil and cook for 2 minutes, stirring constantly. Remove from heat.
5. Drain hot ribs and pour barbecue sauce over ribs. Cover and marinate overnight or at least 1 hour.
6. Grill ribs until browned, basting with excess sauce every 30 seconds. Serve.

Chitterlings/Hogmans

Kenneth F. Hudson
Lancaster, PA
South Christian Street Mennonite
Church

Makes 10-12 servings

5 lbs. chitterlings
5 lbs. hogmans
Water
2 cups vinegar
4 green peppers, sliced
2 large onions, diced
1 Tbsp. seasoned salt
1 Tbsp. meat tenderizer
1 cup hot water
1/3 cup hot sauce

1. Cut chitterlings and hogmans into long, thin strips.
2. Bring large pot of water with 1 cup vinegar to a boil. Drop strips of meat into boiling water and boil for 15 minutes. Remove meat and drain. Cut away any fat or waste.
3. Turn crockpot on high heat. Add 1/2 cup vinegar, 2 green peppers, 1 onion and meat strips.
4. In a medium bowl combine 1/2 cup vinegar, 2 peppers, 1 onion, salt, tenderizer, 1 cup water and hot sauce. Mix well and pour over meat in crockpot.
5. Cover and cook on high for 1 hour. Make sure meat is covered with sauce. Add water if necessary. Reduce heat to low and cook for 9 more hours.

Barbecued Beef

Carolyn Baer
Conrath, WI

Makes 8 or more servings

3-lb. chuck roast *or* round
  steak
Cooking oil
1 cup chopped onion
1/2 cup chopped celery
2 cups beef broth or
  bouillon

Sauce:
1 1/2 cups beef broth
1 clove garlic, minced
1 tsp. salt
3/4 cup ketchup
4 Tbsp. brown sugar
2 Tbsp. vinegar
1 tsp. dry mustard
1/2 tsp. chili powder
3 drops Tabasco sauce
1 bay leaf
1/4 tsp. paprika
1/4 tsp. garlic powder
1 tsp. Worcestershire sauce

1. Brown beef roast in hot oil on both sides. Add onion and celery for the last minute.

2. Spoon beef, vegetables and 2 cups beef broth into covered Dutch oven or crockpot. Cover and simmer 3-4 hours or until tender.

3. Remove meat and vegetables from broth and cool. Skim fat from broth and set aside. Shred beef, separating it into strands.

4. In a large saucepan combine beef, vegetables and skimmed broth. Add all sauce ingredients. Simmer until heated through. Remove bay leaf before serving.

5. Pack mixture into crockpot for transporting to fellowship meal. Plug in on low.

6. Serve with potato rolls or buns.

Beef Stew

Anna C. Gehman
Bally, PA

Makes 10-12 servings

1 1/2 lb. beef cubes
1 medium onion, chopped
2 large carrots, chopped
4 medium potatoes, cubed
Salt and pepper to taste
1 can golden mushroom
  soup
16-oz. can peas

1. Put beef cubes in roasting pan. Cover with onion, carrots and potatoes. Season with salt and pepper. Pour mushroom soup over ingredients.

2. Bake at 350 F. for 3 1/2 hours. Add water if needed.

3. Approximately 1/2 hour before end of baking time, add undrained peas.

Waldorf Astoria Stew

Barbara Longenecker
New Holland, PA
New Holland Mennonite Church

Makes 6 servings

2 lbs. pot roast, cubed
1 medium onion, chopped
1 cup celery, diced
2 carrots, diced
4 medium potatoes, diced
1 can tomato soup
1/3 cup water
3 Tbsp. minute tapioca
1 tsp. salt
Pepper to taste

1. Layer cubed meat, onion, celery, carrots and potatoes into small roaster. Add tomato soup and water. Sprinkle tapioca and seasonings over top.

2. Cover and bake at 250°. for 4 1/2-5 hours. Do not lift lid while baking.

3. Serve.

Beef with Chinese Broccoli

Boulieng Luangviseth
Regina, SK
Laotian Fellowship

Makes 4 servings

2 Tbsp. cooking oil
1 clove garlic, minced
1 tsp. chopped ginger root
1 cup cubed raw beef
2 Tbsp. soy sauce
2 Tbsp. oyster sauce
1 tsp. salt
1 tsp. white sugar
3-4 cups chopped broccoli

1. Heat wok. Add oil, garlic and ginger. Stir fry until garlic turns brown.
2. Add meat, soy sauce, oyster sauce, salt and sugar. Stir fry until meat turns brown.
3. Add broccoli and cook until soft. Add water if needed.

Feijoada

Richard J. Harris
Manhattan, KS
Manhattan Mennonite Fellowship

Makes 8-10 servings

1 lb. dried black beans
1 lb. beef stew meat, cubed
¾-1 lb. link sausage, sliced
Salt and pepper to taste
1 onion, chopped

1. Soak beans overnight. Pour beans and water into crockpot.
2. Brown beef and sausage. Drain excess fat.
3. Stir all ingredients into beans in crockpot.
4. Cook on low for 6-10 hours. Check occasionally and add water if necessary.
5. Serve with rice.

This is an easy version of the Brazilian national dish.

Sukiyaki

Cindy Jordan
Ambler, PA
Line Lexington Mennonite Church

Makes 8 servings

4 ozs. thin spaghetti
3 eggs
2 small onions, sliced
12-16 green onions, sliced
½ lb. mushrooms, sliced
5 stalks celery, diced
1 lb. spinach, torn in pieces
2 lbs. boneless beef steak
½ cup soy sauce

2 Tbsp. sugar
¼ cup cooking oil
2 Tbsp. sesame oil

1. Cook spaghetti according to directions. Rinse and drain.
2. Make an omelet with eggs. Cut into ½-inch squares. Set aside.
3. Prepare all vegetables. Set aside.
4. Trim fat from steak and cut into thin slices.
5. In a 10-inch frying pan combine and heat soy sauce, sugar, cooking oil and sesame oil. Add meat and vegetables and cook until tender, stirring frequently. Immediately before serving, fold in egg.
6. Serve over cooked spaghetti.

Baked Moussaka

Rhoda Atzeff
Harrisburg, PA
Steelton Mennonite Church

Makes 10-12 servings

1½ lbs. round steak, minced
2 Tbsp. butter
¼ cup chopped green pepper
½ cup chopped onion
1 clove garlic, minced
½ cup uncooked rice
1 cup stewed tomatoes
1 tsp. salt
½ tsp. pepper
½ tsp. paprika
½ tsp. dried mint
2 cups hot water

3 eggs
Juice of ½ lemon

1. In a saucepan brown meat with butter. Add green pepper, onion, garlic, rice, tomatoes and seasonings. Sauté for 5 minutes.
2. Add water and mix well. Pour into baking dish.
3. Beat eggs well and stir in lemon juice. Pour over meat mixture.
4. Bake at 350° for 1 hour.

Corned Beef Casserole

Elsie N. Miller
Gulfport, MS
Gulfhaven Mennonite Church

Makes 6 servings

6-oz. pkg. noodles
1 can cream of mushroom soup
1 cup milk
1 lb. Velveeta cheese, sliced
12-oz. can corned beef, chopped
¼ cup grated onion
¾ cup buttered bread crumbs

1. Cook noodles according to directions and drain.
2. Mix soup, milk and cheese. Heat until cheese has melted. Add corned beef, onion and noodles. Spoon into greased casserole dish. Top with bread crumbs.
3. Bake at 350° for 30 minutes.

Dried Beef Casserole

Ruth Zercher, Grantham, PA;
Arlene Eberly, East Earl, PA;
Ulonda Jones, La Grange, IN;
Ruth Ann Zeiset, Mohnton, PA

Makes 4-6 servings

1 can cream of mushroom soup
1 cup milk
1 cup shredded cheddar cheese
3 Tbsp. chopped onion
1 cup uncooked macaroni
⅛ lb. dried beef, cut up
2 hard-boiled eggs, sliced

1. Stir soup until creamy. Add milk, cheese, onion, uncooked macaroni and dried beef. Fold in eggs. Turn into greased 1½-quart baking dish.
2. Refrigerate 3-4 hours or overnight.
3. Bake, uncovered, at 350° for 1 hour and 15 minutes.

Variations:
Substitute 1½ cups frozen peas for the hard-boiled eggs.
Anna S. Eby
Lititz, PA

Double the recipe and add 1 small can diced pimentos and 1 cup finely chopped celery.
Arlene Egli
Morton, IL

Crockpot Wieners with Macaroni and Cheese

Kathy Martin
Lansdale, PA
Line Lexington Mennonite Church

Makes 8 servings

8-oz. pkg. macaroni
2 Tbsp. cooking oil
1 can evaporated milk
1½ cups milk
1 tsp. salt
3 cups shredded cheese
¼ cup melted butter
2 Tbsp. minced onion
1 lb. wieners, cut up

1. Cook macaroni according to directions and drain.
2. Toss cooked macaroni in cooking oil. Add all remaining ingredients. Pour into lightly greased crockpot. Stir well.
3. Cover and cook on low 3-4 hours.

I plug in the crock as soon as we arrive at church and give it a stir between the church service and Sunday school. I especially like this dish because I know my children will eat it.

Barbecued Sauerkraut and Wieners

Doris Ebersole
Archbold, OH
Zion Mennonite Church

Makes 6 servings

2 Tbsp. margarine
2 small onions, chopped
3 Tbsp. brown sugar
¾ cup ketchup
¾ cup water
1-2 lbs. sauerkraut, drained
1 pkg. wieners *or* turkey
   franks

1. Sauté onions in margarine. Add brown sugar, ketchup and water and cook for 5 minutes.
2. Cut wieners or turkey franks into 1-inch chunks. Add sauerkraut and wieners to sauce.
3. Cover and cook on top of stove for about 30 minutes.

Barbecued Wieners

Ruth Liechty
Goshen, IN
Berkey Avenue Mennonite Church

Makes 12-24 servings

¼ cup chopped onion
2 Tbsp. margarine
2 Tbsp. brown sugar
1 cup ketchup
½ cup water
2 Tbsp. vinegar
3 tsp. Worcestershire sauce
½ tsp. mustard
½ cup diced celery
12-24 wieners

1. Sauté onion in margarine. Add all remaining ingredients except wieners. Cook several minutes.
2. Split wieners open and layer into casserole dish. Pour sauce over wieners.
3. Bake at 375° for 50-60 minutes. Serve with wiener rolls.

Zucchini Crust Pizza

Ruth Brunk
Sarasota, FL
Bahia Vista Mennonite Church

Makes 8-12 servings

12-oz. pkg. corn muffin mix
1 cup flour
½ cup grated Parmesan
   cheese
⅔ cup milk
1 large egg, beaten
2 cups shredded zucchini
1 lb. turkey sausage
8-oz. jar sliced mushrooms
1 onion, sliced
3 cups shredded mozzarella
   cheese
¾ cup pizza sauce

1. In a bowl combine corn muffin mix, flour and Parmesan cheese. Add milk, egg and zucchini and mix well. Spread into greased 14-inch pizza pan.
2. Bake at 400° for 18-20 minutes.
3. Brown sausage and remove from skillet. Sauté mushrooms and onion in sausage drippings.
4. Spread ⅔ of cheese over baked crust. Add pizza sauce and spread to within 1 inch of edges. Top with sausage, mushroom and onion mixture. Top with remaining cheese.
5. Return to oven and bake 10 more minutes.

Mini Pizzas

Helene Funk
Laird, SK
Tiefengrund Rosenort Mennonite Church

Makes 12 servings

½ lb. bacon, cut up
½ lb. ground beef
½ green pepper, chopped
1 medium onion, chopped
½ lb. pepperoni
1 cup mushrooms
1 cup tomato soup
1 cup grated mozzarella
   cheese
Salt and pepper to taste
6 whole wheat rolls, halved
Shredded cheese

1. Combine all ingredients except rolls and shredded cheese. Freeze in 2-cup containers for future use or use immediately.
2. Spread meat sauce on each half of roll. Sprinkle with shredded cheese. Arrange on cookie sheet.
3. Broil for 3-5 minutes until meat is well browned and cheese is bubbly.

Bean Main Dishes

❖

A Baked Bean Cele-bration

Baked beans are a hot item at church fellowship meals. We received more than 50 different baked bean recipes, and after thinking about this unexpected phenomenon identified several reasons for it. Many churches have annual summertime picnics, and baked beans continue to be standard North American picnic food. Baked bean recipes are economical. They can be thrown together at a moment's notice and are easily stretched to serve more people. Most bean recipes continue to taste good even when they are no longer piping hot. Many enthusiastic submitters suggested preparing the dish in advance, wrapping it in newspaper or a Turkish towel and not bothering with it again until the dinner was being served.

From sweet and sour beans to calico beans to best-in-the-west beans we found the names as intriguing as the recipes. We also discovered that while each person's recipe seemed to have its own unique twist, many of the recipes were quite similar. Consequently, we decided to choose a small group of basic bean recipes and list the variations as best we could, acknowledging that there would be slight shifts in balance from the original submissions. Happy bean baking!

❖

Best-in-the-West Beans

Lorraine Martin
Dryden, MI
Bethany Mennonite Fellowship

Makes 8-10 servings

½ lb. ground beef
10 slices bacon, chopped
½ cup chopped onion
⅓ cup brown sugar
⅓ cup white sugar
¼ cup ketchup
¼ cup barbecue sauce
2 Tbsp. mustard
2 Tbsp. molasses
½ tsp. salt
½ tsp. chili powder
½ tsp. pepper
1 lb. kidney beans
1 lb. butter beans
1 lb. pork and beans

1. Brown ground beef and bacon. Drain. Add onion and cook until tender. Add all other ingredients except beans and mix well.
2. Drain kidney beans and butter beans. Add all beans to meat mixture. Pour into crockpot or 3-quart casserole dish.
3. To prepare in crockpot cook on high for 1 hour. Reduce heat to low and cook for 4 hours.
4. To prepare in oven bake at 350° for 1 hour.

❖

Hearty Three-Bean Bake

Winifred Wall
Freeman, SD
Salem-Zion Mennonite Church

Makes 10-12 servings

1 lb. ground beef
4 slices bacon, cut up
½ cup chopped onion
½ cup brown sugar
½ cup ketchup
1 Tbsp. vinegar
1 tsp. prepared mustard
1 lb. pork and beans
1 lb. kidney beans, undrained
1 cup cooked soybeans

1. In a large skillet brown ground beef and bacon. Drain excess fat, reserving a small amount.
2. Sauté onion in reserved drippings.
3. Combine all ingredients in 2-quart casserole dish and mix well.
4. Cover and bake at 350° for 30 minutes.

Calico Beans

Anna S. Petersheim, Paradise, PA;
Janice Crist, Quinter, KS; Diena
Schmidt, Henderson, NE; Margaret
Oyer, Gibson City, IL; Jean Wissler,
New Holland, PA

Makes 10 servings

1 lb. ground beef
¼ lb. bacon
1 medium onion, diced
1 lb. pork and beans
1 lb. butter beans
1 lb. kidney beans
½ cup ketchup
½ cup brown sugar
2 Tbsp. vinegar
½ tsp. salt

1. Brown ground beef, bacon and onion in a skillet.
2. Combine ketchup, brown sugar, vinegar and salt.
3. Combine all ingredients and mix well. Pour into casserole dish or crockpot.
4. To prepare in oven bake at 375° for 1 hour. To prepare in crockpot cook on low 4-5 hours.

Variations:
Add 1 Tbsp. mustard to sauce mixture.
Anna Kathryn Reesor, Markham, ON;
Irene Riegsecker, Sarasota, FL;
Margaret Janzen, Minneapolis, MN;
Allie Guengerich, Kalona, IA; Betty
Lou Eberly, Reading, PA; Lorraine
Stutzman Amstutz, Bluffton, OH

Use 2 10-oz. pkgs. frozen lima beans instead of 1 lb. butter beans.
Elizabeth Yutzy
Wauseon, OH

Make a very simple sauce with 1 cup ketchup and 1 cup brown sugar.
Lydia Yoder
London, OH

Use ½ cup brown sugar, 1 cup ketchup and 1 tsp. mustard for the sauce in this recipe.
Retha Schlabach
Millersburg, OH

Calico Baked Beans for a Crowd

Erma Wenger
Lancaster, PA
Mellinger Mennonite Church

Makes 10-12 servings

2 cups green limas
2 cups large dry limas
2 cups red kidney beans
1 quart pork and beans
6 slices bacon, diced
1½ cups chopped onion
¾ cup brown sugar
2 tsp. salt
1 tsp. dry mustard
1 clove garlic, minced
½ cup vinegar
½ cup ketchup

1. Cook and drain each of the beans except pork and beans. Reserve bean liquid.
2. Fry bacon. Drain excess fat. Add onions and sauté. Add brown sugar, salt, mustard, garlic, vinegar and ketchup. Simmer at least 5 minutes.
3. Combine all beans with bacon and onion mixture in a large casserole dish. Add enough reserved bean liquid to barely cover beans.
4. Bake, uncovered, at 325° for 1½ hour, adding additional liquid if beans become too dry.

Variation:
Omit salt and dry mustard. Substitute 2 tsp. Worcestershire sauce for vinegar. Combine all beans with bacon and onion mixture. Cube ¼ lb. processed cheese and sprinkle over top of dish. Cover and bake at 350° for 1 hour.
Maxine Miller
Wakarusa, IN
College Mennonite Church

Baked Bean Casserole

Helen Siemens
Winnipeg, MB

Makes 10-12 servings

1 lb. bacon
1 lb. ground beef
2 onions
Salt and pepper to taste
1 cup brown sugar
¼ cup white sugar

4 Tbsp. molasses
2 tsp. dry mustard
½ cup ketchup
1 lb. lima beans
1 lb. green beans
2 lbs. kidney beans
2 lbs. pork and beans

1. Chop and brown bacon. Remove from drippings. Brown ground beef in bacon drippings for flavoring. Drain all excess fat from ground beef.
2. Combine all ingredients in large casserole dish.
3. Bake at 350° for 1½ hours.

Sweet and Sour Baked Beans

Twila Nafziger
Wadsworth, OH
Bethel Mennonite Church

Anne Long
Harrisburg, PA
Stauffer Mennonite Church

Makes 10-12 servings

8 slices bacon
1 cup brown sugar
½ tsp. garlic powder
½ cup vinegar
1 tsp. dry mustard
1 tsp. salt
3-4 onions, sliced
1 lb. butter beans
1 lb. green beans
1 lb. kidney beans
2 lbs. baked beans

1. Fry bacon slices to a crisp. Drain.
2. To the bacon drippings add brown sugar, garlic pow-

der, vinegar, mustard, salt and onions. Simmer about 20 minutes.
3. Drain butter, green and kidney beans.
4. Combine all ingredients.
5. Bake at 350° for 1 hour.

Variation:
Add ¼ cup ketchup to the bacon dripping mixture.

Darlene Janzen
Butterfield, MN
Evangelical Mennonite Brethren

❖

Baked Lima Beans

Helen Bowman
Columbiana, OH
Midway Mennonite Church

Makes 6-8 servings

1 lb. dry lima beans
1 tsp. salt
½ lb. bacon
1 onion, chopped
¾ cup brown sugar
¾ cup ketchup

1. Soak beans overnight or several hours in warm water. Drain. Add fresh water and ½ tsp. salt. Cook until tender. Drain and save liquid.
2. Sear bacon and onion and add to beans. Add brown sugar, ketchup, ½ tsp. salt and 1½ cups reserved bean liquid. Spoon into baking dish and cover with several strips uncooked bacon.
3. Bake at 250-275° for several hours. If beans become dry, add more water.

Variation:
Substitute 3 Tbsp. molasses and 3 Tbsp. brown sugar for ¾ cup brown sugar.

Gladys D. Kulp
Middletown, VA
Stephens City Mennonite Church

Crockpot Beans

Carol Weber
Lancaster, PA
Charlotte Street Mennonite Church

Makes 6 servings

½ lb. kidney beans
½ lb. baked beans
1 pint lima beans
1 pint green beans
4 slices bacon, crumbled
½ cup ketchup
½ cup white sugar
½ cup brown sugar
2 Tbsp. vinegar
Salt to taste

1. Combine beans and bacon in a crockpot.
2. Stir together ketchup, sugars, vinegar and salt. Add to beans and mix well.
3. Cover and cook 8-10 hours on low.

Variation:
Brown ½ lb. ground beef. Drain excess fat. Stir ground beef in with beans and bacon.

Joan Diller
Bluffton, OH
First Mennonite Church

Baked Navy Beans

Gloria Julien
Cornell, MI

Makes 15-20 servings

2 lbs. navy beans
½ lb. bacon, cut up
1 cup ketchup
2 tsp. vinegar
1 onion, chopped
¾ cup brown sugar
Salt and pepper to taste

1. Wash and sort beans. Soak beans overnight or at least 8 hours. Bring beans to a boil in same liquid and cook until slightly tender, approximately ¾ hour.
2. Spoon beans into a 5-quart crockpot and add all remaining ingredients.
3. Cook on low for 8-10 hours.

Home Baked Beans

Barbara A. Hershey
Lancaster, PA
Rossmere Mennonite Church

Makes 8-10 servings

1 lb. Great Northern navy
    beans
1 tsp. salt
½ tsp. baking soda
1 small onion, minced
2 Tbsp. molasses
½ cup brown sugar
½ cup ketchup
1½ cups tomato juice
½ lb. bacon

1. Rinse and sort beans. Cover with 3 inches water and let soak overnight.
2. In the morning add salt and baking soda and bring beans to a boil. Cook for 1 hour or until tender. Add more water if needed. Drain beans and pour into 2-quart casserole dish.
2. Add all remaining ingredients except bacon.
3. Fry bacon until crisp. Crumble and add along with bacon fat to other ingredients.
4. Bake at 350° for 1 hour.

Baked Beans in a Crockpot

Betty Herr
Beallsville, MD
Dawsonville Mennonite Church

Makes 12 or more servings

1½ lbs. ground beef
½-1 cup chopped onion
3 lbs. pork and beans
1 lb. kidney beans
1 cup ketchup
¼ cup brown sugar, packed
3 Tbsp. vinegar

1. Brown ground beef and onion in a skillet. Drain excess fat. Spoon into a crockpot. Add all other ingredients and mix.
2. Cover and cook on low for 4-6 hours. Stir occasionally.

Red Beans and Rice

Rhoda Byler Yoder
Jackson, MS

Makes 15-20 servings

1 Tbsp. cooking oil
1 large onion, diced
3 lbs. bulk sausage
6 15-oz. cans red beans
1 tsp. pepper
1 tsp. salt
½ tsp. red pepper
1 tsp. cumin
½ tsp. oregano
1 tsp. cooking oil
4 ½ cups uncooked rice
1 tsp. salt
9 cups water

1. Sauté onion in 1 Tbsp. oil. Add sausage and brown. Drain excess fat.
2. Add beans, pepper, 1 tsp. salt, red pepper, cumin and oregano. Simmer at least 2 hours, stirring occasionally. Or simmer in crockpot on low 8-10 hours.
3. Approximately ½ hour before mealtime stir 1 tsp. oil into rice in a large saucepan. Add salt and water. Bring to a rolling boil and stir well with a fork. Reduce heat to simmer. Cover and cook 20 minutes without lifting cover.
4. Serve beans and rice together.

Baked Beans

Pauline A. Bauman
Bluffton, OH
First Mennonite Church

Makes 8-10 servings

2 lbs. pork and beans
$\frac{1}{4}$ cup ketchup
$\frac{1}{4}$ cup brown sugar
1 medium onion, minced
1 tsp. dried parsley
$\frac{1}{2}$ lb. cubed ham *or*
   sliced wieners (optional)

1. Combine all ingredients in a 2-quart casserole dish.
2. Bake at 275-300° all morning, providing there is room in your church oven. If not, bake at 375° for 40 minutes and take to fellowship meal either hot or cold.

Triple Bean Bake

Phyllis Eller
LaVerne, CA

Makes 8-10 servings

1 cup chopped onion
$\frac{1}{2}$ cup chopped celery
2 Tbsp. butter *or* margarine
1 lb. pork and beans
1 lb. kidney beans, rinsed
   and drained
2 10-oz. pkgs. lima beans,
   thawed
$\frac{1}{2}$ cup ketchup
1 Tbsp. brown sugar
1 Tbsp. vinegar
$1\frac{1}{2}$ tsp. dry mustard
1 tsp. salt
$\frac{1}{8}$ tsp. garlic powder
$1\frac{1}{2}$ cups shredded
   Monterey Jack cheese

1. Sauté onions and celery in butter until tender, about 5 minutes. Add pork and beans, kidney beans, lima beans, ketchup, brown sugar, vinegar, mustard, salt, garlic powder and 1 cup cheese. Pour into 2-quart casserole dish.
2. Bake, uncovered, at 350° for 40-50 minutes or until hot and bubbly. Remove from oven.
3. Sprinkle with remaining $\frac{1}{2}$ cup cheese. Let stand 5 minutes before serving.

Calico Baked Beans

Emily Peachey
Scottdale, PA
Kingview Mennonite Church

Makes 10-12 servings

2 cups green limas
2 cups dry limas
2 cups red kidney beans
1 quart pork and beans
$1\frac{1}{2}$ cup chopped onion
1 Tbsp. cooking oil
$\frac{3}{4}$ cup brown sugar
2 tsp. salt
1 tsp. dry mustard
1 clove garlic, minced
$\frac{1}{2}$ cup vinegar
$\frac{1}{2}$ cup ketchup

1. Cook drained limas. Drain other beans. Reserve all bean liquid.
2. Sauté onion in cooking oil. Add brown sugar, salt, mustard, garlic, vinegar and ketchup. Simmer at least 5 minutes.
3. Combine all beans in large casserole dish. Pour sauce over beans. Add enough reserved bean liquid to barely cover beans.
4. Bake at 325° for $1\frac{1}{2}$ hours. Add more bean liquid as needed.

Variation:
Substitute 1 quart vegetarian beans for pork and beans.

Keith Pentz
Sarasota, FL
Bahia Vista Mennonite Church

Pasta Main Dishes

Irish Lasagna

Lorna Sirtoli
Cortland, NY
Nazarene Church of Cortland

Makes 12 servings

1 lb. ground beef
6 ozs. ground pork
¾ cup chopped onion
1 clove garlic, minced
¾ cup chopped green
    pepper
1 lb. tomatoes
1 quart tomato sauce
2 Tbsp. parsley flakes
1 tsp. salt
2 Tbsp. sugar
1 tsp. basil
8-oz. pkg. lasagna noodles
2 Tbsp. cooking oil
12 ozs. cottage cheese
12 ozs. ricotta cheese
8 ozs. Parmesan cheese
1½ cups chopped fresh
    spinach
1 tsp. oregano
¾ lb. mozzarella cheese,
    shredded
Parsley

1. In a large saucepan brown beef, pork, onion, garlic and pepper until all meat is cooked and vegetables are tender. Drain fat. Add tomatoes and break up into meat. Add tomato sauce, parsley, salt, sugar and basil. Mix well. Bring to a boil, stirring occasionally. Simmer without lid for 1 hour or until thickened.

2. While sauce cooks, boil lasagna in water with 2 Tbsp. cooking oil. Drain.

3. Combine cottage cheese, ricotta cheese and Parmesan cheese. Add fresh spinach and oregano.

4. Place ⅓ of noodles into ungreased 9" x 13" baking pan. Add ⅓ of cheese mixture and ⅓ of sauce mixture. Cover with ⅓ of mozzarella cheese. Repeat layers twice, ending with mozzarella cheese. Sprinkle with Parmesan cheese and a little parsley.

5. Bake, uncovered, at 350° for 45 minutes. Let stand 15-20 minutes before serving.

Variation:

To make a plain lasagna substitute 2 beaten eggs and 2 Tbsp. parsley flakes for the spinach and oregano in the cottage cheese mixture.

Karen and Leonard Nolt
Boise, ID
Marilyn Yoder
Archbold, OH

Mexican Lasagna

Sara Fretz-Goering
Silver Spring, MD
Hyattsville Mennonite Church

Makes 6 servings

1 lb. ground beef
17-oz. can corn
15-oz. can tomato sauce
1 cup salsa
1 Tbsp. chili powder
1½ tsp. cumin
16 ozs. cottage cheese
2 eggs, beaten
¼ cup Parmesan cheese
½ tsp. garlic salt
12 corn tortillas
1 cup grated cheddar cheese
Salt and pepper to taste

1. Brown ground beef and drain. Add corn, tomato sauce, salsa, chili powder and cumin. Simmer about 5 minutes, stirring frequently.

2. Combine and mix cottage cheese, eggs, Parmesan cheese and garlic salt.

3. Arrange 6 tortillas on bottom and up the sides of lightly greased 9" x 13" baking pan. Top with half of meat mixture. Spoon cheese mixture over meat. Add another layer tortillas. Top with remaining meat.

4. Bake at 350° for 30 minutes. Remove from oven and top with cheddar cheese. Let stand 10 minutes before serving.

Microwave Lasagna

Mary Ethel Lahman Heatwole
Harrisonburg, VA
Harrisonburg Mennonite Church

Makes 8 servings

½ lb. ground beef
32-oz. jar spaghetti sauce
½ cup water
1½ cups cottage cheese
1 egg
½ tsp. pepper
¼ tsp. oregano
½ Tbsp. parsley flakes
8 lasagna noodles
½ lb. mozzarella cheese, sliced
½ cup Parmesan cheese

1. Microwave ground beef on high for 2-3 minutes. Stir 2-3 times while cooking. Drain excess fat. Add spaghetti sauce and water and set aside.
2. Combine cottage cheese, egg, pepper, oregano and parsley flakes. Set aside.
3. Pour small amount of meat sauce into bottom of 9" x 13" baking pan. Add ½ of noodles, ½ of cottage cheese mixture, ½ of mozzarella cheese and ½ of remaining meat sauce. Repeat layers. Top with Parmesan cheese.
4. Cover dish with plastic wrap, making a tight seal with a small air vent in one corner.
5. Microwave on high for 8 minutes. Reduce to 50% power for 30 minutes. Rotate dish frequently so noodles will not become crisp around the edges.

Beef Lasagna

Edith Stoltzfus
Mantua, OH
Aurora Mennonite Church

Makes 12 servings

2 lbs. ground beef
1 medium onion, chopped
16-oz. can tomatoes
2 8-oz. cans pizza sauce
1 tsp. salt
½ tsp. basil
1 tsp. oregano
8 ozs. lasagna noodles
2 cups cottage cheese
2 cups grated mozzarella cheese
½ cup Parmesan cheese

1. Brown ground beef and onion. Drain excess fat. Add tomatoes, pizza sauce, salt and spices. Cover and cook for 20 minutes, stirring occasionally.
2. Cook lasagna noodles according to directions. Drain.
3. Place 1 cup meat sauce into greased 9" x 13" baking pan and reserve 1 cup meat sauce. Top with ½ of noodles, ½ of remaining meat mixture, ½ of cottage cheese, ½ of mozzarella cheese and ½ of Parmesan cheese. Repeat layers. Distribute reserved 1 cup meat sauce over top. Sprinkle with remaining Parmesan cheese.
4. Bake at 350° for 30 minutes. Let stand 10 minutes before serving.

Spinach Lasagna

Joy Sutter
Iowa City, IA
First Mennonite Church

Makes 8 servings

1 pkg. spaghetti sauce mix
6-oz. can tomato paste
6-oz. can tomato sauce
2 cups water
10-oz. pkg. frozen spinach
1 lb. cottage cheese
½-1 cup Parmesan cheese
2 eggs, beaten
½ lb. lasagna noodles
½ lb. mozzarella cheese, grated

1. Combine spaghetti sauce mix, tomato paste, tomato sauce and water in a saucepan. Simmer for 20 minutes or until thickened.
2. Thaw spinach and squeeze dry.
3. Combine spinach, cottage cheese, ¼-½ cup Parmesan cheese and eggs. Set aside.
4. Cover bottom of greased 9" x 13" baking pan with ½ of tomato sauce mixture. Layer ½ of uncooked noodles, ½ of cheese and spinach mixture and ½ of mozzarella cheese. Repeat layers. Sprinkle top with remaining Parmesan cheese.
5. Cover and bake at 350° for 1 hour.

Layered Spinach Mostaccioli

Linda Welty
La Junta, CO
Emmanuel Mennonite Church

Makes 6-8 servings

8-oz. pkg. mostaccioli noodles
20-oz. jar spaghetti sauce
¼ cup Parmesan cheese
10-oz. pkg. frozen spinach
2 cups shredded mozzarella
   cheese

1. Cook noodles according to package directions. Drain.
2. Combine noodles, sauce and Parmesan cheese.
3. Layer ½ of noodles, ½ of spinach and ½ of mozzarella cheese into 2½-quart casserole. Repeat noodle and spinach layers. Reserve remaining cheese.
4. Cover and bake at 350° for 30 minutes.
5. Top casserole with remaining cheese and return to oven. Bake until cheese has melted.

Stuffed Spinach Shells

Janet Suderman
Indianapolis, IN
First Mennonite Church

Makes 10-12 servings

12-oz. pkg. jumbo shells
32-oz. jar spaghetti sauce
2 cups cottage cheese

2 cups shredded mozzarella
   cheese
½ cup Parmesan cheese
1 small onion, diced
2 Tbsp. parsley flakes
1 Tbsp. oregano
½ tsp. garlic powder
10-oz. pkg. frozen spinach

1. Cook jumbo shells according to package directions. Drain and set aside.
2. Pour ½ of spaghetti sauce into bottom of crockpot.
3. Combine all remaining ingredients. Stuff each shell with spinach mixture and layer into crockpot.
4. Pour remaining spaghetti sauce over shells.
5. Cook on low for 4 hours or until heated and bubbly.

Inside Outside Ravioli

Rachel W. Martin
Mechanicsburg, PA

Makes 10 servings

1 lb. ground beef
½ cup chopped onion
10-oz. pkg. frozen, chopped
   spinach
8-oz. can tomato sauce
6-oz. can tomato paste
½ tsp. salt
Dash pepper
1-lb. jar spaghetti sauce
3 cups shell macaroni,
   cooked
1 cup grated cheddar cheese
½ cup soft bread crumbs
2 eggs, beaten
1 Tbsp. cooking oil

1. Brown ground beef and onion.
2. Cook spinach according to package directions. Drain, reserving liquid. Add enough water to liquid to make 1 cup.
3. Add 1 cup spinach liquid, tomato sauce, tomato paste, salt, pepper and spaghetti sauce to ground beef. Simmer for 10 minutes.
4. Combine spinach with cooked macaroni, cheddar cheese, bread crumbs, eggs and cooking oil. Spread into 9" x 13" baking pan. Top with meat sauce.
5. Bake at 350° for 30 minutes. Let stand 10 minutes before serving.

Spaghetti with Celantri

Jean Yan
Regina, SK
Chinese Fellowship

Makes 6 servings

1 lb. spaghetti
2 eggs
½ tsp. salt
Dash pepper
4 Tbsp. cooking oil
2 tsp. Chinese pepper
½ tsp. salt
30 stalks celantri
1 Tbsp. chopped ginger
   root
2 Tbsp. oyster sauce
4 green onions, sliced

1. Cook spaghetti according to directions. Drain and set aside.

2. Beat eggs. Add ½ tsp. salt and a dash of pepper.

3. Heat 1 Tbsp. oil in large frying pan. Pour ½ of egg mixture into pan, making a large egg pancake. Remove pancake and set aside. Repeat procedure with other half of egg mixture. Cut egg pancakes into strips and set aside.

4. Heat 3 Tbsp. oil in a frying pan. Add Chinese pepper. Heat until it turns dark, dark brown. Remove pepper from oil and discard pepper.

5. To the cooking oil add ½ tsp. salt, spaghetti, eggs, celantri, ginger root, oyster sauce and green onions. Stir fry until heated through. Serve.

Spaghetti in a Crockpot

Sarah Grieser
Akron, PA
Blossom Hill Mennonite Church

Makes 12-15 servings

1 lb. ground beef
1 onion, chopped
2 tsp. salt
1 tsp. garlic powder
2 15-oz. cans tomato sauce
2½ tsp. Italian seasoning
½ lb. mushrooms, sliced
6 cups tomato juice
8 ozs. spaghetti noodles

1. Brown ground beef and onion. Drain excess fat. Place all ingredients except spaghetti in crockpot.

2. Cook 6-8 hours on low or 3-5 hours on high. For the last ½ hour add dry spaghetti and cook on high.

Baked Spaghetti

Rosanna J. Ranck
Christiana, PA
Andrews Bridge Mennonite Fellowship

Makes 12 servings

1 medium onion, chopped
2 Tbsp. cooking oil
1 lb. ground beef
2 tsp. salt
1 tsp. sugar
3 cups cooked tomatoes
8 ozs. spaghetti noodles
½ cup grated sharp cheese

1. Sauté onion in oil until yellow. Add ground beef and cook until browned. Drain excess fat. Add salt, sugar and tomatoes.

2. Cook spaghetti noodles according to directions. Drain. Add to meat mixture. Pour into greased baking dish. Sprinkle with grated cheese.

3. Bake at 350° for 30-40 minutes.

Smokehouse Spaghetti

Yvonne E. Martin
Mechanicsburg, PA
Grantham Brethren in Christ

Makes 6 servings

¼ lb. bacon
1 lb. ground beef
1 medium onion, chopped
2 8-oz. cans tomato sauce
4-oz. can mushrooms with juice
1½ tsp. salt
⅛ tsp. pepper
½ tsp. oregano
½ tsp. garlic salt
8 ozs. spaghetti noodles
¼ lb. Provolone cheese
¼ lb. cheddar cheese

1. Fry, drain and crumble bacon.

2. Brown ground beef and onion. Drain excess fat. Add bacon pieces, tomato sauce, mushrooms and spices. Simmer for 15 minutes.

3. Cook spaghetti according to directions. Drain. Fold spaghetti into meat sauce. Spoon into greased 2-quart casserole dish, alternating with cheeses. Top with cheese.

4. Bake at 375° for 20-25 minutes.

Spaghetti Cheese Bake

Eileen Heintz
Sarasota, FL
Bayshore Mennonite Church

Makes 12-15 servings

1 lb. ground beef
1 large onion, chopped
1-lb. can tomatoes, drained
6-oz. can tomato paste
1 clove garlic
1 tsp. salt
½ tsp. basil
½ tsp. oregano
¼ tsp. thyme
8 ozs. spaghetti noodles
1 cup Parmesan cheese
2 cups milk
3 eggs, beaten
½ tsp. salt
Dash of pepper
1 cup grated mozzarella
   cheese

1. Brown ground beef with onion. Drain well. Add tomatoes, tomato paste, garlic and seasonings. Simmer 15 minutes until thickened.

2. Cook spaghetti according to directions. Drain well and spread into a 9" x 13" baking pan. Sprinkle with Parmesan cheese.

3. In separate bowl combine milk, eggs, salt and pepper. Pour over spaghetti. Spread meat sauce over milk sauce. Sprinkle with mozzarella cheese.

4. Bake at 375° for 40-45 minutes. Let stand 10 minutes and cut into squares before serving.

Spaghetti Casserole

Marian R. Denlinger
Willow Street, PA
River Corner Mennonite Church

Makes 10 servings

1 lb. spaghetti
1 lb. ground beef
28-oz. can tomatoes
½ lb. Velveeta cheese, cubed
1 can cream of mushroom
   soup

1. Cook spaghetti in salt water until tender. Drain.

2. Brown ground beef and drain excess fat.

3. Combine spaghetti, ground beef, tomatoes, cheese and soup in a casserole dish.

4. Bake at 350° for 30 minutes.

Spaghetti Pizza

Sandy Tinsler
Wauseon, OH
Central Mennonite Church

Makes 10-12 servings

12 ozs. spaghetti noodles
2 eggs
½ cup milk
1 cup grated mozzarella
   cheese
¾ tsp. garlic powder
½ tsp. salt
1 lb. ground beef
30-oz. jar spaghetti sauce
1½ tsp. oregano
3 cups grated mozzarella
   cheese
Sliced pepperoni

1. Break spaghetti into 2-inch pieces. Cook and drain.

2. In large bowl mix eggs, milk, 1 cup mozzarella cheese, garlic powder and salt. Fold in spaghetti. Spread into greased 9" x 13" baking pan.

3. Bake at 350° for 10 minutes.

4. Brown ground beef. Drain excess fat. Spread ground beef over spaghetti crust.

5. Pour spaghetti sauce over other ingredients. Sprinkle with oregano and cheese. Arrange pepperoni slices over top. If desired, freeze for serving at a later time.

6. Bake at 350° for an additional 25-30 minutes.

Variation:
Substitute 2 cups grated cheddar cheese and 2 cups grated mozzarella cheese for the 4 cups grated mozzarella cheese.

Jan Pembleton
Arlington, TX
Hope Mennonite Church

Harriet Swank's Homemade Spaghetti Sauce

Harriet Swank
Scottdale, PA
Kingview Mennonite Church

½ bushel tomatoes
3 lbs. onions, chopped
1 pint cooking oil
1½ cups sugar
Pinch cayenne pepper
2 Tbsp. oregano
2 cloves garlic, minced

2 Tbsp. basil leaves
½ cup salt

1. Cook tomatoes into a juice. Dip excess water off top.
2. Sauté onions in oil for ½ hour.
3. Combine all ingredients and put into large roaster.
4. Bake, uncovered, at 325° for 2 hours, stirring occasionally.
5. Pour into 1-quart jars and seal.
6. When ready to use, mix 2 6-oz. cans tomato paste with 1 quart spaghetti sauce.

Crockpot Pasta

Bertha Rush
Hatfield, PA

Makes 6 servings

12-oz. pkg. spiral pasta
2 16-oz. cans stewed tomatoes
10¾-oz. can chicken broth
2 tsp. cooking oil
1 ¼ tsp. Italian seasoning

1. Cook pasta according to directions. Rinse and drain.
2. Combine all ingredients in a crockpot.
3. Cook on low 3-4 hours.

Rigatoni in Crockpot

Harriet Swank
Scottdale, PA
Kingview Mennonite Church

Makes 20 servings

2 lbs. rigatoni
2 quarts homemade spaghetti sauce
4 6-oz. cans tomato paste

1. Cook rigatoni according to directions until tender. Drain.
2. Combine all ingredients in a crockpot. Turn to low and cook during church service.

Baked Ziti

Gail U. Pentz
Sarasota, FL
Bahia Vista Mennonite Church

Makes 8-10 servings

1 lb. ziti
1 lb. cottage cheese
2 Tbsp. Parmesan cheese
1 egg
1 tsp. parsley flakes
⅛ tsp. pepper
⅛ tsp. salt
¼ tsp. granulated garlic
4 cups tomato sauce
½ lb. mozzarella cheese, grated

1. Cook ziti according to directions.
2. Blend cottage cheese, Parmesan cheese, egg and spices. Add ziti and mix lightly.
3. Pour 1½ cups tomato sauce into 9" x 13" baking pan. Add ziti mixture. Pour remaining tomato sauce over top. Sprinkle with mozzarella cheese.
4. Bake at 375° for 25-30 minutes.

Variation:
Substitute spaghetti sauce for tomato sauce.

Gladys Rutt
Blue Ball, PA

Noodles and Chives Casserole

Hazel N. Hassan
Goshen, IN
College Mennonite Church

Makes 12 servings

10-12 ozs. noodles
2 Tbsp. margarine
1 cup sour cream
1 cup milk
2 cups cottage cheese
¼ tsp. pepper
1 tsp. salt
¼ cup chopped chives

1. Cook noodles according to directions. Drain. Add margarine immediately and toss noodles until well coated.
2. Stir in sour cream, milk, cottage cheese, pepper and salt. Gently fold in chives. Spoon into ungreased casserole dish.
3. Bake at 350° for 25 minutes.

Baked Macaroni and Cheese (large recipe)

Laura Siemens
Rosenort, MB

Makes 50 servings

6-8 lbs. macaroni
1 lb. margarine
2½ cups flour
¼ cup salt
1 tsp. black pepper
2½ gallons milk
5 lbs. cheese, cubed
Buttered bread crumbs
    (optional)

1. Cook macaroni according to directions until just tender. Drain, rinse and drain again.
2. Make a thin white sauce by melting margarine. Stir in flour, salt and pepper. Gradually add milk, stirring constantly until slightly thickened.
3. Combine macaroni, white sauce and ⅔ of cheese. Spread mixture into five greased 10" x 16" baking pans. Sprinkle remaining cheese over top of each dish. Add buttered bread crumbs if desired.
4. Bake at 250° for 20-30 minutes or until thoroughly heated and lightly browned on top.

Macaroni and Cheese

Hazel Mast
Phoenix, AZ
Trinity Mennonite Church

Makes 8-10 servings

8-oz. pkg. elbow macaroni
2 cups cottage cheese
1 cup sour cream
¾ tsp. salt
2 cups shredded sharp
    cheddar cheese
Paprika

1. Cook macaroni according to directions. Drain and rinse.
2. Combine cottage cheese, sour cream, salt, cheese and macaroni. Mix well. Pour into 2-quart casserole dish. Sprinkle with paprika.
3. Bake at 350° for 45 minutes.

Variation:
Add 1 slightly beaten egg and 3 Tbsp. minced onion to the ingredients before baking.
Kathy Falk
Champaign, IL

Substitute ¾ cup sour cream and ¼ cup plain yogurt for 1 cup sour cream. Use low-fat cottage cheese. Substitute 2 cups shredded American cheese for sharp cheddar cheese.
Marilyn Langeman
Akron, PA

Baked Macaroni and Cheese (small recipe)

Mabel Neff
Quarryville, PA

Makes 6-8 servings

8-oz. pkg. elbow macaroni
3 Tbsp. butter
⅓ cup all-purpose flour
½ tsp. salt
Dash pepper
2 cups milk
8 ozs. cheddar cheese,
    shredded

1. Cook macaroni according to directions. Drain.
2. In 1½-quart saucepan melt butter. Blend in flour, salt and pepper, stirring until bubbly. Remove from heat and gradually stir in milk. Return to heat and cook, stirring constantly until thickened. Add 1½ cups shredded cheese. Stir until melted.
3. Turn cheese sauce and macaroni into casserole dish. Sprinkle with remaining shredded cheese.
4. Bake at 325° for 40 minutes.

Breakfast Foods

Ham and Cheese Soufflé

Catharine Leatherman
Mount Joy, PA

Jean E. Bender
Williamsville, NY
Harris Hill Mennonite Fellowship

Makes 10-12 servings

16 slices bread, cubed
1 lb. cooked ham, sliced
1 lb. sharp cheddar cheese, grated
1½ cups chopped Swiss cheese
6 eggs
3 cups milk
⅓ tsp. onion salt
½ tsp. dry mustard
3 cups crushed cornflakes
½ cup melted butter

1. Spread ½ of bread cubes into bottom of greased 9" x 13" glass baking dish. Add ham and both cheeses and cover with remaining bread cubes.
2. Combine eggs, milk, onion, salt and mustard and pour evenly over bread cubes. Refrigerate overnight.
3. Combine cornflakes and melted butter. Immediately before baking, sprinkle cornflake topping over casserole dish.
4. Bake at 375° for 40 minutes.

Breakfast Soufflé

Freda Friesen
Hillsboro, KS
Hillsboro Mennonite Brethren Church

Makes 10-12 servings

1½ lbs. pork sausage
9 eggs
3 cups milk
1½ tsp. dry mustard
1 tsp. salt
3 slices bread, cubed
1½ cups grated cheddar cheese

1. Brown pork sausage and drain excess fat. Set aside.
2. Combine eggs, milk, mustard and salt. Add sausage, bread and cheese. Spoon into greased 9" x 13" pan. Cover and refrigerate overnight.
3. Bake, uncovered, at 350° for 1 hour.

Variation:
Use only ¾ lb. sausage, bacon, ham or chicken and ¾ cup grated cheddar cheese. Add ¾ cup grated Swiss cheese and a bit of chopped onion.

Alice Suderman
New Hope, MN
New Hope Mennonite Brethren Church

Night Before Breakfast

Melodie Davis
Harrisonburg, VA
Trinity Presbyterian

Makes 10-12 servings

1 lb. mild sausage
4 slices bread, cubed
1 cup grated sharp cheese
6 eggs
2 cups milk

1. Brown sausage and drain. Set aside.
2. Arrange cubed bread in bottom of greased 9" x 13" baking dish. Place sausage over bread and sprinkle cheese over sausage.
3. Beat eggs and milk together and pour over casserole dish. Refrigerate overnight.
4. Bake at 350° for 45 minutes.

Variations:
Add 1 tsp. dry mustard and 1 tsp. salt to egg and milk mixture.

Ellen Steiner
Temperance, MI
Monroe Street United Methodist

Substitute 2 cups plain croutons for cubed bread. Add 4 slices bacon. Fry bacon to a crisp; drain and crumble it. Sprinkle bacon over top of casserole dish.

Iona S. Weaver
Lansdale, PA
Norristown New Life Church

Extra Egg Brunch

Viola Weidner
Allentown, PA
First Mennonite Church

Makes 8-12 servings

6 eggs, beaten
3 cups milk
1½ tsp. dry mustard
2 Tbsp. parsley
3 Tbsp. chopped onion
¼ tsp. salt
6 slices bread, cubed
¾ lb. grated Colby cheese
2 cups chopped ham, chicken *or* shrimp

1. Gently fold together all ingredients. Pour into greased 9" x 13" casserole dish. Refrigerate overnight.
2. Bake uncovered at 350° for 40-45 minutes.

Breakfast Casserole

Sharon Anders
Alburtis, PA
Hampden Mennonite Church

Makes 6 servings

3 medium potatoes
½ lb. cubed, cooked ham
1 cup grated cheddar cheese
4 eggs, slightly scrambled
Parsley flakes (optional)

1. Cook, peel and grate the potatoes.
2. In 1½-quart casserole dish layer ham, potatoes, cheese and eggs. Top with parsley.

3. Bake at 375° for 15 minutes.

Variation:
Substitute ½ lb. hot sausage, fried and drained, for ham.
Add ½ cup cottage cheese to layers.

Marlene Smucker
Arvada, CO

Easter Breakfast Casserole

Arlene M. Mark
Elkhart, IN
Prairie Street Mennonite Church

Makes 12 large servings

4 cups dried bread cubes
2 cups shredded cheddar cheese
¾-1 lb. chopped ham
8 eggs, beaten
4 cups milk
1 tsp. salt
½ tsp. pepper
1 tsp. dry mustard

1. Combine bread cubes, cheddar cheese and ham. Spread into 9" x 13" baking dish.
2. Blend together all remaining ingredients. Pour over first layer. Refrigerate overnight.
3. Bake at 325° for 1 hour.

Tortilla de Patatas

Elaine Klaassen
Minneapolis, MN
Faith Mennonite Church

Makes 4-6 servings

1½ cups cooking oil
6 medium potatoes, thinly
　sliced
2 medium onions, chopped
1 Tbsp. salt
4 large eggs

1. Begin heating oil in a 10" cast-iron skillet. Slice potatoes into skillet with sharp knife. Add onions. Let potatoes and onions boil in the oil. Do not brown. Add salt. Stir with spatula and break sliced potatoes as they begin to soften. When potatoes and onions are soft, drain oil.

2. In a bowl beat eggs. Stir in potatoes and onions.

3. Pour ½ of mixture into lightly greased 8" skillet. Smooth it flat and shake skillet as mixture cooks. Turn and cook other side, shaking skillet as it cooks. Repeat process with other half of ingredients.

4. Cut each omelet into several pieces and serve.

Baked Oatmeal

Miriam M. Witmer
Manheim, PA
Erisman Mennonite Church

Makes 10 servings

½ cup cooking oil
2 eggs, beaten
1 cup sugar
3 cups oatmeal
2 tsp. baking powder
1 tsp. salt
1 cup milk

1. Combine cooking oil, eggs and sugar. Add oatmeal, baking powder, salt and milk.

2. Bake at 350° for 30-35 minutes. Serve.

Apple Sausage Breakfast Ring

Ina Eigsti
Hesston, KS
Hesston Mennonite Church

Makes 8-10 servings

2 lbs. bulk sausage
2 large eggs
1½ cups crushed Ritz
　crackers
1 cup grated apples
½ cup minced onion
¼ cup milk
Scrambled eggs
Parsley

1. Combine all ingredients except scrambled eggs and parsley. Press into a 2½-quart ring pan. Chill over-

night or at least several hours.

2. Bake at 350° for 45 minutes to 1 hour. Pour off all excess fat.

3. Mix your favorite scrambled eggs recipe.

4. Put baked sausage ring out on round serving dish. Fill center of ring with scrambled eggs. Garnish with parsley.

Oklahoma Cheese Grits

Marlene Smucker
Arvada, CO

Makes 6-8 servings

1 cup quick-cooking grits
4 cups boiling water
1 tsp. salt
2 Tbsp. margarine
2 eggs, beaten
½ cup milk
½ lb. sharp cheddar cheese,
　grated
Paprika

1. Cook grits in boiling, salted water according to directions on package. Add margarine, stirring until melted. Remove from heat.

2. Combine eggs and milk. Add to grits. Fold in grated cheese, reserving ½ cup. Spoon into greased 1½-quart casserole dish. Sprinkle with remaining cheese and paprika.

3. Bake at 350° for 30-40 minutes.

Easy Quiche

Becky Bontrager Horst
Goshen, IN
College Mennonite Church

Makes 6 servings

¼ cup chopped onion
¼ cup chopped mushroom (optional)
1 Tbsp. cooking oil
4 ozs. cheese, shredded
2 Tbsp. bacon bits, chopped ham or browned sausage
4 eggs
½ tsp. salt
1½ cups milk
½ cup whole wheat flour
2 Tbsp. margarine

1. Sauté onion and mushroom in cooking oil. Combine cheese, meat and vegetables in greased 9" pie pan.
2. Combine remaining ingredients in medium bowl. Pour over meat and vegetable mixture.
3. Bake at 350° for 45 minutes. This quiche will make its own crust.

Quiche

Marjorie Weaver Nafziger
Harman, WV

Makes 6 servings

9" unbaked pie shell
2 cups chopped tomatoes, green beans, onions *or* mushrooms
½-¾ cup chopped chicken, sausage, ham, bacon *or* ground beef
½ tsp. basil, sage, thyme *or* oregano
1 tsp. salt
Dash pepper
1 cup grated Swiss, cheddar *or* a mixture of cheeses
2 eggs, slightly beaten
2 Tbsp. flour
1 cup evaporated milk

1. Bake pie shell for 10 minutes.
2. Lightly saute choice of vegetables and meats. Spoon into pie shell. Sprinkle choice of seasonings over vegetable mixture. Add salt and dash of pepper. Cover with choice of grated cheese.
3. Combine eggs, flour and milk. Pour over ingredients.
4. Bake at 375° for 40-45 minutes or until set. Let sit at least 5 minutes before serving.

Variation:
The secret to this quiche is using the combination of ingredients you prefer.

Instead of using regular pie shell, combine 3 Tbsp. cooking oil with 3-4 cups grated potatoes. Press mixture into 9" pie pan and bake at 425° for 15 minutes.

Impossible Quiche

Georgia L. Martin
Lancaster, PA
Charlotte Street Mennonite Church

Makes 6-8 servings

½ lb. bacon
1 cup shredded cheese
⅓ cup chopped onion
2 cups milk
1 cup Bisquick
4 eggs
¼ tsp. salt
⅛ tsp. pepper

1. Fry, drain and crumble bacon. Sprinkle over bottom of pie plate. Sprinkle with shredded cheese and chopped onion.
2. Combine milk, Bisquick, eggs, salt and pepper. Beat for 1 minute. Pour over bacon, cheese and onion. Mix all ingredients.
3. Bake at 350° for 50 minutes.

Ham Quiche

Lucille Taylor
Hutchinson, KS
First Mennonite Church

Makes 8-12 servings

24-oz. pkg. frozen hash brown potatoes
4 Tbsp. butter, melted
½ lb. ham, cubed
12 ozs. Monterey Jack cheese, shredded
4 ozs. hot pepper cheese, shredded

1 cup half-and-half
5 eggs, slightly beaten
½ tsp. seasoned salt

1. Partially thaw potatoes. Drain any liquid. Press potatoes into greased 9" x 13" pan. Drizzle melted butter over potatoes.

2. Bake at 425° for 25 minutes.

3. Combine ham and cheeses. Spread over potato crust.

4. Combine half-and-half, eggs and salt. Pour over ham and cheese mixture.

5. Bake at 350° for 30-40 minutes.

Spinach Quiche

Geraldine A. Ebersole
Hershey, PA
Akron Mennonite Church

Makes 35 appetizer servings

Pastry Crust:
3 ¾ cups all-purpose flour, sifted
1½ tsp. salt
1 cup vegetable shortening, chilled
¾ cup water
1 egg, beaten
1 Tbsp. milk

Spinach Filling:
2 cups grated Swiss cheese
10-oz. pkg. frozen, chopped spinach
1¾ cups light cream
4 eggs, beaten
1 Tbsp. margarine, melted
1 tsp. salt
⅛ tsp. pepper
⅛ tsp. ground nutmeg

1. To prepare pastry crust place sifted flour and salt in large mixing bowl. Cut in shortening with a pastry blender until mixture resembles coarse crumbs.

2. Sprinkle water over crumbs, 1-2 Tbsp. at a time, and mix lightly with fork until pastry holds together.

3. On lightly floured surface roll out pastry into 13" x 18" rectangle. Fit into a 10½" x 15½" jelly roll pan. Prick bottom and sides with fork.

4. Beat egg with 1 Tbsp. milk and brush crust with egg.

5. Bake at 425° for 20 minutes or until lightly browned. Cool completely.

6. When crust has cooled, sprinkle grated cheese evenly over bottom.

7. Combine all remaining ingredients. Pour evenly over cheese.

8. Bake at 425° for 15 minutes. Reduce heat to 350° and bake another 10-15 minutes or until top is golden brown and knife inserted comes out clean. Cool at least 10 minutes before cutting into squares or diamonds.

I often prepare this several days in advance, wrapping and freezing it. To serve unwrap frozen quiche and heat at 325° for 25 minutes or until quiche is hot.

Pies

Amish Vanilla Pies

A. Catharine Boshart
Lebanon, PA
Hereford Mennonite Home Church

Makes 2 9" pies

1 cup white sugar
4 Tbsp. flour
1 egg, beaten
1 cup molasses
2 cups water
1 tsp. vanilla
2 cups flour
1 cup brown sugar
1 tsp. baking soda
1 tsp. cream of tartar
¼ cup butter *or* margarine
¼ cup lard *or* shortening
2 9" unbaked pie shells

1. In a saucepan combine white sugar, 4 Tbsp. flour, egg, molasses, water and vanilla. Bring to a full, rolling boil. Set aside to cool.
2. In a large bowl combine 2 cups flour, brown sugar, baking soda, cream of tartar, butter and lard. Rub together with fingers to make crumbs.
3. Pour ½ of cooked mixture into each unbaked pie shell. Cover each pie with crumbs.
4. Bake at 350° for 40-45 minutes.

I like taking this pie to fellowship meals because it makes a great conversation piece. Also I can make it ahead of time and it is easy to serve.

Impossible Custard Pie

Clara L. Hershberger
Goshen, IN
Goshen Mennonite Church

Makes 1 deep 9" pie

½ cup Bisquick
½ cup sugar
4 eggs
2 cups milk
1 tsp. vanilla
3 Tbsp. butter *or* margarine, melted

1. Combine all ingredients in a blender. Mix for 2 minutes.
2. Pour ingredients into greased 9" deep pie plate.
3. Bake at 400° for 25-30 minutes or until custard is set.

Custard Pie

Verda Swartzendruber
Kalona, IA
Iowa Mennonite School

Makes 1 9" pie

2¼ cups milk
4 eggs
½ cup sugar
1 tsp. vanilla
½ tsp. salt
Nutmeg
1 9" unbaked pie shell

1. Scald the milk.
2. In medium bowl beat the eggs. Add milk, sugar, vanilla and salt and mix well.
3. Pour custard into pie shell. Sprinkle with nutmeg.
4. Bake at 475° for 5 minutes. Reduce oven temperature to 425° and bake 15 minutes longer.

Peanut Butter Cream Pie

Mary I. Smucker
Goshen, IN
College Mennonite Church

Makes 1 9" pie

6-oz. pkg. instant vanilla pudding
¾ cup powdered sugar
½ cup peanut butter
Whipped topping
1 9" baked pie shell

1. Prepare pudding according to package directions.
2. Crumble sugar and peanut butter together.
3. Put ⅔ cup peanut butter crumbs into baked pie shell. Fill with chilled pudding. Top with whipped topping. Sprinkle remaining peanut butter crumbs over topping.
4. Keep refrigerated until ready to serve.

Peanut Butter Pie

Jeanette Harder
Garland, TX

Makes 1 9" pie

16-20 Oreo cookies, crushed
¼ cup butter
3 ozs. cream cheese
⅓ cup peanut butter
1 cup powdered sugar
½ cup milk
¾ cup whipped topping
Chocolate shavings

1. Mix crushed cookies with butter. Press into pie plate.
2. Bake at 400° for 5 minutes. Cool.
3. Combine cream cheese, peanut butter, sugar and milk. Stir until smooth. Pour into Oreo cookie crust. Refrigerate.
4. Immediately before serving, top with whipped topping and sprinkle with chocolate shavings.

French Silk Pie

Ila Yoder
Hesston, KS
Whitestone Mennonite Church

Makes 1 10" pie

8 Tbsp. margarine, softened
¾ cup sugar
4-5 Tbsp. cocoa
1 Tbsp. vanilla
2 eggs
½ pint whipping cream
Chocolate shavings
1 10" baked pie shell

1. Cream margarine until smooth. Gradually add sugar and cream well. Add cocoa and vanilla and cream well.
2. Add 1 egg and beat 5 minutes. Add 1 egg and beat an additional 5 minutes. Pour mixture into baked pie shell. Chill.
3. Whip cream. Immediately before serving, top with whipped cream and sprinkle with chocolate shavings.

Chocolate Chess Pie

Rosemary K. Hartzler
High Point, NC
Greensboro Mennonite Church

Makes 2 deep 9" pies

7 Tbsp. cocoa
3 cups sugar
8 Tbsp. butter *or* margarine, melted
4 eggs
13-oz. can evaporated milk
1 tsp. vanilla
2 9" unbaked pie shells

1. Combine cocoa, sugar, melted butter, eggs, milk and vanilla in blender. Mix well on low speed.
2. Pour into 2 9" deep pie shells.
3. Bake at 350° for 35 minutes.

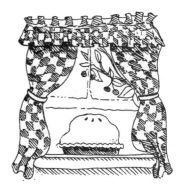

Chocolate Mousse Pie

Lillian F. Gardner
Crystal, MN
New Hope Mennonite Brethren

Makes 1 9" pie

2 squares chocolate
½ cup butter *or* margarine
¾ cup sugar
3 eggs
4-oz. container whipped topping
1 9" baked pie shell

1. Melt chocolate in double boiler. Cool.
2. Cream butter. Gradually add sugar and beat until light and fluffy. Add melted chocolate. Add eggs, one at a time, beating at high speed for 5 minutes after each addition.
3. Fold whipped topping into mixture. Spoon into baked pie shell.
4. Chill until firm, at least 4 hours. Serve.

Chocolatetown Pie

Elizabeth Yutzy
Wauseon, OH
Inlet Mennonite Church

Makes 1 9" pie

½ cup butter *or* margarine, softened
2 eggs, beaten
2 tsp. vanilla
1 cup sugar or less
½ cup all-purpose flour
1 cup semi-sweet chocolate chips
1 cup chopped pecans
Whipped topping (optional)
1 9" unbaked pie shell

1. In small bowl cream butter. Add eggs and vanilla and mix well.
2. Combine sugar and flour. Add to creamed mixture. Fold in chocolate chips and pecans. Pour into unbaked pie shell.
3. Bake at 350 F. for 45-50 minutes or until golden. Cool at least 1 hour.
4. Garnish with whipped topping if desired.

French Rhubarb Pie

Hettie Conrad
Colorado Springs, CO

Makes 1 9" pie

1 egg
1 cup white sugar
1 Tbsp. flour
1 tsp. vanilla
3 cups diced rhubarb

¾ cup flour
⅓ cup margarine
½ cup brown sugar
1 9" unbaked pie shell

1. Combine egg, white sugar, 1 Tbsp. flour and vanilla and mix well. Fold in diced rhubarb. Spoon into unbaked pie shell.
2. Combine ¾ cup flour, margarine and brown sugar. Crumble with fingers. Spread over rhubarb mixture.
3. Bake at 400° for 10 minutes. Reduce oven temperature to 350° and bake 40 minutes longer.

Rhubarb Pie

Vera Kuhns
Harrisonburg, VA
Parkview Mennonite Church

Makes 1 9" pie

4 cups rhubarb
¾ cup white sugar
½ cup brown sugar
4½ Tbsp. cornstarch
1 tsp. cinnamon
1 Tbsp. butter *or* margarine
1 9" unbaked pie shell

1. In a medium bowl combine rhubarb, sugars, cornstarch, cinnamon and butter. Spoon into unbaked pie shell.
2. Bake at 375° for about 1 hour or until bubbly and brown. Serve warm with milk.

Louisiana Sweet Potato Pie

Dorothy L. Ealy
Los Angeles, CA
Calvary Christian Fellowship

Makes 2 9" pies

2 ½ cups cooked, mashed
   sweet potatoes
½ cup butter
2 cups sugar or less
½ tsp. salt
1 tsp. nutmeg
2 eggs, beaten
⅔ cup evaporated milk
2 9" unbaked pie shells

1. Combine sweet potatoes and butter, mixing until well blended. Add sugar, salt and nutmeg. Fold in eggs and milk and mix well.
2. Pour mixture into 2 unbaked pie shells.
3. Bake at 325° for 60 minutes.

Pumpkin Pie

Beth Shank
Wellman, IA
Wellman Mennonite Church

Makes 1 9" pie

16-oz. can pumpkin
½ tsp. salt
1 ½ cups milk
3 eggs, beaten
1 cup white sugar
1 tsp. cinnamon
½ tsp. nutmeg
½ tsp. ginger
1 9" unbaked pie shell

1. Combine all ingredients except pie shell in blender or mixer and mix well. Pour into unbaked pie shell.
2. Bake at 425° for 50-55 minutes.

Variation:
Substitute 1¾ cups well-strained squash for the pumpkin. Add 1 Tbsp. melted butter to the ingredients when using squash.

Impossible Pumpkin Pie

Miriam Christophel
Battle Creek, MI
Pine Grove Mennonite Church

Makes 1 10" pie

¾ cup sugar
½ cup Bisquick
2 Tbsp. butter *or* margarine
13-oz. can evaporated milk
2 eggs

16-oz. can pumpkin
1½ tsp. pumpkin pie spices
2 tsp. vanilla

1. Beat all ingredients until smooth, 1 minute in blender or 2 minutes with hand beater. Pour into greased 10" pie plate.
2. Bake at 350° until knife inserted in center comes out clean, 50-55 minutes.

Many calories are cut by not using a regular crust. I substitute skim milk for evaporated milk which also reduces fat content.

Pumpkin Pecan Pie

Viola Stauffer
Milford, NE
Bellwood Mennonite Church

Makes 1 9" pie

4 eggs
16-oz. can pumpkin
¾ cup sugar
½ cup dark corn syrup
1 tsp. cinnamon
¼ tsp. salt
1 cup pecans
1 9" unbaked pie shell

1. In a large bowl beat eggs lightly. Stir in pumpkin, sugar, corn syrup, cinnamon and salt and mix well. Pour into unbaked pie shell. Arrange pecans on top.
2. Bake at 350° for 45-55 minutes or until filling is set and a knife inserted in center comes out clean.

Pecan Pie

Linda Welty
La Junta, CO
Emmanuel Mennonite Church

Makes 1 9" pie

¾ **cup white sugar**
2 **Tbsp. flour**
¾ **tsp. salt**
1 **cup dark corn syrup**
2 **eggs, beaten**
½ **cup evaporated milk**
1 **cup pecans**
1 **tsp. vanilla**
1 **9" unbaked pie shell**

1. Mix all ingredients and pour into unbaked pie shell.
2. Bake at 350° for 50 minutes or until firm.
3. Serve with ice cream or whipped topping.

Sour Cream Raisin Pie

Diena Schmidt
Henderson, NE
Bethesda Mennonite Church

Makes 1 10" pie

1 **cup raisins**
1 **cup brown sugar**
⅓ **cup cornstarch**
2 **eggs, beaten**
1 **cup sour cream**
Dash salt
4 **cups whipped topping**
1 **10" baked pie shell**

1. Cook raisins in water until plump. Drain, reserving liquid. Measure 1 cup liquid (add water if needed)
2. Add 1 cup liquid and brown sugar to raisins and bring to a boil.
3. Dissolve cornstarch in water and stir into raisin mixture, stirring constantly to avoid scorching. Slowly add eggs, stirring until eggs are cooked. (Mixture will be quite thick.) Cool.
4. When mixture has cooled, add sour cream. Fold in 2 cups whipped topping. Spoon into pie shell.
5. Chill. Immediately before serving, top with remaining whipped topping.

Peach Praline Pie

Ginny Miller
Goshen, IN
Sunnyside Mennonite Church

Makes 1 9" pie

1 **Tbsp. lemon juice**
4 **cups sliced peaches**
½ **cup white sugar**
2 **Tbsp. tapioca flour**
½ **cup flour**
¼ **cup brown sugar**
¼ **cup butter**
½ **cup broken pecans**
1 **9" unbaked pie shell**

1. Sprinkle lemon juice over peaches.
2. Combine white sugar and tapioca flour. Toss with peaches and let stand about 15 minutes.
3. Mix flour, brown sugar and butter until crumbly. Add pecans. Sprinkle ½ of this crumb mixture into bottom of unbaked pie shell. Add peaches and top with remaining crumbs.
4. Bake at 375° for 40-45 minutes.

Creamy Peach Pie

Laura Nisly
Grantham, PA
Slate Hill Mennonite Church

Makes 1 9" pie

3-**oz. pkg. peach gelatin**
¾ **cup boiling water**
1 **cup peach ice cream**
4-**oz. pkg. instant vanilla
  pudding**
1 **cup milk**
1 **cup whipped topping**
Peach slices
1 **9" baked pie shell**

1. Dissolve gelatin in boiling water. Add ice cream and stir until melted.
2. In a small bowl combine dry pudding mix and milk. Beat slowly for about 2 minutes. Add gelatin mixture and whip until thick and fluffy. Fold in ½ cup whipped topping. Spoon into baked pie shell. Chill at least 2 hours.
3. Garnish with ½ cup whipped topping and peach slices before serving.

Lemon Chiffon Pie

Mary Herr and Elsie Lehman
Three Rivers, MI
The Hermitage Community Chapel

Makes 1 9" pie

4 egg yolks, slightly beaten
½ cup sugar
⅔ cup water
⅓ cup lemon juice
1 pkg. unflavored gelatin
1 Tbsp. grated lemon rind
4 egg whites
½ tsp. cream of tartar
½ cup sugar
Whipped topping (optional)
1 9" baked pie shell

1. In a saucepan mix slightly beaten egg yolks, ½ cup sugar, water, lemon juice and gelatin. Heat to boiling point over medium heat, stirring constantly. Remove from heat.
2. Stir in lemon rind. Place saucepan in bowl of ice water. Stir occasionally until mixture mounds when dropped from a spoon.
3. Beat egg whites and cream of tartar until foamy. Beat in ½ cup sugar, 1 Tbsp. at a time. Continue beating until stiff and glossy. Fold in lemon mixture. Mound into pie shell.
4. Refrigerate until set, at least 3 hours. Serve with whipped topping if desired. (Leftover pie should be refrigerated immediately.)

Lemon Meringue Pie

Alma C. Ranck
Paradise, PA
Paradise Mennonite Church

Makes 1 9" pie

2 cups water
1½ cups white sugar
⅓ cup cornstarch
4 egg yolks
1 Tbsp. lemon rind
¼ cup lemon juice
4 egg whites
¼ tsp. cream of tartar
½ cup white sugar
1 9" baked pie shell

1. Bring water to a boil.
2. Combine 1½ cups sugar with cornstarch. Add a little boiling water and stir. Stir cornstarch mixture into remaining water and bring to a boil again.
3. Combine small amount of thickened mixture with egg yolks. Add egg yolk mixture to kettle and bring to a boil again. Remove from heat.
4. Add lemon rind and juice. Mix well. Spoon hot mixture into baked pie shell.
5. Beat the egg whites and cream of tartar. Add sugar gradually. When stiffened, spread over lemon filling. Seal the edges so pie will not weep.
6. Brown meringue at 350° for 15 minutes.

Apple Crumb Pie

Maxine Hershberger
Dalton, OH
Salem Mennonite Church

Makes 1 9" pie

6 tart apples
½ cup white sugar
1 tsp. cinnamon
½ cup brown sugar
¾ cup flour
⅓ cup butter
1 9" unbaked pie shell

1. Pare apples and slice into eighths.
2. Combine white sugar and cinnamon and toss with apples. Spoon mixture into unbaked pie shell.
3. Combine brown sugar and flour. Add butter and rub together until fine crumbs are formed. Sprinkle crumbs over apples.
4. Bake at 425° for 15 minutes. Reduce oven temperature and bake at 350° for 40 minutes longer.

Apple Cream Pie

Miriam Showalter
Salem, OR
Salem Mennonite Church

Makes 1 9" pie

2 Tbsp. flour
1/8 tsp. salt
1/2 cup sugar
1 cup cream *or* half-and-half
1 egg
1/2 tsp. vanilla
2 cups finely chopped
    apples
1/4 cup sugar
1/4 cup flour
3 Tbsp. margarine
1 tsp. cinnamon
1 9" unbaked pie shell

1. Sift 2 Tbsp. flour, salt and 1/2 cup sugar together.

2. Beat cream, egg and vanilla together. Add sifted dry ingredients and apples. Spoon into pie shell.

3. Bake at 400° for 15 minutes. Reduce oven temperature to 350° and bake 30 minutes longer.

4. Combine 1/4 cup sugar, 1/4 cup flour, margarine and cinnamon with pastry blender. Sprinkle over baked pie and return to oven for 10 more minutes.

Diabetic Apple Pie

Faye Pankratz
Inola, OK
Eden Mennonite Church

Makes 1 9" pie

Pastry:
1/2 cup low-fat ricotta
    cheese
5 pkgs. artificial sweetener
3 Tbsp. skim milk
1 egg white
2 Tbsp. cooking oil
1 1/2 tsp. vanilla
Dash salt
2 cups flour
2 tsp. baking powder
2 Tbsp. water

Filling:
6-8 apples
1/4 cup flour
1/2 tsp. cinnamon
10-12 pkgs. artificial
    sweetener

1. Mix pastry ingredients in the order given. Divide pastry into two equal pieces. Chill dough.

2. Roll each piece of dough into a 10-inch circle. Place 1 piece of pastry in pie pan.

3. Peel and slice apples. Toss with flour, cinnamon and sweetener. Spoon into pie shell.

4. Use remaining pastry for a top crust. Slit in several places.

5. Bake at 375° for 20 minutes. Reduce temperature to 325° and bake 25 minutes longer. (The edges of this pastry tend to get hard.)

Apple Custard Pie

Loren J. Zehr
Ft. Myers, FL

Makes 2 9" pies

2 cups sour cream
14 ozs. evaporated milk
1/4 cup frozen apple juice
    concentrate, thawed
2 egg whites
1/4 cup chopped pecans
2 tsp. vanilla
1 tsp. cinnamon
3 large apples
2 Tbsp. margarine
1/2 cup brown sugar
2 9" unbaked pie shells

Glaze:
1/2 cup frozen apple juice
    concentrate, thawed
2 tsp. cornstarch
1 tsp. cinnamon

1. Bake pie shells at 375° for 15 minutes.

2. In a bowl combine sour cream, milk, apple juice, egg whites, pecans, vanilla and cinnamon. Mix until smooth. Pour into pie shell.

3. Bake at 375° for 30 minutes or until custard has set. Cool.

4. Prepare and slice apples. Sauté in margarine until crisp. Sprinkle brown sugar over apple slices. Arrange on top of pie.

5. To prepare glaze combine apple juice, cornstarch and cinnamon in small saucepan. Heat over low heat, stirring constantly until thickened.

6. Pour glaze over apple pie and serve.

Fruit Salad Pie

Freda Friesen
Hillsboro, KS
Hillsboro Mennonite Brethren
Church

Verna Shoemaker
Hesston, KS
Hesston Mennonite Church

Makes 2 9" pies

3-oz. pkg. raspberry jello
1 cup boiling water
21-oz. can cherry pie filling
20-oz. can crushed
    pineapple, undrained
1 cup crushed pecans
3 bananas
Whipped topping
2 9" baked pie shells

1. Dissolve jello in boiling water. Add pie filling, pineapple with juice and pecans. Stir well and refrigerate until partially set.
2. When partially set, slice in bananas. Stir gently, but well. Spoon into baked pie shells. Top with whipped topping and serve.

Lazy Morning Pie

Susan Ortman Goering
Boulder, CO
Boulder Mennonite Church

Makes 12-15 servings

½ cup margarine
1 cup sugar
1 cup flour
2 tsp. baking powder
½ tsp. salt
¾ cup milk
1 quart canned fruit

1. Melt margarine in 9" x 13" baking pan.
2. Sift all dry ingredients together. Mix well with milk. Pour into baking pan, but do not stir with melted butter.
3. Pour choice of fruit with its juice over batter. (My personal favorite is pineapple.) Do not stir.
4. Bake at 350° for 1 hour.

Grandma's Pie Crust

Bernice Hertzler
Phoenix, AZ
Sunnyslope Mennonite Church

Makes 3 9" pie shells

3 cups flour
½ tsp. salt
1 tsp. sugar
1 cup shortening
½ cup water
¼ cup oil
¼ cup milk

1. Mix all dry ingredients.
2. Cut in shortening until small crumbs form.
3. Combine wet ingredients, then stir into crumbs until a ball is formed.
4. Divide into three parts. Roll out one part on floured board to make one pie shell.

Never Fail Pie Dough

Vera Kuhns
Harrisonburg, VA
Parkview Mennonite Church

Makes 4 9" pie shells

3 cups flour
1 tsp. salt
1½ cups shortening
⅓ cup cold water
1 Tbsp. vinegar
1 egg, beaten

1. Mix flour and salt. Cut in shortening.
2. Combine remaining ingredients and stir into shortening mixture. Let stand a few minutes.
3. Roll dough to desired thickness on floured board. Use with favorite pie recipe.

Pecan Tarts

Edna E. Brunk
Upper Marlboro, MD
Hyattsville Mennonite Church

Makes 48 servings

Cheese pastry:
6-oz. pkg. cream cheese
¾ cup margarine
2 cups sifted flour

Filling:
2 eggs
1½ cups brown sugar
2 Tbsp. butter
2 tsp. vanilla
Pinch of salt
1½ cups chopped pecans
Powdered sugar

1. To prepare pastry mix all ingredients. Chill at least 1 hour.

2. Pinch off into small balls and press into small tart pans.

3. To prepare filling mix all ingredients except pecans and powdered sugar. Fold in 1 cup pecans, reserving ½ cup.

4. Fill tarts and sprinkle pecans over top of each tart.

5. Bake at 325° for 25 minutes. Cool and remove from tart pans. Sift a light dusting of powdered sugar over cooled tarts.

Vanilla Chip Fruit Tarts

Ruth Hershey
Paradise, PA
Paradise Mennonite Church

Makes 10-12 servings

¾ cup butter *or* margarine, softened
½ cup powdered sugar
1½ cups all-purpose flour
1⅔ cups vanilla chips
¼ cup whipping cream
8-oz. pkg. cream cheese, softened
¼ cup white sugar
1 Tbsp. cornstarch
½ cup pineapple juice
½ tsp. lemon juice
Assortment of fresh fruit

1. Beat butter or margarine and powdered sugar until light and fluffy. Blend in flour.

2. Press mixture into bottom and up sides of a 12" round pizza pan. Bake at 300° for 20-25 minutes or until lightly browned. Cool completely.

3. In top of double boiler melt the vanilla chips. Stir in whipping cream and cream cheese. Spread vanilla filling over cooled crust and chill.

4. In a saucepan combine white sugar and cornstarch. Stir in pineapple and lemon juice. Cook over medium heat, stirring constantly until thickened. Set topping aside to cool.

5. Slice and arrange assortment of fruit over vanilla filling on crust. Pour topping over fruit.

Butter Tarts

Ferne Burkhardt
Petersburg, ON
Mannheim Mennonite Church

Makes 30-35 mini tarts

Crust:
¾ cup lard
½ cup brown sugar
¼ cup sour milk
½ tsp. baking soda
1 egg
¼ tsp. salt
3 cups all-purpose flour, sifted

Filling:
½ cup butter, melted
½ cup brown sugar
1 cup maple *or* corn syrup
2 eggs
1 tsp. vanilla

1. To prepare crust cream together lard and brown sugar.

2. Dissolve baking soda in sour milk. Add egg and milk to sugar mixture. Add salt and flour. Mix and roll out.

3. Cut dough into rounds with cookie cutter and line mini muffin tins with dough. Gather up bits of dough, roll again and cut more rounds.

4. To prepare filling mix all ingredients and fill tart shells.

5. Bake at 400° for about 5 minutes. Reduce heat to 325° and continue baking until pastry is brown and filling bubbles, about 10-12 minutes.

Cakes

Amy's Chocolate Cake

Dawn Roggie
Lowville, NY
Lowville Mennonite Church

Makes 15-20 servings

Cake:
2 ½ cups flour
2 cups sugar
2 tsp. baking soda
2 tsp. vanilla
2 Tbsp. vinegar
10 Tbsp. cocoa
10 Tbsp. cooking oil
2 cups cold water

Frosting:
2 cups powdered sugar
1 Tbsp. butter, melted
1 cup peanut butter
1 tsp. vanilla
Milk to spread

1. Combine all cake ingredients and beat until well blended.
2. Bake at 350° for 30 minutes.
3. To prepare frosting cream together sugar, butter and peanut butter. Add vanilla and enough milk to make frosting spread easily.
4. Cool cake before frosting.

Chocolate Brownie Cake

Eleanor Kathler
Steinbach, MB

Makes 24-30 servings

Cake:
1 cup margarine
¼ cup cocoa
1 cup water
2 cups flour
1½ cups brown sugar
1 tsp. baking soda
¼ tsp. salt
2 eggs, slightly beaten
½ cup buttermilk
1 tsp. vanilla

Frosting:
¼ cup cocoa
¼ cup margarine
⅓ cup buttermilk
1 rounded Tbsp. flour
1 cup powdered sugar
Chopped nuts

1. To prepare cake bring margarine, cocoa and water to a boil.
2. Combine flour, brown sugar, baking soda and salt and pour hot mixture over dry ingredients. Add eggs, buttermilk and vanilla and mix thoroughly.
3. Pour into greased 13" x 18" cookie sheet. Bake at 350° for 20-30 minutes.
4. To prepare frosting bring cocoa, margarine, buttermilk and flour to a boil. Remove from heat and cool. Add powdered sugar. Spread frosting over warm cake. Sprinkle nuts over top.

Chocolate Sheet Cake

Phyllis Lyndaker, Watertown, NY;
Marilyn Yoder, Archbold, OH;
Thelma Harley, Goshen, IN

Makes 35-40 servings

Cake:
2 cups flour
2 cups sugar
12 Tbsp. margarine
4 heaping Tbsp. cocoa
1 cup water
$\frac{1}{2}$ cup buttermilk
1 tsp. baking soda
1 tsp. vanilla
2 eggs, lightly beaten

Frosting:
8 Tbsp. margarine
6 Tbsp. milk
2 heaping Tbsp. cocoa
1 lb. powdered sugar
1 cup chopped nuts
1 tsp. vanilla

1. To prepare cake sift together flour and sugar.
2. Melt together margarine, cocoa and water and bring to a brisk boil. Pour into dry ingredients. Add buttermilk, baking soda, vanilla and eggs. Beat well and pour into greased 11" x 16" baking sheet.
3. Bake at 400° for 20 minutes.
4. To prepare frosting mix margarine, milk and cocoa and bring to a boil. Add powdered sugar, nuts and vanilla. Mix well.
5. Spread frosting on hot cake just as it comes from oven.

Chocolate Chip Applesauce Cake

Lois Cressman
Plattsville, ON
Nith Valley Mennonite Church

Ruby Lehman
Towson, MD
North Baltimore Mennonite Church

Makes 20-24 small servings

Cake:
$1\frac{1}{2}$ cups white sugar
$\frac{1}{2}$ cup cooking oil
2 eggs
2 cups applesauce
2 cups flour
$1\frac{1}{2}$ tsp. baking soda
$\frac{1}{2}$ tsp. cinnamon
2 Tbsp. cocoa

Topping:
3 Tbsp. white sugar
$\frac{1}{2}$ cup chopped nuts
1 cup chocolate chips

1. To prepare cake batter combine sugar, oil, eggs and applesauce. Beat lightly. Add all dry ingredients and stir to mix.
2. Pour into greased 9" x 13" pan. Mix topping ingredients and sprinkle over batter.
3. Bake at 350° for 40 minutes.

Chocolate Oatmeal Cake

Dorothy R. Hess
Coolidge, AZ
Coolidge Church of the Nazarene

Makes 20-24 small servings

1 cup oatmeal
$1\frac{1}{2}$ cups boiling water
$\frac{1}{2}$ cup shortening
2 cups sugar
2 eggs
1 cup unsifted flour
$\frac{1}{2}$ tsp. salt
1 tsp. baking soda
$\frac{1}{2}$ cup cocoa
1 tsp. vanilla
$\frac{1}{2}$ cup chopped nuts
6-oz. pkg. chocolate chips

1. Pour boiling water over oatmeal in large mixing bowl and let stand for 5-10 minutes.
2. Add shortening, sugar and eggs. Mix well. Add flour, salt, baking soda, cocoa and vanilla. Pour into greased and floured 9" x 13" baking pan.
3. Sprinkle nuts and chocolate chips over batter.
4. Bake at 350° for about 35 minutes.

Crazy Cake

Darlene Janzen
Butterfield, MN
Evangelical Mennonite Brethren
Church
Beth Selzer
Hesston, KS
Whitestone Mennonite Church

Makes 15-20 servings

Cake:
2 cups sugar
3 cups flour
1 tsp. salt
2 tsp. baking soda
1/3 cup cocoa
1 tsp. vanilla
2 tsp. vinegar
3/4 cup cooking oil
2 cups cold water

Frosting:
3 squares unsweetened
   chocolate
3 Tbsp. butter
3 cups powdered sugar
1/8 tsp. salt
7 Tbsp. milk
1 tsp. vanilla
12 marshmallows, cut in
   small pieces

1. To prepare cake batter combine all dry ingredients in 9" x 13" cake pan. Make 3 wells or depressions. Put vanilla in first depression, vinegar in second and oil in third. Pour cold water over the entire mixture. Mix with a fork until all ingredients are gently blended.

2. Bake at 350° for 35-40 minutes. Test for doneness. Cool before frosting.

3. To prepare frosting melt chocolate and butter in a double boiler.

4. In a separate bowl combine sugar, salt, milk and vanilla. Blend well.

5. Add the chocolate mixture. Mix well. Fold in marshmallows and let stand, stirring occasionally until of spreading consistency. Add more milk if the frosting is too thick for spreading.

Variation:
I usually bake this cake in 3 8-inch layer cake pans because it always falls if I bake it in a larger pan.

Grace Krabill
Goshen, IN
College Mennonite Church

Chocolate Eclair Cake

Evie Hershey Atglen, PA; Pat Bishop, Bedminster, PA; Kerry Stutzman Skudneski, Littleton, CO

Makes 20 servings

Cake:
2 3-oz. pkgs. instant vanilla
   pudding
3 cups milk
1 cup whipped topping
1 box graham crackers

Frosting:
2 Tbsp. butter
3 Tbsp. cocoa
2 tsp. light corn syrup
1 tsp. vanilla
1½ cups powdered sugar
3 Tbsp. milk

1. Mix pudding and milk with mixer. Fold in whipped topping.

2. Put layer of graham crackers in bottom of 9" x 13"

pan. Pour half of pudding mixture over crackers. Cover with another layer of crackers. Pour remaining pudding over crackers and cover with another layer of crackers.

3. Mix all frosting ingredients and layer over crackers. Chill for 10-12 hours before serving.

Chocolate Zucchini Cake

Arlene Eberly
East Earl, PA
Groffdale Mennonite Church

Makes 15-20 servings

½ cup margarine, softened
½ cup cooking oil
1 cup brown sugar
½ cup white sugar
3 eggs
1 tsp. vanilla
2 cups grated raw zucchini
2 ½ cups flour
2 tsp. baking soda
½ tsp. salt
½ tsp. cinnamon
4 Tbsp. cocoa
½ cup buttermilk
½-1 cup chocolate chips

1. Combine all ingredients except chocolate chips. Pour into 9" x 13" pan. Sprinkle chocolate chips on top of batter before baking.

2. Bake at 325° for 45 minutes.

Zucchini Bread Cake

Anna S. Eby
Lititz, PA
Lititz Mennonite Church

Makes 15-20 servings

3 eggs
2 cups sugar
1 cup cooking oil
3 tsp. vanilla
2 cups shredded zucchini
3 cups flour
¼ tsp. baking powder
1 tsp. salt
1 tsp. baking soda
3 tsp. cinnamon
½ cup chopped nuts

1. Beat the eggs. Add sugar, oil and vanilla. Stir in zucchini. Blend in all dry ingredients. Fold in nuts.
2. Bake in greased 9" x 13" pan at 350° for 1 hour.

Variations:

Substitute 1 tsp. cinnamon, ½ tsp. nutmeg and ⅛ tsp. cloves for 3 tsp. cinnamon.

Substitute ½ cup raisins or dates for ½ cup nuts.

Substitute green tomatoes, carrots or pumpkin for zucchini.

Mocha Cake

Polly Johnson
Driftwood, ON
Hunta Mennonite Church

Makes 15-20 servings

Cake:
2 ½ cups flour
2 cups brown sugar, packed
½ cup cornstarch
6 Tbsp. cocoa
2 tsp. baking soda
2 tsp. instant dry coffee
1 tsp. salt
⅔ cup cooking oil
2 Tbsp. vinegar
1 tsp. vanilla
2 cups water

Frosting:
3 Tbsp. margarine
1½ cups powdered sugar
2 Tbsp. cocoa
½ tsp. vanilla
½ tsp. instant dry coffee
1 Tbsp. milk

1. To prepare cake batter mix all ingredients with whisk until well blended. Pour into 9" x 13" pan.
2. Bake at 325° for 40 minutes or until center springs back when lightly touched. Cool.
3. Mix all frosting ingredients, stirring until smooth. Add more milk if necessary.

My 12- and 14-year old daughters often make this quick and simple cake when I find myself pressed for time before a fellowship meal.

Poppy Seed Cake

Lee Snyder
Harrisonburg, VA
Community Mennonite Church

Makes 12-15 servings

2 cups flour
1 tsp. salt
1 tsp. baking powder
2 eggs
3/4 cup cooking oil
1½ cups sugar
1 cup milk
1 Tbsp. poppy seeds
1 tsp. vanilla
1 tsp. almond flavoring

1. Mix all ingredients and beat 2 minutes.
2. Pour into 2 small loaf pans or into 1 bundt pan.
3. Bake at 350° for 1 hour or until done (top will split). Cool 5-8 minutes before removing from pan.

This is an elegant, one-step dessert which is easy to whip up the night before the meal.

Orange Poppy Seed Cake

Lois Brubacher
Waterloo, ON
Rockway Mennonite Church

Makes 10-12 servings

½ cup unsalted butter
3/4 cup sugar
2 large eggs
½ cup sour cream
⅓ cup poppy seeds

¼ cup orange juice
1 Tbsp. grated orange rind
1 tsp. vanilla
1 ¼ cups all-purpose flour
½ tsp. baking powder
¼ tsp. baking soda
Pinch salt
Powdered sugar

1. In a mixing bowl cream together butter and sugar until mixture is light and fluffy. Beat in eggs, one at a time. Beat in sour cream, poppy seeds, orange juice, orange rind and vanilla.

2. Sift together flour, baking powder, baking soda and salt. Add to batter and mix well.

3. Pour into greased and floured 1-quart decorative ring mold.

4. Bake at 350° for 40 minutes or until cake tests done. Let stand for 5 minutes, invert onto a rack and let cool completely. Dust with powdered sugar.

Shoo-Fly Cake

**Twila Nafziger, Wadsworth, OH;
Eileen Lehman, Kidron, OH;
Fannie Longenecker,
Mechanicsburg, PA**

Makes at least 12 servings

2 ½ cups boiling water
1 cup light molasses
1 Tbsp. baking soda
4 cups flour
2 ¼ cups brown sugar
½ tsp. salt
3/4 cup cooking oil

1. Mix boiling water, molasses and baking soda and set aside.

2. In large bowl mix flour, brown sugar, salt and oil. Blend into crumbs the size of peas. Reserve 1 cup crumbs for topping.

3. Combine remaining crumbs with molasses mixture and mix well.

4. Pour into ungreased 9" x 13" baking pan. Sprinkle crumbs over top of cake.

5. Bake at 350° for 45 minutes.

Spice Cake

**Polly Johnson
Driftwood, ON**
Hunta Mennonite Church

Makes 15-20 servings

Cake:
2 ½ cups flour
2 cups brown sugar, packed
½ cup cornstarch
2 tsp. baking soda
2 tsp. allspice
2 tsp. cinnamon
1 tsp. cloves
1 tsp. salt
⅔ cup cooking oil
2 Tbsp. vinegar
2 cups water

Caramel Frosting:
½ cup margarine
1 cup brown sugar, packed
4 Tbsp. milk
½ cup + 3 Tbsp. powdered sugar

1. Mix all cake ingredients with whisk until well blended. Pour batter into 9" x 13" pan.

2. Bake at 325° for 35-40 minutes. Cool cake before frosting.

3. To prepare frosting melt margarine and brown sugar over low heat, stirring for 2 minutes. Add milk and bring to a boil. Remove from heat and cool slightly. Slowly add powdered sugar, beating until smooth and creamy.

Sour Cream Pound Cake

**Sharon Anders
Alburtis, PA**
Hampden Mennonite Church

Makes 1 large loaf pan

1 cup butter *or* margarine
2 ½ cups sugar
½ tsp. baking soda
1 cup sour cream
2 tsp. vanilla *or* lemon extract
6 eggs
3 cups flour

1. Cream butter or margarine and sugar together. Add baking soda, sour cream and flavoring. Mix well.

2. Add 2 eggs and 1 cup flour and mix well. Repeat three times. Beat well. Pour batter into large greased and floured loaf pan.

3. Bake at 325° for 1 ¼ hours.

Carrot Pineapple Cake

Irene Epp
Kindersley, SK
Superb Mennonite Church

Makes 15-20 servings

Cake:
1 cup cooking oil
1 cup sugar or less
3 eggs, beaten
2 cups grated carrots
1½ cups crushed pineapple, drained
1 cup flour
1 cup whole wheat flour
1 tsp. salt
1 tsp. baking soda
1 tsp. cinnamon
1 cup raisins
1 cup chopped nuts
2 tsp. vanilla

Frosting:
4-oz. pkg. cream cheese
1 tsp. vanilla
3 Tbsp. margarine
1½ cups powdered sugar
½ cup coconut (optional)

1. Combine oil, sugar, eggs, carrots and pineapple and blend well.

2. Combine all dry ingredients, including raisins and nuts, and add to batter. Add vanilla.

3. Pour batter into greased 9" x 13" baking pan.

4. Bake at 350° for about 45 minutes.

5. To prepare frosting beat cream cheese, vanilla and margarine for 3 minutes. Add powdered sugar and coconut and mix well. Spread over cooled cake.

Carrot Cake with Cream Cheese Frosting

Virginia Bender, Dover, DE; Grace
A. Zimmerman, Reinholds, PA;
Lola L. Miller, Quakertown, PA

Makes 15-20 servings

Cake:
2 cups flour
2 cups sugar or less
2 tsp. baking soda
1 Tbsp. cinnamon
1 tsp. salt
1½ cups cooking oil
4 eggs
3 cups grated carrots

Frosting:
8 ozs. cream cheese, softened
2 Tbsp. margarine
2 cups powdered sugar
1 tsp. vanilla

1. To prepare cake sift all dry ingredients together. Add oil and eggs and mix well. Add carrots and mix again. Pour into greased and floured 9" x 13" baking pan.

2. Bake at 350° for 50-60 minutes. Cool cake.

3. To prepare frosting melt cream cheese and margarine together. Cool. Blend in remaining ingredients and mix until smooth. Spread frosting over cake after it has cooled.

Variation:
Substitute buttermilk glaze for cream cheese frosting. To prepare glaze combine 1 cup white sugar, ½ cup buttermilk, ½ cup butter, 1 Tbsp. white corn syrup and ½ tsp. baking soda in a saucepan. Bring to a boil. Boil 5-6 minutes until thick and syrupy. Add vanilla. Poke holes in top of cake with wooden pick and pour glaze over top while cake is hot. Serve warm or cold.

Ruth Brunk
Sarasota, FL
Bahia Vista Mennonite Church

Oatmeal Cake

Phyllis Lyndaker, Watertown, NY;
Marnetta Brilhart, Scottdale, PA;
Adeline Schiedel, Cambridge, ON

Makes 16 or more servings

Cake:
1 ¼ cups boiling water
1 cup quick oatmeal
8 Tbsp. margarine
1 cup brown sugar
1 cup white sugar
2 eggs
1½ cups flour
½ tsp. salt
1 tsp. baking soda

1 scant tsp. baking powder
1/2 tsp. nutmeg
1 tsp. cinnamon

Frosting:
6 Tbsp. margarine
1/2 tsp. vanilla
1/4 cup cream *or* evaporated milk
1/2 cup chopped nuts
1 cup coconut
1 cup brown sugar

1. Mix together boiling water, oatmeal and margarine. Cover and let stand 20 minutes. Add sugars and eggs and mix well.

2. Sift together all dry ingredients and add to batter. Mix well. Pour into greased and floured 9" x 13" baking pan.

3. Bake at 350° for 35 minutes or until done.

4. To prepare frosting mix all ingredients and spread over cake while still hot. Put cake under broiler to brown frosting. Be careful not to burn it.

Banana Cake

Lolly Arceneaux
Des Allemands, LA

Makes 20 servings

Cake:
1 1/2 cups sugar
1/2 cup cooking oil
2 eggs
1 cup mashed bananas
2 cups flour
2 1/2 tsp. baking soda
1 tsp. salt

1/4 cup buttermilk *
1 tsp. vanilla
2 medium bananas, sliced

Frosting:
5 Tbsp. flour
1/2 cup sugar
1 cup milk
1/2 cup sugar
1 cup margarine, softened
1 tsp. vanilla

If you do not have buttermilk, add 1 tsp. vinegar to 1/4 cup milk.

1. Beat together sugar and oil until well blended. Mix in eggs and mashed bananas until thoroughly blended.

2. In separate bowl mix together dry ingredients.

3. Mix dry ingredients into wet ingredients. Stir in buttermilk and vanilla and cream well.

4. Pour batter into 3 greased 9" cake pans.

5. Bake at 350° for 30 minutes or until center springs back when lightly touched.

6. To prepare frosting combine flour, 1/2 cup sugar and milk in a saucepan. Heat, stirring constantly until mixture thickens. Set aside until thoroughly cooled.

7. In a bowl cream 1/2 cup sugar, margarine, and vanilla. Stir in thickened mixture and beat at least 5 minutes.

8. Slice bananas between each layer of cake. Spread frosting over top and serve.

Pumpkin Cake

Ruth Schmidt
Walton, KS
Tabor Mennonite Church

Makes 15-20 servings

Cake:
2 cups flour
2 cups sugar
2 tsp. baking soda
1 tsp. baking powder
1/2 tsp. salt
4 eggs
1 cup cooking oil
2 cups cooked pumpkin

Frosting:
4 Tbsp. margarine, softened
4-oz. pkg. cream cheese, softened
1 cups powdered sugar
1 tsp. vanilla
1/2 cup chopped nuts

1. To prepare cake sift together all dry ingredients and set aside.

2. Beat eggs in large mixing bowl. Add oil and pumpkin and beat slightly. Add sifted dry ingredients and mix gently. Spread into ungreased 9" x 13" baking pan.

3. Bake at 350° for 35 minutes.

4. To prepare frosting blend all ingredients except nuts with mixer. Fold in nuts. Spread over cooled cake.

Raw Apple Cake

Kathryn Yoder
Minot, ND
Fairview Mennonite Church

Makes 15-20 servings

Cake:
4 cups diced apples
2 cups brown sugar
½ cup cooking oil
1 cup nuts (optional)
2 eggs, beaten
2 tsp. vanilla
2 cups whole wheat flour
2 tsp. baking soda
2 tsp. cinnamon
1 tsp. salt

Hard Sauce:
¼ cup margarine
¾ cup brown sugar
1 heaping Tbsp. flour
Dash salt
1½ cups water
1 tsp. maple flavoring

1. To prepare cake combine apples and brown sugar and mix thoroughly. Add oil, nuts, eggs and vanilla.
2. Mix all dry ingredients and add to batter. Place in greased and floured 9" x 13" pan.
3. Bake at 350° for 40-50 minutes or until done.
4. To prepare hard sauce melt margarine in saucepan. Add all other ingredients and cook until mixture thickens. Pour over warm cake. Serve.

German Apple Cake

Ruth S. Weaver
Reinholds, PA
South Seventh Street Mennonite Church

Makes 15-20 servings

Cake:
½ cup shortening
1 cup white sugar
½ cup brown sugar
2 eggs
2 ¼ cups flour
2 tsp. cinnamon
2 tsp. baking soda
1 cup sour cream
2 cups chopped apples

Topping:
½ cup brown sugar or less
¼ cup white sugar or less
½ tsp. cinnamon
½ cup pecans

1. To prepare cake cream together shortening, sugars and eggs. Add dry ingredients and sour cream and mix well. Fold in apples.
2. Pour batter into greased 9" x 13" baking pan.
3. To prepare topping mix all ingredients. Sprinkle over cake batter before baking.
4. Bake at 350° for 50-55 minutes.

Apple Dabble Cake

Joyce G. Slaymaker
Strasburg, PA
Refton Brethren in Christ Church

Makes 15-20 servings

Cake:
3 eggs
2 cups sugar
1 cup cooking oil
2 tsp. vanilla
3 cups flour
1 tsp. baking soda
1 tsp. cinnamon
¼ tsp. salt
3 cups chopped apples
1 cup chopped nuts

Topping:
2 Tbsp. margarine *or* butter
1 cup brown sugar
¼ cup cream *or* milk

1. Beat together eggs and sugar. Add oil, vanilla and all dry ingredients. Fold in apples and nuts. Pour into greased 9" x 13" baking pan.
2. Bake at 350° for 45 minutes to 1 hour.
3. Mix all topping ingredients and bring to a boil. Boil 4 minutes and pour over cake while still hot.

Variation:
Add 1 cup coconut to cake ingredients with apples and nuts.

Laura Nisly
Grantham, PA
Slate Hill Mennonite Church

Pineapple Layer Cake

Mrs. A. Krueger
Richmond, BC
Bakerview Gospel Chapel

Makes 12 servings

Cake:
3/4 cup margarine
2 cups sugar
5 egg yolks
2 2/3 cups all-purpose flour
1/2 tsp. salt
3 tsp. baking powder
1 cup pineapple juice
1 tsp. lemon juice
3 egg whites
3/4 cup crushed pineapple, drained

Filling:
1 cup pineapple juice
3 Tbsp. cornstarch
1/4 cup sugar
1/4 tsp. salt
1 Tbsp. butter
20-oz. can crushed pineapple, drained

1. To prepare cake batter cream margarine and sugar together. Add egg yolks, one at a time. Beat well after each addition.

2. Sift dry ingredients together and add alternately with pineapple and lemon juice.

3. Beat egg whites until stiff. Fold into batter. Add crushed pineapple.

4. Divide batter evenly into 3 greased and floured layer cake pans. Bake at 350° for 30 minutes or until done.

5. While cake bakes, prepare filling. In a saucepan combine pineapple juice and dry ingredients. Cook until thickened, stirring constantly. Add butter and crushed pineapple and mix well. Cool filling.

6. Spread filling between each layer of cake. Use frosting of your choice for top layer.

Hawaiian Pineapple Cream Cheese Cake

Lorna Sirtoli, Cortland, NY;
Elaine Unruh, Moundridge, KS;
Doris Risser, Orrville, OH;
Edwina Stoltzfus, Narvon, PA

Makes 15-20 servings

Cake:
2 cups sugar
2 cups flour
2 tsp. baking soda
1 tsp. vanilla
2 eggs
1/2 tsp. salt
20-oz. can crushed pineapple with juice
1/2-1 cup chopped nuts

Frosting:
1/2 cup margarine *or* butter
8-oz. pkg. cream cheese
1 cup powdered sugar
1 tsp. vanilla

1. Mix all cake ingredients and pour into greased 9" x 13" baking pan.

2. Bake at 350° for 35-40 minutes.

3. Mix all frosting ingredients and beat thoroughly. Spread over cooled cake.

Health-Conscious Variation:
To make this a health-conscious recipe delete salt. Top with low-fat whipped topping or frozen yogurt instead of frosting. Bake in an ungreased 9" x 13" baking pan.

Lucille Taylor
Hutchinson, KS
First Mennonite Church

Arnold's Cake

Melodie Davis
Harrisonburg, VA
Trinity Presbyterian Church

Makes 16 servings

Cake:
1 yellow cake mix
11-oz. can mandarin oranges, undrained
4 eggs
1/2 cup cooking oil

Frosting:
1 cup whipped topping
16-oz. can crushed pineapple, drained
6-oz. pkg. instant vanilla pudding

1. To prepare cake batter mix all ingredients. Pour into three, round, greased and floured 9-inch cake pans.

2. Bake at 300° for 20-25 minutes or until done.

3. To prepare frosting mix all ingredients. (Do not prepare pudding. Simply add dry powder to mixture.)

4. Spread frosting between cooled layers of cake and frost top and sides. Keep refrigerated until ready to serve.

Hawaiian Wedding Cake

Cheryl Benner
Honeybrook, PA
Christian Fellowship Church

Makes 15-20 servings

1 yellow cake mix
20-oz. can crushed pineapple
3-oz. pkg. instant vanilla
  pudding
2 cups cold milk
8-oz. pkg. cream cheese,
  softened
1 cup whipped topping
1 cup shredded coconut
Crushed nuts (optional)

1. Prepare and bake cake mix according to package directions.
2. Pour crushed pineapple with juice over cooled cake. Set aside.
3. In a bowl combine pudding, milk and cream cheese, beating until well mixed. Pour over cake and pineapple.
4. Spread whipped topping over cream cheese mixture. Sprinkle generously with coconut. If desired, sprinkle with crushed nuts.
5. Chill and serve.

Royal Raspberry Cake

Miriam Christophel
Battle Creek, MI
Pine Grove Mennonite Church

Makes 15-20 servings

Cake:
2 cups flour
½ tsp. salt
1 Tbsp. baking powder
⅓ cup margarine, softened
1 cup sugar
1 egg, room temperature
1 cup milk, room
  temperature
1 tsp. vanilla
3 ½ cups red raspberries

Glaze:
1½ cups powdered sugar
2 Tbsp. cream *or* milk
1½ Tbsp. margarine, melted
1 tsp. vanilla

1. Sift together flour, salt and baking powder. Set aside.
2. Cream margarine with mixer. Add sugar gradually, beating well after each addition. Stir in egg.
3. Combine milk and vanilla.
4. Add dry ingredients to margarine mixture, alternating with milk and vanilla and beating well after each addition.
5. Spread cake batter into greased 9" x 13" pan. Spread berries evenly over the top.
6. Bake at 350° for 30-35 minutes or until center of cake springs back when lightly touched. Cool 5 minutes.
7. Combine all glaze ingredients and spread over cake.
8. Serve warm with ice cream or frozen yogurt.

Mary R. Greene's Blueberry Cake

Bonnie Heatwole
Springs, PA
Springs Mennonite Church

Makes 16 servings

Cake:
2 ½ cups flour
1 tsp. baking powder
½ tsp. baking soda
1 cup margarine, softened
1¼ cups sugar
1 tsp. vanilla
½ tsp. grated lemon rind
2 eggs
1 cup sour cream

Filling:
2 Tbsp. sugar
1 cup blueberries

Topping:
1 Tbsp. sugar
½ tsp. cinnamon

1. Combine flour, baking powder and baking soda. Set aside.
2. Cream margarine, 1¼ cups sugar, vanilla and lemon rind. Beat in eggs, one at a time. Add sour cream and mix well. Gradually beat in dry ingredients.
3. To prepare filling mix sugar and blueberries.
4. Turn about ⅓ of cake batter into greased bundt pan. Sprinkle with ½ of blueberry filling. Repeat layers. Spread with remaining batter.
5. To prepare topping mix sugar and cinnamon. Sprinkle topping over last layer of cake batter and press into batter.
6. Bake at 350° for about 50 minutes.

Blueberry Spice Cake

Rosalee M. Otto
Champaign, IL

Makes 15-20 servings

1 pint blueberries
2 cups flour
2 tsp. baking powder
1 tsp. baking soda
½ tsp. cinnamon
½ tsp. cloves
½ tsp. allspice
½ tsp. salt
⅓ cup butter, softened
1 cup white sugar
1 egg, room temperature
3 Tbsp. molasses
1 cup buttermilk *or* sour
   milk
¼ cup powdered sugar

1. Toss berries in a little flour.
2. Sift flour, measuring 2 cups. Resift flour with baking powder, baking soda, cinnamon, cloves, allspice and salt.
3. Cream butter and white sugar. Beat egg and add to batter. Gradually beat in molasses. Add this mixture alternately with milk to dry ingredients. Fold in blueberries. Spread batter into greased and floured 9" x 13" pan.
4. Bake at 375° for 30 minutes. Cool on rack.
5. Immediately before serving, dust with powdered sugar.

Strawberry Shortcake

Gladys D. Kulp
Middletown, VA
Stephens City Mennonite Church

Makes 3 dozen slices

1 lb. butter
3 cups sugar
6 eggs
3 cups flour
½ tsp. salt
¼ tsp. baking soda
1 cup sour cream
1 tsp. vanilla
Strawberries
Whipped topping

1. Cream butter and sugar. Add eggs, one at a time, beating thoroughly after each addition.
2. Sift dry ingredients. Add to batter, alternating with sour cream. Beat until smooth and and blend in vanilla. Pour into 3 greased and floured loaf pans.
3. Bake at 325° for approximately 1 hour.
4. Slice into ½-inch thick pieces. Serve with strawberries and whipped topping.

Plantation Cake

Edith Yordy
Hinsdale, IL
Lombard Mennonite Church

Makes 15-20 servings

1 cup chopped, pitted
   prunes
1 cup walnuts (optional)
2 cups flour
1 tsp. allspice
1 tsp. cinnamon
1 tsp. nutmeg
1 tsp. baking soda
1 tsp. baking powder
½ tsp. salt
3 eggs
1½ cups sugar
1 ¼ cups cooking oil
1 tsp. vanilla
1 cup buttermilk
Powdered sugar (optional)

1. Combine prunes with walnuts. Stir and mix well. Set aside.
2. Combine flour, spices, baking soda, baking powder and salt. Set aside.
3. In a large bowl beat eggs with sugar until well blended. Beat in oil and vanilla. Add dry ingredients alternately with buttermilk and mix thoroughly. Stir in the prune and nut mixture. Pour into greased and floured 9" x 13" pan.
4. Bake at 350° for 40-45 minutes or until top of cake springs back when lightly touched. Cool cake for 10 minutes and sprinkle with powdered sugar, if desired.

Ravenea

Rhoda Atzeff
Harrisburg, PA
Steelton Mennonite Church

Makes 10-12 servings

Cake:
6 egg whites, room
  temperature
1 cup farina
6 egg yolks, room
  temperature
1 tsp. vanilla
¼ tsp. almond flavoring
  (optional)

Syrup Topping:
5 cups water
1½ cups sugar
1 tsp. lemon juice
½ tsp. grated lemon rind

1. Beat egg whites until
stiff, but not dry. Fold in farina. Set aside.
2. Beat egg yolks until
light and lemon colored.
Add flavorings and fold egg
yolks into egg white mixture.
Pour into 7" x 11" baking pan.
3. Bake at 375° for 25 minutes or until cake tests done.
Remove from oven and cut
into diamond-shaped pieces.
4. While cake bakes, pre-
pare syrup by combining all
syrup ingredients in a saucepan. Bring to a boil. Turn to
simmer and cook for 15 minutes, stirring occasionally.
5. Pour warm syrup over
cake very slowly so syrup
will be absorbed by cake. Let
cool completely before serving.

Blintz Loaf

Kirsten Zerger
Berkeley, CA
First Mennonite Church of
San Francisco

Makes 15-20 servings

Batter:
½ cup butter, softened
½ cup sugar
2 eggs
1 cup flour
1 Tbsp. baking powder
1 tsp. vanilla
⅛ tsp. salt
¾ cup milk

Cheese Filling:
2 8-oz. pkgs. cream cheese,
  softened
16-oz. container cottage
  cheese
2 eggs
½ cup sugar, scant
½ tsp. vanilla

Topping:
½ cup sugar
1 tsp. cinnamon

1. Using a mixer, combine
all batter ingredients in one
bowl and all filling ingredients in another bowl.
2. Spread 1 ¼ cups of batter into greased 9" x 13" baking pan. Drop cheese filling
over batter by spoonful.
Drizzle remaining batter
over top. Sprinkle with sugar
and cinnamon topping.
3. Bake at 325° for 45-60
minutes or until set. Serve
warm or cool.

Pluckit Cake

Rosetta Martin
Columbiana, OH
Midway Mennonite Church

Makes 20 servings

Dough:
1 pkg. yeast
¼ cup warm water
½ cup sugar
⅓ cup margarine, melted
1 cup scalded milk
3 eggs, beaten
½ tsp. salt
4 cups flour

Topping:
1 cup sugar
½ cup finely chopped nuts
3 Tbps. cinnamon
Melted margarine

1. Dissolve yeast in warm
water. Mix together ½ cup
sugar, margarine and
scalded milk. Cool mixture.
2. Add yeast, eggs, salt
and flour and mix thor-
oughly. Cover and let rise until double. Stir down and let
rise again.
3. To prepare topping mix
sugar, nuts and cinnamon.
4. Take walnut-sized
lump of dough, dip it in
melted margarine, roll in
sugar mixture and put into
angel food or bundt cake
pan. Pile balls loosely until
all dough is used.
5. Let rise 30 minutes.
Bake at 400° for 10 minutes.
Reduce heat to 350° and bake
for 30 minutes. Turn upside
down onto plate immedi-
ately after removing from
oven.

Filled Cupcakes

Anita Falk
Mountain Lake, MN
Bethel Mennonite Church

Makes 36 servings

Batter:
⅔ cup cooking oil
2 cups water
2 tsp. vanilla
2 Tbsp. vinegar
3 cups flour
2 cups sugar
½ cup cocoa
2 tsp. baking soda
1 tsp. salt

Filling:
8-oz. pkg. cream cheese
1 egg
⅓ cup sugar
⅛ tsp. salt
1 cup chocolate chips

1. To prepare batter combine oil, water, vanilla and vinegar. Add all dry ingredients and mix well.
2. To prepare filling mix all ingredients except chocolate chips and beat well with mixer. Stir in chocolate chips.
3. Fill each cupcake liner ½ full. Drop 1 tsp. filling in center of each cupcake.
4. Bake at 350° for 20-25 minutes.

Apple Cupcakes

Makes 24 cupcakes

Cake:
1 cup whole wheat flour
1 ¼ cups white flour
1 cup sugar
1½ tsp. baking soda
⅜ tsp. baking powder
1 tsp. cinnamon
½ tsp. cloves
⅔ cup margarine *or* oil
2 eggs
⅔ cup milk
1½ tsp. vanilla
3 cups chopped apples
½ cup raisins (optional)

Topping:
1 Tbsp. margarine, melted
⅓ cup brown sugar
½ cup chopped nuts
2 tsp. cinnamon
2 tsp. flour
¼ cup quick oats

1. To prepare cake combine all dry ingredients in a bowl. Add margarine, eggs, milk and vanilla and beat well. Fold in apples and raisins. Fill greased and floured muffin cups at least ½ full.
2. Mix all topping ingredients and put 1 tsp. topping on each cupcake.
3. Bake at 350° for 20-25 minutes.

Light Chocolate Cupcakes

Helen Claassen
Elkhart, IN
First Norwood Mennonite Church

Makes 20 cupcakes

2 cups all-purpose flour
1 Tbsp. cocoa
½ tsp. salt
1 ¼ cups sugar
¾ cup shortening
2 eggs
1 tsp. vanilla
1 tsp. baking soda
1 cup water
1-1½ cups chocolate chips

1. Sift together flour, cocoa and salt. Set aside.
2. Cream together sugar and shortening. Add eggs and vanilla. Set aside.
3. Combine baking soda and water. Add alternately with dry ingredients to batter.
4. Line 20 cupcake cups with paper baking cups. Fill about ½ full with batter. Sprinkle chocolate chips over each cupcake.
5. Bake at 375° for 15 minutes.

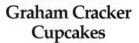

Graham Cracker Cupcakes

Esther Smucker
West Liberty, OH
Oak Grove Mennonite Church

Makes 16-18 cupcakes

½ cup shortening
1 cup sugar
2 eggs
32 graham crackers, crushed
2 tsp. baking powder
1 cup nuts (optional)
1 tsp. vanilla
1 cup milk
1 cup unsweetened, crushed
    pineapple
1 cup sugar

1. Cream shortening and sugar. Add eggs, graham crackers, baking powder, nuts, vanilla and milk. Mix well.
2. Spoon batter into greased or paper-lined muffin tins.
3. Bake at 350° for 20-25 minutes.
4. While cupcakes bake, cook unsweetened pineapple and sugar about ten minutes. Spoon small amount of pineapple mixture onto each cupcake. Let sit at least a day before serving.

Cinnamon Coffee Cake

Evie Hershey
Atglen, PA
Christiana Mennonite Church

Makes 12-15 servings

3 cups flour
1 cup brown sugar
½ cup white sugar
1 Tbsp. cinnamon
1 cup butter
1 tsp. salt
1 tsp. vanilla
1 tsp. baking soda
2 eggs
1 cup buttermilk

1. In large bowl mix flour, brown sugar, white sugar and cinnamon. Cut butter into dry ingredients and mix until crumbly. Reserve one cup crumbs.
2. Add all other ingredients and beat well with a spoon.
3. Pour into greased and floured tube pan. Sprinkle with one cup crumbs.
4. Bake at 350° for 45 minutes.

Sour Cream Coffee Cake

Susie Janzen
Wichita, KS
Lorraine Avenue Mennonite Church

Makes 15-20 servings

Cake:
8 Tbsp. margarine
1 cup white sugar
1 cup sour cream
2 eggs, slightly beaten
2 cups sifted flour
1 tsp. baking powder
1 tsp. baking soda
1 tsp. vanilla

Filling:
⅓ cup brown sugar
¼ cup white sugar
1 tsp. cinnamon

Frosting:
1 cup powdered sugar
2 tsp. margarine
Few drops vanilla
Milk

1. To prepare cake cream margarine until soft. Add sugar and sour cream and mix until fluffy. Add eggs.
2. Mix flour, baking powder and baking soda. Add to creamed mixture. Stir in vanilla. Pour batter into greased 9" x 13" pan.
3. To prepare filling mix all ingredients and sprinkle evenly over batter. With a fork swirl filling into batter.
4. Bake at 350° for 20-25 minutes.
5. To prepare frosting mix all ingredients, adding enough milk to make it smooth and easy to spread. Spread over cooled cake.

Cherry Swirl Coffee Cake

Ila Yoder
Hesston, KS
Whitestone Mennonite Church

Makes 24-30 servings

Cake:
1½ cups sugar
½ cup margarine, softened
½ cup shortening
1½ tsp. baking powder
1 tsp. vanilla
1 tsp. almond extract
4 eggs
3 cups flour
21-oz. can cherry pie filling

Glaze:
1 cup powdered sugar
1-2 Tbsp. milk

1. Mix all cake ingredients except pie filling. Stir until just mixed.
2. Generously grease jelly roll pan or two 9-inch cake pans. Spread ⅔ of batter into pan. Spread pie filling over batter. Drop remaining batter by tablespoonsful onto pie filling. Spread tablespoons of batter together as much as possible. (Not all of pie filling will be covered.)
3. Bake at 350° for 30-40 minutes or until done.
4. Combine glaze ingredients and drizzle over cake while still warm.

Overnight Coffee Cake

Freda Friesen
Hillsboro, KS
Hillsboro Mennonite Brethren Church

Makes 15-20 servings

Cake:
2 cups flour
1 tsp. baking powder
1 tsp. baking soda
1 tsp. cinnamon
½ tsp. salt
⅔ cup margarine
1 cup white sugar
½ cup brown sugar
2 eggs
1 cup buttermilk

Topping:
½ cup brown sugar
½ cup chopped nuts
½ tsp. cinnamon
¼ tsp. nutmeg

1. Mix flour, baking powder, baking soda, cinnamon and salt and set aside.
2. Cream margarine and sugars until light and fluffy. Add eggs, one at a time, beating well.
3. Add dry ingredients and buttermilk and blend. Spread batter into greased and floured 9" x 13" pan.
4. Mix all ingredients for topping and sprinkle over batter. Refrigerate overnight or for at least 8 hours.
5. Bake at 350° for 45-50 minutes.

Apple Coffee Cake

Janet Suderman
Indianapolis, IN
First Mennonite Church

Makes 15-20 servings

2 cups sugar
2 eggs, beaten
¾ cup cooking oil
1 tsp. vanilla
2 ½ cups flour
2 tsp. baking powder
1 tsp. baking soda
1 tsp. salt
1 tsp. cinnamon
4 cups finely diced apples
1½ cups chopped nuts
6-oz. pkg. butterscotch chips

1. Mix together sugar, eggs, oil and vanilla. Set aside.
2. Mix together flour, baking powder, baking soda, salt and cinnamon. Add to sugar mixture and mix well.
3. Fold in apples and chopped nuts. Pour into greased and floured 9" x 13" baking pan. (Mixture will be crumbly). Sprinkle with butterscotch chips.
4. Bake at 350° for 35-40 minutes or until done.

Carrot Fruitcake

Margaret Wenger Johnson
Keezletown, VA
Harrisonburg Friends Meeting

Makes 2 small loaves

1 cup grated carrots
1 cup raisins
3/4 cup honey
2 Tbsp. margarine
1 tsp. cinnamon
1 tsp. allspice
1 tsp. salt
½ tsp. nutmeg
¼ tsp. cloves
1½ cups water
1½ cups whole wheat flour
1 tsp. baking soda
½ cup wheat germ
½ cup chopped walnuts

1. Cook carrots, raisins, honey, margarine and spices in 1½ cups water for 10 minutes. Let cool.

2. Combine flour, baking soda, wheat germ and walnuts. Add dry ingredients to batter and mix well. Pour into 2 small, well-greased loaf pans.

3. Bake at 300° for 45 minutes.

Bars and Cookies

Double Chocolate Crumble Bars

Marlene J. Byers
Ladysmith, WI
Shiloh Mennonite Fellowship

Arlene Egli
Morton, IL
Trinity Mennonite Church

Makes 15-20 servings

½ cup margarine
¾ cup white sugar
2 eggs
1 tsp. vanilla
¾ cup flour
2 Tbsp. cocoa
¼ tsp. baking powder
¼ tsp. salt
2 cups mini marshmallows
1 cup chocolate chips
1 cup peanut butter
1½ cups Rice Krispies

1. Combine margarine and sugar. Beat in eggs and vanilla. Add flour, cocoa, baking powder and salt and mix well.

2. Spread into greased 9" x 13" pan. Bake at 350° for 15-20 minutes.

3. Sprinkle mini marsh-mallows evenly over bars and bake 3 minutes longer.

4. In a double boiler melt chocolate chips and peanut butter. Stir in Rice Krispies. Spread over top of cooled bars. Chill before serving.

Variation:
Add ½ cup chopped pecans to the bar mixture before baking.

Bertha Selzer
Hesston, KS
Whitestone Mennonite Church

Fudge Nut Bars

Gladys Stoesz
Akron, PA
Akron Mennonite Church

Makes 60 Bars

Batter:
1 cup margarine
2 cups brown sugar
2 eggs
2 tsp. vanilla
2½ cups sifted flour
1 tsp. baking soda
1 tsp. salt
3 cups quick oats

Fudge Filling:
12-oz. pkg. chocolate chips
1 can evaporated milk
2 Tbsp. margarine
½ tsp. salt
1 cup chopped nuts
2 tsp. vanilla

1. Mix all batter ingredients. Set aside.

2. In a saucepan over hot water, melt chocolate chips with evaporated milk, margarine and salt. Stir until smooth. Fold in nuts and vanilla.

3. Spread ⅔ of batter in bottom of a jelly roll pan. Cover with fudge filling.

4. Dot with remaining ⅓ of batter. Swirl batter over fudge filling.

5. Bake at 350° for 25-30 minutes.

Chocolate Chip Oatmeal Bars

Nancy S. Lapp
Goshen, IN
Assembly Mennonite Church

Makes 40-60 servings

½ cup shortening
½ cup margarine
⅓ cup peanut butter
½ cup white sugar
½ cup brown sugar
2 eggs
1 tsp. vanilla
1 cup white flour
½ cup whole wheat flour
1 tsp. baking soda
½ tsp. salt
2 cups rolled oats
1¼ cups chocolate chips

1. Cream together shortening, margarine, peanut butter, sugars, eggs and vanilla. Add remaining ingredients and mix well.
2. Spread batter on a jelly roll pan.
3. Bake at 375° for 20-25 minutes. Cool and cut into bars before serving.

Peanut Butter Bars

Betty Pellman
Millersville, PA
Rossmere Mennonite Church

Makes 15-20 servings

½ cup margarine
1¼ cups flour
½ cup brown sugar
1 cup peanut butter
6 ozs. chocolate chips
3 Tbsp. water

1. Blend well margarine, flour and brown sugar. Press into 9" x 13" pan.
2. Bake at 350° for 20 minutes. Cool.
3. Spread peanut butter over cooled cake. Melt chocolate bits and water and spread over peanut butter. Cool and cut into bars.

Peanut Butter Cake Bars

Sharon Lantzer
Galeton, PA
Hebron Tabernacle

Makes 24-30 servings

4 eggs
2 cups sugar
1 tsp. butter
1 cup heated milk
1 tsp. vanilla
2 cups flour
2 tsp. baking powder
1½ cups peanut butter
4-6 plain, milk chocolate bars

1. Beat eggs well. Add sugar slowly, beating well.
2. Melt butter in milk and add to batter along with vanilla, flour and baking powder. Place on greased and floured cookie sheet or jelly roll pan.
3. Bake at 350° for 20-25 minutes.
4. Remove from oven and immediately spread with peanut butter. Place chocolate bars over top of peanut butter. Return to oven just long enough to melt bars. Spread chocolate over peanut butter. Cool and cut into squares before serving.

Cocoa Cinnamon Bars

Doris Loganbill
Moundridge, KS
West Zion Mennonite Church

Makes 24-30 bars

Batter:
2 cups flour
2 cups white sugar
2 tsp. cinnamon
½ tsp. salt
¼ cup cocoa
1 cup water
½ cup cooking oil
½ cup margarine
2 eggs, beaten
1 tsp. vanilla
½ cup buttermilk
1 tsp. baking soda

Frosting:
½ cup margarine
6 Tbsp. milk
¼ cup cocoa

2 cups powdered sugar
1 cup pecans *or* coconut

1. Mix flour, sugar, cinnamon and salt in a bowl. Set aside.
2. Combine cocoa, water, cooking oil and margarine in saucepan and bring to a boil. Cool slightly before mixing well with dry ingredients.
3. Add eggs, vanilla, buttermilk and baking soda. Stir well and pour into a 10" x 16" jelly roll pan.
4. Bake at 350° for 15-20 minutes. Cool before frosting.
5. To prepare frosting combine margarine, milk and cocoa in a saucepan and bring mixture to a boil. Remove from heat.
6. Using a mixer, add up to 2 cups powdered sugar, until frosting reaches spreading consistency. Fold in pecans or coconut.
7. Spread frosting over cooled cake. Cut into bars.

Butterscotch Nut Bars

Edith Denlinger
Holtwood, PA
River Corner Mennonite Church

Makes 15-20 servings

$\frac{1}{2}$ cup margarine
$1\frac{1}{2}$ cups brown sugar
2 eggs
1 tsp. vanilla
$1\frac{1}{2}$ cups flour
2 tsp. baking powder
1 cup chopped nuts
Powdered sugar (optional)

1. Melt margarine and add sugar. Add eggs one at a time, beating well. Add vanilla, flour and baking powder. Stir to mix thoroughly. Fold in nuts.
2. Pour into greased 9" x 13" baking pan.
3. Bake at 350° for 25-30 minutes. Let cool and cut into bars.
4. If desired, coat with powdered sugar immediately before serving.

Walnut Bars

Barbara A. Yoder
Indianapolis, IN
First Mennonite Church

Makes 15-20 servings

Crust:
$\frac{1}{2}$ cup soft butter *or* margarine
$\frac{1}{2}$ cup brown sugar, packed
1 cup flour

Walnut Filling:
2 eggs
1 cup brown sugar, packed
1 tsp. vanilla
1 Tbsp. flour
$\frac{1}{4}$ tsp. salt
$\frac{1}{4}$ tsp. baking powder
$1\frac{1}{2}$ cups chopped walnuts

1. To prepare crust cream together butter and brown sugar in a small bowl. Add flour and mix well. Pat crust into bottom of an 8" x 10" baking pan.
2. Bake at 350° for 10-12 minutes. Let cool.
3. To prepare walnut filling beat eggs until light. Gradually add sugar. Add vanilla, flour, salt and baking powder, beating until just combined.
4. Fold in nuts and spread over crust.
5. Turn oven temperature to 375° and bake for 20 minutes or until brown and set. Cool and cut into small squares.

Date Nut Bars

Anna A. Yoder
Millersburg, OH
Son Light Chapel Conservative Mennonite

Makes 24 servings

2 eggs
1 cup sugar or less
$\frac{1}{2}$ cup butter, melted
$\frac{3}{4}$ cup whole wheat flour
$\frac{1}{4}$ tsp. baking powder
1 cup chopped nuts
1 cup chopped dates

1. Beat eggs and add sugar, mixing well. Add melted butter.
2. Sift together flour and baking powder and add to batter. Beat gently. Fold in nuts and dates. Pour into greased 9" x 13" pan.
3. Bake at 350° for about 15-20 minutes. Cool, cut and serve.

Pumpkin Bars

Susan Ortman Goering
Boulder, CO
Boulder Mennonite Church

Makes 32-40 servings

Batter:
2 cups flour
2 tsp. baking powder
½ tsp. salt
1 tsp. baking soda
4 eggs
1 cup chopped walnuts
2 cups canned pumpkin
2 cups white sugar
1 cup cooking oil
1 tsp. cinnamon

Topping:
3-oz. pkg. cream cheese
4 Tbsp. margarine
1 ¾ cups powdered sugar
1-2 Tbsp. milk

1. Mix all batter ingredients and blend well. Spread into greased jelly roll pan.
2. Bake at 350° for 25 minutes.
3. To prepare topping cream together cream cheese, margarine and powdered sugar. Add enough milk to make topping spread easily. Frost cake and cut into bars.

This delicious, moist desert serves lots of people. When I worry that there will not be enough food, this is what I take.

Apricot Bars

Shirley Thieszen
Lakin, KS
Garden Valley Church
Virginia Bender
Dover, DE
Presbyterian Church of Dover

Makes 16 or more servings

1 egg, beaten
½ cup margarine
1 tsp. baking powder
1 cup flour
¾ cup sugar
1¼ cups quick oats
1 cup apricot jam *or* preserves
¾ cup sugar
1 egg, beaten
4 Tbsp. margarine
2 cups coconut

1. Combine 1 egg, ½ cup margarine, baking powder, flour, ¾ cup sugar and quick oats. Press into greased 9" x 13" baking pan.
2. Spread batter with apricot jam.
3. Mix together ¾ cup sugar, 1 egg, 4 Tbsp. margarine and coconut. Spread this mixture over apricot jam.
4. Bake at 350° for 40-45 minutes. Cut when cool.

Variation:
Add ⅓ cup pecan or walnut pieces and ½ tsp. vanilla to ingredients in step 3.
Loren J. Zehr
Ft. Myers, FL

Lemon Bars

Kirsten L. Zerger
Berkeley, CA
First Mennonite Church of San Francisco

Makes 16-32 servings

Crust:
1 cup butter
½ cup powdered sugar
2 cups flour

Topping:
2 cups sugar
4 eggs, beaten with juice and rind of 2 lemons
¼ tsp. nutmeg
4 Tbsp. flour
¼ tsp. salt
Powdered sugar

1. To prepare crust cream together butter and sugar and add flour. Press into 9" x 13" baking pan.
2. Bake at 350° for 25 minutes.
3. Mix well all ingredients for topping. Pour over baked crust. Bake at 350° for 25 more minutes or until lightly browned on edges and no longer runny in center. Cool and dust with powdered sugar.

Variation:
Add 1 cup chopped pecans or hickory nuts to topping mixture.
Betty Hostetler
Belleville, PA

Granola Bars

Hettie Conrad
Colorado Springs, CO

Makes 15-20 servings

2 cups coconut flakes
$1\frac{1}{2}$ cups rolled oats
$1\frac{1}{2}$ cups raisins
2 cups sunflower seeds
$\frac{1}{2}$ cup sesame seeds
$\frac{3}{4}$ cup peanuts *or* soy nuts
$\frac{1}{2}$ cup dried fruit *or*
   chocolate bits (optional)
$\frac{1}{2}$ tsp. salt
1 cup honey
1 tsp. vanilla
1 cup peanut butter

1. Mix all dry ingredients well.
2. Blend honey, vanilla and peanut butter until smooth. Add to dry ingredients, greasing hands and mixing thoroughly by hand.
3. Press firmly into greased 9" x 13" pan. Bake at 275° until golden. Cool on rack and cut with a hot knife.

Brownies

Becky Bartel
Lenexa, KS
Rainbow Mennonite Church

Lorraine Stutzman Amstutz
Bluffton, OH
First Mennonite Church

Makes $2\frac{1}{2}$-3 dozen brownies

Batter:
$\frac{1}{2}$ cup butter *or* margarine
1 cup sugar
4 eggs
16-oz. can chocolate syrup
1 cup + 1 Tbsp. flour
1 cup pecans (optional)

Frosting:
$1\frac{1}{2}$ cups sugar
6 Tbsp. milk
6 Tbsp. butter
$\frac{1}{2}$ cup semi-sweet chocolate chips

1. Combine butter or margarine, sugar and eggs and beat until light. Add chocolate syrup, flour and pecans. Pour into cake or jelly roll pan.
2. Bake at 350° for 20-30 minutes.
3. To prepare frosting bring sugar, milk and butter to a boil. Boil for 30 seconds. Add chocolate chips. Stir until melted. Pour over brownies immediately. Cool and serve.

Cocoa Brownies with Dark Chocolate Frosting

Linda Sponenburgh
DeLand, FL

Makes 16 servings

Batter:
1 cup sugar
$\frac{1}{2}$ cup soft butter
2 eggs
$\frac{1}{4}$ tsp. salt
1 tsp. vanilla
$\frac{1}{4}$ cup cocoa
$\frac{3}{4}$ cup all-purpose flour
$\frac{1}{2}$ cup chopped nuts
Pecans

Frosting:
$1\frac{1}{2}$ cups powdered sugar
$\frac{1}{4}$ cup cocoa
$\frac{1}{4}$ cup soft butter
3 Tbsp. cream *or* milk
$\frac{1}{2}$ tsp. vanilla

1. To prepare batter cream together sugar and butter. Add eggs, salt, vanilla and cocoa. Stir in flour and $\frac{1}{2}$ cup chopped nuts. Pour into lightly greased 8-inch square baking pan.
2. Bake at 350° for 30 minutes. Cool.
3. To prepare frosting mix sugar and cocoa. Cream butter until shiny. Add sugar and cocoa mixture alternately with cream to butter. Beat thoroughly. Add vanilla.
4. To make frosting shiny heat over very low heat for about 5 minutes, stirring constantly. Cool for a minute or two and spread over brownies. Place a pecan half on top of each brownie.

Chocolate Brownies

Sandy Zeiset Richardson
Leavenworth, WA

Makes 16 servings

2 eggs
¾ cup white sugar
½ tsp. vanilla
½ cup chocolate syrup
⅓ cup cooking oil
¾ cup flour
½ tsp. salt
½ cup chopped nuts

1. Beat eggs until foamy. Add sugar and vanilla. Beat.
2. Add chocolate syrup and cooking oil. Beat.
3. Add flour and salt. Mix thoroughly. Fold in nuts.
4. Spread into 8-inch square nonstick pan.
5. Bake at 350° for 30 minutes.

Chocolate Chip Blond Brownies

Mary Ellen Musser
Reinholds, PA
Gehmans Mennonite Church

Makes 24 servings

⅔ cup butter
2 Tbsp. hot water
2 cups brown sugar
2 eggs
2 tsp. vanilla
2 cups flour
1 tsp. baking powder
¼ tsp. baking soda
1 tsp. salt

½ cup chopped nuts
½ cup chocolate chips

1. Melt butter in a saucepan.
2. In a bowl combine melted butter, hot water and brown sugar, stirring until thoroughly mixed. Cool slightly.
3. Add eggs and vanilla and beat well. Add flour, baking powder, baking soda and salt and mix well.
4. Fold in nuts and spread batter into greased 9" x 13" baking pan.
5. Sprinkle chocolate chips over top.
6. Bake at 350° for 25-30 minutes. Cool slightly and cut into squares. These will be chewy in center.

Rainbow Blonde Brownies

Alta M. Ranck
Lancaster, PA

Makes 24-30 servings

½ cup margarine *or* butter
1½ cups light brown sugar
1½ Tbsp. hot water
1½ tsp. vanilla
2 eggs, slightly beaten
1½ cups flour
¾ tsp. baking powder
¼ tsp. baking soda
½ tsp. salt
1 cup plain M&M chocolate candies, coarsely chopped
¾ cup chopped nuts

1. Melt margarine in heavy saucepan over medium heat. Remove from heat. Stir in sugar, water and vanilla. Cool slightly.
2. Blend in eggs. Set aside.
3. Combine flour, baking powder, baking soda and salt. Gradually add dry ingredients to batter, mixing well after each addition. Fold in ½ cup candies and ¾ cup nuts.
4. Spread batter into greased 9" x 13" baking pan. Sprinkle remaining candies over top of batter.
5. Bake at 350° for 20-25 minutes or until lightly browned. Cool thoroughly and cut into squares.

Apple Date Nut Blonde Brownies

Judith E. Bartel
North Newton, KS
Bethel College Mennonite Church

Makes 3-4 dozen servings

1-lb. box light brown sugar
¾ cup butter *or* margarine
2 eggs
2 Tbsp. vanilla
2 medium cooking apples
2½ cups flour
2 tsp. baking powder
½ tsp. salt
½ cup chopped pecans
½ cup chopped fresh dates

1. Combine sugar and butter in large, heavy saucepan. Cook over low heat 20 minutes, stirring constantly until sugar dissolves. Remove from

heat and cool to room temperature.

2. Beat in eggs and vanilla.

3. Peel, core and dice apples. Toss apples in ¼ cup flour. Set aside.

4. Add remaining 2 ¼ cups flour, baking powder and salt to sugar mixture. Mix well.

5. Fold in apples, pecans and dates. Pour batter into greased 10" x 15" jelly roll pan.

6. Bake at 350° for 35 minutes or until wooden toothpick inserted in center comes out clean. Cool completely before cutting into squares.

Buttertart Squares

Lydia Konrad
Edmonton, AB
Lendrum Mennonite Brethren Church

Makes 24 servings

2½ cups flour
½ cup brown sugar
1 cup butter
2 Tbsp. flour
½ cup butter
2 cups brown sugar or less
2 tsp. vanilla
2 cups raisins
2 eggs, beaten
4 Tbsp. cream
Whipped cream

1. Mix together flour, ½ cup brown sugar and 1 cup butter. Press into 9" x 13" baking pan.

2. Mix together all remaining ingredients and spread over crust.

3. Bake at 375° for 30-40 minutes. (If you use a glass baking dish, lower baking temperature to 350°.)

Cherry Squares

Edith Petri
Wood Dale, IL
Lombard Mennonite Church

June Marie Weaver
Harrisonburg, VA
Harrisonburg Mennonite Church

Makes 24 servings

1 cup butter
1½ cups sugar
4 eggs
2 cups all-purpose flour
1 tsp. baking powder
1 tsp. vanilla *or* 1 tsp. lemon extract *or* 1 tsp. almond extract
24 Tbsp. cherry pie filling
Powdered sugar

1. In large mixing bowl cream butter and sugar until light and fluffy. Add eggs one at a time. Add flour, baking powder and your choice of flavoring. Pour into well-greased jelly roll pan.

2. Mark 24 squares and put 1 Tbsp. cherry filling into each square.

3. Bake at 350° for 45-50 minutes. Cool and cut into squares. Immediately before serving, dust with powdered sugar.

Pineapple Squares

Pauline Settee
Selkirk, MB
Selkirk Christian Fellowship

Makes 16 servings

14-oz. can crushed pineapple
½ cup butter, softened
1 egg
1 cup all-purpose flour
1 tsp. baking powder
¼ cup white sugar
2 eggs
1 Tbsp. butter, melted
1 cup white sugar
2 cups coconut

1. Pour pineapple into strainer and drain excess juice. When drained, pineapple should measure 1½ cups. Set aside.

2. In medium-sized bowl beat ½ cup butter and 1 egg together.

3. In separate bowl combine flour, baking powder and ¼ cup sugar. Beat dry ingredients into butter and egg mixture until well blended. Press into lightly greased 8-inch square baking pan.

4. Spread pineapple evenly over crust.

5. Beat together 2 eggs, 1 Tbsp. butter and 1 cup sugar. Stir in coconut. Spread over pineapple layer.

6. Bake at 325° for 35-40 minutes or until top is evenly browned and batter seems set when pan is jiggled.

German Blueberry Kuchen

Mrs. A. Krueger
Richmond, BC
Bakerview Gospel Chapel

Makes 18-20 servings

Batter:
3 cups flour
1½ cups sugar
4 tsp. baking powder
½ tsp. salt
½ cup margarine
1⅓ cups milk
2 eggs
2 tsp. vanilla
1 tsp. nutmeg
Grated rind of 1 lemon
4 cups fresh *or* frozen
   blueberries

Crumb Topping:
1½ cups sugar
1 cup flour
½ cup margarine

1. To prepare batter combine flour, sugar, baking powder, salt, margarine and milk in large bowl. Beat 2 minutes with electric mixer or 300 strokes by hand. Add eggs, vanilla, nutmeg and lemon rind. Mix thoroughly.

2. Pour batter into greased and floured 12" x 16" baking pan. (Do not use a smaller pan.) Sprinkle with blueberries.

3. To prepare crumb topping rub together sugar, flour and margarine until mixture is crumbly. Sprinkle over layer of blueberries.

4. Bake at 350° for 40-45 minutes. Cut into squares.

Pumpkin Pie Squares

Jewel Showalter
Irwin, OH
Mechanicsburg Christian Fellowship

Annabelle Kratz
Clarksville, MD
Hyattsville Mennonite Church

Makes 15-20 servings

Crust:
1 cup flour
½ cup oatmeal
½ cup brown sugar
½ cup margarine

Filling:
¾ cup white sugar
½ tsp. salt
1 tsp. cinnamon
½ tsp. ginger
¼ tsp. cloves
2 cups canned pumpkin
13½-oz. can evaporated
   milk
2 eggs

Topping:
½ cup chopped nuts
½ cup brown sugar
2 Tbsp. margarine, melted

1. Combine all crust ingredients and mix until crumbly. Press into ungreased 9" x 13" baking pan.

2. Bake at 350° for 15 minutes.

3. Combine all filling ingredients and mix well. Pour over crust.

4. Bake at 350° for 15 minutes or until almost set. Remove from oven.

5. Combine all topping ingredients and sprinkle over filling. Return to oven for several minutes.

6. Cool and cut into squares. If desired, serve with whipped topping.

Pumpkin Squares

Lorraine Martin
Dryden, MI
Bethany Mennonite Fellowship

Makes 15-20 servings

1 pkg. yellow cake mix
1 egg
¼ cup margarine, melted
2 cups canned pumpkin
2 eggs
½ cup white sugar
⅔ cup milk
½ cup white sugar
1 tsp. cinnamon
¼ cup margarine, melted

1. Reserve 1 cup yellow cake mix. Mix together remaining cake mix, 1 egg and ¼ cup margarine which has been melted and cooled. Press batter into ungreased 9" x 13" baking pan.

2. Combine pumpkin, 2 eggs, ½ cup white sugar and milk. Spread over layer of batter.

3. Combine reserved 1 cup cake mix, ½ cup white sugar, cinnamon and ¼ cup margarine which has been melted and cooled. Crumble over pumpkin layer.

4. Bake at 350° for 40-45 minutes.

Oatmeal Pan Squares

Helen White
Edmonton, AB
Holyrood Mennonite Church

Makes 30 squares

1 cup all-purpose flour
1 tsp. baking soda
½ tsp. salt
½ tsp. cinnamon
1 cup margarine, softened
¾ cup white sugar
¾ cup brown sugar
2 eggs
1 tsp. vanilla
3 cups rolled oats
6-oz. pkg. chocolate chips
6-oz. pkg. butterscotch chips

1. In small bowl combine flour, baking soda, salt and cinnamon. Set aside.
2. In large bowl combine margarine, sugars, eggs and vanilla. Beat until light. Add dry ingredients. Fold in oats along with chocolate and butterscotch chips. Spread into greased 10" x 13" baking pan.
3. Bake at 375° for 20-25 minutes. Cool and cut into squares.

Sour Cream Squares

Verla Fae Haas
Bluesky, AB

Makes 20-25 servings

1 cup soured cream
1½ cups sugar
1 large egg
4 scant cups flour

2 tsp. cream of tarter
1¼ tsp. baking soda
⅛ tsp. salt
1 tsp. vanilla
1 cup raisins

1. Beat together soured cream, sugar and egg.
2. Sift all dry ingredients together and add to sour cream mixture. Stir in vanilla and raisins. Spread or pat thinly on greased cookie sheet or jelly roll pan.
3. Bake at 350° for 20-25 minutes or until nicely browned. Cut into squares.

I try to make these using ingredients I have on hand. We buy milk directly from a farmer so I always have plenty of soured cream.

Chocolate Honey Squares

Tena Neufeld
Delta, BC
Peace Mennonite Church

Makes 16 squares

⅓ cup butter *or* margarine
½ cup cocoa
⅓ cup honey
3 cups miniature marshmallows
1 tsp. vanilla
4 cups Rice Krispies
1 cup peanuts (optional)

1. Melt butter in large saucepan. Blend in cocoa. Stir in honey and add marshmallows. Cook over low heat, stirring constantly, until marshmallows melt and mixture is smooth.
2. Remove from heat and stir in vanilla. Add Rice Krispies and peanuts. Stir until Rice Krispies and peanuts are thoroughly coated.
3. Press lightly into greased 9-inch square cake pan. Cool and cut into squares.

Peanut Cereal Squares

Audrey J. Brubaker
York, PA
Church of the Nazarene

Makes 24 servings

½ cup sugar
½ cup light corn syrup
½ cup peanut butter
½ tsp. vanilla
3 cups crisp, unsweetened cereal
1 cup salted peanuts

1. Combine sugar and corn syrup. Cook, stirring constantly, until mixture comes to full, rolling boil.
2. Remove from heat and stir in peanut butter and vanilla.
3. Mix together cereal and peanuts. Pour peanut butter mixture over cereal and peanuts.
4. Pat into greased pan. Cool and cut into squares.

Scotcheroos

Priscilla Falb, Dalton, OH;Gladys
Sprunger, Berne, IN;Thelma P.
Plum, Waynesboro, PA;Ethel O.
Yoder, Goshen, IN;Carolyn
Slaubaugh Yoder, Wellman, IA

Makes 40 1-inch squares

1 cup sugar
1 cup light corn syrup
1 cup peanut butter
6 cups Rice Krispies
1 cup chocolate chips
1 cup butterscotch bits

1. In large saucepan cook
sugar and corn syrup over
moderate heat, stirring frequently until mixture boils.
Do not overcook. Remove
from heat.

2. Stir in peanut butter.
Add Rice Krispies and stir
until well coated.

3. Press into greased 9" x
13" pan.

4. In a double boiler or microwave melt chocolate chips
and butterscotch bits, stirring
until well blended. Spread
evenly over Rice Krispies
mixture. Cut into bars and
serve.

Chocolate Chip Pizza

Becky Bixler
Iowa City, IA
First Mennonite Church

Makes 16 servings

1 cup sifted flour
½ tsp. baking powder
⅛ tsp. baking soda
½ tsp. salt
⅓ cup butter *or* margarine,
    melted
1 cup brown sugar, firmly
    packed
1 egg
1 Tbsp. hot water
1¼ tsp. vanilla
½ cup chopped nuts
6-oz. pkg. semi-sweet
    chocolate chips
1 cup miniature
    marshmallows

1. Sift together flour, baking powder, baking soda and
salt. Set aside.

2. Cream melted butter
and brown sugar together in
mixing bowl. Beat at me-
dium speed until blended.
Add egg, hot water and vanilla. Mix well.

3. Add dry ingredients, ⅓
at a time, mixing well after
each addition. Fold in
chopped nuts. Spread into 2
greased 9" pie plates. Sprinkle each pie with half the
chocolate chips and half the
marshmallows.

4. Bake at 350° for 20 minutes. Cool on rack. Cut each
pie into 8 pieces and serve.

Chewy Chocolate Cookies

Sharon Hartman
Winston-Salem, NC
Oak Hill Mennonite Church

Makes 4 dozen cookies

1¼ cups margarine,
2 cups sugar
2 eggs
2 tsp. vanilla
2 cups flour or more
¾ cup cocoa
1 tsp. baking soda
½ tsp. salt
2 cups (12-oz. pkg.) chocolate
    chips

1. In large mixing bowl
cream margarine and sugar
until light and fluffy. Add
eggs and vanilla and beat
well.

2. Combine flour, cocoa,
baking soda and salt. Gradually blend into creamed mixture. Fold in chocolate chips.

3. Drop by teaspoonsful
onto ungreased cookie sheet.

4. Bake at 350° for 8-9 minutes. (Do not overbake; cookies will puff while baking
and flatten while cooling.)
Cool slightly before removing from cookie sheets. Cool
fully on wire rack.

Chocolate Oatmeal Drops

Erma J. Sider
Fort Erie, ON
Riverside Chapel Brethren in Christ

Makes 30-35 cookies

1/2 cup margarine
1/2 cup milk
2 cups sugar
1/3 cup cocoa
1 tsp. vanilla
1/4 tsp. salt
3 cups instant rolled oats
1/2 cup coconut
1/3 cup chopped walnuts

1. Combine margarine, milk, sugar, cocoa, vanilla and salt in saucepan. Bring to a boil and boil for 5 minutes.
2. Remove from heat and add remaining ingredients. Stir well.
3. Drop by teaspoonsful onto wax paper. Serve.

Chocolate Chip Cookies

Carolyn Slaubaugh Yoder
Wellman, IA
West Union Mennonite Church

Makes approximately 3 dozen cookies

1 cup shortening
3/4 cup brown sugar
3/4 cup white sugar
2 eggs
1 tsp. vanilla

1 tsp. baking soda
3 Tbsp. hot water
3 cups flour
1/2 tsp. salt
1 cup chocolate chips

1. Combine shortening, sugars and eggs. Add vanilla.
2. Dissolve baking soda in hot water. Add baking soda, flour, salt and chocolate chips to batter. Mix well.
3. Drop by teaspoonsful onto greased baking sheet at least 1 inch apart.
4. Bake at 350° for approximately 10 minutes. Do not overbake.

Chocolate Peanut Cookies

Edna M. Detwiler
Honeybrook, PA
West Chester Mennonite Church

Makes 7-9 dozen cookies

1 cup margarine
1 cup peanut butter
1 cup white sugar
1 cup brown sugar
2 eggs
2 cups flour
1 tsp. baking soda
6-oz. pkg. chocolate chips
1 cup peanuts

1. Cream margarine and peanut butter until fluffy. Gradually add sugars and beat until blended. Beat eggs into mixture.
2. Combine flour and baking soda and add to batter. Fold in chocolate chips and peanuts.

3. Drop by teaspoonsful onto ungreased cookie sheet, approximately 2 inches apart. Flatten with back of spoon.
4. Bake at 325° for 15-20 minutes.

Chocolate Chip Oatmeal Cookies

Phoebe M. Yoder
Bristol, IN
Tri Lakes Community Church

Makes 8-9 dozen cookies

2 cups white sugar
2 cups brown sugar
2 cups shortening
1/2 cup peanut butter
4 eggs
2 tsp. vanilla
1 tsp. maple flavoring
3 cups flour
2 tsp. baking soda
2 tsp. salt
3 cups rolled oats
12-oz. pkg. chocolate chips

1. In a very large mixing bowl combine sugars, shortening, peanut butter, eggs and flavorings and mix thoroughly.
2. Sift flour, baking soda and salt together. Stir dry ingredients into batter. Add rolled oats and chocolate chips. Batter will be stiff.
3. Drop by spoonsful onto greased cookie sheet. Flatten each cookie.
4. Bake at 350° for 10-15 minutes.

Raisin Chocolate Chip Oatmeal Peanut Butter Cookies

Joan Hall
Johnson, VT
Second Congregational Church

Makes 6-8 dozen cookies

1 cup margarine
1/3 cup peanut butter
1/2 cup white sugar
1/2 cup brown sugar
2 eggs
1 tsp. vanilla
1 1/2 cups flour
1 tsp. baking soda
1/2 tsp. salt
2 cups rolled oats
2 cups chocolate chips
1 cup raisins

1. Cream together margarine, peanut butter, sugars, eggs and vanilla. Add all other ingredients and mix well.
2. Drop by teaspoonsful onto greased cookie sheet.
3. Bake at 375° for 8-9 minutes.

Brown County Oatmeal Cookies

Mary Hochstedler
Kokomo, IN
Parkview Mennonite Church

Makes 3-4 dozen cookies

1 cup shortening *or* cooking oil
1 cup brown sugar
1 cup white sugar
2 eggs
1 tsp. vanilla
1 1/2 cups flour
1 tsp. baking soda
1 tsp. salt
1 tsp. cinnamon
1/2 cup buttermilk
4 cups oatmeal
2 cups sunflower seeds
1 cup sesame seeds
1 cup broken nuts

1. Cream shortening and sugars. Add eggs and vanilla.
2. In separate bowl combine flour, baking soda, salt and cinnamon. Add dry ingredients alternately with buttermilk to batter. When well blended, add oatmeal, seeds and nuts. Let stand at room temperature for at least 1 hour.
3. Drop by spoonsful onto greased cookie sheet.
4. Bake at 375° for about 10 minutes or until lightly browned.

Sunflower Cookies

Anna Kathryn Reesor
Markham, ON

Makes 5 dozen cookies

1/2 cup butter *or* margarine
3/4 cup brown sugar, lightly packed
3/4 cup white sugar
1 egg, beaten
1/2 tsp. vanilla
1/2 tsp. baking soda
2 tsp. hot water
1 cup sunflower seeds, unsalted and shelled
1/2 cup all-purpose flour
1/2 cup rolled oats
1/2 cup chocolate chips
1/2 cup raisins
1/3 cup natural wheat bran
1/3 cup wheat germ
1 tsp. salt

1. In large bowl cream butter or margarine and sugars until fluffy. Stir in egg, vanilla and baking soda dissolved in hot water. Add all other ingredients and mix thoroughly.
2. Drop by spoonsful onto lightly greased cookie sheet.
3. Bake at 350° for approximately 10 minutes.

Mom's Cookies

Arlene Wiens
Newton, KS
Goessel Mennonite Church

Makes 4-5 dozen cookies

1 cup white sugar
1 cup brown sugar
1 cup shortening
3 eggs
1 tsp. vanilla
2 cups flour
1 tsp. baking soda
1/2 tsp. baking powder
1/2 tsp. salt
2 cups quick oats
2 cups shredded coconut
2 cups Rice Krispies
1/2 cup nuts, chopped

1. Cream sugars and shortening. Stir in eggs and vanilla.

2. Sift together flour, baking soda, baking powder and salt. Add dry ingredients to creamed mixture, alternating with oats, coconut, Rice Krispies and nuts.

3. Drop onto greased cookie sheets.

4. Bake at 375° for 10-12 minutes.

Old-Fashioned Sour Cream Drops

Susie Janzen
Wichita, KS
Lorraine Avenue Mennonite Church

Makes 5 dozen or more cookies

Batter:
½ cup shortening, softened
1½ cups sugar
2 eggs
1 cup thick sour cream
1 tsp. vanilla
2 ¾ cups sifted flour
½ tsp. baking soda
½ tsp. baking powder
½ tsp. salt

Frosting:
2 cups powdered sugar
4 tsp. margarine
1 tsp. vanilla
1-2 Tbsp. milk *or* cream
Chopped nuts

1. Combine shortening, sugar and eggs and beat thoroughly. Add sour cream and vanilla.

2. In separate bowl combine flour, baking soda, baking powder and salt. Add to batter. Chill at least 1 hour.

3. Drop rounded teaspoonsful, leaving dough mounded high, onto lightly greased baking sheet.

4. Bake at 425° for 8-10 minutes or until almost no imprint remains when touched lightly with finger.

5. To prepare frosting beat together powdered sugar, margarine, vanilla and enough milk or cream to make frosting spread easily.

6. Frost each cookie. Sprinkle with chopped nuts.

Soft Sugar Cookies

Mrs. Elmer S. Yoder
Hartville, OH
Cornerstone Mennonite Church

Makes 6-7 dozen cookies

1½ cups sugar
1 cup butter, softened
¾ tsp. salt
4 eggs
1 tsp. baking soda
2 Tbsp. hot water
1 cup sour cream
4 cups all-purpose flour
1 tsp. baking powder
1 tsp. nutmeg
Red gelatin *or* powdered sugar
Walnut pieces (optional)

1. Cream sugar, butter, salt and eggs together.

2. Dissolve baking soda in hot water. Add with sour cream to butter mixture. Add flour, baking powder and nutmeg and mix well.

3. Dough will be sticky. Chill several hours.

4. Drop by teaspoonsful onto greased cookie sheet. Sprinkle with dry red gelatin mix or colored sugar. Top each cookie with a walnut piece if desired.

5. Bake at 350° for 8-10 minutes.

Easy Roll Out Sugar Cookies

Joyce Hofer
Morton, IL
Trinity Mennonite Church

Makes 5 dozen cookies

3 cups sugar
2 cups margarine
2 eggs
1 tsp. almond extract
5 cups flour
2 tsp. baking soda
2 tsp. cream of tartar
Colored sugar

1. Cream together sugar and margarine. Add eggs and almond extract and beat well.

2. Mix together flour, baking soda and cream of tartar and add to batter. Refrigerate at least 3 hours or overnight.

3. Roll out dough and cut into desired shapes (Christmas, valentines, shamrocks, flowers or animals). Sprinkle with colored sugar.

4. Bake at 375° for 7-8 minutes. Watch carefully.

Black Walnut Cookies

Grace E. Hess
Lititz, PA
Millport Mennonite Church

Makes 3-5 dozen cookies

1 cup brown sugar
½ cup butter
2 eggs
¼ cup milk
1 tsp. vanilla
¾ tsp. baking soda
2 cups flour
¾ cup walnuts

1. Cream sugar and butter. Add eggs and beat well. Add milk and vanilla.
2. Mix baking soda and flour, then add to batter. Fold in walnuts.
3. Drop by teaspoonsful onto ungreased baking sheet.
4. Bake at 350° for 15 minutes.

Forgotten Cookies

Penny Blosser
New Carlisle, OH
Huber Mennonite Church

Makes 25-30 cookies

2 egg whites
⅔ cup sugar
Pinch salt
1 tsp. vanilla
½ cup chopped nuts
½ cup chocolate chips

1. Preheat oven to 350°.
2. Beat egg whites until foamy. Gradually add sugar,

beating until stiff. Fold in remaining ingredients.
3. Drop cookies onto foil-lined cookie sheet. Place in oven.
4. Turn oven *off* immediately. Let cookies in oven until cooled completely or overnight. Do not forget cookies on Sunday morning!

Cherry Winks

Berdella Miller
Millersburg, OH
Berlin Mennonite Church

Makes 5 dozen cookies

2 ¼ cups flour
1 tsp. baking powder
1 tsp. baking soda
½ tsp. salt
¾ cup shortening
1 cup sugar
2 eggs
2 Tbsp. milk
1 tsp. vanilla
¾ cup chopped nuts
1 cup chopped dates
1 cup maraschino cherries
2½ cups crushed cornflakes

1. Combine flour, baking powder, baking soda and salt. Set aside.
2. Combine shortening and sugar and mix well. Blend in eggs, milk and vanilla. Add nuts, dates and ⅓ cup maraschino cherries. Add dry ingredients and mix well.
3. Drop 1 teaspoon cookie dough at a time into crushed cornflakes. Roll into ball and

place on cookie sheet. Continue until cookie sheet is filled. Place ¼ of a maraschino cherry on each cookie.
4. Bake at 350° for 10-12 minutes. Cool and serve.

Cornmeal Cookies

Doris Schrock
Goshen, IN
Yellow Creek Mennonite Church

Makes 3 dozen cookies

¾ cup margarine
½ cup sugar
1 egg
1 cup flour
1 cup cornmeal
1 tsp. baking soda
¼ tsp. salt
1 tsp. vanilla
½ cup raisins (optional)

1. Mix margarine and sugar. Add egg and beat well. Add all other ingredients and mix well.
2. Drop by teaspoonsful onto greased cookie sheet.
3. Bake at 350° for 15 minutes or until lightly browned.

Butter Cookies

Anna A. Yoder
Millersburg, OH
Son Light Chapel Conservative
Mennonite

Makes 100 small cookies

1 lb. margarine *or* butter
1¼ cups sugar
3 egg yolks
5 cups sifted flour
¼ tsp. baking soda

1. Cream together margarine and sugar. Add egg yolks and beat well. Add flour and baking soda and mix thoroughly.
2. Press small cookies onto baking sheet.
3. Bake at 400° for about 10 minutes.

Chinese Almond Cookies

Geraldine A. Ebersole
Hershey, PA
Akron Mennonite Church

Makes 4½ dozen cookies

2¾ cups all-purpose flour
1 cup sugar
½ tsp. salt
½ tsp. baking soda
1 cup butter *or* margarine
1 egg, slightly beaten
1 tsp. almond extract
⅓ cup unblanched, whole almonds

1. Sift together flour, sugar, salt and baking soda.

Cut in butter or margarine until mixture resembles cornmeal. Add egg and almond extract and mix well.
2. Shape dough into 1-inch balls and place 2 inches apart on ungreased cookie sheet. Place an almond on each cookie and press down to flatten slightly.
3. Bake at 325° for 15-18 minutes. Cool on rack.

Welsh Cakes

Rita Baechler
Stratford, ON
Avon Mennonite Church

Makes 4 dozen cookies

1 cup shortening
1¼ cups white sugar
3 cups all-purpose flour
2 tsp. baking powder
1 tsp. salt
1 cup currants
2 eggs, beaten

1. Cream together shortening and sugar.
2. Combine flour, baking powder and salt and add dry ingredients to creamed mixture. Fold in currants.
3. Add eggs slowly, beating after each addition.
4. Roll out as you would for pastry dough and cut out shapes with cookie cutters.
5. Grease frying pan with cooking oil and heat oil on low for several minutes. Put in cookies and fry until light brown on one side. Flip over and fry until light brown on other side. Cool and serve.

New Year's Cookies

Bernice Friesen
Henderson, NE

Makes 5-7 dozen cookies

2 pkgs. yeast
¼ cup warm water
3 eggs, slightly beaten
2 cups warm milk
1 tsp. salt
1 tsp. baking powder
½ cup sugar
4½-5 cups flour
2 cups raisins
Cooking oil
Sugar

1. Dissolve yeast in warm water. Let set at least 5 minutes.
2. Beat eggs; add milk and mix. Stir in yeast.
3. Mix together salt, baking powder, sugar and flour. Add to yeast mixture. Beat well with wooden spoon. Fold in raisins. Let rise in warm place until double in bulk.
4. Heat cooking oil in deep fryer to 350°. Dip batter by tablespoonsful into oil. Brown and turn. Cool on rack. Serve plain or dredged in sugar.

According to tradition, the women and children stayed home on New Year's Day and made these special fritters while the men went to the annual church business meeting. Even today many Mennonite cooks serve these only on New Year's Day.

Peppernuts

Marie I. Kaufman
Glendale, AZ

Makes 2 gallons peppernuts

3 cups white sugar
1 cup brown sugar
1½ cups butter
3 eggs
1½ tsp. baking soda
1 tsp. mace
1 tsp. nutmeg
1 tsp. cloves
1 tsp. cinnamon
1 tsp. ginger
1 tsp. allspice
1 tsp. cardamom
1 tsp. oil of anise
9-10 cups flour

1. Cream together sugars and butter. Add eggs. Set aside

2. Sift together all dry ingredients. Add to creamed mixture along with oil of anise.

3. Knead thoroughly on lightly floured board.

4. Roll dough into long ropes, ¾ inch in diameter. Using a scissors, snip into ½-inch pieces.

5. Bake at 325° for about 12 minutes. Store in gallon containers.

I like taking these to fellowship meals because some people do not know what they are. I like watching the reaction when they taste one.

Black Walnut Peppernuts

Ruth Schmidt
Walton, KS
Tabor Mennonite Church

Makes 1 gallon peppernuts

½ tsp. salt
1 tsp. baking soda
4 cups flour
8 Tbsp. margarine *or* butter
2½ cups sugar or less
3 eggs, beaten
1 Tbsp. white syrup
1 Tbsp. vanilla
1 cup raisins
½ cup black walnuts

1. Sift together salt, baking soda and flour. Set aside.

2. Cream margarine and sugar until fluffy. Add eggs, syrup and vanilla.

3. Wet the raisins and run through food grinder with walnuts. Add to batter and mix well. Gradually add dry ingredients and knead thoroughly on lightly floured board.

4. Roll dough into thin ropes and freeze. Slice into ½-inch pieces and place on greased baking sheet.

5. Bake at 325° for 10-12 minutes.

Desserts and Candies

❖

Super Dessert

Helen M. Peachey
Harrisonburg, VA
Lindale Mennonite Church

Elsie Neufeldt
Saskatoon, SK
Nutana Park Mennonite Church

Makes 12-15 servings

Layer 1:
1 cup flour
½ cup margarine
½-1 cup chopped nuts

Layer 2:
8-oz. pkg. cream
   cheese, softened
1 cup powdered sugar
1 cup whipped topping

Layer 3:
1 small pkg. instant vanilla
   pudding
1 small pkg. instant
   chocolate pudding
3 cups milk

Layer 4:
1 cup whipped topping
½ cup chocolate shavings

1. Combine all ingredients for layer 1 and press into 9" x 13" pan.
2. Bake at 350° for 15 minutes. Cool.
3. Combine ingredients for layer 2. Spread over crust.
4. Combine ingredients for layer 3 and spread over layer 2.
5. Spread whipped topping and chocolate shavings over layer 3.
6. Chill and serve.

Variations:
Substitute 2 small pkgs. instant butterscotch pudding for vanilla and chocolate pudding. Substitute ½ cup chopped nuts for chocolate shavings.
Mabel Neff
Quarryville, PA

Grace A. Zimmerman
Reinholds, PA
Bowmansville Mennonite Church

Substitute 2 small pkgs. instant pistachio pudding for vanilla and chocolate pudding. Use pecans for the nuts in the first layer. Delete chocolate shavings.
Pauline Wyatt
Tangent, OR
Albany Mennonite Church

Substitute ½ cup quick oats and ⅓ cup brown sugar for the nuts in the first layer. Change layer 3 ingredients to 2 small pkgs. instant vanilla pudding, 1½ cups canned pumpkin, 2 cups milk and ½ tsp. cinnamon. Substitute 1½ tsp. pumpkin pie spices for the chocolate shavings in layer 4. Sprinkle ½ cup chopped nuts over top before serving.
Betty Herr
Beallsville, MD
Dawsonville Mennonite Church

Substitute 2 small pkgs. instant lemon pudding for vanilla and chocolate pudding in third layer. Delete chocolate shavings from fourth layer.
Marcella Stalter
Flanagan, IL
Waldo Mennonite Church

Viola K. Shore
Louisville, OH
Beech Mennonite Church

Heath Candy Bar Dessert

Topeka, KS
Southern Hills Mennonite Church

Makes 15-20 servings

Crust:
12 soda crackers
12 graham crackers
8 Tbsp. margarine, melted
¼ tsp. butter flavoring

Pudding:
2 cups cold milk
2 small pkgs. instant vanilla
   pudding
2 cups vanilla ice cream
½ tsp. vanilla

Topping:
2 cups whipped topping
4 frozen Heath candy bars

1. To prepare crust crush crackers. Add margarine and flavoring and mix well. Press into 9" x 13" greased baking dish. Refrigerate.
2. To prepare pudding combine cold milk and instant pudding. Add ice cream and vanilla. Spoon over crust.
3. Top with whipped topping.
4. Crush 4 frozen candy bars and sprinkle over whipped topping. Refrigerate until ready to serve.

Eclairs

Anna Hochstetler
Kalona, IA
Iowa Mennonite School

Makes 12 servings

8 Tbsp. margarine
1 cup water
1 cup flour
4 eggs
1 small pkg. instant vanilla
   pudding
8-oz. pkg. cream cheese
1 cup whipped topping
1 chocolate bar

1. Melt margarine with water over medium heat. Bring to a boil. Immediately add flour and stir hard and fast while removing from heat. Stir until smooth. (The mixture will form a ball.) Beat in one egg at a time.
2. Spread into greased 9" x 13" pan and pull up along the sides.
3. Bake at 350° for 30 minutes. Cool. (The mixture will be lumpy when baked.)
4. Prepare instant pudding according to directions and add softened cream cheese, mixing well. Push down lumps in crust and spread pudding over crust. Top with whipped topping and shavings from chocolate bar.

Der Tod vor Schokolade

Joy Sutter
Iowa City, IA
First Mennonite Church

Makes 15-20 servings

9" x 13" pan brownies
2 pkgs. chocolate mousse,
   prepared
2 cups whipped topping
8 Heath Bars, crushed
1 cup chopped pecans

1. Prepare brownies. Cool. Crumble and place ½ of crumbs in large glass bowl.
2. Prepare chocolate mousse according to directions and spread ½ of mousse over crumbled brownies. Spread ½ of whipped topping over mousse. Spread ½ Heath Bars and pecans. Repeat all layers.
3. Refrigerate for several hours or overnight. Serve.

Chocolate Peanut Butter Dessert

Selma Sauder
Pettisville, OH
Tedrow Mennonite Church

Makes 20 servings

2 cups graham cracker
   crumbs
6 Tbsp. margarine
1 cup crunchy peanut butter
1½ cups powdered sugar
1 large pkg. chocolate
   pudding
2 large pkgs. vanilla
   pudding
2 cups whipped topping

1. Combine graham
cracker crumbs and marga-
rine. Press into 9" x 13" baking pan.
2. Bake at 350° for 10 minutes. Cool.
3. Combine peanut butter
and sugar and spread over
cooled crust.
4. Prepare puddings ac-
cording to package direc-
tions. Spread over peanut
butter mixture. Top with
whipped topping.

Peanut Butter Delight

Winifred Wall
Freeman, SD
Salem-Zion Mennonite Church

Makes 15-20 servings

⅔ cup chopped peanuts
8 Tbsp. margarine
1 cup flour
⅓ cup peanut butter
8 ozs. cream cheese
1 cup powdered sugar
1 cup whipped topping
1 small pkg. instant
   chocolate pudding
1 small pkg. instant vanilla
   pudding
1 cup whipped topping
½ cup chopped peanuts

1. Combine ⅔ cup pea-
nuts, margarine and flour
and press into 9" x 13" baking dish.
2. Bake at 350° for 15 minutes. Cool.
3. Cream together peanut
butter, cream cheese, sugar
and 1 cup whipped topping.
Spread over crust.
4. Prepare puddings ac-
cording to package direc-
tions. Combine two pud-
dings quickly. Spread over
cream cheese layer. Let stand
until firm, about 45 minutes.
5. Top with whipped top-
ping. Garnish with ½ cup
chopped peanuts.

Date Delight

Grace Glick
Millersburg, OH
Walnut Creek Mennonite Church

Makes 10-12 servings

4 Tbsp. flour
3 cups milk
4 egg yolks, beaten
⅛ tsp. salt
1 cup brown sugar
¼ cup white sugar
4 egg whites
2 Tbsp. white sugar
½ tsp. vanilla
¾ cup chopped dates
½ cup chopped pecans *or*
   walnuts

1. Combine flour and milk
and bring to a boil. Combine
½ cup hot milk mixture with
beaten egg yolks.
2. Add egg yolk mixture
and salt to remaining milk
and flour and cook 2 min-
utes. Add brown sugar and
¼ cup white sugar, stirring
until thoroughly mixed.
Pour into an 8-inch square
baking dish.
3. Beat egg whites until
stiff. Add 2 Tbsp. sugar and
vanilla and mix well. Fold in
dates and pecans. Pour over
custard.
4. Bake at 300° until
puffed up and brown, about
15-20 minutes.

Date Pudding

Wanda Good
Harrisonburg, VA
Mt. Clinton Mennonite Church

Makes 12-15 servings

1 cup boiling water
1 cup chopped dates
1 tsp. baking soda
1 cup sugar or less
1 egg
1 Tbsp. butter
1 cup flour
½ cup chopped pecans
4 bananas, sliced
1 pint whipping cream

1. Pour boiling water over dates and baking soda. Cool.
2. Mix sugar, egg, butter, flour and pecans. Add cooled dates and mix well. Pour into greased 9" baking pan.
3. Bake at 350° for 20-25 minutes. Cool and cut into small cubes. Carefully fold in sliced bananas.
4. Whip cream and carefully fold into date pudding. Serve.

Graham Cracker Pudding

Lois Fenton
Philadelphia, MO
Pea Ridge Mennonite Church

Makes 12-15 servings

12 graham crackers, crushed
⅓ cup white sugar
8 Tbsp. margarine, melted
3 Tbsp. cornstarch *or* 6 Tbsp. flour
1 quart milk
⅔ cup white sugar
2 egg yolks, beaten
1 tsp. vanilla
2 egg whites

1. Combine crushed graham crackers, ⅓ cup sugar and margarine and mix well. Spoon into 9" x 13" baking dish and cover sides and bottom of pan.
2. In a saucepan combine cornstarch with ½ cup milk, mixing until smooth paste forms. Add ⅔ cup sugar, egg yolks and remaining milk. Heat until mixture thickens, stirring constantly. Remove from heat.
3. Stir in vanilla and pour over crust.
4. Beat egg whites to a stiff meringue and spread over pudding. Sprinkle with 1 crushed graham cracker and brown lightly in moderate oven. Cool before serving.

Mother's Cracker Pudding

Erma Kauffman
Cochranville, PA
Media Mennonite Church

Makes 10 servings

2 egg yolks
1 quart milk
1 cup finely crushed saltines
½ cup coconut (optional)
½ cup sugar
1 tsp. vanilla
2 egg whites
2 Tbsp. sugar

1. Combine egg yolks, milk, crushed saltines, coconut and ½ cup sugar in 3-quart saucepan. Bring to a boil and cook until mixture thickens, stirring constantly. (Stirring is very important as mixture sticks easily). Remove from heat and add vanilla.
2. Pour into 2-quart casserole dish.
3. Beat egg whites until stiff, gradually adding 2 Tbsp. sugar.
4. Spread beaten egg whites over pudding and brown in 375° oven for a few minutes.

Variation:
Use whole eggs in pudding. Substitute 1 cup whipped topping for the meringue topping.

Miriam Nolt
Chambersburg, PA
Pond Bank Mennonite Church

Graham Cracker Delight

Loretta Lapp
Kinzer, PA

Makes 8 servings

1 pkg. vanilla pudding
1 cup whipped topping *or* **1 cup sour cream**
Crumbled graham crackers
1 cup whipped topping
Maraschino cherries

1. Prepare pudding according to directions. Fold in 1 cup whipped topping or sour cream.
2. In a dessert dish arrange layer graham crackers, ½ of pudding mixture, graham crackers and remaining pudding.
3. Top with 1 cup whipped topping and maraschino cherries.

Variation:
Add 4 sliced bananas to this recipe. Alternate layers of bananas with other ingredients. Omit maraschino cherries.
Joanna Yoder
Springs, PA
Oak Grove Mennonite Church

Old-Fashioned Cracker Pudding

Joan Ranck
Christiana, PA
Maple Grove Mennonite Church

Makes 10-12 servings

4 Tbsp. margarine
7 cups milk
1¾ cups sugar
28 2-inch soda crackers
4 eggs
2 Tbsp. cornstarch
1 cup milk
2 cups coconut (optional)
1 Tbsp. vanilla

1. Melt margarine. Add 7 cups milk, sugar and soda crackers. Bring to a boil.
2. Beat together eggs, cornstarch and 1 cup milk. Add slowly to hot mixture. Bring to a boil again. After mixture has thickened, fold in coconut and vanilla. Chill before serving.

Egg Custard

Carolyn Fitzwater
Kidron, OH
Salem Mennonite Church

Makes 8 servings

4 cups milk
6 eggs
½ cup sugar
Pinch of salt
1 tsp. vanilla
Marshmallows

1. Scald milk.
2. Beat eggs slightly; add sugar, salt and vanilla. Pour mixture into milk and mix well. Pour into baking dish. Arrange marshmallows over top.
3. Place baking dish in a pan of water, and bake at 350° for 45 minutes.

Flan

Pat Augsburger Blum
Berkeley, CA

Makes 10 servings

1 quart milk
¾ cup sugar
⅛ tsp. salt
6 large eggs, well beaten
1 tsp. vanilla
½ cup sugar

1. In a saucepan combine milk, ¾ cup sugar and salt. Bring to a boil and boil vigorously for 10 minutes. Remove from heat and add mixture to well-beaten eggs, a little at a time, beating constantly. Continue beating for 3 more minutes. Stir in vanilla.
2. In a saucepan melt ½ cup sugar over low heat, stirring constantly. Pour into greased 9" x 12" pan. Pour pudding mixture over sugar sauce. Place 9" x 12" pan in larger pan, ½ full of hot water.
3. Bake at 300° for 1½ hours or until knife inserted in center comes out clean.

Spanish Cream

Lydia S. Martin
Harrisonburg, VA
Lindale Mennonite Church

Makes 8 servings

½ **cup sugar**
3 cups milk
Pinch of salt
1 Tbsp. plain gelatin
3 eggs, separated
1 tsp. vanilla

1. Put sugar, milk and salt in top of double boiler. Sprinkle gelatin over milk. Let soak for 5-10 minutes. Bring mixture almost to a boiling point.

2. Beat the egg yolks and stir into mixture until spoon is coated. Remove from heat and add vanilla. Cool.

3. Beat egg whites until stiff. Fold into cream mixture. Pour into a large dish or mold. Refrigerate overnight or until set.

Rice Custard

Marcella Klaassen
Hillsboro, KS
Hillsboro First Mennonite Church

Makes 6-8 servings

½ **cup uncooked rice**
½ **cup sugar**
½ **tsp. cinnamon**
3 cups milk
1 Tbsp. butter
½ **cup raisins or more**
3 eggs, beaten
1 tsp. vanilla

1. Cook rice according to directions.

2. In small bowl combine sugar and cinnamon.

3. Scald milk and melt butter in scalded milk.

4. Combine all ingredients and pour into greased 2½-quart casserole dish.

5. Place in pan of hot water and bake, uncovered, at 350° for 1 hour or until knife inserted in center comes out clean.

Quick Rice Pudding

A. Catharine Boshart
Lebanon, PA
Hereford Mennonite Home Church

Makes 8 servings

⅓ **cup sugar**
2 Tbsp. cornstarch
⅛ **tsp. salt**
2 cups milk
2 egg yolks, slightly beaten
2 Tbsp. butter *or* margarine
2 tsp. vanilla
⅛ **tsp. cinnamon**
½ **cup uncooked rice**
1 ¾ **cups water**
½ **tsp. salt**
⅓ **cup raisins (optional)**

1. Blend sugar, cornstarch and salt in saucepan.

2. In separate bowl combine milk and egg yolks. Gradually stir into sugar mixture. Cook over medium heat, stirring constantly, until mixture thickens and comes to a boil. Boil for 1 minute, stirring constantly.

Remove from heat and add butter, vanilla and cinnamon. Set aside.

3. Cook rice with water, adding salt. Fold in raisins. (You mau substitute 1½ cups leftover rice.)

4. When rice is done, stir into pudding. Cool before serving.

Mom's Sweet Rice

Bonnie and Vern Ratzlaff
Tuba City, AZ
Moencopi Mennonite Church

Makes 4-6 servings

1 cup uncooked rice
3 cups water
⅔ **cup sugar**
1 tsp. vanilla
¼ **tsp. salt**
4 cups milk

1. Cover rice with water. Over high heat bring to a full, rolling boil. Stir with a fork. Reduce heat to simmer, cover and do not stir or lift lid for 20 minutes.

2. Remove from heat and stir in sugar, vanilla and salt.

3. Add milk and cook mixture until it thickens.

4. Chill before serving.

Grapenut Pudding

Joan Hall
Johnson, VT
Second Congregational Church

Makes 8-10 servings

4 eggs, slightly beaten
⅔ cup sugar
¼ tsp. salt
4 cups milk, scalded
1 tsp. vanilla
⅔ cup grapenuts
Cinnamon
Nutmeg

1. In a 2-quart baking dish combine eggs, sugar and salt. Add scalded milk gradually. Fold in vanilla and grapenuts. Sprinkle with cinnamon and nutmeg.
2. Place in pan of hot water and bake at 325° for 1 hour and 20 minutes or until knife inserted along the edge comes out clean. (Center of pudding will set as it cools.)
3. Serve with whipped cream or crushed fruit.

Ozark Pudding

Lois Hallman
Goshen, IN
College Mennonite Church

Makes 15-20 servings

2 eggs
1⅓ cups sugar
⅔ cup flour
½ tsp. salt
3 tsp. baking powder
2 cups chopped raw apples
1 cup chopped walnuts
Whipped topping

1. Beat eggs until thick and lemon colored. Gradually beat sugar into the eggs.
2. Combine flour, salt and baking powder and fold dry ingredients into egg mixture. Fold in apples and walnuts. Spoon into greased 9" x 13" baking pan.
3. Bake at 350° for 35-40 minutes. (Pudding will fall slightly after baking.)
4. Serve with whipped topping.

Chocolate Vanilla Pudding

Joyce G. Slaymaker
Strasburg, PA
Refton Brethren in Christ

Makes 6-8 servings

3 cups milk
1 cup sugar or less
¼ tsp. salt
2½ Tbsp. cornstarch
3 egg yolks
1 Tbsp. butter
1 tsp. vanilla
3 egg whites
5 Tbsp. sugar
1 oz. unsweetened chocolate, melted

1. Scald 2½ cups milk in top of double boiler.
2. Combine 1 cup sugar, salt and cornstarch. Add ½ cup cold milk to make a smooth paste. To this mixture add a small amount of scalded milk and mix thoroughly.
3. Add paste to remaining scalded milk and cook until thickened, stirring constantly.
4. Beat egg yolks and add to pudding. Cook for 2 minutes. Remove from heat. Add butter and vanilla and mix well.
5. Chill pudding while preparing meringue.
6. To prepare meringue beat egg whites until stiff. Add 5 Tbsp. sugar and melted chocolate. Beat meringue until it has sheen. Spread over pudding and serve.

Oreo Cookie Dirt

Theda Brunk
Dayton, VA
Living Water Mennonite Fellowship

Makes 12 servings

1 lb. Oreo cookies
12 ozs. cream cheese, softened
3 pkgs. instant vanilla pudding
1 quart milk
12-oz. container whipped topping

1. Freeze cookies and grind them in food processor until mixture looks like dirt.
2. Combine softened cream cheese, pudding, milk and whipped topping. Beat until smooth, about 3 minutes.
3. Put a layer of cookie mixture in bottom of a new, sterilized flower pot. Add layer of pudding mixture. Repeat layers as often as needed, ending with layer of cookie mixture. Chill 3-4 hours or overnight.
4. To serve push a few stems of silk flower blossoms into center of flower pot. Use dish as a centerpiece.

This dish always gets a lot of laughs. I usually put a spoon into flowerpot and that makes people ask what is going on. Children enjoy this, but so do the adults.

Cookie Salad

Annetta Weaver
Berlin, OH
Martins Creek Mennonite Church

Makes 12 servings

2 3-oz. pkgs. instant vanilla pudding
2 cups buttermilk
2 cups whipped topping
12 fudge cookies, broken up
2 11-oz. cans mandarin oranges, drained

1. Whisk pudding and buttermilk together with a wire whisk. Fold in whipped topping.
2. Fold in cookies and well-drained oranges. Serve.

Ice Cream Pudding

Lula Swartzentruber
Millersburg, OH

Makes 15-20 servings

1/4 cup butter
1 cup brown sugar
2 1/2 cups crushed cornflakes
1/2 cup crushed nuts
8 ozs. coconut
1/2 gallon soft ice cream

1. Melt butter and brown sugar together. Combine all ingredients except ice cream.
2. Press 1/2 of mixture into bottom of 9" x 13" pan. Spread ice cream over mixture.
3. Mix remaining 1/2 of cornflake mixture by hand

until crumbly. Sprinkle crumbs over ice cream. Store in freezer until immediately before serving.

Rhubarb Torte

Carla Koslowsky
Hillsboro, KS
Parkview Mennonite Church

Makes 15-20 servings

Crust:
1 cup butter *or* margarine, melted
2 cups flour
1/2 tsp. salt
4 Tbsp. powdered sugar

Pudding:
4 1/2 cups diced rhubarb
2 1/2 cups sugar
6 egg yolks
1 cup cream *or* milk
4 Tbsp. flour

Meringue:
6 egg whites
1/2 cup sugar

1. To prepare crust melt butter in 9" x 13" pan in the oven. Add flour, salt and powdered sugar. Mix and press flat into pan.
2. Bake at 350° for 15-20 minutes.
3. On stove top cook rhubarb, 2 1/2 cups sugar, egg yolks, cream and flour until thick and clear, stirring occasionally.
4. While pudding is cooking, beat egg whites until stiff peaks form. Gradually add sugar.

5. Pour pudding over hot crust and top with meringue.

6. Brown meringue in 350° oven for 15-20 minutes. Serve cold.

Rhubarb Crunch

Marie I. Kaufman
Glendale, AZ

Makes 15-20 servings

1 cup oatmeal
1 cup brown sugar
Pinch of salt
1 cup flour
¾ cup butter *or* margarine
4 cups diced rhubarb
1 cup white sugar
2 Tbsp. cornstarch
1 cup water
1 tsp. almond flavoring
21-oz. can cherry pie filling
Chopped nuts

1. Combine oatmeal, brown sugar, salt and flour. Cut in butter and mix by hand until crumbly. Press into bottom of 9" x 13" baking pan. Reserve 1 cup for topping.

2. Spread rhubarb over crust.

3. Combine white sugar and cornstarch. Add water, flavoring and pie filling and mix until smooth. Pour over rhubarb. Sprinkle with reserved topping and nuts.

4. Bake at 350° for 45 minutes.

5. Serve with whipped topping or ice cream.

Scalloped Rhubarb

Louise A. Bartel
North Newton, KS
Bethel College Mennonite Church

Ruth Schmidt
Walton, KS
Tabor Mennonite Church

Makes 8-10 servings

6 cups diced bread
16 Tbsp. margarine, melted
2 cups sugar or less
4 cups diced rhubarb
3-oz. pkg. strawberry gelatin
4 Tbsp. water

1. Mix bread and margarine thoroughly. Add sugar and rhubarb and mix well. Add ½ of the dry strawberry gelatin. (Save remaining gelatin for future use.) Spoon into 9" x 13" baking dish and put 1 Tbsp. water in each corner of pan.

2. Bake at 325° for 45 minutes or until most of the moisture has cooked down.

Rhubarb Tapioca

Carol Weber
Lancaster, PA
Charlotte Street Mennonite Church

Elaine Gibbel
Lititz, PA
Lititz Church of the Brethren

Makes 6-8 servings

2 Tbsp. tapioca
⅓ cup cold water
2 cups chopped rhubarb
½ cup sugar

¾ cup water
1 pint frozen strawberries
Whipped topping

1. Soak tapioca in ⅓ cup cold water for 20 minutes.

2. Cook rhubarb, sugar and ¾ cup water until rhubarb is soft, about 5 minutes. Add tapioca slowly. Cook until mixture is transparent.

3. Fold in strawberries. Cool and top with whipped topping.

Pumpkin Dessert

Sharon Reber
Newton, KS

Makes 15-20 servings

16-oz. can pumpkin
4 eggs
12-oz. can evaporated milk
½ cup sugar
2 tsp. cinnamon
1 tsp. ginger
½ tsp. nutmeg
1 pkg. yellow cake mix
1 cup margarine *or* butter, melted
1 cup chopped nuts

1. Mix together pumpkin, eggs, milk, sugar and spices. Pour into 9" x 13" pan. Sprinkle cake mix evenly over top of pumpkin mixture. Pour melted margarine over all and top with chopped nuts.

2. Bake at 350° for 1 hour.

Pumpkin Cake Roll

A. Catharine Boshart
Lebanon, PA
Hereford Mennonite Home Church

Makes 8 servings

3 eggs
1 cup white sugar
⅔ cup pumpkin
1 tsp. lemon juice
¾ cup flour
1 tsp. baking powder
2 tsp. cinnamon
1 tsp. ginger
½ tsp. nutmeg
½ tsp. salt
1 cup finely chopped
walnuts
Powdered sugar

Filling:
1 cup powdered sugar
2 3-oz. pkgs. cream cheese
4 Tbsp. butter or margarine
½ tsp. vanilla

1. Beat eggs at high speed for 5 minutes. Gradually add sugar. Stir in pumpkin and lemon juice.

2. Combine flour, baking powder, cinnamon, ginger, nutmeg and salt. Fold dry ingredients into pumpkin mixture. Spread into greased and floured 10" x 15" baking pan. Top with chopped walnuts.

3. Bake at 375° for 15 minutes. Turn out onto towel which has been sprinkled with powdered sugar. Beginning at narrow end, roll towel and cake together. Cool. Unroll for filling and remove towel.

4. To prepare filling combine all ingredients. Beat un-

til smooth. Spread over cooled cake and roll up again. Chill.

5. Slice immediately before serving.

Pumpkin Torte

Anna Weinhold
Ephrata, PA
Ephrata Mennonite Church

Makes 15-20 servings

2 cups graham cracker
crumbs
⅓ cup sugar
½ cup butter
8-oz. pkg. cream cheese,
softened
¾ cup sugar
2 eggs, beaten
2 cups pumpkin
3 egg yolks
½ cup sugar
½ cup milk
Pinch salt
2 tsp. cinnamon
1 pkg. plain gelatin
¼ cup cold water
3 egg whites
¼ cup sugar
Whipped topping

1. Combine cracker crumbs, ⅓ cup sugar and butter and mix by hand. Press into 9" x 13" baking pan.

2. Cream together cream cheese and ¾ cup sugar. Add eggs slowly and mix until creamy. Pour mixture over crust.

3. Bake at 350° for 20 minutes. Remove from oven and cool.

4. Combine pumpkin, egg yolks, ½ cup sugar, milk, salt and cinnamon in a saucepan. Cook several minutes until mixture thickens, stirring constantly. Remove from heat.

5. Dissolve gelatin in cold water. Add to pumpkin mixture and cool.

6. Beat egg whites until stiff, gradually adding ¼ cup sugar. Fold egg whites into pumpkin mixture and pour over cooled crust.

7. Refrigerate at least 1 hour before serving. Top with whipped topping.

Hot Pineapple Fruit Dish

Mary Ann Gaeddert
Georgetown, KY
Faith Baptist Church

Makes 8-10 servings

2 15¼-oz. cans pineapple
tidbits
½ lb. grated cheddar cheese
½ cup sugar
⅓ cup flour
½ cup pecans

1. Combine all ingredients, including juice from pineapples, and mix well. Spoon into 9-inch square baking dish.

2. Bake at 350° for 40 minutes. Serve while still hot.

Cherry Delight

Pearl Martin
Sheldon, WI
Shiloh Mennonite Church

Makes 15-20 servings

32 graham crackers, crushed
6 Tbsp. butter *or* margarine
6 Tbsp. sugar
8-oz. pkg. cream cheese
1 cup powdered sugar
1 tsp. vanilla
1 cup dry whipped topping
1 cup water
1½ cups sugar
3 Tbsp. clear gel
1 quart cherries

1. Combine graham crackers, butter and 6 Tbsp. sugar until crumbly. Press into 9" x 13" pan.
2. In large mixing bowl combine cream cheese, powdered sugar and vanilla.
3. In small bowl combine dry whipped topping and water. Beat until thick and combine with cream cheese mixture. Pour over crumbs.
4. In a saucepan combine 1½ cups sugar and clear gel. Add some of the cherry juice and mix well. Cook until thickened. Fold in cherries and cool. Spoon over cream cheese layer and chill before serving.

Variation:
Substitute 2 cups cherry pie filling for the homemade cherry mixture.

Marian R. Denlinger
Willow Street, PA
River Corner Mennonite Church

Substitute 2 cups flour, ½ cup brown sugar, 1 cup margarine and 1 cup chopped nuts mixed together for the graham cracker crust. Bake at 400° for 15 minutes.

Irma Bowman
Akron, PA
Akron Mennonite Church

Cherry Swirl

Ellen Steiner
Temperance, MI
Monroe Street United Methodist

Makes 20 servings

1½ cups sugar
½ cup margarine
½ cup shortening
1 tsp. vanilla
1 tsp. almond flavoring
4 eggs
2 cups flour
1½ tsp. baking powder
21-oz. can cherry pie filling

1. Blend sugar, margarine, shortening, vanilla, almond flavoring and eggs in large bowl. Beat 3 minutes.
2. Combine flour and baking powder and fold dry ingredients into batter. Spread ⅔ of batter into well-greased jelly roll pan. Spread cherry filling over top. Drop remaining batter by spoonsful over cherry layer.
3. Bake at 350° for 45-50 minutes. Cool about 30 minutes. Drizzle with thin powdered sugar frosting.

Cranberry Refrigerator Dessert

Louise A. Bartel
North Newton, KS
Bethel College Mennonite Church

Makes 8-10 servings

2 cups ground cranberries
1 large banana, sliced
⅔ cup sugar
2 cups crushed vanilla wafers
½ cup margarine
2 cups powdered sugar
2 eggs
½ cup chopped nuts
2 cups whipped topping

1. Combine cranberries, sliced banana and sugar. Set aside.
2. Place ½ of crushed wafers into 9-inch square pan.
3. Cream margarine, sugar and eggs and beat until fluffy. Spread mixture over crushed wafers. Top with cranberry mixture and sprinkle with nuts. Spread whipped topping over nuts. Sprinkle with remaining crushed wafers.
4. Chill overnight before serving.

Raspberry Dessert

Kirsten L. Zerger
Berkeley, CA
First Mennonite Church of
San Francisco

Makes 15-20 servings

2 10-oz. pkgs. frozen red
  raspberries
1 cup water
½ cup sugar
2 tsp. lemon juice
4 Tbsp. cornstarch
¼ cup cold water
50 large marshmallows
1 cup milk
2 cups heavy cream
1¼ cups graham cracker
  crumbs
¼ cup chopped nuts
¼ cup melted butter

1. Combine raspberries, 1
cup water, sugar and lemon
juice and heat slowly in a
saucepan.
2. Dissolve cornstarch in
¼ cup cold water. Stir into
berry mixture and cook until
thick and clear. Cool.
3. Melt marshmallows and
milk in double boiler or in
saucepan over boiling water.
Cool.
4. Whip cream. Fold into
marshmallow mixture.
5. Combine graham crack-
ers, nuts and butter in 9" x
13" pan. Press into bottom.
Spread marshmallow cream
mixture over crumbs. Spread
raspberry mixture over top.
Chill until firm.

Raspberry Delight

Barbara A. Yoder
Indianapolis, IN
First Mennonite Church

Makes 12-16 servings

2 pkgs. frozen red
  raspberries
2 3-oz. pkgs. red raspberry
  gelatin
2 small pkgs. vanilla
  pudding
4 cups boiling water
Whipped topping (optional)

1. Place all ingredients except whipped topping in a
large saucepan and let come
to a full, rolling boil, stirring
constantly. Remove from
heat and cool.
2. Spoon into a 9" x 13"
pan or pretty glass bowl. Refrigerate at least 24 hours.
Add whipped topping if desired.

Raspberry Bavarian

Joyce Hofer
Morton, IL
Trinity Mennonite Church

Makes 6-8 servings

3-oz. pkg. raspberry gelatin
1 cup boiling water
½ cup cold water
2 cups fresh *or* frozen
  raspberries
2 cups whipped topping

1. Dissolve gelatin in boiling water. Add cold water.
Cool.

2. Fold in raspberries.
Chill until partially set. Fold
in whipped topping. Chill
and serve.

Variation:
*Substitute 1 lb. frozen black-
berries for the raspberries.*
Ellen S. Peachey
Harpers Ferry, WV
Hyattsville Mennonite Church

Blueberry Cream
Dessert

Margaret Oyer
Gibson City, IL
East Bend Mennonite Church

Makes 15-20 servings

18-oz. box white cake mix
½ cup finely chopped nuts
½ cup graham cracker
  crumbs
½ cup margarine, melted
21-oz. can blueberry pie
  filling
1 cup sour cream
1 egg
¼ tsp. nutmeg

1. In large mixing bowl
combine cake mix, nuts,
cracker crumbs and marga-
rine. Mix on low speed until
crumbly. Reserve 1½ cups
for topping.
2. Press remaining mix-
ture into bottom of greased
9" x 13" baking pan. Spread
pie filling over crust.
3. In small mixing bowl
combine sour cream, egg and
nutmeg. Pour over pie filling
and sprinkle with reserved
crumbs.

4. Bake at 350° for 40-50 minutes or until topping is golden.

5. Serve warm or cold.

Blueberry Dessert

Doris Risser
Orrville, OH
Martins Mennonite Church

Makes 12 servings

2 3-oz. pkgs. grape *or* blackberry gelatin
2 cups boiling water
20-oz. can crushed pineapple
21-oz. can blueberry pie filling
8-oz. pkg. cream cheese
1/2 pint sour cream
1/2 cup sugar
1/2 cup chopped nuts
1 tsp. vanilla

1. Prepare gelatin with boiling water. Add pineapple and pie filling. Spoon into 9" x 13" pan. Let cool until mixture sets.

2. Combine cream cheese, sour cream, sugar, nuts and vanilla. Spread over gelatin mixture. (This is a very thick, rich topping.)

3. Serve.

Blackberry Rolypoly

Elaine Gibbel
Lititz, PA
Lititz Church of the Brethren

Makes 10-12 servings

2 cups flour
2 tsp. baking powder
1/2 tsp. salt
1 Tbsp. sugar
Dash nutmeg
4 Tbsp. butter
3/4 cup milk
2 Tbsp. butter, melted
6 cups blackberries
1 cup sugar
1/2 tsp. salt
Whipped topping

1. Combine flour, baking powder, 1/2 tsp. salt, sugar and nutmeg. Work 4 Tbsp. butter into dry ingredients with fingers. Gradually stir in milk until dough holds together but is soft. Turn out onto floured board and roll into a 1/2-inch thick rectangle.

2. Brush with 2 Tbsp. melted butter.

3. Combine berries, sugar and 1/2 tsp. salt. Sprinkle 1/2 fruit mixture over dough. Roll up like a jelly roll.

4. Place in greased 8" x 12" pan, seam side down. Spoon remaining fruit mixture around roll.

5. Bake at 425° for 30 minutes. Cut into slices and serve with whipped topping.

Strawberry Pretzel Dessert

Emma Kauffman
Lake Odessa, MI
Media Mennonite Church

Gertrude Ziegler
Hatfield, PA
Line Lexington Mennonite Church

Makes 15-20 servings

3 Tbsp. sugar
3/4 cup margarine
2 1/2 cups crushed pretzels
8-oz. pkg. cream cheese
1 cup sugar
2 cups whipped topping
6-oz. pkg. strawberry gelatin
2 cups boiling water
2 10-oz. pkgs. frozen strawberries

1. Cream together 3 Tbsp. sugar and margarine. Fold crushed pretzels into mixture. Press into 9" x 13" pan.

2. Bake at 350° for 10 minutes. Cool completely.

3. Cream together cream cheese, 1 cup sugar and whipped topping. Pour over cooled crust.

4. Combine strawberry gelatin, boiling water and strawberries and spoon over cream cheese mixture. Chill until set.

Apple Raisin Crisp

Bob Litt
London, OH

Makes 8 servings

5 cups sliced, pared, tart
  apples
¼ **cup raisins**
1 cup brown sugar
¾ **cup flour**
¾ **cup quick oats**
1 tsp. cinnamon
½ **cup margarine**

1. Arrange apples in
greased 9" pie pan. Sprinkle
raisins over apples.
2. Combine sugar, flour,
oats and cinnamon. Cut in
margarine until mixture is
crumbly. Press over apples
and raisins.
3. Bake at 350° for 45 minutes.

Happy Apple Crisp

Betty J. Rosentrater
Nappanee, IN
Iglesia Menonita del Buen Pastor

Makes 12-15 servings

10-12 apples, sliced
¼ **cup orange juice**
1 cup flour
½ **cup white sugar**
¾ **cup brown sugar**
1 tsp. cinnamon
½ **tsp. nutmeg**
8 Tbsp. butter

1. Place sliced apples 1½"
deep in a 9" x 13" baking dish.

Pour orange juice over them.
2. In large mixing bowl
combine all dry ingredients.
Add butter, cutting in with 2
table knives or with fingers.
3. Stir the apples and
cover with crumbled mix-
ture.
4. Bake at 350° for 30 minutes or until apples are soft.

Apple Crunch

Lorene Good
Armington, IL
Hopedale Mennonite Church

Makes 12 servings

8-10 apples
⅓ **cup brown sugar**
⅓ **cup white sugar**
Cinnamon
Butter *or* margarine
1 cup flour
⅔ **cup white sugar or less**
1 tsp. baking powder
¼ **tsp. salt**
1 egg

1. Peel and slice apples.
Arrange in 9" x 13" baking
pan. Sweeten with ⅓ cup
brown and ⅓ cup white
sugar. Sprinkle with cinnamon and dot with butter.
2. Sift together flour, ⅔ cup
white sugar, baking powder
and salt. Add egg and mix
with fork or fingers until
crumbly. Pour over apples.
Shake slightly so mixture will
settle down through apples.
3. Bake at 350° for about
40 minutes.
4. Serve with ice cream or
whipped topping.

Apple Cranberry Crisp

Kathy Hertzler
Lancaster, PA
Charlotte Street Mennonite Church

Makes 8-10 servings

3 cups chopped apples,
  unpeeled
2 cups raw cranberries
¾ **cup white sugar**
1½ **cups old-fashioned *or***
  quick cooking oats
½ **cup brown sugar**
⅓ **cup flour**
⅓ **cup chopped pecans**
½ **cup butter *or* margarine,**
  melted
Whipped topping (optional)

1. Combine apples, cran-
berries and white sugar in an
8" baking dish or 2-quart casserole dish. Mix thoroughly
to blend. Set aside.
2. Combine oats, brown
sugar, flour, pecans and butter. Mix until crumbly and
spread evenly over fruit.
3. Bake at 350° for 1 hour
or until fruit is fork-tender.
Serve as is or with whipped
topping.

Autumn Surprise

Jeanette Friesen
Loveland, CO
Boulder Mennonite Church

Makes 10-12 servings

2 cups chopped apples
1 cup sugar
½ cup cooking oil
1 egg
1 tsp. vanilla
1½ cups flour
½ tsp. salt
½ tsp. cinnamon
1 tsp. baking soda
½ tsp. nutmeg
½ cup chopped nuts
½ cup flaked coconut

1. Mix apples and sugar and let stand for 20 minutes.
2. Combine cooking oil, egg and vanilla. Add all dry ingredients and mix well. Fold in apples, nuts and coconut and mix well. Spoon into an 8" x 12" baking pan.
3. Bake at 350° for 30 minutes.

Easy Bake Apples

Willard and Alice Roth
Elkhart, IN
Southside Fellowship

Makes 12 servings

12 baking apples
½ cup raisins
½ cup chopped nuts
1 cup brown sugar
½ tsp. nutmeg

1 tsp. cinnamon
3 slices fresh lemon
1 ¼ cups boiling water

1. Wash and core whole apples. Starting at the stem, peel about ⅓ of the way down.
2. Fill each apple with raisins and nuts. Stack into crockpot.
3. Combine sugar, nutmeg and cinnamon in small saucepan. Add lemon slices and pour boiling water over everything. Boil ingredients together for about 5 minutes. Pour over apples in crockpot.
4. Cover and cook on low 6-8 hours. Serve hot or cold.

Apple Kuchen

Elaine Gibbel
Lititz, PA
Lititz Church of the Brethren

Makes 15-20 servings

¼ cup margarine, softened
1 pkg. yellow cake mix
½ cup coconut *or* oatmeal
2½ cups sliced, pared baking apples
½ cup sugar
1 tsp. cinnamon
1 cup sour cream
1 egg

1. Cut margarine into cake mix until crumbly. Add coconut or oatmeal. Pat mixture lightly into ungreased 9" x 13" pan, building up sides slightly.
2. Bake at 350° for 10 minutes.

3. Arrange apple slices over warm crust.
4. Combine sugar and cinnamon and sprinkle over apples.
5. Blend sour cream and egg together and drizzle over apples.
6. Bake at 350° for 25 minutes or until the edges are light brown. Do not overbake. Serve warm or cold.

Variation:
Substitute fresh peaches for apples and use a white cake mix.

Fruit Tapioca

Anna Weber
Atmore, AL
Mennonite Christian Fellowship

Makes 15-20 servings

7 cups water
1 cup minute tapioca
1 cup sugar
12-oz. can frozen orange concentrate
2 bananas, sliced
1 peach, sliced
2 oranges, diced

1. Bring water to a boil and add tapioca. Boil for 1 minute or until tapioca appears clear. Remove from heat and add frozen concentrate. Mix well and cool.
2. Immediately before serving, fold in fruit slices.

Tapioca Dessert

Samay Phommalle
Toledo, OH

Makes 16 servings

1 lb. tapioca
1½-2 cups sugar
16 ozs. coconut milk
1 Tbsp. vanilla
¼ tsp. salt

1. Cook tapioca according to directions. Chill.
2. In separate saucepan combine sugar and coconut milk. Heat until sugar has dissolved. Add vanilla and salt.
3. Immediately before serving, combine tapioca with syrup mixture.

Grandma's Old-Fashioned Pearl Tapioca

Willard and Alice Roth
Elkhart, IN
Southside Fellowship
Lois Mast
Indianapolis, IN

Makes 20-25 servings

5 cups water
1 cup pearl tapioca
3-oz. pkg. fruit-flavored gelatin
1 cup whipping cream
½ cup sugar
1 Tbsp. vanilla
Chopped pecans *or* fresh berries

1. Bring water to a boil and cook tapioca with water over low heat, stirring every few minutes until tapioca is clear (about 1 hour!).
2. Remove from heat and stir in gelatin until dissolved. Cool, stirring occasionally.
3. Beat whipping cream. Add sugar and vanilla. Fold into cooked, cooled tapioca. Pour into large glass serving bowl and garnish with pecans or berries.

This recipe can be used with imagination, depending on fruits and flavors in season.

Variation:
I like to make this recipe with 3-oz. pkg. strawberry gelatin When adding gelatiun and sugar, I also add an 8-oz. can drained, crushed pineapple. Immediately before serving, I fold in 3 sliced bananas.
Ruth Sommers
Kokomo, IN
Parkview Mennonite Church

Fruit Cobbler

Verna Birky
Albany, OR
Albany Mennonite Church

Makes 10-15 servings

4 cups fresh fruit
½ cup sugar
½ tsp. cinnamon
1 egg, beaten
½ cup milk
⅓ cup cooking oil
1 cup flour
1 cup sugar

1 tsp. baking powder
¼ tsp. salt
1-2 Tbsp. minute tapioca (optional)

1. Arrange choice of fruit in greased 9" x 13" pan. Sprinkle with ½ cup sugar and cinnamon.
2. Combine egg, milk and oil.
3. Combine dry ingredients, add minute tapioca only if the fruit is quite juicy. Stir egg mixture into dry ingredients. Pour over layer of fruit.
4. Bake at 325° for 45 minutes or longer, depending on choice of fruit.

Mississippi Mud

Erma Kauffman
Cochranville, PA
Media Mennonite Church

Makes 8 servings

1 cup brown sugar
1 Tbsp. butter
¼ cup water
3 egg yolks
4 Tbsp. flour
2½ cups milk
1 tsp. vanilla
12 graham crackers
3 egg whites
2 Tbsp. white sugar

1. Melt brown sugar and butter together. Add water and boil for several minutes, stirring constantly.
2. Combine egg yolks, flour and milk. Add to syrup and boil until mixture is

thick, stirring constantly. Stir in vanilla.

3. Roll graham crackers into very fine crumbs. Layer ½ of crumbs into bottom of greased casserole dish. Add pudding and top with remaining crumbs.

4. Beat egg whites until stiff, adding white sugar. Spread over dish. Brown meringue at 375° for 7 minutes.

Princess Poppy Torte

Lola L. Miller
Quakertown, PA
West Swamp Mennonite Church

Makes 15-20 servings

½ cup butter
1 cup flour
¼ cup brown sugar
¾ cup chopped nuts
1½ Tbsp. unflavored gelatin
½ cup cold water
1½ cups milk
1 cup white sugar or less
5 egg yolks, slightly beaten
¼ cup poppy seeds
2 Tbsp. cornstarch
¼ tsp. salt
½ tsp. vanilla
5 egg whites
½ tsp. cream of tartar
½ cup white sugar or less
Whipped topping

1. Cut butter into flour and brown sugar. Add nuts and mix well. Press into greased 9" x 13" baking pan.

2. Bake at 350° for 12-15 minutes or until golden. Cool.

3. Soften gelatin in cold water.

4. Combine milk, 1 cup white sugar and egg yolks in double boiler. Stir to dissolve sugar. Add poppy seeds, cornstarch and salt. Cook until mixture thickens and coats spoon.

5. Stir softened gelatin into mixture and blend well. Add vanilla. Cool until partially set.

6. Beat egg whites until frothy. Add cream of tartar and beat until soft peaks form. Gradually beat in ½ cup white sugar. Beat until very stiff. Fold into partially set poppy seed custard. Pour over baked crust.

7. Chill until firm. Garnish with whipped cream before serving.

Fruit Delight

Joan Ranck
Christiana, PA
Maple Grove Mennonite Church

Makes 10-15 servings

1 pkg. graham crackers, crushed
¼ lb. butter, melted
½ tsp. unflavored gelatin
1 tsp. powdered sugar
2 cups whipped topping
8-oz. pkg. cream cheese
½ cup powdered sugar
Fruit *or* pie filling

1. Combine graham crackers, butter, gelatin and 1 tsp. powdered sugar. Press into 9" x 13" pan.

2. Bake at 350° for 10-12 minutes or until golden brown.

3. Combine whipped topping, cream cheese and ½ cup powdered sugar and spoon over graham cracker crust. Top with choice of fruit or pie filling.

Spiced Peaches

Clara L. Hershberger
Goshen, IN
Goshen Mennonite Church

Makes 10-15 servings

29-oz. can peach halves
¾ cup brown sugar, packed
½ cup vinegar
1 Tbsp. whole cloves
1 Tbsp. whole allspice

1. Drain syrup from peaches.

2. To syrup add sugar, vinegar and spices. Bring to a boil and boil for 5 minutes.

3. Add fruit and simmer for 5 more minutes.

4. Chill before serving.

Grape Mush

Edna Mast
Cochranville, PA
Maple Grove Mennonite Church

Makes at least 12-15 servings

1 quart home-canned grape juice
½ cup sugar
¼ tsp. salt
6 Tbsp. minute tapioca
2 bananas, sliced

1. Combine all ingredients except bananas and let sit for 5 minutes. Cook over medium heat, stirring frequently, until mixture comes to a full boil and tapioca becomes clear.
2. Chill at least 1 hour or overnight.
3. Immediately before serving, top with sliced bananas.

Ambrosia Parfait

Nancy Roth
Colorado Springs, CO
Remnant of Israel Congregation

Makes 6 servings

1 small pkg. instant vanilla pudding
1 cup cold milk
1 cup miniature marshmallows
1 banana, sliced
8-oz. can crushed pineapple, undrained
11-oz. can mandarin oranges, drained

½ cup sliced almonds (optional)
½ cup coconut (optional)

1. No longer than an hour before serving, beat together pudding mix and milk.
2. Fold in all remaining ingredients.
3. Refrigerate and serve.

Plumamooss

Elsie M. Pankratz
Mountain Lake, MN
Bethel Mennonite Church

Makes 20 servings

4 quarts water
2 cups raisins
½ lb. dried peaches *or* dried apricots
1 lb. prunes
1 stick cinnamon
2-3 points star anise
1 cup sugar
1 cup cream
½ cup flour

1. To the water add fruits, spices and sugar. Simmer until fruit is soft, but do not overcook.
2. Blend cream and flour thoroughly in a shaker. Add a small amount of water and a small amount of hot Mooss to the shaker and stir well.
3. Pour cream thickening into saucepan with Mooss, stirring gently to keep fruit from breaking apart.
4. Chill and serve.

Fruit Gelatin Whip

Karen and Leonard Nolt
Boise, ID
Hyde Park Mennonite Church

Makes 12 servings

2 3-oz. pkgs. unflavored gelatin
1 cup cold orange *or* pineapple juice
2½ cups hot apricot nectar
⅔ cup sugar or less
¼ tsp. salt
1-2 cups whipped topping

1. Soften gelatin in cold juice for 5 minutes. Add hot apricot nectar, sugar and salt. Stir until gelatin dissolves.
2. Refrigerate until set. Garnish with whipped topping.

Merry Fruit Compote

A. Catharine Boshart
Lebanon, PA
Hereford Mennonite Home Church

Makes 18-20 servings

2 12-oz. pkgs. pitted prunes
12-oz. bottle gingerale
8-oz. pkg. dried apricots
1 cup raisins
1 cup orange juice
1 tsp. minced, peeled ginger root *or* ¼ tsp. ground ginger
1 stick cinnamon
20-oz. can pineapple chunks
16-oz. can pear halves
½ cup light corn syrup

1. In 5-quart saucepan combine prunes, gingerale, apricots, raisins, orange juice, ginger and cinnamon. Bring to boiling over high heat. Reduce heat to low; cover and simmer 15 minutes or until fruit is tender.

2. Drain pineapple chunks and pear halves. Cut each pear in half lengthwise.

3. To fruit mixture in saucepan add pineapple, pears and corn syrup. Stir gently with rubber spatula to mix well.

4. Cool at least 30 minutes before serving or refrigerate and serve chilled.

Fresh Fruit Pudding

Doris Schrock
Goshen, IN
Yellow Creek Mennonite Church

Makes 12-15 servings

½ cup sugar or less
3 Tbsp. butter *or* margarine
1 cup flour
1 tsp. baking powder
1 tsp. salt
½ cup milk
1 quart fresh berries
1 cup sugar or less
2 Tbsp. cornstarch
2 cups boiling water

1. Cream butter and ½ cup sugar together.

2. Combine dry ingredients and add to creamed mixture, alternating with milk. Mix well.

3. Place washed and drained fruit in bottom of greased 9" x 13" baking dish. Pour batter over fruit.

4. Combine 1 cup sugar and cornstarch and sprinkle over batter. Pour boiling water over all.

5. Bake at 350° for 40-45 minutes. Serve warm or cold.

Fruit Salad with Dressing

Julie Hurst
Leola, PA

Makes 6 servings

Fruit Dressing:
3 cups sugar or less
3 eggs, well beaten
Juice and grated rind of 3 oranges
Juice and grated rind of 2 limes
Juice and grated rind of 2 lemons

Fruit Salad:
3 11-oz. cans mandarin oranges, drained
3 apples, peeled and sliced
3 bananas, sliced
18 dates
½ cup walnut chips

1. In a saucepan combine sugar, eggs, juice and grated rind of oranges, limes and lemons. Blend well, stirring constantly until mixture comes to a boil. Boil for 1 minute. Remove from heat and cool. Refrigerate until ready to serve.

2. To prepare fruit salad dip sliced bananas in lemon juice. Combine all fruit salad ingredients.

3. Serve fruit salad and dressing in separate bowls and allow persons to help themselves.

Frozen Fruit

Anna A. Yoder
Millersburg, OH
Son Light Chapel Conservative Mennonite

Makes 15-20 servings

3 cups water
1½ cups sugar
8 bananas, sliced
20-oz. can crushed pineapple
6-oz. can frozen orange juice

1. Combine water and sugar and let stand to dissolve.

2. Combine bananas and pineapple. Set aside.

3. Add orange juice to sugar water. Pour mixture over bananas and pineapple, stirring gently until mixed. Pour into 9" x 13" baking dish with a lid. Cover dish and freeze.

4. Remove from freezer 2 hours before serving.

Variation:
Add some sliced fresh peaches and a small bottle of maraschino cherries. Pour gingerale over slush immediately before serving.

Veva Zimmerman Mumaw
Hatfield, PA

Refreshing Fruit Cup

Polly Johnson
Driftwood, ON
Hunta Mennonite Church

Makes 20-24 servings

2 large apples, cored and diced
1 red grapefruit, peeled, sectioned and cut up
2 oranges, peeled, sectioned and cut up
2-3 kiwi fruit, sliced
1 lb. red *or* green seedless grapes
1 honeydew melon, peeled and sliced
10-oz. pkg. frozen strawberries
10-oz. pkg. frozen raspberries
10-oz. pkg. frozen blueberries
20-oz. can pineapple tidbits with juice

1. Combine all ingredients and seal container tightly.
2. Refrigerate until ready to serve. May be served with ice cream.

If prepared in the morning, the frozen fruit acts as a cooler and the container will not require refrigeration. The fruit will be icy cold and refreshing 2-3 hours later. A real hit on hot summer Sundays!

Fruit Slush

Yvonne E. Martin
Mechanicsburg, PA
Grantham Brethren in Christ

Makes 3 quarts

12-oz. can unsweetened frozen orange juice concentrate
3 cans water
2 20-oz. cans crushed pineapple
4-5 large bananas, sliced

1. Mix all ingredients together and freeze.
2. Thaw slightly before serving.

Slush

Betty Hartzler
Toano, VA
Williamsburg Mennonite Church

Makes 15-20 servings

6 ripe bananas, mashed
20-oz. can crushed pineapple
12-oz. can frozen orange juice
2 cups sugar
2 29-oz. cans apricots
1 pint strawberries, crushed
2 Tbsp. lemon juice

1. In a large bowl combine all ingredients, including juice from pineapple and apricots. Mix well.
2. Freeze until slushy. Serve.

Mixed Fruit

Lois Taylor Erb
Morgantown, PA

Makes 30 servings

16-oz. can peaches
16-oz. can pears
20-oz. can unsweetened pineapple chunks
11-oz. can mandarin oranges
1 lb. seedless red grapes
1 lb. seedless white grapes
3 kiwi fruit, peeled and sliced

1. Drain and wash peaches and pears in cold water. Cut into bite-sized pieces.
2. Combine all ingredients, including the pineapple and mandarin orange juices, in a large glass serving dish.
3. Cover and chill thoroughly.

Fruit Pudding

Penny Blosser
New Carlisle, OH
Huber Mennonite Church

Phoebe M. Yoder
Bristol, IN
Tri Lakes Community Church

Makes 8-10 servings

8-oz. can pineapple, undrained
11-oz. can mandarin oranges, undrained
17-oz. can fruit cocktail, undrained
½ cup coconut

2 Tbsp. lemon juice
1 small pkg. lemon instant
  pudding
1 cup milk
2 bananas, sliced

1. Combine pineapple, mandarin oranges, fruit cocktail, coconut and lemon juice.

2. Combine pudding and milk and mix well.

3. Combine fruit mixture with pudding mixture and stir gently to combine all ingredients.

4. Immediately before serving, fold in sliced bananas

Light Fruit Pizza

Doreen Snyder
Waterloo, ON
Erb Street Mennonite Church

Makes 15-20 servings

Crust:
⅔ cup shortening
¾ cup sugar
1 tsp. vanilla
1 egg
4 tsp. milk
2 cups flour
¼ tsp. salt

Topping:
8-oz. pkg. cream cheese
3 Tbsp. powdered sugar
Variety of fruit

Glaze:
1½ cups fruit juice
1½ Tbsp. cornstarch

1. To prepare crust cream together shortening, sugar

and vanilla. Beat in egg and milk.

2. Sift together flour and salt and stir into batter. Spread on greased cookie sheet.

3. Bake at 375° for 10 minutes until cooked, not browned. Cool.

4. To prepare topping beat together cream cheese and powdered sugar and spread over cooled crust. Arrange sliced fruit over topping.

5. To prepare glaze combine fruit juice and cornstarch and heat until clear. Cool slightly and pour evenly over fruit. Refrigerate overnight and cut before serving.

Fruit Pizza

Frances Bumgardner
Morton, IL
First Mennonite Church

Makes 15-20 servings

Crust:
½ cup cooking oil
½ cup white sugar
½ cup powdered sugar
½ cup margarine
1 egg
½ tsp. baking soda
½ tsp. cream of tartar
2 ¼ cups flour
¼ tsp. salt

Topping:
8-oz. pkg. cream cheese
½ cup white sugar
1 tsp. vanilla
2 cups whipped topping
Variety of fruit pieces

Glaze:
1 cup sugar
2 Tbsp. cornstarch
¼ cup lemon juice
1 cup orange juice
½ cup water
Dash of salt

1. To prepare crust combine oil, sugars and margarine. Mix well. Add egg.

2. Sift together dry ingredients and add to batter, beating until all ingredients are well blended. Spread into 10" x 15" jelly roll pan, sealing edges.

3. Bake at 375° for 12 minutes. Cool.

4. To prepare topping bring cream cheese to room temperature and blend with sugar. Add vanilla. Fold in whipped topping. Spread over cooled crust.

5. Place fruit over topping in interesting color arrangements, using a variety of fruits such as bananas, mandarin oranges, melons, berries and peaches.

6. Combine all glaze ingredients in a saucepan. Bring to a boil over medium heat, stirring constantly. Cool slightly and pour over fruit. Refrigerate overnight if possible. Cut and serve.

Homemade Ice Cream

Shirley Thieszen
Lakin, KS
Garden Valley Church

Makes 1 gallon

5 eggs
1 cup sugar
½ tsp. salt
2 14-oz. cans Eagle Brand milk
5-oz. can evaporated milk
2 Tbsp. vanilla
2 quarts whole milk or more

1. Beat eggs well. Add sugar and salt and beat well. Add 3 cups regular milk and pour into double boiler. Cook until thickened. Cool.

2. Pour cooled mixture, Eagle Brand milk, evaporated milk, vanilla and remaining regular milk into ice cream freezer. Mix well.

3. Freeze according to directions given with your ice cream freezer.

Musli

Marjorie Nafziger
Harmon, WV

Margaret Wenger Johnson
Keezletown, VA
Harrisonburg Friends Meeting

Makes 8-12 servings

2 cups yogurt
1 cup rolled oats
½ cup flaked coconut
1½ cups canned fruit (cherries, peaches, pears or whatever fruit you desire)
½ cup blueberries
½ cup strawberries
4 ozs. orange juice concentrate
¼ cup honey
Raisins (optional)

1. Combine yogurt, oats and coconut and refrigerate overnight or at least 3 hours.

2. Approximately 1 hour before serving, add all remaining ingredients. Chill.

This adaptable recipe makes a wonderful, not-too-sweet dessert.

Cheesecake

Ruth Schmidt, Walton, KS; Eva Blosser, Dayton, OH; Hazel L. Miller, Hudson, IL; Velma Zehr, Eureka, IL

Makes 15-20 servings

3-oz. pkg. lemon gelatin
1 cup boiling water
32 graham crackers
8 Tbsp. butter, melted
2 Tbsp. powdered sugar

12-oz. can evaporated milk, chilled
1 cup white sugar
8-oz. pkg. cream cheese
2 tsp. vanilla

1. Dissolve gelatin in boiling water. Cool to room temperature.

2. Crush crackers with rolling pin. Mix with butter and powdered sugar. Reserve ½ cup crumbs. Press remaining crumbs into 9" x 12" baking pan.

3. When evaporated milk has been thoroughly chilled, whip until stiff. Set aside.

4. Cream white sugar and cream cheese, adding 2-3 Tbsp. gelatin mixture.

5. Slowly add remaining gelatin to whipped milk. Fold in cream cheese and add vanilla. Pour over crust and sprinkle reserved crumbs over top of batter. Chill overnight in refrigerator.

Variations:

Substitute 1½ cups whipping cream for evaporated milk.

Add 3 tsp. lemon juice for extra flavoring.

Margaret Willms
Coaldale, AB

Mini Cheesecakes

Lorraine Stutzman Amstutz
Bluffton, OH
First Mennonite Church

Makes 18-20 servings

2 8-oz. pkgs. cream cheese,
  softened
¾ cup sugar
2 eggs
1 Tbsp. lemon juice
1 tsp. vanilla
18-20 cupcake liners
18-20 vanilla wafers
21-oz. can pie filling

1. Beat together cream
cheese, sugar, eggs, lemon
juice and vanilla until light
and fluffy.

2. Line cupcake pans with
liners. Place 1 vanilla wafer
in the bottom of each liner.

3. Fill liners approxi-
mately ¾ full with cream
cheese mixture.

4. Bake at 375° for 15-20
minutes.

5. Top with pie filling and
chill before serving. (Or use
homemade pie filling as a
variation if you like.)

*These cheesecakes are attrac-
tive, fun and easy for the kids!*

Maple Pumpkin Cheesecake

Jeanette Harder
Garland, TX

Makes 15-20 servings

1¼ cups graham cracker
  crumbs
¼ cup sugar
¼ cup butter, melted
3 8-oz. pkgs. cream cheese,
  softened
14-oz. can sweetened
  condensed milk
16-oz. can pumpkin
3 eggs
1 cup maple syrup
1½ tsp. cinnamon
1 tsp. nutmeg
½ tsp. salt
1 cup whipping cream
½ cup pecans, chopped

1. Combine cracker
crumbs, sugar and butter.
Press firmly into 9" x 13" pan.

2. In large mixing bowl
beat cream cheese until fluffy.
Gradually add condensed
milk, beating until smooth.
Add pumpkin, eggs, ¼ cup
maple syrup, cinnamon, nutmeg and salt. Mix well. Pour
into graham cracker crust.

3. Bake at 300° for 1 hour
and 15 minutes or until edge
springs back when lightly
touched. Cool and chill.

4. In a saucepan combine
remaining ¾ cup maple
syrup and whipping cream.
Bring to a boil. Boil rapidly
for 15-20 minutes or until
thickened, stirring occasionally. Fold in chopped pecans.
Spread this glaze over
chilled cheesecake.

Blueberry Cheesecake

Myrtle Miller Fricke
McMinnville, OR
First Baptist Church

Makes 15-20 servings

16 graham crackers, crushed
4 Tbsp. margarine, melted
¾ cup white sugar
2 8-oz. pkgs. cream cheese
1 cup white sugar
2 eggs, beaten
1 tsp. vanilla
21-oz. can blueberry
  pie filling
2 cups whipped topping

1. Combine graham crack-
ers, margarine and ¾ cup
white sugar until crumbly.
Press into 9" x 13" baking pan.

2. Cream together cream
cheese and 1 cup sugar. Add
eggs and vanilla and mix well.
Spread cream mixture over
graham cracker crust.

3. Bake at 375° for 25-30
minutes or until toothpick inserted in center comes out
clean. Cool at least 15 minutes.

4. Spread blueberry pie filling over cake. Chill for several
hours. Immediately before
serving, spread with whipped
topping.

Variation:

*After baking, cool for 15 min-
utes. Mix together 1½ cups sour
cream, ½ cup white sugar and ½
Tbsp. vanilla. Spread over cooled
cheesecake. Return to oven and
bake another 15 minutes. Cool
and spread with pie filling before
serving. Omit whipped topping.*

Mary Zehr
Mt. Pleasant, PA
Mennonite Church of Scottdale

Coffee Chews

Debbie Rowley and Leanora Harwood
Lancaster, PA
South Christian Street Mennonite Church

Makes 12-15 servings

¾ **cup flour**
½ **tsp. salt**
1 tsp. baking powder
1 Tbsp. instant coffee
2 eggs
1 cup sugar
½ **cup margarine, melted**
1 tsp. vanilla

1. Sift together flour, salt, baking powder and coffee.
2. In separate bowl beat eggs until foamy. Gradually add sugar and continue beating until stiff. Stir in melted margarine, vanilla and dry ingredients. Mix until blended.
3. Pour into a greased 8-inch square baking pan.
4. Bake at 350° for 30 minutes.

Dried Fruit Morsels

Joan Gingrich
Landisville, PA

Makes 30-35 pieces

30-35 moist dried prunes and apricots
4 ozs. cream cheese
2-3 Tbsp. powdered sugar
1-2 Tbsp. frozen orange juice concentrate

1. Flatten and "cup" prunes and apricots and arrange on a serving plate.
2. Beat cream cheese, sugar and orange juice until thoroughly mixed.
3. Using a cake decorator, dab a bit of filling on each piece of fruit.

Variations:
Garnish each piece of fruit with nuts.Let some pieces of fruit undecorated for persons who need to be careful about cholesterol.

Tandy Takes

Elaine Gibbel
Lititz, PA
Lititz Church of the Brethren

Makes 40-50 servings

2 cups sugar
4 eggs
2 tsp. cooking oil
1 tsp. vanilla
2 cups flour
Dash salt
2 tsp. baking powder
1 cup milk
8 Tbsp. peanut butter
7-oz. Hershey chocolate bar
1 Tbsp. shortening

1. Beat together sugar, eggs, oil and vanilla. Add flour, salt, baking powder and milk and beat again.
2. Pour into greased and floured 15-inch jelly roll pan. Bake at 350° for 20-25 minutes.
3. Spread peanut butter over hot cake. Cool in refrigerator.

4. Melt chocolate and shortening in double boiler. Spread over cooled cake. Cut into 2-inch squares.

Children love Tandy Takes. They are easy to eat.

Scotch Toffies

Margaret Rich
North Newton, KS
Bethel College Mennonite Church

Makes 15-20 servings

⅓ **cup margarine, melted**
2 cups oatmeal, uncooked
½ **cup brown sugar**
¼ **cup dark corn syrup**
1½ **tsp. vanilla**
1 cup semi-sweet chocolate chips
¼ **cup nuts, chopped**

1. Pour melted margarine over oatmeal and mix thoroughly. Add all remaining ingredients and mix well.
2. Pack firmly into well-greased 9" x 13" baking pan.
3. Bake at 350° about 15-20 minutes or until mixture is a rich brown color. (At this stage it will be bubbling.)
4. Remove from oven and cool slightly in pan. Cut into squares. If toffies harden before they are cut, reheat slightly and cutting will be easy.

Rainbow Finger Jello

Georgia L. Martin
Lancaster, PA
Charlotte Street Mennonite Church

Makes 25-30 servings

3-oz. pkg. black cherry
   gelatin
3-oz. pkg. cherry gelatin
3-oz. pkg. lime gelatin
3-oz. pkg. lemon gelatin
3-oz. pkg. orange gelatin
½ pint dairy sour cream
5 cups boiling water

1. Dissolve black cherry gelatin with 1 cup boiling water. Pour ⅔ of mixture into an 8" x 8" pan. Chill about ½ hour until set.
2. To remaining third of black cherry gelatin, add 2 Tbsp. sour cream and beat until thoroughly mixed. Pour over first layer. Chill until set.
3. Cut gelatin into squares or use small cookie cutters to make shapes children will enjoy.
4. Follow steps 1 to 3 for each flavor of gelatin.

Sesame Candy

Colleen Heatwole
Burton, MI
New Life Christian Fellowship

Makes 30-50 servings

3 cups sesame seeds
2 cups coconut
1 cup chopped nuts
1 cup sunflower seeds
1 cup honey
½ cup dry milk
1 tsp. vanilla
¼ tsp. salt (optional)

1. Lightly grease a 10" x 15" jelly roll pan. Toast sesame seeds at 375° for 5 minutes. Add coconut, nuts and sunflower seeds.
2. Toast mixture, stirring frequently, until ingredients are golden brown, approximately 20 minutes.
3. In a saucepan mix honey and dry milk and bring to a boil over medium heat, stirring constantly. Remove from heat.
4. Combine all ingredients in a large bowl, stirring until dry ingredients are completely coated.
5. Press firmly into large flat container, using plastic wrap as mixture is quite sticky.
6. Cool at least ½ hour in refrigerator. Cut into small pieces, separating each piece.

Despite unusual appearance of this candy, it is a nutritious, filling confection that does not leave a sugar-laden "high."

Easy Fake Heath Bars

Sara Fretz-Goering
Silver Spring, MD
Hyattsville Mennonite Church

Makes 10-12 servings

½ box graham crackers
16 Tbsp. margarine
½ cup brown sugar
½ cup chopped pecans
12-oz. pkg. chocolate chips
½ pkg. brickle chips

1. Line greased cookie sheet with graham crackers.
2. Bring margarine, brown sugar and pecans to a boil. Boil for 3 minutes. Pour over graham crackers.
3. Bake at 325° for 8 minutes. Remove from oven and turn off heat.
4. Top with chocolate chips. Return tray to oven for 2 minutes to melt chocolate chips.
5. Top with brickle chips. Cool and break into pieces.

Easy Fudge

Betty Hartzler
Toano, VA
Williamsburg Mennonite Church

Makes 60-65 small pieces

12-oz. pkg. semi-sweet
chocolate chips
14-oz. can sweetened,
condensed milk
1 tsp. vanilla (optional)
1 cup chopped nuts
(optional)

1. In a double boiler melt chocolate and milk together and continue cooking 15-20 minutes until thickened.

2. Stir in vanilla and nuts if desired.

3. Pour into 9-inch square pan.

4. Refrigerate and cut into squares before serving.

Barfi (Indian Fudge)

Florence Nafziger
Goshen, IN
College Mennonite Church

Makes approximately 50 pieces

12-oz. can evaporated milk
1½ cups sugar
Dash of salt
½ tsp. ground cardamom
1½ tsp. margarine
4-5 cups dry skim milk

1. In a saucepan mix evaporated milk, sugar, salt and cardamom together. Bring to boil and boil for 3 minutes, stirring constantly.

2. Remove from heat and stir in margarine. Gradually stir in dry milk until mixture becomes thick enough to follow spoon and begins to set.

3. Quickly pour into lightly greased 9" x 13" baking pan. Press into pan with greased fingers.

4. Cool and cut into 1½-inch squares. Store in covered container in refrigerator or freezer.

Appetizers and Snacks

Crab Spread

Alice Suderman
New Hope, MN
New Hope Mennonite Brethren
Church

Makes 20 servings

8-oz. pkg. cream cheese
2 Tbsp. mayonnaise
1 Tbsp. lemon juice
2 tsp. grated onion
2 tsp. Worcestershire sauce
3-oz. bottle cocktail sauce
6-oz. can crab meat
Parsley flakes

1. Soften cream cheese and add mayonnaise, lemon juice, onion and Worcestershire sauce. Spread on dinner plate.
2. Top with cocktail sauce.
3. Drain and crumble crab over top. Top with parsley flakes.
4. Serve with favorite crackers.

Chicken Salad Spread

Lois W. Benner
Lancaster, PA
Rossmere Mennonite Church

Makes 6-8 servings

2 cups shredded, cooked
  chicken
1/2 cup mayonnaise
1/2 tsp. cream-style
  horseradish
1/2 tsp. prepared mustard
1/2 tsp. Worcestershire sauce
1 tsp. white sugar
1/2 tsp. salt
1 Tbsp. finely chopped
  onion
1 Tbsp. finely chopped
  celery

1. Prepare cooked chicken by removing all skin, bones and tendons. Save broth and chunks of chicken. Shred chicken chunks in blender. Set aside and cool thoroughly.
2. Combine all other ingredients.
3. Add cooled, shredded chicken to mayonnaise mixture. If consistency is too thick to spread easily, add small amounts of chicken broth until it spreads easily.
4. Spread filling generously between bread rolls.

Tuna Cheese Spread

Elizabeth Yutzy
Wauseon, OH
Inlet Mennonite Church

Makes 10-15 servings

1/4-1/2 cup margarine
8-oz. pkg. cream cheese
7-oz. can tuna, drained
1 onion, minced
1/2 tsp. Worcestershire sauce
1/8 tsp. thyme
1/8 tsp. basil
1/8 tsp. marjoram
Pinch parsley

1. Cream together margarine and cream cheese. Add tuna and all other ingredients and mix well.
2. Chill and serve with your favorite crackers.

Bunwiches

Betty Pellman
Millersville, PA
Rossmere Mennonite Church

Makes 12 servings

½ lb. boiled *or* baked ham
½ lb. sharp cheese
6-8 sweet pickles
1 small onion
2 hard-boiled eggs
½ cup ketchup
12 hamburger rolls

1. Put ham, cheese, pickles, onion and eggs through food chopper. Stir in ketchup and mix well.
2. Spread on hamburger rolls. Wrap each one in aluminum foil and heat at 250° until cheese melts, about 20 minutes. Serve.

Ham and Cheese Sandwiches

Lois Hallman
Goshen, IN
College Mennonite Church

Makes 12 servings

4 Tbsp. margarine
1 tsp. grated onion
1 tsp. mustard
½ tsp. poppy seeds
12 fresh potato buns
1½ lbs. chipped ham
12 thin slices cheese

1. Mix margarine, onion, mustard and poppy seeds. Spread on cut sides of buns.
2. Fill buns with ham and cheese. Wrap in foil and heat in 350° oven for 15 minutes.

Crock Cheese for Finger Food Sandwiches

Elsie Regier
Newton, KS

Makes 6 servings

24-oz. container cottage cheese
½ tsp. salt
¼ tsp. baking soda
½ tsp. caraway seed (optional)
1½ Tbsp. butter *or* margarine
3-4 Tbsp. evaporated milk
½ cup grated cheddar cheese

1. Drain cottage cheese in colander or cloth bag for 4 hours.
2. Place cheese in crock and crumble until fine. Add salt, baking soda and caraway seed to cheese and let stand for another 3 hours.
3. Melt margarine or butter in skillet and add cottage cheese mixture, evaporated milk and cheddar cheese. Cook for several minutes. If mixture has not blended, pour into blender and mix on high for a short time until blended and smooth.
4. Pour into glass jar and cover to cool. Serve as open-faced sandwiches with homemade rye or whole wheat bread.

Many old-timers made this cheese with homemade curds. My mother would let it ripen for 5 days after it was in the crock. She stirred and crumbled it every morning. How we enjoyed it!

Vegetable Pizza

Ruth Ann Swartzendruber, Hydro, OK; Edith Stoltzfus, Mantua, OH; Ruth Hershey, Paradise, PA; Colleen Heatwole, Burton, MI; Becky Bixler, Iowa City, IA; Beth Selzer, Hesston, KS; Shirley Hochstetler, Kidron, OH; Edwina Stoltzfus, Narvon, PA; Doris Ebersole, Archbold, OH

Makes 15-20 servings

2 8-oz. pkgs. crescent rolls
2 8-oz. pkgs. cream cheese
1 cup salad dressing
1 pkg. dry Hidden Valley dressing

1 cup chopped broccoli
1 cup chopped cauliflower
1 cup chopped green pepper
1 cup chopped tomatoes
1/2 cup grated carrots
1 cup shredded cheddar
  cheese

1. Spread crescent rolls on a large cookie sheet to form crust. Bake at 350° for 10 minutes or until brown. Set aside to cool.

2. Combine cream cheese, salad dressing and Hidden Valley dressing. Spread over cooled crust. Sprinkle vegetables over top and sprinkle with cheddar cheese. Pat into dressing mixture.

3. To serve cut into small squares.

Party Rye Pizzas

Louise A. Bartel
North Newton, KS
Bethel College Mennonite Church

Makes approximately 50 servings

1 lb. sharp cheddar cheese,
  shredded
10-15 ripe *or* green olives,
  chopped
4-oz. can diced chilies
8-oz. can tomato sauce
1/4 cup cooking oil
2 Tbsp. vinegar
1/2 cup chopped onion
6 drops Tabasco sauce
Party Rye bread

1. Combine all ingredients except bread.

2. Spread sauce over bread slices.

3. Place under broiler for 3-5 minutes or until mixture becomes bubbly. Watch closely because it burns easily.

4. Sauce keeps well in refrigerator, or it may be frozen for future use.

Cheesy Garlic Bread

Loretta Krahn
Mountain Lake, MN
Bethel Mennonite Church

Makes 10-12 servings

4 Tbsp. butter *or* margarine
4 Tbsp. Parmesan cheese
1 Tbsp. Italian seasoning
1/2 Tbsp. finely chopped
  onion
1/2 tsp. garlic powder
1/2 tsp. salt
1 loaf French bread

1. Warm butter until softened. Stir in all remaining ingredients except bread.

2. Slice bread and spread mixture thinly on each slice.

3. Warm in microwave or slow oven immediately before serving.

Herb Toast

Hazel N. Hassan
Goshen, IN
College Mennonite Church

Makes 20-25 servings

1/2 cup margarine, melted
1 1/2 tsp. curry powder
1/4 tsp. paprika
1 tsp. savory
1/4 tsp. thyme
1 loaf Roman meal bread *or*
  other thinly sliced bread

1. Mix margarine and seasonings either a few hours or a day ahead.

2. Spread mixture on thin slices of bread.

3. Toast at 300° for 30-40 minutes.

4. Serve in basket lined with a cloth napkin.

Shrimp Stuffed Celery Stalks

Lois W. Benner
Lancaster, PA
Rossmere Mennonite Church

Makes 25 servings

1 lb. fresh shrimp
3 cups boiling water
1 tsp. salt
1/4 cup vinegar
Dash pepper
3-oz. pkg. cream cheese, softened
1 Tbsp. grated onion
1/2 tsp. Worcestershire sauce
1/3 cup mayonnaise
1 Tbsp. sweet pickle juice
1/2 tsp. horseradish
Dash garlic salt (optional)
Celery stalks
Cherry tomatoes, olives *or* small radishes

1. Rinse shrimp thoroughly. Cook shrimp for 5 minutes in boiling water to which has been added salt, vinegar and pepper. Drain water. Cool shrimp, take off outer shells and shred in blender.

2. Combine cream cheese, onion, Worcestershire sauce, mayonnaise, pickle juice, horseradish, garlic salt and shredded shrimp. Mix well and chill.

3. Fill celery stalks with shrimp mixture and arrange in an attractive manner on a platter. Add either cherry tomatoes, olives or radishes for additional color.

Ham Roll Ups

Jennie Stutzman
Corry, PA
Beaverdam Mennonite Church

Makes many appetizer servings

1 lb. boiled ham
8-oz. pkg. cream cheese, softened
1 1/2 bunches green onions

1. Spread cream cheese over ham slices. Place one green onion in the center of each slice.

2. Roll up ham with onion in it. Slice in pinwheels.

3. Chill at least 1/2 hour to let flavors blend.

Appetizer Tortilla Pinwheels

Carol Sommers
Millersburg, OH
Martins Creek Mennonite Church

Makes about 50 servings

8-oz. container sour cream
8-oz. pkg. cream cheese, softened
4-oz. can diced green chilies
4-oz. can chopped black olives
1 cup grated cheddar cheese
1/2 cup chopped green onions
Garlic powder to taste
Seasoned salt to taste
5 10-inch flour tortillas
Fresh parsley
Salsa sauce (optional)

1. Make sure chilies and black olives are well drained. Mix together sour cream, cream cheese, chilies, olives, cheddar cheese, onions, garlic powder and seasoned salt.

2. Divide the filling into 5 parts and spread evenly over each tortilla. Roll up tortillas. Cover tightly with plastic wrap, twisting the ends. Refrigerate for several hours.

3. Unwrap the tortillas and cut into 1/2- to 3/4-inch slices. Lay these tortilla pinwheels flat on glass serving plate. Garnish with parsley.

4. If desired, put small bowl of salsa sauce in center of plate.

French Cheese Stick

Ferne Burkhardt
Petersburg, ON
Mannheim Mennonite Church

Makes 10-12 servings

Bread:
1 loaf French bread
1/3 cup butter, melted
1 tsp. celery seed
1 1/2 tsp. dry mustard
1/4 tsp. onion salt
1/2 lb. processed cheese

Optional Topping:
2 Tbsp. butter, melted
1 Tbsp. lemon juice
1/4 cup finely chopped parsley

1. Slice French bread into 3/4-inch slices.

2. Blend ⅓ cup butter, celery seed, dry mustard, onion salt and cheese in food processor.

3. Spread each slice of bread with cheese mixture and stack with spread sides facing each other. Wrap as a loaf in aluminum foil and bake at 350° for 15-20 minutes. (Lay on top of the casseroles already heating in the church oven).

4. If desired, mix all topping ingredients and keep warm by setting bowl near a crockpot or oven vent.

5. About five minutes before the end of baking time, remove loaf from oven. Drizzle the optional topping onto the bread and return to oven for several minutes.

Kate's Philadelphia Cream Sticks

Grace Glick
Millersburg, OH
Walnut Creek Mennonite Church

Makes 10-12 servings

8-oz. pkg. Philadelphia
  cream cheese
½ tsp. vanilla
2 Tbsp. sugar or less
1 egg yolk
1 small loaf white bread
Melted butter

1. Cream softened cream cheese, vanilla, sugar and egg yolk together.

2. Cut the crusts off each piece of bread. Roll each slice flat with rolling pin. Cut

each slice in half. Spread cream cheese mixture on bread. Roll bread into a stick. Dip each piece in melted butter. Bake at 350° for 10 minutes.

Corn Sticks

Judith E. Bartel
North Newton, KS
Bethel College Mennonite Church

Makes 20 servings

2 cups buttermilk baking
  mix
8½-oz. can cream-style corn
¼ cup grated Parmesan
  cheese
1 tsp. powdered garlic
1 Tbsp. dill weed seed
4 Tbsp. margarine, melted

1. Combine baking mix, corn, Parmesan cheese, garlic and dill weed and mix well.

2. Knead 15-20 strokes on lightly floured board. Roll into large rectangle with rolling pin. Cut into 1" x 3" strips. Place strips 1½ inches apart on ungreased cookie sheet. Brush with melted margaring.

3. Bake at 450° for 10-12 minutes.

Egg Rolls

Li' Traung
Kokomo, IN

Makes 30-40 egg rolls

1½ lbs. plain ground pork
2 pkgs. bean thread, soaked
  in cold water
3 dried black mushrooms,
  soaked in hot water
3 ozs. crab meat
1 Tbsp. garlic powder
1 tsp. salt
1 tsp. pepper
4 medium carrots, shredded
1 Tbsp. sugar
1 large onion, chopped
1-2 Tbsp. fish sauce
1 egg, slightly beaten
30-40 egg roll skins
Oil for deep frying

1. In a large bowl mix together ground pork, bean thread, mushrooms, crab meat, garlic powder, salt, pepper, carrots, sugar and onion. Check flavoring and add fish sauce to taste. Add egg and mix thoroughly.

2. Place 1 heaping tablespoon filling on each egg roll skin. Fold in the ends and the sides to make each egg roll about ½" x 4".

3. Pour oil into pan deep enough to cover ½ of egg roll. Heat to 350°. Turn each egg roll once with tongs.

4. Place egg rolls upright in a strainer to drain excess oil. Serve.

Mini Ham or Cream Puffs

Ila Yoder
Hesston, KS
Whitestone Mennonite Church

Makes approximately 80-85 mini servings

Cream Puffs:
8 Tbsp. margarine
1 cup water
1 cup flour
4 eggs

Ham Filling:
2 8-oz. pkgs. cream cheese, softened
2 pkgs. dry ranch dressing
3-4 celery ribs, chopped
2 cups ground ham
2 Tbsp. 7-up
2 Tbsp. chopped green onions

Cream Filling:
1 pkg. instant vanilla pudding
½ pint whipping cream
½ tsp. vanilla
Powdered sugar

1. To prepare cream puffs bring margarine and water to a boil. Add flour and stir over low heat until mixture forms a ball, about 1 minute.

2. Remove from heat and add eggs, beating until smooth.

3. Drop by small teaspoonsful onto greased cookie sheet. Bake at 400° for 30-40 minutes.

4. When cream puffs have cooled, cut off tops and carefully clean out inside of puff.

5. Fill half with ham filling and half with cream filling.

6. To prepare ham filling mix all ingredients together and fill cream puffs. Serve.

7. To prepare cream filling make pudding according to directions and refrigerate until set. Whip the cream, adding vanilla and powdered sugar to taste. Combine cream filling and whipped cream and fill cream puffs. Dust the top of each cream puff with powdered sugar. Serve.

Strawberry Cream Puffs

Barbara Hershey
Lancaster, PA
Rossmere Mennonite Church

Makes 12-15 puffs

Cream Puffs:
½ cup margarine
1 cup boiling water
1 cup flour
¼ tsp. salt
4 eggs

Strawberry Filling:
3 ½-oz. pkg. instant strawberry pudding
1¼ cups milk
1 cup heavy whipping cream

Chocolate Glaze:
½ cup chocolate chips
1 Tbsp. butter *or* margarine
1½ tsp. milk
1½ tsp. light corn syrup

1. To prepare cream puffs combine margarine and boiling water in pan. Keep on low heat until margarine has melted.

2. Sift flour and salt and add to water, stirring vigorously until mixture leaves sides of pan and forms a ball. Remove from heat and add unbeaten eggs, one at a time. Beat thoroughly after each addition.

3. Drop by tablespoonsful onto a greased baking sheet. Place about 2 inches apart.

4. Bake at 400° about 30-40 minutes or until beads of moisture no longer appear on top. Turn oven off and let cream puffs in oven an additional 15 minutes.

5. To prepare filling combine strawberry pudding and milk.

6. Whip cream and fold into pudding mixture.

7. To prepare chocolate glaze combine all ingredients and heat in double boiler or microwave until melted. Stir occasionally.

8. Slice off top of each cream puff. Remove any remaining egg and fill with strawberry filling. Top with chocolate glaze.

Soft Pretzels

Jane Miller
Minneapolis, MN
St. Paul Mennonite Fellowship

Makes 16 servings

Pretzels:
2 cups warm water
2 Tbsp. yeast
½ cup sugar
¼ cup margarine
1 egg
6 ½ cups flour

Topping:
1 egg yolk
2 Tbsp. water
Coarse salt

1. Dissolve yeast in warm water.
2. Beat sugar, margarine, egg and yeast mixture with several cups flour. Knead in the remaining flour. Cover dough with aluminum foil and refrigerate from 2 to 24 hours.
3. Divide dough into 16 pieces. Roll into 20-inch long strips and shape into pretzels. Place on greased cookie sheet.
4. Combine egg yolk and water and brush each pretzel. Sprinkle with coarse salt.
5. Let rise 20 minutes. Bake at 350° for 20 minutes.

Take the dough to children's worship and let them create their own shapes (letters, animals, braids). The "pretzels" can bake during during the fellowship meal and be ready for dessert.

Popcorn

Rosetta Martin
Columbiana, OH
Midway Mennonite Church

Makes 15 or more servings

2 tsp. salt
2 tsp. garlic powder
2 Tbsp. cheese powder
½ cup margarine, melted
8 quarts *popped* popcorn
2 cups small cheese crackers or cheese curls

1. Mix together salt, garlic powder and cheese powder.
2. Pour melted margarine over popcorn. Pour seasonings over popcorn and mix well.
3. Add cheese crackers or curls and serve.

Microwave Caramel Corn

Deb Kauffman
Topeka, IN
Topeka Mennonite Church

Mary Ethel Lahman Heatwole
Harrisonburg, VA
Harrisonburg Mennonite Church

Makes 1 gallon popcorn

Non-stick cooking spray
1 gallon *popped* popcorn
¼ cup dark Karo syrup
1 cup brown sugar
8 Tbsp. margarine
¼ tsp. salt
¼ tsp. baking soda

1. Spray the inside of a large brown bag with non-stick cooking spray. Put the popped popcorn into the bag and set aside.
2. Put syrup, sugar, margarine and salt into a 1½-quart microwave dish. Do not mix ingredients. Microwave for 1 minute. Stir. Microwave for 2 minutes. Stir. Microwave for 2 more minutes, then add soda and stir well.
3. Pour mixture over popcorn, but do not mix or shake. Microwave for 1½ minutes. Remove bag and shake well. Microwave for 1 minute and shake well again. Microwave for 45 seconds and shake well. Microwave for 30 more seconds.
4. Pour into large container to cool and fluff until separated.

Oven Caramel Corn

Verna Birky
Albany, OR
Albany Mennonite Church

Makes 8-10 quarts popcorn

2 cups brown sugar
½ cup light corn syrup
1 cup margarine
Pinch of cream of tartar
1 tsp. baking soda
8-10 quarts *popped* popcorn

1. Cook sugar, syrup, margarine and cream of tartar for 5 minutes, stirring constantly. Add baking soda and mix well.

2. Pour popcorn into a large greased roasting pan. Pour caramel sauce over popcorn, stirring until popcorn is thoroughly coated.

3. Bake at 250° for 1 hour, stirring well every 15 minutes.

4. Break up large pieces as the popcorn cools. Serve.

Roasted Soybeans

Gladys Sprunger
Berne, IN
First Mennonite Church

Makes 12 or more servings

2 cups soybeans
Oil for frying
Seasoned salt

1. Soak soybeans in water overnight.

2. Blot dry the soybeans while bringing the cooking oil to 350°.

3. Fry small amount of soybeans for 10 minutes at a time.

4. Drain on paper towels and salt with seasonings of your choice. We enjoy barbecue flavoring.

Snack Crackers for a Crowd

Faye Nyce
Grantham, PA
Slate Hill Mennonite Church

Makes multiple servings

2 12-oz. pkgs. oyster crackers
1 pkg. Original Ranch dressing
¾ cup cooking oil

1. Mix all ingredients together several days ahead of time.

2. Store in airtight container and stir occasionally to blend flavors.

This dish requires no last-minute Sunday morning fuss, no need for an oven or a crockpot and it is easy to eat.

Cracker Treat

Georgia L. Martin
Lancaster, PA
Charlotte Street Mennonite Church

Makes 50-60 servings

1 box club crackers
2 cups ground nuts
8 Tbsp. margarine
⅓ cup sugar

1. Spread crackers on cookie sheets and put ground nuts on each cracker.

2. On low heat melt margarine and add sugar. Bring to a rolling boil for 1 minute.

3. Spoon melted butter over each cracker. Put in cold oven and bake at 350° for 10 minutes.

4. Remove from cookie sheets immediately and place on waxed paper to cool.

TV Scramble

Ethel Mumaw
Walnut Creek, OH
Berlin Mennonite Church

Makes multiple servings

1 lb. mixed nuts
12-oz. pkg. bite-sized shredded wheat
10½-oz. pkg. Cheerios
5¼-oz. pkg. slim pretzels
6½-oz. pkg. Rice Chex
6½-oz. pkg. pretzel bits
1 cup butter-flavored shortening
1 cup margarine
2 Tbsp. Worcestershire sauce

½ Tbsp. celery salt
½ Tbsp. garlic powder
1 Tbsp. seasoned salt

1. Mix nuts, shredded wheat, Cheerios, pretzels, Rice Chex and pretzel bits.

2. Melt shortening and margarine. Add Worcestershire sauce, celery salt, garlic powder and seasoned salt and mix well.

3. Pour mixture over dry ingredients and stir until dry ingredients are thoroughly coated.

4. Bake at 200 to 250° for 1 hour. Stir every 15 minutes.

Caramel Cereal Snack

**Margaret Oyer, Gibson City, IL;
Jane M. Zimmerman, Blue Ball, PA;
Julia Horst, Gordonville, PA**

Makes about 3 quarts

3 cups Cheerios
2 cups shredded wheat cereal
2 cups shredded rice cereal
2 cups toasted corn cereal
1 cup raisins
1 cup walnut *or* pecan pieces
½ cup margarine
1⅓ cups brown sugar, firmly packed
¼ cup Karo
2 tsp. cinnamon
½ tsp. salt

1. Toss cereals, raisins and nuts together in large greased bowl.

2. Combine margarine, brown sugar, Karo, cinnamon and salt in heavy 1-quart saucepan. Bring to a boil over medium heat, stirring constantly. Boil 3 minutes.

3. Pour hot syrup over mixture and stir well to coat cereals completely. Spread on 2 greased cookie sheets to cool. When completely cool and firm, break into pieces.

Puppy Chow

**Mattie Miller
Sugarcreek, OH**
Walnut Creek Mennonite Church

Makes 10 servings

2 cups chocolate chips
½ cups margarine
1 cup peanut butter
12 cups Rice Chex cereal
2 cups powdered sugar

1. Heat chocolate chips, margarine and peanut butter on low heat. Stir constantly until smooth.

2. Pour sauce over cereal and mix well.

3. Place chocolate-coated cereal in a bag with powdered sugar. Toss until well coated.

Cheeses and Dips

Cheese Ball

Mrs. Lewis L. Beachy
Sarasota, FL
Bahia Vista Mennonite Church

Makes 20 servings

5 ozs. blue cheese
2 8-oz. pkgs. cream cheese
6 ozs. cheddar cheese, grated
1 tsp. minced onion
1 tsp. Worcestershire sauce
½ cup finely chopped
    pecans

1. Mix all ingredients, except pecans, thoroughly.
2. Roll into two balls and cover each ball with pecans.
3. Refrigerate until two hours before serving.
4. Serve with a variety of crackers.

Variation:
Instead of using blue cheese in above recipe, increase cheddar cheese to 1 cup and add 1 Tbsp. horseradish and ½ cup shredded ham.

Frances Schrag
Newton, KS
First Mennonite Church

Pineapple Cheese Ball

Betty Pellman, Millersville, PA;
Jeanne Heyerly, Reedley, CA; Edna
Brunk, Upper Marlboro, MD

Makes 10-12 servings

2 8-oz. pkgs. cream cheese,
    softened
½ cup grated cheddar cheese
8-oz. can crushed pineapple,
    thoroughly drained
2 Tbsp. chopped green
    pepper
2 Tbsp. chopped onion
1 tsp. seasoned salt
½ cup chopped nuts

1. Combine all ingredients except nuts. Mix well. Refrigerate for a few hours.
2. When chilled, shape into a ball. Roll ball in chopped nuts. Wrap in plastic wrap and keep cold until serving time. Serve with crackers.

Salmon Roll

Miriam Showalter
Salem, OR
Salem Mennonite Church

Makes 16-20 servings

1-lb. can salmon
8-oz. pkg. cream cheese,
    softened
1 Tbsp. lemon juice
1 tsp. liquid smoke
¼ tsp. salt
¼ tsp. dry dill weed
    (optional)
1 heaping tsp. minced onion
½ cup chopped nuts
⅓ cup parsley

1. Drain salmon and remove skin and bones. Flake and mix with softened cream cheese. Add lemon juice, liquid smoke, salt, dill weed and onion. Mix well and chill. Shape into log or ball.
2. Mix nuts and parsley and roll salmon ball in mixture.
3. Chill several hours or overnight.
4. Serve with crackers, cocktail breads or celery wedges.

Dried Beef Cheese Ball

Elaine Unruh
Moundridge, KS
First Mennonite Church

Makes 1 large cheese ball

2 8-oz. pkgs. cream cheese, softened
3-oz. pkg. dried beef
2 Tbsp. mayonnaise
2 tsp. prepared mustard
2 Tbsp. dry onion soup mix
Parsley *or* chopped nuts (optional)

1. Mix all ingredients well except parsley or nuts. Shape into a ball. If desired, roll in either parsley or chopped nuts.
2. Serve with a variety of crackers.

Broccoli and Cheese Dip

Faye Nyce
Grantham, PA
Slate Hill Mennonite Church

Makes 1½ cups dip

2 slices bacon
2 pkgs. Lipton broccoli and cheese cup-a-soup
½ cup milk
8-oz. pkg. cream cheese, softened
¼ cup diced green onions

1. Cook bacon until crisp. Set aside to drain, then crumble it.

2. In small bowl blend cup-a-soup, milk and cream cheese or use a blender to cream mixture. Stir in green onions and bacon.
3. Chill and serve with crisp, fresh vegetables or potato chips.

Variations:
Add ½ tsp. pepper and ½ tsp. seasoned salt to mixture. Also increase amount of bacon to 5 slices.

Kerry Stutzman Skudneski
Littleton, CO

Creamy Spinach Dip in Loaf of Bread

Marilyn Yoder
Archbold, OH
West Clinton Mennonite Church

Makes at least 12 servings

8-oz. container sour cream
1½ cups mayonnaise
½ tsp. celery salt
½ tsp. dill weed
¼ tsp. onion salt
¼ cup chopped green onions
3 Tbsp. chopped red pepper
2 10-oz. pkgs. frozen spinach, thawed and well drained
8-oz. can water chestnuts, chopped
Round loaf of rye or pumpernickel bread

1. Mix all ingredients except bread thoroughly. Refrigerate until completely chilled.
2. Cut the top and center out of bread. Be sure to let at least ½ inch all around.
3. Pour dip into the hollow loaf of bread. Use bread pieces which you have cut out of center for dippers. Or prepare a plate of vegetables and crackers for dippers.

Variation:
Substitute 1 pkg. Knorr's Vegetable Soup Mix for celery salt, dill weed and onion salt.

Irma Bowman
Akron, PA
Akron Mennonite Church

Edith Seibert's Vegetable Dip

Edith Williams Seibert
Bedford, VA
Main Street Methodist Friendship Bible Class

Makes 16 servings

1 cup creamed cottage cheese
2 Tbsp. lemon juice
2 Tbsp. milk
2 Tbsp. mayonnaise
2 Tbsp. chopped green onion
¼ cup parsley
½ tsp. tarragon leaves
Dash of pepper

1. Mix all ingredients until smooth and creamy.
2. Serve with a variety of vegetables, such as carrots, celery, cucumbers, broccoli, cauliflower or zucchini.

Veggies and Dip

Dolores Metzler
Belleville, PA
Allensville Mennonite Church

Fannie Bender
Accident, MD
Cherry Glade Mennonite Church

Makes 1 quart dip

2 cups mayonnaise
2 cups sour cream
3 Tbsp. parsley flakes
3 Tbsp. onion flakes
1½ tsp. seasoning salt
3 tsp. dill weed

1. Mix all ingredients well. Chill for one hour before serving.
2. Serve with an assortment of raw vegetables such as turnips, celery sticks, carrot sticks, radishes and cucumber slices.

Always keep pre-sliced veggies immersed in cold water until just before you arrange them on a tray for serving.

Laura Bauman's Vegetable Dip

Laura Bauman
Elmira, ON
Floradale Mennonite Church

Makes approximately 4½ cups dip

24 ozs. jar Hellmans
  mayonnaise
1½ cups sour cream
1½ Tbsp. lemon juice
¾ tsp. salt

¾ tsp. paprika
¾ tsp. garlic powder
¾ cup chopped fresh parsley
3 Tbsp. grated onion
3 Tbsp. chopped chives
1½ tsp. Worcestershire
  sauce
⅜ tsp. curry powder

1. Mix all ingredients thoroughly. Flavor improves if made well in advance of using.
2. Serve with vegetables or potato chips.

Raw Vegetable Dip

Judy Hall
Molalla, OR
Zion Mennonite Church

Makes 3 cups dip

4 green onions
⅓ to 1 bunch fresh parsley
1½ tsp. dill weed
1¼ tsp. Bon Appetit *or*
  Beau Monde
¼ tsp. curry powder
1¼ cups mayonnaise
1 cup sour cream *or* plain
  yogurt

1. Gradually add green onions, parsley, dill weed, Bon Appetit, curry powder and ¼ cup mayonnaise to the blender. Begin blending with the help of a small amount of water.
2. After ingredients are thoroughly blended, stir in remaining 1 cup mayonnaise and sour cream or yogurt.
3. Serve with a variety of vegetables.

Asparagus Spears and Dip

Joan Gingrich
Landisville, PA

Makes 10-15 servings

20-30 asparagus spears
2 eggs
1½ Tbsp. sugar
2 Tbsp. vinegar
¼ tsp. salt
1 Tbsp. butter
8-oz. pkg. cream cheese
½ green pepper, chopped
1 small onion, chopped

1. Cook asparagus in salt water for 1-2 minutes. It should still be firm. Plunge in cold water until chilled. Set aside.
2. Beat eggs. Add sugar, vinegar, salt and butter. Cook mixture in double boiler until thickened. Set aside to cool.
3. Beat softened cream cheese. Add pepper and onion. Blend with cooled egg mixture.
4. Arrange asparagus spears on a platter around bowl of dip.

Dill Dip for Vegetables

Rhoda H. Sauder
York, PA
Stony Brook Mennonite Church

Betty Pellman
Millersville, PA
Rossmere Mennonite Church

Makes 2 cups dip

8 ozs. sour cream
1 cup mayonnaise
1 Tbsp. dry minced onion
1 Tbsp. dry parsley flakes
2 tsp. dry dill weed
1 tsp. seasoned salt

1. Combine all ingredients and chill.
2. Serve with a large tray of raw vegetables such as carrots, celery, cauliflower, broccoli and radishes.

Yogurt Dill Dip

Margaret Wenger Johnson
Keezletown, VA
Harrisonburg Friends Meeting

Makes 3 cups dip

2 cups yogurt
1 cup mayonnaise
1/2 tsp. dried onion
1/2 tsp. dried garlic
1/2 tsp. salt
1 1/2 tsp. dill weed
1 Tbsp. vinegar

1. Mix all ingredients together, mashing soft lumps.
2. Serve as a dip with raw vegetables.

Dill Shrimp Dip

Myrtle Miller Fricke
McMinnville, OR
First Baptist Church

Makes 10 servings

2 4-oz. cans cooked
  shrimp, drained
1 Tbsp. lemon juice
8 ozs. cream cheese, softened
1/4 cup milk
1/4 cup mayonnaise
2 Tbsp. chopped green
  onions
1/2 tsp. dry dill weed
6 drops hot pepper sauce
Dash of salt

1. Combine all ingredients except shrimp. Beat with an electric mixer for several minutes.
2. Fold in shrimp.
3. Serve dip in a bowl with an assortment of crackers.

Shrimp Dip

Helen Bowman
Columbiana, OH
Midway Mennonite Church

Makes 20-30 servings

1/4 cup water
3-oz. pkg. unflavored gelatin
1 can tomato soup
8-oz. pkg. cream cheese,
  softened
1/2 cup chopped celery
1/2 cup chopped onion or less
1 cup mayonnaise
1 lb. tiny, canned shrimp

1. Bring water, gelatin and tomato soup to a boil. Stir in cream cheese, celery onion, mayonnaise and shrimp.
2. Chill in a mold.
3. Serve with crackers.

Polynesian Crab Dip

Hulda G. Stucky
Wichita, KS
Lorraine Avenue Mennonite Church

Makes 3 cups dip

1 cup sour cream
1 cup mayonnaise
4-oz. can sliced mushrooms
7-oz. can crabmeat *or*
  1/2 lb. shredded seafood
1 cup flaked coconut
1 Tbsp. minced onion
1 tsp. lemon juice
2 Tbsp. chopped parsley
1/4 tsp. curry powder
Salt and pepper to taste

1. Blend sour cream and mayonnaise. Add all remaining ingredients and stir well.
2. Chill before serving.
3. Serve with assortment of vegetables or crackers.

Curry Dip

Ferne Miller
Landisville, PA
Landisville Mennonite Church

Edna Brunk
Marlboro, MD
Hyattsville Mennonite Church

Makes 2 ½ cups dip

2 cups mayonnaise
½ cup sour cream
¼ tsp. turmeric
1-2 Tbsp. curry powder
½ tsp. garlic powder
4 tsp. sugar
1 tsp. salt
2 tsp. lemon juice

1. Mix all ingredients together.
2. Refrigerate for at least 24 hours before serving.
3. Serve with assortment of fresh vegetables.

Every fellowship meal needs at least one tray with fresh veggies. My kids will eat more if I serve this dip with the relish tray.

Chipped Beef Dip

Mary E. Martin
Goshen, IN
Benton Mennonite Church

Makes 6-8 servings

8-oz. pkg. cream cheese, softened
3-oz. pkg. chipped beef
5-6 green onions, chopped
1 tsp. Accent
1 tsp. Worcestershire sauce

1. Mix all ingredients thoroughly and chill.
2. Serve with an assortment of crackers or vegetables.

Hummus bit Tahini

Lorraine J. Kaufman
Moundridge, KS
West Zion Mennonite Church

Makes 6-8 servings

1 can garbanzo beans
2-3 cloves garlic
1 tsp. salt or less
½ cup lemon juice, freshly squeezed
1 cup tahini (toasted sesame)
Olive oil
Parsley, freshly chopped
Several loaves pita bread

1. Drain beans. Process garlic, salt and lemon juice in blender. Add drained garbanzo beans and process. Blend in tahini.
2. If the mixture is very thick, add a small amount of water and vinegar, making it the desired consistency for dipping.
3. Serve in a flat dish, making a slight depression in center. Fill depression with olive oil and garnish with parsley. Dip pita bread.

Hot Cheese Dip

Anita Schauer
Plain City, OH
Shalom Community Church

Makes 8 servings

¼ cup finely chopped onion
1 Tbsp. margarine *or* butter
1 tsp. cornstarch
¼ tsp. pepper
½ cup milk
1 Tbsp. Worcestershire sauce
2 cups cubed, processed cheese
3-oz. pkg. cream cheese, cubed
1 Tbsp. snipped parsley

1. In a 1½-quart casserole dish combine onion and margarine or butter. Cover and cook in microwave for 1½-2 ½ minutes or until onion is tender, stirring once.
2. Stir in cornstarch and pepper. Add milk and Worcestershire sauce. Cook, uncovered, for 2-5 minutes or until slightly thickened and bubbly, stirring every minute. (Mixture will appear curdled).
3. Stir in processed cheese, cream cheese and parsley. Cook, uncovered, for 4-5 minutes or until cheese is melted and mixture is heated through, stirring every minute.
4. Keep dip warm in fondue pot or reheat in casserole dish.
5. Serve with crackers, chips or vegetables.

Tostado Dip

Bernice Hertzler
Phoenix, AZ
Sunnyslope Mennonite Church

Alice Suderman
New Hope, MN
New Hope Mennonite Brethren
Church

Makes 15-20 servings

16-oz. can refried beans
1 pkg. dry taco seasoning
1 cup sour cream
2 avocados, mashed
½ cup chopped green
   onions
4-oz. can diced black olives
4-oz. can diced green chilies
1 cup grated cheddar cheese
2 fresh tomatoes, chopped
1 cup alfalfa sprouts
   (optional)
Tortilla chips

1. Stir dry taco seasoning
into refried beans and mix
well.
2. Combine mashed avoca-
dos with sour cream and mix
well.
3. Layer ingredients on a
flat serving plate in the following order: Refried beans,
sour cream, onions, olives,
chilies, cheddar cheese, tomatoes and alfalfa sprouts.
4. Circle the plate with tortilla chips. Serve.

Taco Dip

Elaine Gibbel
Lititz, PA
Lititz Church of the Brethren

Makes 20 or more servings

8 oz. pkg. cream cheese,
   softened
½ cup sour cream
⅓ cup taco sauce
⅓ cup shredded cheddar
   cheese
¼ cup chopped green
   pepper
¼ cup chopped red pepper
¼ cup chopped onion
1 tomato, chopped
Taco *or* tortilla chips

1. Mix cream cheese and
sour cream together and
spread on 9-inch serving
plate. Spread taco sauce over
top.
2. Reserve 2 Tbsp. ched-
dar cheese. Layer other items
on plate in following order:
cheese, peppers, onion and
tomato. Top with reserved
cheese.
3. Serve with firm and
fresh chips to prevent breaking when persons scoop out
dip.

Variation:
*For the layers in this dish, I
like to use chopped lettuce,
chopped tomatoes, green or
black olives and cheese.*
Lee Snyder
Harrisonburg, VA
Community Mennonite Church

Guacamole

Mabel E. De Leon
La Junta, CO
Emmanuel Mennonite Church

Makes 4 servings

3 avocados
1 clove garlic, chopped
2 Tbsp. grated onion
4-oz. can diced green chilies
1 tsp. salt
1 small tomato, chopped
Lime juice to taste

1. Peel avocados and
mash with a fork until they
are smooth. Add all other ingredients and mix thor-
oughly. Or combine all ingredients in blender and mix until smooth.
2. Serve as a dip.

Salsa Sauce

Ginny Buckwalter
Scarborough, ON
Warden Woods Mennonite Church

Makes 2 cups sauce

28-oz. can canned tomatoes
2-4 carrots, chopped
½ onion, sliced
2 Tbsp. chili powder or more
2 tsp. cumin or more
1 tsp. salt

1. Purée all ingredients in
blender to desired sauce consistency.
2. May be used as a dip
for vegetables or nachos.

Orange Cheese Dip

Ila Yoder
Hesston, KS
Whitestone Mennonite Church

Makes 2 cups dip

11-oz. can mandarin
oranges, drained
8-oz. pkg. cream cheese,
softened

1. Purée mandarin oranges in blender.
2. Combine cream cheese and oranges and chill.
3. Serve with a platter of assorted fruit or with tortilla chips and crackers.

Fruit Dip

Edna E. Brunk
Upper Marlboro, MD
Hyattsville Mennonite Church

Makes approximately 3 cups

1 pkg. instant vanilla
pudding
1 cup milk
½ cup orange juice
1 cup sour cream

1. Place all ingredients in blender and blend for 45-60 seconds. Chill and keep refrigerated.
2. Serve with pieces of fresh fruit such as pineapple, apples, bananas, cherries and strawberries.

Fresh Fruit and Dip

Cheryl Rutschilling
West Liberty, OH

Makes 2 cups dip

Fruits:
Melon slices
Apple wedges
Peach slices
Grapes
Banana chunks
Pear slices
Sweet cherries

Dip:
8-oz. pkg. cream cheese,
softened
¼ cup milk
3 Tbsp. sugar
3 Tbsp. lemon juice
¾ tsp. cardamom

1. Combine all dip ingredients in small bowl and beat until smooth.
2. Arrange fruit on platter. Place bowl of dip in center of platter. Serve.

Caramel Apple Dip

Sharon Reber
Newton, KS

Makes 1½ cups dip

8-oz. pkg. cream cheese,
softened
¾ cup brown sugar or less
¼ cup white sugar or less
1 tsp. vanilla

1. Blend together all ingredients until smooth and creamy.
2. Serve with fresh apple slices or an assortment of fruit slices. (Slice apples immediately before serving to keep them from becoming discolored.)

Pepper Jelly

Marjorie Anderson
Lima, OH

Makes 2 ½ pints

6 medium red *or* green
peppers, chopped
¾ cup cider vinegar
2 tsp. hot pepper sauce
1¾ ozs. powdered fruit
pectin
3 ½ cups sugar

1. Process peppers in food chopper with medium blade. Drain. Measure 2 cups peppers into large saucepan. Add vinegar, pepper sauce and pectin. Bring to hard boil over high heat, stirring constantly.
2. Stir in sugar. Bring to a full, rolling boil and boil for 1 minute, stirring constantly.
3. Alternately skim and stir for 5 minutes to cool slightly and prevent peppers from floating.
4. Ladle into sterilized glasses. When using paraffin, leave ½ inch headspace and pour ⅛ inch paraffin into jar.
5. Served with cream cheese and crackers, this makes a unique finger food.

Beverages

Fruit Punch

Lucille Taylor
Hutchinson, KS
First Mennonite Church

Makes 25 servings

2 cups sugar or less
2 quarts water
3-oz. pkg. lemon gelatin
6-oz. can frozen orange juice
¾ cup lemon juice
46-oz. can pineapple juice
2 quarts gingerale

1. Bring sugar and water to a boil. Add gelatin and cool.
2. Stir in all other juices. Pour half of mixture into each of two-gallon jugs. Freeze.
3. Four hours before serving take out of freezer.
4. Add 1 quart gingerale to each gallon jug.

Frozen Gelatin Punch

Pauline A. Bauman
Bluffton, OH
First Mennonite Church

Makes 50 punch cup servings

5½ quarts water
5 3-oz. pkgs. strawberry gelatin
12-oz. can frozen lemonade
5 cups white sugar or less
46-oz. can pineapple grapefruit juice
20-oz. can crushed pineapple
Gingerale to taste

1. Heat just enough water to dissolve the gelatin and thaw the lemonade, stirring constantly. Add remaining water, sugar, juice and crushed pineapple. Mix thoroughly.
2. Freeze in 4 half-gallon milk cartons or other suitable containers.
3. To serve thaw to a slushy consistency and add gingerale to taste.
4. Refreeze any unused punch at the end of the meal.

My Mother's Holiday Punch

Geraldine A. Ebersole
Hershey, PA
Akron Mennonite Church

Makes 25 servings

3 cups sugar or less
3 cups water
4 cups cranberry juice cocktail
6-oz. can frozen lemon juice
6-oz. can frozen orange juice
3 cups pineapple juice
Ice
1 quart gingerale
Sprigs of mint (optional)

1. Make a sugar syrup with sugar and water. Bring to a boil and cool.
2. Add all fruit juices to cooled sugar syrup. When ready to serve, pour mixture over ice in punch bowl and add gingerale.
3. If desired, garnish with sprigs of mint.

Very Simple Punch

Mrs. Lewis L. Beachy
Sarasota, FL
Bahia Vista Mennonite Church

Makes 50-60 servings

46-oz. can pineapple juice
46-oz. can grapefruit juice
46-oz. can orange juice
2 quarts gingerale
1 quart orange sherbet

1. Mix all liquids together.
2. Immediately before serving, cut sherbet into chunks and add to punch.

Slush Punch

Ethel Shank
Ephrata, PA
Akron Mennonite Church

Makes 20 servings

4 cups water
2 cups sugar
5 bananas
1½ cups orange juice
1½ cups lemon juice
1½ cups pineapple juice
7-up

1. Combine water and sugar in saucepan and bring to a boil. Stir until sugar dissolves.
2. Blend bananas in blender with ½ cup sugar water.
3. Combine all ingredients except 7-up and mix well. Pour into quart or pint containers. Freeze.
4. Immediately before serving, put 5-6 large spoonsful frozen mix into punch bowl. Fill with 7-up and serve.

Refresher Drink

Lois E. Harsh
Lorida, FL
Lorida Church of the Brethren

Makes 24 servings

2 cups sugar
4 cups water
2 cups orange juice
¼ cup lemon juice
Rind from 2 oranges, grated
Gingerale

1. Boil sugar and water for 20 minutes. Add orange juice, lemon juice and orange rind. Stir to blend.
2. Freeze in ice cube trays.
3. Put 2 cubes in each glass. Fill glasses with gingerale.

Lemonade

Ruth R. Nissley
Mount Joy, PA
Bethel Mennonite Church

Makes 60 servings

3 cups Realemon
6 ozs. frozen orange juice
6 cups sugar
Water to fill 3 gallons

1. Mix Realemon, orange juice and sugar.
2. Add water and ice to make an ice-cold drink.

One Pot Meals

Soup Carry-In

Phyllis Lyndaker
Watertown, NY
Watertown Mennonite Church

An idea we tried for a soup carry-in was to have each person bring a beef broth soup. We combined all of the soups. It made the best beef broth soup I have ever eaten!

Stir Fry Potluck

Sandy Zeiset Richardson
Leavenworth, WA

We are currently part of a small non-Mennonite faith community. We meet weekly, though not always on Sunday, and we try to meet once a month for meals.

Sometimes when we do a stir fry potluck, we designate one person to bring enough cooked rice for the group. At other times we ask persons to bring enough rice for themselves.

We suggest a variety of other ingredients. People often bring whatever they have around or what they think might be good. Ingredients which need to be chopped or marinated should be prepared in advance. Following are suggested ingredients:

Rice
Garlic
Onions
Carrots
Red, green *or* **yellow**
    peppers
Mushrooms
Cabbage
Marinated chicken, beef *or*
    pork
Tofu
Raisins
Pineapple slices
Sliced almonds
Sunflower seeds
Curry
Basil
Parsley
Salt
Red *or* **black pepper**
Cooking oil

Each person fills his or her plate from the uncooked potluck of ingredients. After filling plate, persons go to a wok which has been started with cooking oil.

We arrange to have an average of one wok for 4-5 people. Each plate of food is stir fried separately either by a designated cook or by each person.

We have found this works well for a small group, but it will also work for 40-50 people.

Potluck Fondue

Kate Emerson
Strasburg, PA

Ingredients:
Beef *or* **chicken broth**
Chicken bits
Beef cubes
Meatballs
Broccoli, cut up
Cauliflower, cut up
Carrots, cut up
Any other meat *or* **vegetable**

Sauces:
Mustard
Ketchup
Barbecue sauce
Vinegar
Mayonnaise
Ailoli-Garlic sauce
Any other sauce

Put broth into a fondue pot or chafing dish and heat. Allow guests to spear meat or vegetables with wooden skewers. Cook each piece of food in pot until it is done. Dip finished food in a sauce before eating it.

With Italian bread and a dessert, you have a great party meal. I have had 45 people in my living room for fondue meals. People enjoy talking while they eat. We always have lots of fun and fellowship at fondue meals.

Ailoli-Garlic Sauce for Fondue

Kate Emerson
Strasburg, PA

Makes 1 cup

4 or more cloves garlic
2 egg yolks
⅛ tsp. salt
1 cup olive oil
½ tsp. cold water
1 tsp. lemon juice

1. Skin and chop cloves of garlic. Beat in egg yolks and salt.
2. Very slowly add olive oil, water and lemon juice, beating constantly as it thickens.

Pizza for a Crowd

Sharon Reber
Newton, KS

We sometimes meet with a small group, usually no more than 25 people. We order in enough pizza for the entire group and provide relish plates, beverages and cookies. It is so convenient, and most people enjoy pizza. More attention may be given to fellowship and less to food preparation.

Remember to save pizza coupons for these occasions!

Turkey Soup

Verla Fae Haas
Bluesky, AB

Our church always has a large Thanksgiving meal. After the meal, a volunteer boils all the leftover turkey bones and takes off the meat. The broth, turkey meat and any leftover gravy are frozen until our January business meeting.

On the day of the business meeting, volunteers bring vegetables such as potatoes, carrots, turnips, onions and celery to church and add them to the boiling broth. About ½ hour before serving, we add homemade noodles and tomato juice and ask the best soup tasters to adjust the seasoning with salt, pepper, basil, parsley, thyme, rosemary and marjoram.

We serve the soup with open-faced sandwiches and a dessert such as apple crisp or bread pudding. People are asked to bring the desserts and filling for sandwiches.

Chili Con Carne Picnic

Verla Fae Haas
Bluesky, AB

One of our congregation's stand-by meals is chili con carne. Different people bring the same chili recipe.

Makes 12-14 servings

2 lbs. hamburger
2 onions, chopped
2 cloves garlic (optional)
2 Tbsp. flour
3 tsp. salt
1½-3 tsp. chili powder
1 quart tomatoes with juice
3-4 cups cooked kidney beans

1. Fry the hamburger. Drain excess fat. Add onion and garlic and sauté. Add flour, salt and chili powder and mix well. Add tomatoes and simmer for about an hour. If necessary, add water.
2. Add beans and bring to a boil. This chili should be quite thick.

We serve this chili over buns. People eat it with forks. In addition, we have salads, fresh vegetable platters and desserts. Many of our fellowship meals occur outside during the summer months. We usually use our church yard or a designated picnic place.

Potato Salad

Anita Falk
Mountain Lake, MN
Bethel Mennonite Church

In the Mountain Lake, Minnesota area Bethel Mennonite Church has long been known for its good potato salad. We serve it twice a year—on Children's Day and for the Harvest Festival. Twenty-eight different people bring one gallon of potato salad, using approximations of the following recipe. We mix all the salads together and add extra hard-boiled eggs and mayonnaise along with some cream. Eggs and cream are what make a great potato salad.

Makes 6 quarts

1 cup vinegar
1 cup water
1 cup sugar
1 tsp. salt
½ tsp. pepper
1 Tbsp. prepared mustard
8 eggs, well beaten
1 quart mayonnaise
10 lbs. potatoes
12 hard-boiled eggs, chopped
½ cup minced onion
1 tsp. celery seed

1. In a saucepan combine vinegar, water, sugar, salt, pepper and mustard and bring to a boil. Reduce heat. Gradually beat in well-beaten eggs. Cook, stirring constantly, until slightly thickened. Remove from heat and beat in mayonnaise.
2. Cook and cube potatoes. Toss with all remaining ingredients.
3. Pour dressing over potato salad and toss gently. Adjust seasoning. Refrigerate at least 4-6 hours before serving.

Sunday Noon Congregational Soup Lunch

Mary Leatherman
Doylestown, PA
Doylestown Mennonite Church

The hospitality committee asks each family to bring enough soup—either vegetable or chicken noodle—to serve themselves plus two additional people. Those families with names beginning A-K bring enough bread or rolls to serve double their family. Those whose names begin with L-Z carry in a finger food-type dessert such as cookies, bars, cupcakes or fresh fruit—enough to serve double their family. Beverages are provided. Singles and small families are invited to combine efforts in what they bring.

We have two electric roasting ovens in our large church kitchen. We combine all the vegetable soups in one and all the chicken noodle soups in the other. Persons serve themselves directly from the roasters

Mexican Plate

Elda Martens
Fairview, OK
Fairview Mennonite Brethren
Church

Makes 200 servings

35 lbs. ground chuck
10 lbs. potatoes
1 #10 can pinto beans
10 lbs. onions
2 #10 cans tomato sauce
3 9-oz. pkgs. taco seasoning
9-10 heads lettuce
15 lbs. fresh tomatoes
15-20 lbs. shredded cheddar
cheese
20 lbs. nacho chips
1-2 gallons mild picante
sauce

1. Using 3 electric roasters make a meat sauce following these directions.
2. Brown meat.
3. Peel potatoes and shred in food processor. Add potatoes to ground chuck.
4. Purée pinto beans in food processor. Add to ground chuck.
5. Purée onions with tomato sauce and add to ground chuck.
6. Add taco seasoning and water to each roaster to keep sauce at a relatively thin consistency.
7. Shred lettuce and dice tomatoes and put in separate large dishes.
8. Put cheddar cheese, slightly crushed chips and picante sauce in separate containers.
9. Invite individuals to go through serving line and create their own salads.

10. Serve with ice cream or pudding for dessert.

Haystack Dinner

Faye Gerber
Kidron, OH
Salem Mennonite Church

Makes 12-15 servings

Assign one or more persons to bring each of the following ingredients. Increase amounts of recipe for larger groups.

4 cups uncooked rice
3 lbs. ground beef
2 jars spaghetti sauce
2 cans cheddar cheese soup
1½ cups milk
2 heads lettuce, chopped
6 tomatoes, diced
1 large jar olives, diced
½ lb. soda crackers, crushed
2 pkgs. corn chips, crushed
2 cups nuts *or* sunflower
seeds, chopped

1. Cook rice according to directions.
2. Brown ground beef and add spaghetti sauce. Cook until heated through.
3. Add milk to cheddar cheese soup and heat through.
4. Put each item in separate dish and pass in following order: soda crackers, rice, lettuce, corn chips, tomatoes, olives, nuts or sunflower seeds, ground beef and cheddar cheese soup.
5. Guests take a portion of each and slowly build a haystack of ingredients.

I recommend this for groups of 15-20 people. We used it for our Women in Mission sewing lunch. There are always lots of laughs as each person's haystack grows.

Pastor's Soup

Paul Isaak
Rocky Ford, CO
Rocky Ford Mennonite Church

When I first introduced this idea to my congregation, it was tried with a great deal of reservation. I suggested each person or family bring one large or several small cans of soup from the grocery store. The only soup that was off limits was tomato soup.

About an hour before the meal, all the different soups were combined in a kettle. We added water, but not necessarily according to the directions. Several persons brought stew which added to the flavor. The soup was brought to a boil and simmered for about 15 minutes, resulting in an easy and tasty fellowship meal. The last time we did this, three gallons of soup served 25 people.

If You Do Not Cook

Arrange sliced cheeses and summer sausage on a platter.

Pearl Zehr
New Wilmington, PA
Maple Grove Mennonite Church

Stop at grocery store late Saturday night and buy a cheese cake mix and a 21-oz. can of pie filling. Fix the cheese cake mix according to directions. Immediately before serving, top with pie filling.

Pearl Zehr
New Wilmington, PA
Maple Grove Mennonite Church

In a beautiful glass dish arrange fresh grapes—red and seedless green.

Pearl Zehr
New Wilmington, PA
Maple Grove Mennonite Church

Fix a tray with venison trail bologna, cheese and crackers. Cut bologna and cheese on Saturday night and leave space on the tray for crackers.

Shirley Hochstetler
Kidron, OH
Sonnenberg Mennonite Church

If I am running out of time, I buy healthy natural crackers and serve them with a deli cheese such as Brie or Swiss.

Elizabeth Weaver Bonnar
Thorndale, ON
Valleyview Mennonite Church

I buy several jars of baby beets, a liver paté and crackers.

Elizabeth Weaver Bonnar
Thorndale, ON
Valleyview Mennonite Church

If my dessert flops at the last minute, I mix chocolate M&Ms, peanuts, sesame sticks and raisins plus whatever else I have available that fits. I call this "gorp."

Elizabeth Weaver Bonnar
Thorndale, ON
Valleyview Mennonite Church

I take an assortment of fresh fruit and let the food committee cut the fruit into smaller pieces to be served as a finger food.

Barbara Longenecker
New Holland, PA
New Holland Mennonite Church

I have made little "wiennie picks," as I call them. On a toothpick I put a piece of a previously cooked wiener and a cube of cheese. I top this off with any of the following choices: pickle, pineapple tidbit, olive or orange section. The kids love them.

Lois Cressman
Plattsville, ON
Nith Valley Mennonite Church

I take a tray with my home-canned pickled beets and dill pickles. To the tray I add a variety of fresh vegetables, whatever I have on hand.

Helen R. Goering
Moundridge, KS
Eden Mennonite Church of Rural Moundridge

A simple bowl of mixed fruit almost always gets eaten up. I use a combination of fresh fruit to which I add at least one container of canned mixed fruit.

Helen Claassen
Elkhart, IN
First Norwood Mennonite Church

Here is a gourmet idea which does require oven time and monitoring after you get to church. Cut crusts off 10-12 slices sandwich bread. Cut each slice into thirds. Spread with softened cream cheese. Roll or wrap ½ of a bacon strip around each slice and secure bacon with a toothpick. Bake at 325 F. for 20 minutes.

Betty Pellman
Millersville, PA
Rossmere Mennonite Church

Many people in our fellowship are urban, and they welcome fresh fruit. I find whatever fruit is in season and wash, chill and shine it. I serve the fruit in an attractive glass bowl or a basket.

Violet Jantzi
Medina, NY
Harris Hill Mennonite Church

I prepare orange, apple and kiwi slices to which I add small clusters of grapes, bananas cut into chunks, bitesized pieces of melon and strawberries when they are in season. I make an attractive arrangement on a platter and put a small container of toothpicks next to the platter for ease in handling the small pieces of fruit.

Joan Gingerich
Landisville, PA

I buy several loaves of homemade bread and take along some butter and jelly. Children are especially glad to see bread at a fellowship meal.

Carol Sommers
Millersburg, OH
Martins Creek Mennonite Church

I dip dried apricots in melted chocolate and arrange them on a tray.

Ethel O. Yoder
Goshen, IN
College Mennonite Church

Take along several packages frozen peas, green beans or corn and a saucepan. If you really do not enjoy cooking, have committee prepare the vegetables. I usually prepare this at home using my home-grown frozen vegetables.

Grace Gehman
Bechtelsville, PA

Stop at a deli and pick up a salad.

Carol Weber
Lancaster, PA
Charlotte Street Mennonite Church

I take a big dish of fresh celery which I buy at the local farmers' market.

Anne Wilson
Strasburg, PA
New Providence Mennonite Church

I fill my crockpot with a frozen vegetable—peas, lima beans or corn—and plug it in as soon as we arrive at church. Many people enjoy this dish.

Anne Wilson
Strasburg, PA
New Providence Mennonite Church

Scrub 12-15 small potatoes. Wrap them in aluminum foil. Bake at 350° for 1 hour. Wrap well and take to church. Do not forget butter, salt and pepper to serve with potatoes.

Joan Gingerich
Landisville, PA

On a large, flat platter arrange approximately 8-10 individual lettuce leaves. On each leaf put ½ of a canned peach. Fill center of each peach with cottage cheese. Top with ½ of a maraschino cherry and you have an easy, delicious and attractive dessert.

Betty Lou Eberly
Reading, PA
Hampden Mennonite Church

Time Savers, Space Savers and Other Hints

Each year we have a congregational Easter breakfast. The first year I standardized a breakfast casserole recipe from several different ones and circulated the recipe, asking persons to prepare it and to bring the baked casserole ready to serve.

Along with the casserole we offered rolls, juice and hard-boiled eggs which had been decorated by the children. The eggs provided decoration on the tables and were passed around near the end of the meal.

Arlene M. Mark
Elkhart, IN
Prairie Street Mennonite Church

Following are a few suggestions for dealing with limited electrical outlets and refrigeration:

1) Freeze fruit punch or lemonade in several large, plastic containers. Before church service begins, mix up a drink, using frozen punch or lemonade for ice. The drink stays chilled without becoming watered down.

2) Bring a large picnic cooler with a cold pack or ice and pack dishes that need to be kept cool in the cooler.

3) Cook or bake hot dishes at home, wrap them in newspaper and place in a cardboard box.

Eva Burkholder
Markham, ON
Rouge Valley Mennonite Church

Children frequently fill their plates with the usual casserole offerings and often eat very little which wastes a lot of food. When I take

Sloppy Joes, I stand at the beginning of the line and fill buns as the young people come through. They tend to take less "iffy" food when they have a Sloppy Joe. More food is left for the adults, and the line moves much faster.

Arlene M. Mark
Elkhart, IN
Prairie Street Mennonite Church

Our church has two ovens. The food committee keeps one oven turned to warm and sets the other at 350°. The 350° oven is then ready for the many casseroles which need to be baked at 350° for approximately one hour.

Shirley Hochstetler
Kidron, OH
Sonnenberg Mennonite Church

I love potlucks, but I find my children do not care for the adventure of tasting new foods. Managing two or three kids through a line can be a headache for young parents. I have found that taking along large trays helps because one tray will hold two or three plates plus utensils and cups.

Because of the Sunday morning hassle, I have also simplified my own preparation by taking plain, raw vegetables and fruits which children enjoy but will not eat if they are concealed in a fruit salad or other concoction.

Melodie Davis
Harrisonburg, VA
Trinity Presbyterian Church

We rent a chapel in a student residence and have a number of university students who attend our services. Except for the summer months, we have a fellowship potluck once a month and what we call "Soup Sunday" once a month. Everyone who attends the worship service is invited to stay for our meal whether or not they brought food. The students are usually happy for some home cooking.

We have six food committees, each serving for two months at a time. They supply the soup, oversee the potluck and organize coffee, tea

and cookies for the remaining Sundays. Almost every household is involved in a food committee so there is no big burden on anyone.

We try to avoid disposables. We have one dishwasher, but the rest of the dishes are washed and dried by hand. The food committee for that month is responsible for clean-up, but other people always help.

Janice Kreider
Vancouver, BC
Point Grey Fellowship

We have a fellowship meal every Sunday. This allows busy people time to visit and no one feels obliged to invite visitors to their home for Sunday dinner.

Also in the town of Lafayette the food kitchen for the poor is closed on Sundays, so we open our fellowship meal to the local homeless population.

Marjorie Rush
West Lafayette, IN
Lafayette Mennonite Fellowship

We are a group of friends who meet once a week for quilting, embroidery, patchwork or pottery, sometimes known as the The Barn Swallow Quilters. The name comes from our work space—a renovated barn

which houses pottery, woodworking and even old saddles on the ground floor and quilting and "clean" crafts on the second floor.

We usually carry bag lunches, but every now and then we have a potluck to celebrate a special occasion. One of our members takes cups and coffee pot into her house each week and puts them through her dishwasher. Any other dishes that we need, we bring and take home again. No disposables here! The key words at our potlucks are "ready-to-eat" dishes.

Jeanette Zacharias
The Barn Swallow Quilters
Morden, MB

We occasionally plan a breakfast meal, asking persons whose last names begin with A-K to bring fruits and persons whose last names begin with L-Z to bring sweet breads or coffee cakes. The food committee provides coffee and tea.

Joy Kauffman
Goshen, IN
Belmont Mennonite Church

Because of the landfill crisis affecting our country, we have eliminated the use of disposables in our church. One of our church members, Mervin Swartzentruber, built a mug board which hangs under the high windows in the kitchen. It has helped eliminate styrofoam cups which are so detrimental to the environment. We each bring our own plates and flatware and are responsible for our own clean-up.

Alta Dezort
Normalville, PA
Kingview Mennonite Church

her own dish and was served from the group pot.

In Japan rice was prepared and each family brought something to go on top. The food committee served each person by putting rice in a bowl, adding seaweed, vegetables, eggs and whatever else was brought. In a few minutes a beautiful meal was prepared. Since there was no room for tables, we all sat facing each other in a circle.

In Honduras the food was served on banana leaves rather than plates. The leaves were tossed to the hogs after the meal.

In Nicaragua neighbors often got together to do baking so that only one kitchen would have a hot oven. Afterward we traded baked goods. When we planned dinner parties, we often told our neighbors and they would each loan us things like ice cubes, dishes and chairs. That meant all of us had what we needed and all of us lived with less.

Betty J. Rosentrater
Nappanee, IN
Iglesia Menonita del Buen Pastor

I am from a small congregation and we have had fellowship meals without a kitchen for many years. We use crockpots and extension cords. We also take some casseroles or hot dishes to the homes of church members who live within walking distance of the church. We serve the food from Sunday School rooms and use the sanctuary for eating.

We are currently building on and will soon have a kitchen and a place to eat. We cannot wait!

Miriam Nolt
Chambersburg, PA
Pond Bank Mennonite Church

To entertain the children during fellowship meals set up library book displays and ask persons to provide a time of reading books or telling stories. Or set up an art table and let the children draw or paint. Or when the weather is nice, simply let them enjoy a time of playing outside with their friends.

Sharon L. Spicher
Huntingdon, PA
Allensville Mennonite Church

Here are some cross-cultural styles of eating which I have participated in:

In Mexico a huge pot of hominy was prepared and every person brought his or

I have always dreaded having to take a dish to a potluck. However, I finally decided such occasions were not contests or competitions. When I feel like preparing a nice dish, I use a recipe. Just as often I take a plate of fresh fruit or a simple relish plate. Many people seem to like fresh, simple items. The kids love cupcakes, angel food cakes and even something as simple as a bag of chips. Some people love to taste new dishes, but my kids belong to the group who needs to feed on more familiar fare.

Carol Friesen
Wallace, NE
Wallace United Methodist Church

If stove or oven space is limited, use crockpots and electric skillets. If that is not an option due to lack of electrical outlets, make dishes which can be heated in the microwave or eaten cold.

Also do not miss out on fellowship meals because you do not like to cook. Stop at a supermarket deli or even the local fast-food restaurant. Food does not have to be homemade!

Jan Pembleton
Arlington, TX
Hope Mennonite Church

preparation and clean-up. Fellowship meals provide excellent opportunities for working together and serving each other. Everyone should be included and involved.

Rachel Kauffman
Alto, MI
West Odessa Community Church

As the chairperson of a hospitality committee, I have several suggestions:

1) When considering a casserole or dish, think about how it will fit into the oven or refrigerator with other dishes.

2) Food looks wonderful in that special crystal dish, but it certainly makes the food committee nervous.

3) Always start casserole dishes with raw meat at home, so they will finish baking in the same amount of time as most of the other dishes brought to the meal.

4) Avoid writing complicated instructions for the food committee members.

Naomi Headings
West Liberty, OH
South Union Mennonite Church

You may want to appoint someone to be responsible for taking a plate of food to shut-ins. This is a nice way to say, "You are a part of us. We have not forgotten you."

Marnetta Brilhart
Scottdale, PA
Mennonite Church of Scottdale

At church fellowship meals established members need to reach out to new members, visitors, singles and shy people. Ask them to stay for dinner and even to help with setting up, preparing and cleaning up. This helps prevent feelings of exclusiveness, "I don't know what to do" or "I'm not a part of this."

Skilled Mennonite cooks need to be sensitive about people who may not have the same training and understanding of how to prepare a meal as they do. All contributions to the meal should be appreciated and praised, even those which come directly from a grocery store or even fast-food restaurant.

Men and children, as well as the women, should be encouraged to help with food

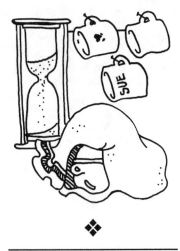

One year we cooked for 35 persons at a church retreat. We asked each person to bring her or his own bowl and mug. We provided one spoon per person. All the meals were one-dish meals which could be eaten with a spoon. On the side we served bread, muffins, fresh fruit, cookies and other finger foods. To make sure no one was overwhelmed with the work, we assigned people to help with preparation and clean-up.

Elaine Gibbel
Lititz, PA
Lititz Church of the Brethren

Recently our church purchased a set of pottery plates which we now usually use at fellowship meals.

Wilma Roeschley
Hinsdale, IL
Lombard Mennonite Church

Each Sunday a different cluster group meets for a fellowship meal. Usually, there are about 20 people and each family brings one main dish and one other dish. All visitors are invited to join the cluster group for the meal.

Joyce Hofer
Morton, IL
Trinity Mennonite Church

At Community Mennonite Church we have fellowship meals once a month. We feel these meals are very important to the growth of our young congregation.

Lee Snyder
Harrisonburg, VA
Community Mennonite Church

We usually have carry-in fellowship meals and everyone is involved in the preparation. People seem to have specialties--Paul brings pasta dishes, Lee brings breads and Don makes shoo-fly pies. We feel like one big family when we eat together.

Ruby Lehman
Towson, MD
North Baltimore Mennonite Church

Recipe Index

Index

Recipes for Serving Large Crowds

Recipes to Please the Children

Recipes That Are Cross-Cultural

Recipes for Finger Foods

Recipes for the Health-Conscious

About the Authors

Phyllis Pellman Good is a *New York Times* bestselling author whose books have sold more than 2 million copies.

Good, a Lancaster County, Pennsylvania, native, is also a highly respected expert on the Amish and Mennonite peoples.

Phyllis Pellman Good has authored or co-authored many cookbooks, including the national #1 bestselling cookbook (with Dawn J. Ranck) *Fix-It and Forget-It Cookbook: Feasting with your Slow Cooker.* Good's other cookbooks include *The Best of Amish Cooking, Delicious Amish Recipes, An Amish Table, From Amish and Mennonite Kitchens, Mennonite Recipes from The Shenandoah Valley, Amish Cooking for Kids,* and *Favorite Recipes with Herbs.*

She and her husband Merle co-authored the bestselling *20 Most Asked Questions about the Amish and Mennonites* as well as *Christmas Ideas for Families.* They edit an annual collection entitled *What Mennonites Are Thinking.*

Among Good's other books are an exquisite photo essay book *Amish Children* (with photographer Jerry Irwin), *Perils of Professionalism, A Mennonite Woman's Life*, a children's picture book *Plain Pig's ABC's: A Day on Plain Pig's Amish Farm*, and the elegant *Quilts from two Valleys: Amish Quilts from the Big Valley and Mennonite Quilts from the Shenandoah Valley.*

Phyllis Pellman Good serves as the curator of the nationally-acclaimed People's Place Quilt Museum. She and Merle are executive directors of The People's Place, The Old Country Store, and several galleries and related shops in the historic village of Intercourse, Pennsylvania, in the heart of the Old Order Amish settlement.

Having come through the Old Order Amish and Beachy Amish line into the Mennonite Church, **Louise Stoltzfus** has attended many church dinners and fellowship meals and has often struggled with knowing what to take. She is a member of Blossom Hill Mennonite Church in Lancaster, Pennsylvania.

Among her other books are *Amish Women: Lives and Stories, The Lancaster County Cookbook, Favorite Recipes from Quilters*, and *Two Amish Folk Artists.*

Good and Stoltzfus previously collaborated on *The Central Market Cookbook.*